Fantasticism. Poetics of Fantastic Literature

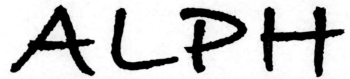

ALPH

Arbeiten zur Literarischen Phantastik
Eine Schriftenreihe der Universität Leipzig

Herausgegeben von Elmar Schenkel und Alexandra Lembert

Band 1

PETER LANG

Frankfurt am Main · Berlin · Bern · Bruxelles · New York · Oxford · Wien

Fanfan Chen

Fantasticism
Poetics of Fantastic Literature

The Imaginary and Rhetoric

PETER LANG
Internationaler Verlag der Wissenschaften

Bibliographic Information published by the Deutsche Nationalbibliothek
The Deutsche Nationalbibliothek lists this publication in the Deutsche Nationalbibliografie; detailed bibliographic data is available in the internet at <http://www.d-nb.de>.

Cover illustration:
Hael Yxxs: *Sign* (2006)

ISSN 1864-323X
ISBN 978-3-631-56514-8

© Peter Lang GmbH
Internationaler Verlag der Wissenschaften
Frankfurt am Main 2007
All rights reserved.

Printed in Germany 1 2 3 4 5   7

www.peterlang.de

Table of Contents

Preface

Il faut se féliciter de voir Mademoiselle Fanfan Chen, professeur chinois de Taiwan, entreprendre une étude passionnante sur les domaines des fantastiques, si peu explorés en Orient. L'intérêt que l'on porte à ces domaines est d'ailleurs récent, en Occident même. Rares ont été les chercheurs qui ont entamé des approches sérieuses sur ce sujet avant naguère. Le premier frémissement pour cet intérêt a été la traduction en anglais de l'ouvrage académique de T. Todorov *Introduction à la littérature fantastique* (1970). Il traçait des espaces spécifiques, où il casait des « genres littéraires» occidentaux, délimitant les frontières des genres merveilleux et fantastiques. Il décrivait un fonctionnement du texte fantastique comme producteur volontaire d'ambiguïté, en exploitant sur le plan théorique la parole attribuée à Madame du Deffant « Je ne crois pas aux fantômes, mais j'en ai peur ». Par la suite, aux USA, E.Rabkin (1976) en particulier, proposait une lecture moins restrictive du terme « fantastic » qui incluait sans distinction aussi bien la science-fiction que l'heroic fantasy, ou les contes merveilleux, dans ce domaine. Mais dans les deux cas, la théorisation se faisait en s'appuyant explicitement et exclusivement sur des textes occidentaux. Et pour sa part, Todorov s'appuyait pour théoriser sur un corpus très étroit de textes, publiés en majorité au XIX° siècle. Depuis, en Occident, de nombreux ouvrages[1] ont entrepris d'explorer plus complètement les domaines des fantastiques, de la science-fiction et de l'heroic fantasy, mais ils sont plus ou moins demeurés enclos dans les textes de leur culture. Au point d'entraîner parfois la question suivante : existe t il des textes fantastiques dans les cultures non-occidentales.[2]

En Occident, on dispose de plusieurs vocables pour nommer de différents types de textes, et on peut considérer que, si des vocables divers existent, ils renvoient à des domaines peut-être proches mais différents. C'est ainsi que l'on a pu opérer des distinctions par l'évolution historique des représentations. Avant le XIX° siècle, le vocable « fantastique » avait le même sens en français qu'en anglais. C'était un adjectif qualifiant ce qui relevait de l'imagination, des inventions des contes merveilleux, dont il se différenciait uniquement par la prise en compte d'une certaine « bizarrerie ». Mais à partir du XIX° siècle et en référence aux textes d'Hoffmann, a été inauguré en France « le fantastique » comme un domaine en soi, devenu par la suite un « genre ». De même à partir de 1939 le terme de « science fiction », inventé aux USA par Hugo Gernsback, donnait une visibilité, éditoriale d'abord, théorique ensuite, à toute une série de

---

[1] Denis Mellier, *L'écriture de l'excès, fiction fantastique et poétique de la terreur*, Paris, Honoré Champion, 1999. Stephen King, *Anatomie de l'horreur*, Paris, J'ai lu, 1995, (*Stephen King danse macabre*, 1981).

[2] Muriel Diétrie, « Les contes 'fantastiques' chinois : questions de genre et de terminologie », p. 199-204 et Roger Bozzetto, « Peut-on parler de « fantastique » dans la littérature chinoise ? », p. 215-233, *Cahiers du CERLI*, No. 7 et 8, 1998.

textes. Ils présentent des aventures et s'appuient sur un vocabulaire à connotations scientifiques. Ils étaient publiés aussi bien dans les magazines comme *Amazing Stories* que par auteurs reconnus comme Aldous Huxley *Le meilleur des mondes* (1932) ou Rosny aîné. Entre temps, des auteurs du début du XX° faisaient jouer à la magie un rôle important comme le roman de Lord Dunsany *La fille du roi des Elfes*. Ce qui a engendré la littérature d'heroic fantasy. Ces trois genres initiaux ont ouvert, en Occident, la voie à une production très importante, ainsi qu'à des tentatives académiques de définition de ces divers « genres ».

La professeur Fanfan Chen emprunte une voie plus originale. D'abord elle entame son analyse à partir des théories et des critiques chinois, qu'elle cite et discute abondamment, ainsi que sur les théories de l'imaginaire des philologues anglais Owen Barfield et J.R.R. Tolkien. Ceci pour de ne pas se focaliser sur les déterminations notionnelles occidentales classiques issues de Todorov. Elle prend aussi en compte les approches des écrivains sud américains comme Borges et Cortázar, puis ose innover au plan des notions utilisées, comme on le voit dans la seconde partie de l'ouvrage. Elle élargit le corpus fictionnel, sur quoi elle va appuyer ses recherches, à des textes chinois, bien que le nombre de textes européens soit important, comme en témoigne la riche bibliographie.

Le second aspect de cette approche originale dans l'exploration du domaine des fantastiques, tient au fait qu'elle ne va pas prendre comme point de départ le déroulement historique, à l'occidentale. Elle prend comme base le fond mythique propre à tous les imaginaires, qu'après Charles Nodier et Gilbert Durand, elle rapprochera de la créativité et de la dynamique onirique. Cette créativité mythopoïétique est présentée comme seule capable d'inventer une infinité de connexions au niveau des images, ou même des thèmes dans le cadre de ce que Freud nomme la condensation (la métonymie) et le déplacement (la métaphore). Images et figures rhétoriques aboutissent à de nouvelles figurations d'un « impossible à dire », qui pourtant fait signe vers une vérité. Le professeur Chen s'appuie dans le même temps sur Platon ainsi que sur Gaston Bachelard, pour établir une rencontre enrichissante entre mythopoïétique et métaphysique.

Le troisième aspect de l'originalité de cette démarche sera de se référer à la Surnature qui caractérise le fond de tous les mythes depuis ceux des premiers hommes et de faire référence au substrat proprement chinois des mythes et des récits qu'elle questionne en prenant en compte le rapport particulier que les écrivains chinois dans leurs textes, présentent un rapport particulier à la Surnature comme à la nature, sans toujours distinguer explicitement les différences dans les textes plus anciens retranscrits par Pu Songling.

La dernière partie de la thèse se propose de donner une lecture originale de la rhétorique propre à produire divers effets de fantastique, ce vocable étant entendu au sens large et appuyé sur la dimension mythique. Elle le fait en jouant sur trois modèles rhétoriques neufs qui entraînent autant de types de récits plus ou moins complexes. Cette partie permet aussi d'aborder les problèmes de focalisation ainsi que les figures de rhétorique issues de la classification de Pierre Fontanier dans *Manuel classique pour l'étude des tropes* (1821) reprise par Genette, et qui sous-tendent le texte fantastique. On y relève l'hyperbole, la litote, l'hypotypose dans les textes classiques et, pour les textes modernes, la prise au pied de la lettre de certaines métaphores.

D'abord en prenant en compte le discours du rêve et de l'imaginaire qui rassemble dans la même perspective onirique les textes de Tolkien et *L'investiture des dieux*, et *Faust* et le *Voyage en Occident*. La comparaison des deux montre, au plan de l'imaginaire, l'importance des substrats culturels différentiels. Le monde du *Voyage* renvoie à un imaginaire traditionnel chinois par le fait que le héros est un bonze, monté sur un cheval dragon, qu'il est accompagné d'un singe et d'un cochon. Ces animaux sont des réincarnations d'individus qui ont commis des fautes dans une vie antérieure, ce qui renvoie aussi à une dimension religieuse bouddhique. Par contre l'imaginaire de Tolkien renvoie au moyen âge occidental, mêlant le substrat nordique et le merveilleux des contes.

En second lieu, le discours du miroir qui s'intéresse, en plus des textes, à la peinture, et à la mise en abyme comme procédé rhétorique produisant de possibles effets de fantastique. Cette partie permet aussi d'aborder les problèmes de focalisation ainsi que les figures de rhétorique qui sous-tendent parfois le texte fantastique: l'hyperbole, la litote, la prise au pied de la lettre de certaines métaphores par exemple. Un développement vers le fantastique cinématographique en aurait été le complément naturel.

Enfin, dans une formulation piquant l'imagination, Fanfan Chen nous propose une description touchant à la prestidigitation, avec le type de discours du magicien faisant surgir un lapin de son chapeau. Ce n'est pas un simple jeu, mais cela permet au texte de supprimer l'ambiguïté possible, et nous sommes là dans une esthétique qui est plus proche du baroque que du fantastique à l'occidentale, mais permet au professeur Chen d'élargir le domaine exploré. C'est ainsi qu'elle permet par cette prise en compte de la rhétorique et par le jeu de ses figures, un regard neuf sur le vaste domaine des merveilles, insistant sur la créativité de la langue même, dans l'invention des imaginaires et des fantastiques.

Par le truchement de cette tripartition des types de récits, Fanfan Chen n'affronte pas directement les distinctions génériques des critiques occidentaux. Elle ne les ignore pas, mais elle n'en tient pas compte. Disons qu'elle choisit une démarche « transversale » par rapport à ces notions. Elle aborde les textes de ce qu'elle prend en compte comme « fantastique », par le biais de la rhétorique, dont elle montre que les textes qu'elle analyse en utilisent les figures de façon inattendue. Elle en montre les diverses approches par une étude du langage, par les métamorphoses qu'il peut induire. Ces analyses, qui ne se situent pas dans des notions pré-établies, permettent alors d'aborder les diverses formes de connaissance possibles permises par ces textes fantastiques.

Le lecteur se retrouve, une fois l'ouvrage terminé, devant un gisement de questions nouvelles, de réponses imprévues, signes de la grande qualité de ce travail, original et enrichissant.

Roger Bozzetto
Professeur émérite de Littérature Générale et Comparée
Université d'Aix-en-Provence, Marseille I

Prelude: Sequel to the Zen Story "What is Stirring?"

Once there was a reverend monk who preached to swarms of servile disciples the quintessence of Buddhist Zen in a wonderful languid afternoon. As the bourdon tone of the solemn speech swung with breeze, lulling the petrified audience, two of the disciples were distracted by the banner fluttered by a waft of wind. The master, seizing the chance to challenge his students, posed the renowned question, "What is stirring?" The first disciple answered naturally, "The banner is stirring." The other confidently replied, "The wind is stirring." After two wise coughs, the master pronounced the enlightening Zen discourse, "It's no banner neither wind but your mind that's stirring." A fit of silence struck the congregation drowned in self-reflection; the monk resumed his tedious lecture by reminding his disciples to rein their mind, since all illusion was stirred by it. Then, all of a sudden, a gust whizzed and whipped right at the master, who tumbled and grumbled; however, the disciples dared not stir, in order to show their comprehension of their master's illumination. Some of them smartly conjectured that this must be another Zen test and concentrated on their meditation, not stirred a whit by the whistle of the wind. It was not until another master passed by and discovered that the lecturer had swooned to the ground that the disciples woke out of their mind-reining meditation. A straggle of students carried away the immobile master. The evacuated ground echoed with swooshes of the disciples' confused mind. The breeze caressed and wafted the banner. Cicadas chanted their Zen amid the fluttering leaves.

"So what do you think is stirring?" Lao Zi came to one disciple, who seemed to awaken from slumbering in meditation during the whole session. He rubbed his eyes, surprised to find the great Daoist[3] philosopher before his eyes. Gaping at the fantastic scene, the disciple replied with absolute silence. He was completely enthralled by the complete metamorphosis of the congregation. "So what is stirring?" Lao Zi asked a second time. The chorus of nature broke the student's reticence. The banner was there fluttering with leaves rustling, cicadas stridulating, bees buzzing and birds warbling. "Listen to the wind!" He understood the language of birds and started to sing with Zephyr. Zephyrus beamed. "I got it!" "I got it!" No sooner had he turned to tell the master that all three were stirring in unison than Lao Zi left with the lingering couplets, "Discard desire to intuit mystery of the Universe; regard desire to deduce knowledge of the Universe." This straggler strode afar in mirth, thenceforth a minstrel telling fantastic tales; he thus named himself Zhuang Zi.

---

[3] We adopt the Beijing phonetic transcription system to transcribe Chinese words. Therefore *Tao*, *Taoist* and *Taoism* are transcribed as *Dao*, *Daoist* and *Daoism* in this book.

Introduction and Theorization of Fantastic Literature
Introduction

The fantastic genre or *le fantastique* "retrieves" its niche in literature following on from postmodernism. The verb "retrieves" implies that the fantastic narrative had effectively enjoyed its prestige in the sanctuary of Classic and Medieval literature. The sparkling ephemeral resurgence of fantastic literature[4] during the course of the Romantic Movement notwithstanding, its position in the literary academy proved to be overshadowed by realism, naturalism and symbolism. Though German authors (such as Tieck, Von Chamisso, Eichendorff, Hoffmann and Goethe) distinguished themselves in the style of fairy tales and exerted an important influence on French writers, especially Hoffmann's *Fantasiestücke* and Goethe's *Faust*, French realistic and naturalistic fiction and symbolist poetry still dominated literature. Charles Nodier inspired many of his contemporaries to excel in the fantastic genre, including great writers such as Gérard de Nerval and Théophile Gautier. Nevertheless, his visionary and universal theory of the fantastic has been ignored under the current focus on realism. In England, writers such as George MacDonald, Andrew Lang and Lord Dunsany had to wait until J. R. R. Tolkien's discovery and creation for a literary resurrection. In Chinese literature, the pejorative epithet of *"Zibuyu* (what Confucius refuses to discourse)" has made the fantastic, *zhiguai* or *shenguai* remain marginal.[5]

The attention swerving towards fantastic literature in academia was actually triggered in German and French worlds by Freud's analysis of Hoffmann's "The Sandman" and Jensen's *Gradiva* and P.-G. Castex's monograph on French romantic fantastic writers in the 20th century, whence emerged and evolved a series of systematic critiques, among others, psychoanalytical, thematic and structuralist. With the postmodern trend questioning all assumed *Weltanschauungen*, this imaginary genre hereafter spread its enchantment and popularity among English-speaking academia, further exercising a sweeping influence on the rest of the world, in particular Asia. Interestingly, this Western stimulation has aroused Chinese scholars and Western sinologists to explore the cultural heritage of the fantastic treasure *zhiguai*, a perpetuating narrative genre since Zhuang Zi, in Chinese literature. The reception and perception of the genre *zhiguai* caused no confusion of theoretical problems except for the debate between the truth of the

---

[4] In light of G. K. Chesterton, who employs "fantastic literature" in his *The Everlasting Man* to refer to the writings of imagination such as myths, fairytales and supernatural tales, I adopt the term "fantastic literature" in this book. The English adjective-noun term thus echoes the generic term in French (*la littérature fantastique*) or in German (*Phantastische Literatur*).

[5] Considering the controversy in the term *zhiguai*, often taken as referring to short stories, modern sinologists like Ouyang Jian and Lin Chen employ the term *shenguai* to include novels in their generic studies of the fantastic.

real and the unreal in Chinese history. Ironically, however, certain modern sinologists even claim that *zhiguai* is not fantastic literature, by forcing the genre
into the procrustean bed of Todorovian theories. The fallacy in evaluating this
literary genre naturally results from a limited linguistic and cultural knowledge
of a literature. Suffice it to adduce the absence of inflection in Chinese verbs and
the non-dualistic thinking mode that divulge the inadequacy in Tzvetan Todorov's theory of fantastic literature. On the contrary, the long disregarded theory of Nodier, who traced the fantastic creation back to myths and Greek epics,
proves to be universal and clairvoyant.

Be it fantasy, fantastic, *fantastique* or *zhiguai*, the thriving terminological
polysemy and interdisciplinary polyphony of the theories and critiques nevertheless induce a perplexing and even fallacious vision of the genre. For example,
the *fantasy* defined by Tolkien (a rather aesthetic term)[6] is received differently
by fantasy readers and emulators. This semantic lapse results in the confusion
and alternation between *fantasy* and *fantastic*. Critiques and research on the fantastic genre continue to burgeon with various phases, such as *la littérature fantastique*, fantastic literature, literature of the fantastic, fantasy, low fantasy or
French fantastic, horror or Gothic, magical realism and science-fiction. Certain
scholars content themselves with referring to some theories and advocating the
theoretical bias by adducing the generally accepted renowned fantastic fictions,
including numerous films. Some others abase fantastic literature by treating it as
an elucidation of psychoanalysis, feminism, deconstruction or cultural studies.
In view of the aforementioned historical evolution, sectarianism of academic
disciplines, bigotry in theories and incompetence in foreign languages and literatures, defining fantastic literature is becoming all the more delicate and "fantastic." A general ignorance of the fantastic imagination and *littérarité* or literariness has resulted in three branches of theorization about fantastic literature.
The thematic studies present an enumeration of analogous images and actions
without delving into the inventive sources and poetics. Psychoanalysis orients
the fantastic into a pathological diagnosis of the creating subject. The structuralist approach along the lines of Todorov, though declaring itself poetic, often
simplifies the fantastic creation into a semiotic or mathematic system, ignorant
of the poetic elements of invention and diction. A reexamination of the critiques
and theories on fantastic/fantasy literature from different cultures will bring to
light the problematic issues concerning the genre circumscription.

Chinese literature features among the world literature the first theoretical reflection on the fantastic genre, *zhiguai*. Writers as well as Daoist philosophers
meditated on the fantastic wisdom in such literary creation. The critical hub in
fact hinges on metaphysical discourses. Our studies of fantastic literature will

---

[6] In his "On Fairy-Stories," Tolkien employs *fantasy* to designate the narrative art that bridges
imagination and the result of the sub-creation. *Fantasy* is apprehended as the aestheticized
imagination, while *Fairy-Story* is treated as the genre.

start with an introduction of Daoist vision, both poetic and metaphysical, on the fantastic and conclude with a return to the metaphysics of *unus mundus* or one-as-whole.[7] Prior to the investigation of Western theories and critiques on the fantastic, it is essential to return to the etymology of the terms germane to the genre in question. Given that French writers and scholars are the first among Western literature to theorize about the fantastic genre and given Todorov's phenomenal influence worldwide, we will commence with French criticism after the exploration of Chinese fantastic literature.

Chinese Critiques and Theories

Historically, Chinese literature has been shaped by pressures towards realism from the preferences of the monarchy, and the dictates of Confucianism. The fantastic *zhiguai*, though defined as the original form of the narrative, had remained ignored under the Confucian criteria. However, Fang Zhengyao, contemporary scholar of Chinese literary criticism, divides Chinese fiction (*xiaoshuo*) into two principal schools: the fantastic theory (*huanqi*) and the realistic theory (*xieshi*). This fantastic theory refers to an aesthetics deriving from the Daoist vision of yin and yang. Different from the strict French perspective of the fantastic that sees the narrative of the improbable, unreal or supernatural as something scandalous or unbearable, the Daoist vision of the fantastic regards such phenomena as a part of Nature. Nevertheless, the Chinese fantastic narrative is different from the narrative mode of a fairy tale.

Although Steinmetz, the first critic to consider the fantastic by referring to other cultures, mentions Chinese *zhiguai* while exploring the etymology of *fantastique* in his work, the meaning of the term is not clarified enough. It is therefore necessary to explore the issue of *zhiguai*. The etymology of the Chinese term originates with the Daoist master Zhuang Zi [*Zhuangzi*, Chapter Xiaoyaoyou]: "Qi Xie, this is a man of *zhiguai* (or a collection of *zhiguai*) (*zhiguai* means to relate abnormal or strange or weird events): He tells the following story: When the Peng flies towards the meridional ocean, it beats water as far as three thousand stages (Chinese *li* = 0.576 Km). It soars up in a spiral along with the ascending wind of ninety thousand stages. It travels in the month of June where the strong wind breathes" [my translation]. The old Chinese dictionary *Shi Wen* explains the term *zhiguai* as: *Zhi* means to relate or to note; *guai* means *yi*, i.e. bizarre, strange, abnormal, unheard-of, inexplicable, absurd and supernatural.

---

[7] With regard the concept of *unus mundus*, please refer to our later discussion in the section of the imaginary of the fantastic and the following arguments.

In the history of Chinese literature, *zhiguai* undergoes three phases of evolution from the adjective *zhiguai* in the Six dynasties, then in the Tang dynasty a term designating all works containing the *zhiguai* elements and eventually, towards the end of the Tang dynasty, *zhiguai* becomes a sub-genre of *xiaoshuo* (fiction), thus *zhiguai xiaoshuo*. Fantastic writer Duan Chengshi first employed *zhiguai* as a genre in his preface of *Youyang zazu* (his collection of fantastic stories). Critic of the Ming dynasty, Hu Yinglin classified Chinese fiction into six sub-divisions, which included *zhiguai*.

In contemporary Chinese literary criticism, the fantastic kind of fiction is termed as "the genre of *zhiguai*" or "the genre of *shenguai* (the divine and the weird or the marvellous and the uncanny)." Or in response to foreign influence on the incremental popularity in the fantastic genre, Taiwanese publishers often consider the genre as a foreign concept by translating the term *fantasy literature* into *qihuan wenxue*, meanwhile also borrowing the Western confusion in the conception of the genre. It appears less baffling if we adopt the traditional definition of the Chinese *zhiguai*, though somewhat superficially and thematically oriented. This simplification and permanence of *zhiguai*'s definition shows that the Chinese fantastic genre has existed since Antiquity and always offers a precise conception of the genre. Unfortunately, this perpetual representation of the fantastic turns out to be a faithful mimesis of literature; *zhiguai* manifests itself as a stylized narrative code. We have to wait until the republic epoch where Western literature exerts a great influence on Chinese literature to see the naissance of a fantastic literature with a paradigm shift.

Defining Chinese fantastic literature is indeed like enumerating the cast of imaginary characters. Most critics take pains to explore the semantic field of these terms related to fantastic phenomena. Since most collections of such tales have *guai* and *yi* in their titles, these terms are usually studied. French sinologist André Lévy, in his preface to the collection of Chinese fantastic tales of the Tang dynasty, elucidates and highlights the particular meaning of *yi* by translating his neologism "superextraordinary." Critic Gao Heng needed to clarify the meaning of *zhiyi* while prefacing Pu Songling's (1604-1715) masterpiece of fantastic tales *Liaozhai zhiyi*: *Zhiyi* signifies "to tell or to render evident what is different from the normality." Modern Scholar Li Jianguo, whose specialty is *zhiguai* before the Tang dynasty, elaborates the etymology and morphology of the essential fantastic phenomena featuring in *zhiguai*. These essential beings featuring in the tales of *zhiguai* are *shen* (god, especially celestial gods), *xian* (Daoist immortal, normally taken as god), *gui* (ghost), *yao* (nonhuman spirits, monsters and devils) and *guai* or *yi* (abnormal phenomena). One of the rare contemporary scholars who write solely on the fantastic genre, Yu Rujie offers the following definition: "*Zhiguai* is a kind of weird, strange, extraordinarily abnormal and absurd tale. The images in the tale are divine and weird; the plots are extraordinary and extraordinarily abnormal because they transgress logic, reason and nature" [Yu, 19].

Such an oversimplification of a genre definition can be attributed to the absence of dialectic argumentation in Chinese philosophy. Without a tradition of Cartesian dualism, the Chinese narrative does not revolve around the antithesis of the real and the unreal or supernatural, but rather the cohabitation of the transiently considered real and unreal or supernatural. Nothing is permanently stable; the truth involves permanent changes, *"yi"* in Daoist *Yi Jing*[8] or *"wuchang"* (impermanence) in Buddhism. Chinese vision reserves the possibility or ruse of reevaluating reality; the interplay between the real and the unreal appears to be insignificant. In this manner, the Daoist writer Guo Pu (276-324) offered the earliest critique on the fantastic in Chinese literature in the preface of *Shanhai Jing (The Classic of Mountains and Seas)*. His discourse is oriented by the genuine meanings of *yi* and *guai*. He argued that the abnormality is not absolutely unreal or nonexistent, for he deemed that all perceiving subjects are relatively objects from the perspective of the Universe. Men are the only subjective beings apt to sunder the objects and beings into normal and abnormal or strange. The concepts in the *yi* vs. non-*yi* or *guai* vs. non-*guai* are relative but not absolute. He questioned human world vision by pronouncing: "Who knows whether it is not man who is the more fantastic than the phenomena that are claimed to be fantastic" [*Shanhai Jing*, preface]. In order to voice opposition to the Confucian contemptuous attitude about fantastic writing, Guo defended *zhiguai* by persuading readers to accept it as something real. After Confucius's famous discourse of *"Zi bu yu guai li luan shen"* (Confucius refuses to discourse about the weird, violence, disorder and gods), Chinese literati have often regarded it as taboo to write *zhiguai* since *guai* here features the first item among Confucius's subjects of refusal. Chinese fantastic literature is thus oppressed to certain extent by the synonym of *Zi Bu Yu* (What Confucius refuses to discourse about). One great writer, Yuan Mei (1716-1797) of the Qing dynasty, ironically entitled his book of fantastic tales as *Zi Bu Yu*.

Most Daoist writers tend to assume *zhiguai* as realistic stories, by questioning who can say that what is fantastic today will not be real in the future and vice versa. Lin Zaiyong, a contemporary critic, follows this philosophical vision to comment on fantastic literature. He focuses on Chinese people's mentality faced with the phenomena of *guai* (weird) and *yi* (superextraordinary) and the process of engendering wisdom. He adduces *zhiguai* stories to show the literature's function as a mirror. The *zhiguai* literature is treated as a literature of evasion that illustrates Chinese wisdom. He underlines the Chinese notion of normal and abnormal:

---

[8] We use the transcription of *Yi Jing* in the present book, according to the Beijing transcription. *Yi Jing* is also transcribed as I Ching or Yi Ching.

> The normal and the abnormal are not fixed and unchangeable notions. The normal is the established order and the phenomenon that is found to be within reach of human wisdom. The abnormal is the subversion of this order. However, this established order is constrained by the barrier of human wisdom; therefore, we are not able to correctly seize the order of the world. The abnormal can also result from the alteration of the world or the Universe; the established order is thus overturned." [my translation, Lin, 9]

For most Daoist writers, the fantastic involves wisdom, mystery and the aesthetics of liberty. For most Confucian writers, the fantastic functions as satire or allegory. For Buddhists, the fantastic is a contrivance to intimidate readers by the abiding karma and retribution to convert to Buddhism. Chinese theories on the fantastic manifest themselves as metaphysical and general when compared with the theorization underpinned by Western formal logic. To examine and review the fantastic theories developed in Western literature, it is necessary to trace back to the etymology of these words: fantastic or *fantastique* and fantasy or *fantaisie* or *merveilleux*. The polysemy of terming the fantastic genre and the polyphony of discoursing the genre are indeed related to the semantic obscurity of the words in question and the severing of meanings.

Etymology of Fantastic/Fantastique *and* Fantasy/Fantaisie

The English word *fantastic* and *fantasy* are indeed derived from the French word *fantastique,* which in turn is from Latin and Greek. The etymology of *fantastic* is presented as follows:

> Fantastic: [obsolete] imaginary XIV; [obsolete] imaginative XV; extravagantly fanciful XVI. – Old French *fantastique* – Medieval Latin *fantasticus,* Late Latin *phantasticus* – Greek *phantastikós,* formed on *phantázein* make visible, *phantázesthai* have visions, imagine; [...]. [Onions, 344]
> Fantastic: c.1387, "existing only in imagination," Middle English fantastic, imagined, from Old French *fantastique,* from Late Latin *phantázein,* imaginary, from Greek *phantastikós,* able to create mental images, from *phantázein* "make visible" (middle voice *phantázesthai* "picture to oneself"), from *phantázesthai,* to appear. Trivial sense of "wonderful, marvellous" first recorded 1938. [Harper]

The term *fantastic* is essentially related to imagination, the imaginary and the creation of visions. *Fantasy*, besides the meanings of imagination and the creation of visions, also focuses on the features of illusion, appearance and desire:

> Fantasy, phantasy: [obsolete] mental apprehension; obsolete phantom; obsolete delusive imagination; baseless supposition XIV; changeful mood XV; imagination XVI. – Old French *fantasie* (modern fantaisie) = Provençal *fantazia,* etc.,

Italian *fantasia* – Latin *phantasia* – Greek *phantasíá* appearance (later, *phantom*), mental process, sensuous perception, faculty of imagination, formed on *phantázein*; [...]. [Onions, 344]

Fantasy: c.1325, "illusory appearance," from Old French *fantasie*, from Latin *phantasia*, from Greek *phantasíá* "appearance, image, perception, imagination," from *phantázesthai* "picture to oneself," from *phantos* "visible," from *phainesthai* "appear," in late Greek "to imagine, have visions," related to *phaos, phos* "light." Sense of "whimsical notion, illusion" is pre-1400, followed by that of "imagination," which is first attested 1539. Sense of "day-dream based on desires" is from 1926, as is fantasize. [Harper]

In view of the fact that English "fantastic" and "fantasy" trace their origin to Old French, Latin and Greek, and that the epithet of the term fantastic as genre is a translation from French *fantastique* to designate the specific imaginary genre, we deem it a requisite to examine the etymology of the French *fantastique* and *fantasie*.

Fantastique: 14th Century Latin adjective *fantasticum*, deriving from Greek verb *phantasein*: "faire voir en apparence" (make perceive apparently), "donner l'illusion" (give illusion), and is applied to the phenomena departing from the ordinary, "appear" and "show." The adjective *phantastikon* "that concerns imagination" could make the substantive *phantstiké*: "the ability to imagine vain things" (Aristotle). The adjective "*fantastique*" is used in the Middle Ages. *Fantasie* in classic French designates imagination until the 19th Century. The *Dictionnaire de l'Académie* of 1831 gives the meaning "chimerical" to *fantastique*: "It also signifies what only has the appearance of a corporal being, without reality." *The Littré* (1863) agrees, and continues to indicate that (1) *fantastique* only exists through imagination (2) it only appears to be a corporal being. The dictionary also specifies that "fantastic tales generally refer to fairy tales, ghost tales and in particular, a genre of tales to be in vogue by German Hoffmann (*Fantasiestücke*), where the supernatural plays an important role. Hoffmann is one of the distinctive writers following the German tradition of the *Märchen*. This definition is also accepted by the *Dictionnaire de l'Académie* of 1878 and the *Trésor de la Langue fraçaise* (1980). Around this epoch (first half of the 19th Century), the word *fantastique* appears as a substantive to name a certain category of literary expression, i.e., a genre. [my translation, *Le Robert*]

This same root gives words like "phantasm", "phantasmagoria", "fantasy" and "phantom", all that belongs to the field of apparition, imagination, and spectre. In this manner, *le fantastique* or the fantastic is essentially related to the morbid part of our imagination, to our incessant search of evasion, to the mixing of the unexpected and the unpredictable [Labbé et Millet]. Rooted in the meanings of "imaginary," "visionary" and "unbelievable," the word *fantastique* or fantastic is concerned with imagining the vain things, as opposed to reality and reason, thus related to madness and strangeness. It makes the nonexistent come to light and renders the invisible visible. The supernatural is naturally one of the attributes of the word *fantastic*.

In Anglophonic culture, the term "fantasy literature" is adopted by more writers and critics of the genre. However, this demonstrates a semantic confusion in the term originally defined by Tolkien. He discerned quite clearly "fantasy" and "fantastic" while writing his treatise on "Fairy-Stories" and did not regard fantasy as a genre but an aesthetic treatment of fairy-stories; viz. the poeticization or aestheticization of fairy-stories is called fantasy, the art that bridges imagination and the final sub-creation. From a semantic and etymological perspective, he connected fantasy with the fantastic. Both involve "images of things that are not only 'not actually present,' but which are indeed not to be found in our primary world at all or are generally believed not to be found there" [Tolkien 1997, 139]. Different from *the fantastic*, a more general term to characterize any inexplicable or unlikely phenomenon, *fantasy* is a polished form of narrative art, which is a requirement to writing fairy-stories.

Considering the etymology of the term and the difference between *fantasy* and *fantastic*, we maintain that fantastic literature is more appropriate to encompass the genre of writing containing non-realistic elements or the imaginary writing germane to the unknown, from the ancient Greek literarized myths (*mythes littérarisés*),[9] the Chinese *zhiguai*, fairy tales, supernatural tales, to the romantic fantastic, modern fantasy, magical realism and science-fiction. If we respect the etymological meanings of "fantastic" and "fantasy," the sundry representations of fantastic literature beget various names for the genre, which can be simply considered as sub-genre of fantastic literature: fantasy, horror story, ghost story, Gothic novel, science-fiction, science-fantasy, low fantasy, magical realism, *le merveilleux* vs. *le fantastique*, etc. The aforementioned linguistic blur of terms and the reception of the fantastic genre may not result from translation problems, but rather from the fundamental *Weltanschauungen*, which expound the differences in theorizing the fantastic genre from different cultures.

French Critiques and Theories

In earlier French theorization of fantastic literature, critics tended to deduce a theory through distinguishing the genre from its neighbouring genre, viz. *le fantastique* from *le merveilleux* (the marvellous). By *le merveilleux* French critics originally meant the fairy tale, whose narrative formula is fixed by commencing

---

[9] According to the *mythocritique* or mythocriticism of the French school, theorists such as Pierre Brunel and André Siganos, *mythes littérarisés* or literarized myths mean the traditional antique myths rewritten into literature. On the contrary, mythes *littéraires* or literary myths refer to the myths created from a repetitive theme by authors in literature, for example, the myth of Don Juan.

the story with "*Il était une fois*" (Once upon a time). However, after Todorov's launching his famous theory, *le merveilleux* was defined as the narrative that falls into the supernatural explanation of unlikely events taking place in the story, as opposed to *l'étrange* (English translation generally adopts Freud's term "uncanny"), if the reader is inclined for a natural explication of the same phenomenon. The vision of fantastic literature hinging on the differentiation from the marvellous among French scholars can be traced to the Cartesian tradition of dualism. Under this bias of finite reasoning, theorizing about an infinite imaginary literary genre would appear to be paradoxical. Thus, Denis Mellier penetrates into the theoretical paradox that he who engages in the critical debate on *le fantastique* would confront. This paradox is quite simple after all: either the critical discourse constructs its Procrustean bed of definition and theory or attempts to avoid the restrictive delimitation by adopting a considerable open approach [Mellier 1999, 71]. We conceive that this paradoxical dualism manifests in French theorization of *la littérature fantastique* in four perspectives: (1) a historical vs. non-historical vision of the fantastic, (2) the distinction between the fantastic and the marvellous, (3) objectivity vs. subjectivity in the intrusion of unlikely phenomena and (4) hesitation as an aesthetics of reception: the reader's engagement. The central aspect highlighted by most critics is the psychological and realistic essence in French fantastic literature in contrast with the superficial and supernatural narration of the marvellous or fairy tale. Except for few writers such as Nodier, Schuhl, Schneider and Caillois, who maintain a historical lineage in fantastic creation and disregard a distinction between the fantastic and the marvellous, nearly all other important critics insist on a historical rupture in the fantastic genre, thus vigorously distinguishing the fantastic from the marvellous. They interpret the so-called supernatural intrusion as nothing but the subjective perception or illusion of the character. With a Cartesian world vision, French readers tend to experience the Todorovian hesitation. We will adduce hence, briefly, certain important definitions of the fantastic proposed by French critics.

Castex, whose study of French fantastic tales (from Nodier to Maupassant) is a landmark in fantastic research, defined from a historical and thematic point of view the fantastic as "a brutal intrusion of the mystery in the setting of real life" (*une intrusion brutale du mystère dans le cadre de la vie réelle*) and assumes that the genre is related to psychological morbidity [Castex, 8]. Albeit anthropologist Roger Caillois compiled a comprehensive anthology of world fantastic literature, he still maintained a strict and French definition of the genre that the intrusion of the fantastic shows a scandal (*scandale*), a tear (*déchirure*) and an unusual irruption (*irruption insolite*) that is unbearable for both the character and the reader in the real world [Caillois 1966, 8-9]. His theoretical paradox emerges as we read through the fantastic tales from his anthology to find that many tales do not fit his definition proposed in the preface to the volumes.

Formalist poetician Todorov defines the fantastic genre by three elements: (1) The text obliges the reader to consider the world of the character as real. The reader has to hesitate between the supernatural (*le merveilleux*) and the natural (*l'étrange*) explanations. (2) The character may also feel this kind of hesitation. Thus the reader identifies with the character. (3) It is significant that the reader adopts a certain attitude towards the text: an allegorical or "poetic" interpretation must be refused. [my translation, Todorov 1970, 37-8]. His assumption that the hesitation felt by a being that knows nothing but natural laws, confronting an apparently supernatural event [ibid., 12] exposes the influence of the Cartesian thinking mode on his fantastic theorization, since the natural laws themselves remain to be questioned. With this perspective and cultural restriction in his theory of the fantastic, Todorov nevertheless bequeaths to the field of fantastic criticism a very precious heritage, viz. an analysis undergirded firmly by structuralist poetics. His analysis of the *énoncé* or enunciated (discourses and figures) and the *énonciation* or enunciation (narrative authority), syntax and semantic of fantastic short stories is a departing point of our present analysis of fantastic poetics.

While Todorov reduces the definition of the fantastic to an ephemeral moment of hesitation, Irène Bessière, another semiotician of fantastic theory, recaptures Sartre's terms of *"thétique"* and *"non-thétique"* to exhibit the antinomy of the fantastic story. The marvellous tale is *non-thétique* because it does not affirm the reality it represents. On the other hand, the fantastic tale is *thétique* when the represented reality is a false hypothesis. The fantastic is imposed with ambiguity and hesitation between the natural and the supernatural. Objecting to Todorov's theory of "hesitation between," she contends that the fantastic is the place of "convergence of *thétique* narration (novel of *realia*) and *non-thétique* narration (the marvellous, fairy tale)" [Bessière, 36-7].

Discriminating from the setting and characters in fairy tales, Louis Vax sees the narrative economy of fantastic fiction as such: "We are at first in our clear, solid and reassuring world, a strange, dreadful and inexplicable event arises unexpectedly; so we know the particular shiver that provokes a conflict between the real and the possible" (*Nous sommes d'abord dans notre monde clair, solide, rassurant, survienne un événement étrange, effrayant, inexplicable ; alors nous connaissons le frisson particulier que provoque un conflit entre le réel et le possible*) [Vax 1974, 5].

For Jacques Finné, the fantastic narrative consists of "logical mysteries that are dissolved by an explanation that brings back to our knowledge system a number of apparently illogical phenomena." With a more general perspective, he raises the issue of cultural differences in the reception of fantastic literature. For example, he brings to light the contrasting receptions of ghost stories in England and France. An English reader undoubtedly accepts the existence of ghosts while reading fantastic stories implying a haunted house. On the contrary, a French reader is more skeptical about the existence of ghosts and the phenomenon of being haunted. This difference is even greater if we compare a Chinese reader with a French reader. A Chinese reader would conclude *without hesitation* that the disquieting invisible phenomenon in Maupassant's "Le Horla" is nothing but a ghost. This is why the story is often included in the collection translated in Chinese language as "Selected ghost stories."

The contemporary studies of *la littérature fantastique* in France manifest an inclination towards a more general definition of the genre, in that fantasy writings and horror or ghost stories have become a fantastic *vedette* and the French style ambiguous fantastic (befitting Todorov's theory) is withering after creative saturation. For example, Mellier conceives of a third perspective, the fantastic as "the writing of excess," to leave the alleged critical paradox. He suggests envisaging the meanings of theoretical differences, viz. exploring the plurality of discourse provided by such differences [Mellier 1999, 71]. By the same token, Roger Bozzetto and Arnaud Huftier seek to cross the boundaries to investigate *le fantastique* and study the approaches to *the unthinkable in literature*. The issue of translations and aesthetic receptions for the generic term with the fantastic effect in different cultures is raised and questioned [Roger 2004, 15]. A universal viewpoint of the imaginary genres is reendowed to fantastic literature. Academic journals such as *IRIS/Gerf*, *GERLI* or *Otrante* (French journals of fantastic literature) publish articles on myriads of fantastic literature. Likewise, the American *Journal of the Fantastic in the Arts* publishes articles on fantastic works in terms of the general definition. If English literature, compared with German and French, appeared slow in its dedication to fantastic literature during the Romantic period, it relays the fantastic creation in the 20th century by its prolific production of horror stories, fantasy and science-fiction. Compared with the strictness and dualism in the French theorization, the theoretical evolution of the fantastic in Anglophonic literature presents a broader perspective, except for critiques along the lines of Todorovian theory.

English Critiques and Theories

Todorov's theory of fantastic literature not only reigns over French theorization of the genre but also influences and intrigues Anglophonic critics. Their theorizing development can be seen as theses for and against Todorov's restrictive definition and theory. In order to include the genres of fantastic stories written by Kafka (*The Metamorphosis*) or Gogol ("The Nose") and to be at the same time faithful to Todorov's structuralist poetics, Brooke-Rose enhances the definition of the latter by modifying it into two modes of narration. The mode of "the real as unreal" refers to Todorovian fantastic; the mode of "the unreal as real" encompasses the fantastic that narrates the unreal events in a realistic way, for

example, the pathetic metamorphosis of Gregor into a bug in the beginning of
the story and the absurd loss of Kovalev's nose and his nose-figure's individual
adventure, both narrated by a heterodiegetic narrator (Todorov argues that fantastic literature should be told by homodiegetic narrators)[10] that excludes hesitation. While Brooke-Rose revolutionizes Todorov's linear model (uncanny / fantastic-uncanny / fantastic-marvellous / marvellous) into a circle to allow realism
and the marvellous to get connected (marvellous / realism / uncanny) so as to
include her assumed mode of "the unreal as real" [Brooke-Rose, 84], Cornwell
modifies both models by returning to Todorov's linear form and extending to the
following scheme: non-fiction / fiction / realism / uncanny realism / fantastic-uncanny / pure fantastic / fantastic-marvellous / marvellous / mythology, etc.
[Cornwell, 39]. He further sub-divides the part of marvellous into three different
narrative modes: (1) What if? (e.g. Kafka's *Metamorphosis*) (2) Fairy story (e.g.
animal stories) and (3) Romance/Fantasy (e.g. sub-creation *à la Tolkienienne*).
[ibid., 40]. In this manner, he circumscribes the literary fantastic as ranging from
fantastic-uncanny to fantastic-marvellous.

Another major branch of fantastic theorization is oriented towards the psychoanalytical approach along the lines of Freud. The combination of Freudian
theory and Todorovian theory is further developed as a vital vision inspiring the
researches of fantastic literature. Rosemary Jackson, with psychoanalysis as a
cornerstone to characterize fantasy as subversion, extends Todorov's theorization from being confined to the poetics (or rather structuralism) of the fantastic
into "a more widely based cultural study of the fantastic" [Jackson, 7]. She defines fantasy as a literary mode, "structural features underlying various works in
different periods of time, [...] from which a number of related genres emerge
[ibid., 35]. We may regard, in terms of linguistics, the sub-genres or various
forms as *paroles* and the mode as *langue*.

Quite close to French semiotician Bessière's theory, also inspired by Sartre,
Jackson places the fantastic as existing "in the hinterland between 'real' and
'imaginary,' shifting the relations between them through its indeterminacy"
[ibid., 35] and concludes that the fantastic "pushes towards an area of
non-signification" [ibid., 41]. This conception parallels Bessière's theory postulated by *thétique* and *non-thétique* as well as the system of signifying without
the signified. Like the two aforesaid critics, Amaryll Chanady's theory is also
based on a dualistic view. Attempting to transcend the ambiguity resulting from
"hesitation," she employs "antinomy" to replace "hesitation" and defines it as
"the simultaneous presence of two conflicting codes in the text" [Chanady, 12].
With this postulate, she further distinguishes the fantastic from magical realism.
Her theory is reminiscent of the differentiation between the fantastic and the
marvellous among French critics.

---

[10] We employ Gérard Genette's terms of narratology in this book.

T. E. Apter, who also espouses psychoanalytical theory, raises the characteristic of uncertainty in fantasy, a vision similar to Todorovian hesitation and ambiguity. She argues that "the impact of fantasy rests upon the fact that the world presented seems to be unquestionably ours, yet at the same time, as in a dream, ordinary meanings are suspended" [Apter, 2-3]. Fantasy is interpreted as the aestheticization of our phantasm. Faithful to Freud's uncanny theory, she asserts that fantasy literature features the following psychoanalytic concepts: employment of associations which are like idiosyncratic associations, satisfaction of unconscious desires, being susceptible to psychoanalytic interpretation of dreams so as to be an exhibition of unconscious processes.

After reviewing the above theories revolving around "hesitation," "antinomy" and "psychoanalysis," we will investigate the more general or eclectic theories. Voicing opposition to the Todorovian vision of the genre, Harold Bloom criticizes Todorov's exclusive theory by denying that we "hesitate" in reading Hoffmann and others [Bloom 1982, 205]. However, without proposing a theory or definition for the genre, his books are confined to treat the fantastic sub-genre: fantasy, mainly Lindsay and most writers of "the Inklings." Fantasy is to him a specific version of romance, the decisive role being played by the author:

> Fantasy, as a belated version of romance, promises an absolute freedom from belatedness, from the anxieties of literary influence and origination, yet this promise is shadowed always by a psychic over-determination in the form itself of fantasy, that puts the stances of freedom into severe question. ... The cosmos of fantasy, of the pleasure/pain principle, is revealed in the shape of nightmare, and not of hallucinatory wish-fulfillment. [ibid., 206]

By extending Tolkien's theory of Fairy-Stories as sub-creation, T. E. Little assumes that fantasy is the sub-creation of a *Tertiary World* when an author's Secondary World "goes beyond that licence [realistic] and becomes other" in comparison with the sub-creation of the Secondary World [Little, 10]. He argues that "all writers of creative fiction are sub-creators of Secondary Worlds. The Secondary World of a non-fantastic writer will be as close to the Primary World as his talents and the needs of his art will allow" [ibid., 9]. However, his concept of "sub-creation" is not exactly what Tolkien defines it to be.

Eric S. Rabkin contends that the work's universe and its characters are crucial to the delineation of the fantasy genre: "the truly fantastic occurs when the ground rules of a narrative are forced to make 180-degree reversal, when prevailing perspectives are directly contradicted" [Rabkin, 12]. He terms the ability of art to create its own interior set of ground rules "decorum," which is what Tolkien calls "sub-creation." He adduces Lewis Carroll's Alice's astonishment underpinned by the diametrically contradicted ground rules to illustrate this possible condition for the fantastic. He further assumes three classes of signal for the fantastic: "signals of the characters (such as Alice's astonishment), signals of the narrator (such as Juster's and Morris' assertions), and signals of the implied author (such as the narrative structures of Borges and Moorcock)" [ibid., 24]. He differentiates between the fantastic and Fantasy by degrees. "In more or less degree, a whole range of narratives uses the fantastic. And at the far end of this range, we find Fantasy, the genre whose centre and concern, whose primary enterprise, is to present and consider the fantastic" [ibid., 41]. Accordingly, Rabkin views the fantastic as a literary technique and Fantasy more a genre. His emphasis on the work's universe shifts the attention to the composition of work instead of a philosophical argumentation hinging on the polar thesis of real and unreal. Like Belgian scholar Finné, Rabkin raises the issue of cultural differences in appreciating the fantastic genre, especially the difference between English speakers and German and French speakers:

> In the world of English speakers, perhaps the paradigmatic Fantasist is the delightful Lewis Carroll. For speakers of German and French, the paradigmatic Fantasist is the ghastly Hoffmann. The continental words for 'fantastic' have a bit of the tone we associate with 'macabre'. Freud and Jung, German speakers, created the modern reception of the fantastic. But we can choose to look at the daylight instead of the gloom. In England, someone can feel 'fantastic!' The fantastic reveals our deepest fears, but also our greatest aspirations; not only our hidden shames, but also our finest hopes. [ibid., 226-7]

Albeit his assertion that fantasy represents a basic mode of human knowing with a polar opposite of Reality, Rabkin reserves his view on the permanence of Reality, which is analogous to Daoist world vision:

> Reality is that collection of perspectives and expectations that we learn in order to survive in the here and now. But the here and now becomes tomorrow; a child grows, a culture develops, a person dreams. In every area of human thought, civilization has evolved a functioning reality, but the universe has suffered no reality to maintain itself unchanged. The glory of man is that he is not bounded by reality. Man travels in fantastic worlds. [ibid., 227]

C. N. Manlove uses the term fantasy to define the narrative genre. To explore the fantasy literature of England, he needs a definition and thus defines fantasy as "a fiction involving the supernatural or impossible, which fits with the English preoccupation with the supernatural" [Manlove 1999, 3] He further clarifies the meanings of the crucial terms: "'supernatural' implies the presence of some form of magic or the numinous, from ghosts and fairies to gods and devils; 'impossible' means what simply could not be [...]: for the purposes of this book 'impossible' will be subsumed under 'supernatural'" [Ibid., 3]. Manlove's definition of the genre appears relatively simple and broad, and resembles the Chinese definition. It is derived from his eclectic perspective on the sundry world visions subject to cultures:

> Those theorists whose definitions differed from mine usually did so because they were applying them to quite different works, or contexts: E.S. Rabkin, for instance, described what he saw as the fantastic in all literature (as, more recently, has Kathryn Hume); Rosemary Jackson discussed 'subversive fantasies' by Poe, Stevenson, Dostoevsky, Kafka, or Pynchon directed at criticism of our world; W.R. Irwin considered fantasies subscribing to his notion of 'play', or 'the game of the impossible'; Tzvetan Todorov was concerned with certain French works of the nineteenth century which produced a hesitation in the reader between 'supernatural' and 'natural' readings. No synthesis of these diverse views is possible; rather we should consider each on its merits as having discovered a genre or a dominant characteristic appearing in numbers of different works, such discoveries at best allowing both increased understanding of individual works and the revelation of some larger cultural impulse. [Manlove 1990, 53-4]

Among the existing theories, Kathryn Hume's definition is relatively universal to encompass a broad spectrum of literary works. Criticizing the common fallacy of assuming fantasy to be a pure phenomenon, she classifies the existing exclusive theories into five categories ranging from one-element definitions to five-element definitions so as to offer her own inclusive definition. With a revolutionary postulate that literature is the product of two impulses, she proposes a working definition that fantasy is any departure from consensus reality, an impulse native to literature and manifested in innumerable variations, from monster to metaphor [Hume, 21]. Consequently, fantasy comprises "transgressions of what one generally takes to be physical facts, technical or social innovations which have not yet taken place, alternate worlds and universes" and "those stories whose marvel is considered 'real'" [ibid., 21].

In responding to the existing heterogeneous theories, Nancy H. Trail proposes an eclectic theory for the fantastic genre in her article "Fictional World of the Fantastic." She develops a comprehensive theory based on four modes of the fantastic: authenticated, ambiguous, disauthenticated and paranormal. The authenticated mode refers to the fictional world "characterized by the copresence of two modally opposite domains, the natural and the supernatural." The ambiguous mode fits in the mostly accepted theories revolving around Todorov's definition of hesitation or ambiguity. The disauthenticated mode includes the narratives often excluded from fantastic literature, namely the fantastic explained, for example, Potocki's *Le Manuscrit Trouvé à Saragosse*. The fourth fantastic mode depicts, by a radical transformation of the dichotomy, a world where "'supernatural' and 'natural' are no longer mutually exclusive." The obscurity between the natural and the supernatural domains will make "a seemingly supernatural event – for example, a character having a precognitive ex-

perience – occurs within the natural domain yet resists explanation under accepted concepts of the physically possible." Maupassant's "Apparition" (1883)
is of this type. Trail's theory of the fantastic appears to be comprehensive, although Tolkien's idiosyncratic fantasy being classified under the same mode as
Lewis's or Gogol's fantastic narratives seem far-fetched.

One of the current theoretical monographs on fantastic literature, Richard
Mathews's *Fantasy – The Liberation of Imagination* contains very rich research
on the historical evolution of the genre from antiquity to the present day. Nevertheless, his book is limited to Morris, Tolkien, White, Howard and Le Guin.
While recognizing the difficulty in defining literary fantasy precisely, Mathews
assumes that it is "a type of fiction that evokes wonder, mystery, or magic – a
sense of possibility beyond the ordinary, material, rationally predictable world in
which we live. As a literary genre, modern fantasy is clearly related to the
magical stories of myth, legend, fairy tale, and folklore from all over the world"
[Mathews, 1]. This is another universal definition similar to the Chinese thematic conception of the genre, both lacking a systematic generic argumentation
with formal examination. Since some critics raise the issue of cultural differences vis-à-vis various visions of the fantastic, it is relevant to get acquainted
with some theories from other linguistic cultures.

Critiques and Theories from Other Western Linguistic Cultures

Mario Praz, a specialist of Romantic literature, contributes important pages in
his *The Romantic Agony* to some discussion on the literature belonging to the
fantastic genre. His approach is thematic and psychological. His focus thus is on
the storyline, psychology and eroticism without a systematic theorization of
fantastic literature. From an unconventional angle, another Italian scholar, Strada
Vittorio, grounded in the philosophy of Plato's myth of the cave, defines the
creation of the fantastic as a general act of human imagination. This is a poetic
procedure that *aestheticizes* superstition – the lost primitive myth. In his view,
Plato's "myth of the cave"

> can point the way to a definition of the fantastic which is a form of invention
> on the part of a poetic reason born in the post-mythic age, an age in which the
> model of knowledge and of truth is constituted from an empirical and positive
> science, from the viewpoint of which myth, deprived of its symbolic signifi-
> cance, turns into pure superstition, or a primitive stage of knowledge – imper-
> fect and superceded. [qtd. Cornwell, 21]

The modern fantastic bears a quality with "a presentiment of another reality, as
an image of the invisible, as code for the unknowable. The fantastic is a form of
consciousness of being in the cave. ... The fantastic is a poetic mythology of a

disenchanted and demythologised world" [ibid., 21]. Strada's idealistic theory of the fantastic mirrors the ideal of Nodier and Tolkien.

Gero von Wilpert, German critic of the fantastic, offers the term *Phantastische Literatur* both general and restrictive definitions:

> (1) In a broader sense, the unreal, the surreal, the marvellous, the dream-like elements, fear and prevision, etc. encompassed in literary works, from horror novel to science-fiction.
>
> (2) In a strict sense, the representation of the marvellous and of the uncanny in a particular manner in literature, where the reader and the character are left undecided between the reality and the imagination, from the value of a suspended aesthetic. For example, E. T. A. Hoffmann, E. A. Poe, J. Potocki, etc. [Wilper, 600][11]

Conscious of the controversy in all possible definitions of the fantastic literature, Von Wilpert presents an eclectic viewpoint on the genre. From a universal perspective, Critics Zondergeld and Wiedenstried, asserting that *Phantastische Literatur* exists in all times and epochs, hold a general view of fantastic literature, which corresponds with the first definition proposed by Wilper.

We have heretofore recapitulated most Western critics and theories on fantastic/fantasy literature. The analytical and dialectic language in theorization underscores the narrative process and the underlying epistemology. In fact, certain Western theorists, such as Vittorio, Rabkin, Manlove and Hume, also embrace a universal view based on the metaphysical differences, from a perspective similar to Chinese critics. We observe that the process of the theorization of fantastic literature resembles the abstraction of language, as Barfield and Tolkien criticized the devaluation of language.[12] Since fantastic creation is quintessentially engrained in imagination, using abstract and rational rules to force the literature into such a limited Procrustean bed proves to be contradictory and ridiculous. Last, we have to listen to the fantastic authors themselves. If we turn our back on the truth in Logos or Words, we would split the semantic unity of language and myth. Likewise, we may miss the imaginary essence of fantastic literature by ignoring the authors' visions (mostly visionary) and their poetic language of the fantastic.

---

[11] (1) im weitesten Sinne jedes Literaturwerk, das irreale, surreale, wunderbare, traumhafte Elemente, Angst und Zukunftsvisionen u.a. enthält, vom Schauerroman bis zur Science Fiction. (2) im engeren Sinne die lit. Darstellung des wunderbaren / unheimlichen in einer Weise, die Leser und Figuren zwischen Realität und Imagination unschlüssig werden lässt und aus dem Schwebezustandästhet Werte zieht, bes. E.T.A. Hoffmann, E.A. Poe, J. Potocki u.a.

[12] Barfield and Tolkien's criticism on language and myth will be elaborated later in the section of periodization and style of recovery.

Creation vis-à-vis Theorization –
Authors' Own Interpretations of the Genre

In the existing theories of the fantastic, except for Tolkien, writers' own theories on the genre had been ignored. The strict theories of the fantastic manifest a gap between existing works and theories. Given that fantastic creation is essentially related to imagination, a rationalistic and dualistic theorization may appear paradoxical. It is time to turn to authors themselves. Evoking fantastic writers' own assertion or definition of the genre may facilitate our understanding of the fantastic virtuosity. Though contemporary theorists insist on the alleged meta-writing or claim writing critiques to be equally valuable as creative writing (a re-creating of the work), we have to hearken unto the writers' own discourses since literary creation and dialectical argumentation can never be the same. Furthermore, writing the fantastic is completely different from theorizing the fantastic, as we can corroborate from the abundant aforementioned theories. It requires authentic imagination, a kind of imagination that is beyond discursive language, which can be apprehended through the Eucharistic process.[13]

Zhuang Zi, the pioneer of *zhiguai*, told stories or fables to illustrate the unfathomable wisdom of Dao but had not developed theoretical argumentation on the genre. Instead, he treated fantastic storytelling as an important means to reveal truth. Given that Zhuang Zi and Lie Zi are classified as philosophers instead of fantastic writers, Gan Bao (?-336) is generally accepted by Chinese scholars as the authentic initiator of *zhiguai xiaoshuo* or the fantastic short story. This different reception results from an exclusive consideration of Zhuang Zi as philosopher instead of a literary writer. Compared with Gan Bao, Zhuang Zi was more an authentic creator of *zhiguai* stories, since he invented his own stories to portray the obscure philosophy of Daoism. As to Gan Bao, according to his own preface to *Soushen ji* (*In Search of Gods and Spirits*), he proclaimed that he faithfully recorded or copied the tales from his predecessors and folks so as to arouse in readers the principle that gods cannot be defiled. Likewise, Pu Songling (1640-1715) took a similar stance towards the fantastic creation by stating that he collected tales from folks and emulated the predecessors of great *zhiguai* and *chuanqi* masters.[14] Slightly different from Gan Bao who bore a stance of historiographer, Pu Songling interpolated, besides recording and imitating, fantastic stories through the supernatural phenomena to express his own aspirations. Indubitably, these two great writers do not bother to defend the genuineness of their tales or discourse a Daoist argumentation about the normal and the abnormal; it is sufficient that they proclaimed their writing as mere re-

---

[13] Please refer to the section "*Unus Mundus* of Harmonism – Music and the Eucharistic Alchemy of Language" for further discussion of "Eucharist."

[14] *Chuanqi* is a special narrative form of short stories developed in the Tang dynasty (618-907).

cording and imitation. This mask is a common *modus operandi* in fantastic storytelling, especially in a China with Confucian core spirit. This declaration is similar to that of the brothers Grimm. They insisted that they did not add anything other than what they recorded while readers can appreciate the linguistic fluidity and art exercised by the writers. The following two writers treated the genre in earnest and endeavoured to develop a convincing theory on *zhiguai*.

Ge Hong (284-364), adept of Daoist alchemy (*shenxianjia*) and author of the famous work *Bao Pu Zi* (Daoist master), defended the genre *zhiguai* by stating that the reader and the tale need to connive to create a new reality. He implied that the reader needs certain wisdom in order to appreciate the art and the mystery of *zhiguai*. His inclination for Daoism in his writing does not abate his emphasis on the artistry of literary creation. He criticized Liu Xiang (79-8 BC, historiographer and *zhiguai* writer) for the deficiency of poeticity in his stories. Through his belief in the reality of *zhiguai*, Ge Hong could be deemed, among others, as the first to concern himself about the profundity, the extraordinary aspects, the aesthetics and poetic form in fantastic writing as well as the circumstances of readers.

Contrary to his predecessors who believed the "reality" in the fantastic, Hong Mai (1123-1202) from the Song dynasty underscored the art of invention in fantastic fiction. He stated that the *zhiguai* aesthetics is an imaginative narrative creation and affirmed that the aesthetic and poetic value of the tale holds a romantic character overflowing the imagination on the strange and the extraordinary. He did not deny that certain of these works implicitly offer profound philosophical ideas as well as allegories. Nevertheless, Hong highlighted the narrative art of the fantastic writing by denying its being abased to be the tool for didacticism.

Like Chinese writers of the fantastic, many Western writers also value the power of the imaginary. Nodier and Hoffmann, as writers of Romanticism, held an original vision of fantastic creation. Lovecraft manifested himself as a master of horror stories. The dominant form of the fantastic in the 20th century is Tolkienian style of fantasy or fairy-story. Along the lines of magical realism and European fantastic writing, Cortázar's unique fantastic writing represents a postmodern combination of the Western fantastic narrative and Oriental mysticism. Revisiting fantastic writers of Antiquity and of Chinese *zhiguai* will track authors' vision of the genre back to the times of primitive representation of fantastic literature.

In the course of the 19th Century, French fantastic writers were themselves interested in establishing a theory of the genre. Nodier, as a famous and influential fantastic storyteller, claimed that a historical analysis of the fantastic brings to light the emergence of the genre as one of the phenomena in the Romantic Movement. Grounded in this linear historical vision on fantastic literature, Nodier further commented on the narrative forms of the genre through the nar-

rators' voice in his tales. The narrator appears as the implied author who argues
for the narrative technique of the genre. Nodier did not bother to discriminate
the fantastic from the marvellous as did most of his fellow critics, but elaborated
the nuance in the fantastic. In one of his fantastic tales, "Histoire d'Hélène Gillet," he distinguishes three modes of narration in fantastic literature: (1)
l'histoire fantastique fausse (false fantastic story), the charm of which results
from a double credulity of the teller and the audience; (2) *l'histoire fantastique
vague* (vague fantastic story), which leaves the soul suspended in a dreaming
and melancholic doubt, lulls it to sleep like a melody and cradles it like a dream;
(3) *l'histoire fantastique vraie* (true fantastic story), the first among all, because
it profoundly shakes our heart without sacrificing our reason. This kind of fantastic story relates an event held as materially impossible that, nevertheless, was
done to the knowledge of everyone [Nodier 1961, 330]. Nodier's avant-garde
and unique vision on fantastic literature seems more applicable to the works of
our times than do his later critics.

With the German heritage of *Märchen* and his musician status, Hoffmann
deems the fantastic tale as a dexterous and unbounded linguistic representation
of the musical fantasia. His art of fantastic storytelling evolves from his art of
music. For him, the art of music is

> the most romantic of all the arts – one might almost say, the only genuinely
> romantic art – for its sole subject is the infinite. The lyre of Orpheus opened
> the gates of Orcus. Music discloses an unknown realm to man, a world that has
> nothing in common with the outer world of the senses that surrounds him, a
> world in which he abandons all definite feelings to surrender himself to an in-
> expressible longing. [Hoffmann 2003, 97]

Disillusioned about his failure to become a great composer, Hoffmann pro-
gressed from writing musical commentaries to stylized storytelling. *Ritter Gluck*,
(1809) his first weird tale, features a musician as the hero of the story. The narration presents a juxtaposition of madness and possession of the hero. Most of
his fantastic tales portray the struggle between the philistine and artistic worlds.
For example, his most famous story (thanks to Freud's scrupulous analysis)
"The Sandman", and also "Don Giovanni" and "The Golden Pot" raise the issue
of the conflict between art and mediocrity. Hoffmann connects the art of storytelling (with its fluent musicality) with music and poetry in his fantastic tales. As
the aforementioned quote that "music discloses an unknown realm to man,"
Hoffmann creates his second art of music by storytelling. He appropriates the
fantastic, with the underlying technique of grotesque images and irony, to disclose to readers another unknown space that human imagination is able to explore. His highlighting the fabulous and ironic as fantastic valences of his storytelling is manifest in his letter to the publisher on the completed manuscript of
"The Golden Pot":

> I am sending you without delay the enclosed, finished fairy tale with the sincere wish that it will please you with its sustained irony! To be sure, the idea of permitting the fabulous to enter boldly into ordinary life is daring and, as far as I know, has not yet been used to this extent by any German author; however, I believe a more profound interpretation lends it the needed weight. [Hoffmann 1977, 221]

It is indeed this "fabulous boldly entering into ordinary life" and "the sustained irony" that intrigues Walter Scott to criticize as "too strongly to the grotesque and fantastic." [Scott 1968, 348]; while he defends (in his essay of 1827) the use of the supernatural in fiction, as long as it remained "rare, brief, indistinct" [ibid, 316]. And it is effectively this grotesque or fantastic that exerts incredible influence on French writers of his times. The idiosyncrasy of Hoffmannian fantastic is its musicality, either as subject matter or as linguistic style. His virtuosity of telling fantastic stories eventually metamorphoses and crystallizes the lofty art of music into dexterous language.

H. P. Lovecraft, American writer of horror tales, holds in high regard the fear of the unknown as the underlying momentum for his fantastic creation. His fantastic writing focuses more on the dark side of imagining the unknown than on other imaginary perspective of the unknown, such as the jubilant fantastic tales of Tolkien. In relief against the fantastic writers like Tolkien, Lovecraft creates his idiosyncratic horror fantasy as his myth of the Cthulhu:

> The oldest and strongest emotion of mankind is fear, and the oldest and strongest kind of fear is fear of the unknown. These few psychologists will dispute, and their admitted truth must establish for all time the genuineness and dignity of the weirdly horrible tale as a literary form. [...]
> The appeal for the spectrally macabre is generally narrow because it demands from the reader a certain degree of imagination and a capacity for detachment from every-day life. Relatively few are free enough from the spell for the daily routine to respond to rappings from outside, and tales of ordinary feelings and events, or of common sentimental distortions of such feelings and events, will always take first place in the taste of the majority; rightly, perhaps, since of course these ordinary matters make up the greater part of human experience. [Lovecraft 1973, 12]

In his essay "On Fairy-Stories," Tolkien defends the narrative genre fairy-story by theorizing the aesthetic elements of the genre. He elaborates his theory of the fairy-story by commencing with a reference to the sources of imagination, the Cauldron of Story. Myth according to his philological understanding is the purest language. This vision reflects Tolkien's emphasis on the middle one of the three faces of fairy-stories: the Mystical towards the Supernatural, the Magical towards Nature, and the Mirror of scorn and pity towards Man [Tolkien 1997, 125]. Besides dismissing the idea that fairy-stories are written for children, he further expounds the four necessary elements of the genre: Fantasy, Recovery, Escape and Consolation or *Eucatastrophe*, amidst which he highlights the last element. Accordingly, fairy stories offer this kind of joy through the imaginative satisfaction of ancient desires. These ancient desires can be traced further to mythic desires and imagination. Tolkien, with his philological background, views language as a disease of myth, which corresponds to Owen Barfield's assumption of myth as a semantic unity. Both see an ultimate truth in myth and language. For Tolkien, "legends and myths are largely made of 'truth'" [Tolkien 1995, 147], which is the very opposite of the popular reception of the word myth – known as imagined and unreal, as *mythos* distinguished from *logos* by Plato. It is noticeable that Tolkien does not use the term *fantasy* as an epithet to his particular writing of the fantastic. According to his treatise, we perceive that *fantasy* was considered as a mediating aesthetic form that is requisite to the genre fairy-story. Tolkien's fantastic creation is idiosyncratic in that he resurrects the style of epic through his mythopoeic fantasy.

Displeased by a psychological and Cartesian interpretation of his works, Julio Cortázar views the fantastic creation as nostalgia "of not being capable of completely opening the doors that, in many occasions, [he] saw ajar for some fugitive seconds" [my translation, Cortázar 1980, 88]. Insisting on "the suspension of disbelief" as proposed by Coleridge, he creates a fantastic narrative in search of the real behind the real, namely the normal real. Inspired by oriental mysticism (Hinduism, Buddhism and Daoism), Cortázar worked on a particular fantastic tale with a delicate balance between literature and dogmatic engagement: "do not let those who share your views force you away from literature and into dogmatic 'commitment'; maintain at all costs that delicate balance that allows your 'commitment' to flower in your art" [Peavler, 129]. Though criticized by Borges for his "spontaneous experimentalism" [Stravans, 37], Cortázar's art of the fantastic fiction is a perfect amalgamation of oriental mysticism and European narrative rhetoric. This shows his better apprehension of the oriental mysticism than Borges's, albeit the latter's writings on the oriental topic are Cortázar's main sources of exotic knowledge. Among examples of oriental mysticism, he admires Chinese Daoist Zhuang Zi's fable of "Zhuang Zhou Dreams of a Butterfly." Out of this Daoist metaphysical standpoint, Cortázar develops rhetoric tripartite syntaxes of a non-dualistic way of addressing subject, space and time. He does not content himself with glancing at the misty apparition of the other dimension, merely revealing a possible world behind the realistic curtain. On the contrary, he audaciously draws the curtain and depicts harmoniously a world shunting between the known and the unknown. The emergence of the Cortázarian fantastic mode departs from the conventional realistic fantastic that sticks to the conventional hesitation or ambiguity between the supernatural and the natural. His fantastic enunciation often glides harmoniously from our presumed reality to the unreal sphere, like the Möbius strip. However, for Cortázar, this unreal space is more real than the normally perceived real.

Cortázar's unique vision on fantastic literature entails a return to Chinese *zhiguai* authors' viewpoints on the creation of the genre. A core influence on Cortázar's nimbleness and mysticism in narration, Zhuang Zi could be considered as the initiator of *zhiguai* writing, given that his fables are both an excellent representation of Daoist philosophy and an artistic storytelling that appertains to the unknown. His vision of the *zhiguai* story is more metaphysical than poetical but his narrative art is poetic. With the communion between Cortázar and Zhuang Zi and other *zhiguai* tales, we would bridge fantastic creation between the East and the West through the present book. Globalization is not only characterized in terms of economy and politics, but also, even essentially, in terms of the universality in human imagination and mythopoeia. Then the idea of universal *Geist* emerges again. To appreciate *zhiguai*, the underlying philosophy requires the reader to reject a dualistic approach to appreciate the world fantastic genre; fantastic tales arouse the reader's imagination to explore the unknown worlds beyond our limited realm. This is indeed the spirit of fantastic creation, which inspires and makes us dream in a universal chorus.

Conclusion: Fantasticism *or Fantastic Poetics*

Different from numerous studies that assume a historical rupture in fantastic literature (a completely new narrative genre emerging just in the late 18th century), this work proposes a return to the assumption that the genre originates with myth (the Greek word *mythos* denotes both imaginary and narrative), legend, fairy tale, epic, saga, ballad and episodic picaresque novel tradition. This harks back to Chinese fantastic theories, or Nodier's analysis. Such a historical vision will be elaborated through a diachronic survey of fantastic works and reinforced by theoretical discourses of the authors and, in particular, the approach of the literary imaginary. Charles Nodier's theory on *le fantastique* and Tolkien's on Fairy-Stories, both writers being philologists and ingenious fantastic storytellers, already offered a historical vision of the genre. A philological perspective will appropriately adumbrate a genuine view of the fantastic genre, in that fantastic literature features the most concrete language in narrating the unknown. We contend that fantastic literature should be an *archetypal literary genre* of the imaginary (generally referring to the unreal imagination or images) in view of the similar kind of literatures created in different cultures. For example, ghost stories are ubiquitous in world literature. The term "archetypal genre" bears a dual signification for the fantastic: the synchronic quintessence (archetype of imagining the unknown) and the diachronic view with perennial metamorphosis.

The evidence that fantastic stories from different cultures resemble each other in representing the invisible phenomena such as dragons, ghosts and the actions of metamorphosis invites a hypothesis of a universal origin of the fantastic imagination. Considering the existing fantastic texts and synthesizing the theories from different linguistic cultures, we accordingly offer a working definition of fantastic literature to facilitate our exploration of the genre as in universal terms. Fantastic literature is thus defined as literary narratives or poeticized storytelling about the imaginary *unknown*. We consider the term *unknown* more appropriate for defining the fantastic genre than other related words that are often employed by critics, such as *unreal* and *irrational*. As the aforementioned Chinese theorists point out, what we judge as unreal today may become real tomorrow and according to our examination of various cultures, what is deemed as irrational in one culture may be rational in another, the word *unknown* holds a clear guideline for readers to judge and appreciate. Moreover, the term already conserves the future possibility in its semantic field: what is unknown today will be known tomorrow and the known comes from the unknown, according to Daoist philosophy.[15] Todorov also shows this changing status of presently unknown phenomena as he clarifies the concept of the marvellous by the unique status of the hyperbolic marvellous, the exotic marvellous and instrumental marvellous; the first may derive from the enunciator's figurative language, the second may be found in another country or time, and the last kind may be invented later [Todorov 1970, 60-2]. Consequently, the choice of the unknown has wider scope than the unreal, the irrational and the marvellous. The idea of the unknown is also employed by Hoffmann. Divulging the unknown through imagination is esteemed by Hoffmann as the value of the lofty art of music that "discloses the unknown realm to man." Following his musical creation, Hoffmann writes fantastic tales to touch upon the unknown realm.

The unknown may refer to all phenomena that heretofore cannot be demonstrated by science or objectively received by figuration of collective consciousness, to employ the term of Owen Barfield. As Bachelard defines the imaginary as the function of the unreal or of deformation of the real, we see that the function of fantastic literature is to arouse readers' imagination so as to probe into the unknown realm. Lao Zi pronounced in his *Dao De Jing*[16] that all existence comes from nothingness and the known comes from the unknown. Plato expressed the difficulty of elucidating the concept of chôra that seemingly refers to the transmuting origin of the nothingness, a status of inception for all possible

---

[15] The underlying concept of Lao Zi's "The unknown is the commencement of all becoming; the known is the mother of all becoming" influences the Daoist writers who defend the genre *zhiguai* by claiming that "what is unreal today could become real in the future."

[16] We adopt the Beijing phonetic transcription system to transcribe Chinese words. Lao Zi's *Dao De Jing* is often translated in English as *Tao Te Ching* or *Tao Te King*.

transformations of the manifestations of existence.[17] The term chôra can be appropriately conceived as the archetype of the unknown. All human science and knowledge effectively comes from the exploration of the unknown since the development of Aristotle's formal logic. The imagination of fantastic literature as well as myth then bridges the known and the unknown.

For psychologists, this gulf-bridging medium would be dream and mystic imagination; for philosopher Bachelard, the nexus lies in material imagination; for anthropologist Durand, this imaginary function is *la fantastisque* (to differentiate from *le fantastique* as a literary genre); for philologists Barfield and Tolkien, poetic diction and fantasy assume the role of articulation and amalgamation. The interrelationships between the imaginary, mythical, fantastic mimesis and chôra will be further elaborated in the next section. With the help of the historical and imaginary approaches, we will be able to trace the fantastic genre back to 2700 BC (*The Epic of Gilgamesh*). Our viewpoint derives from a synthesis of several precursors. These are Nodier's viewpoint on the fantastic, Goethe's division of the human mind into robust, sacred, sensible and common epochs, Barfield's evolutionary stages of human consciousness, Tolkien's view on the connection between myths and fairy-stories, and the Chinese *Yi Jing* aesthetics of changes. A mythopoeic periodization of four epochs of fantastic literature is postulated: the primitive conception, myth as the fabrication of truth, skepticism and truth in mirage. This periodization sheds light on the diverse epochal styles of fantastic imagination and narrative art.

We propose the neologism *Fantasticism*, modelled on Romanticism, to proclaim a resurrection of fantastic literature that arouses *aesthetic imagination* (Barfield) through the quintessence of poetics in terms of its classic meaning: the imaginary as the fantastic *inventio*, the fantastic *dispositio* as the rhetoric of dream, mirror and magician's hat and the fantastic style. By making up another "-ism", we ironically parallel contemporary discourses on the subject. *Fantasticism* is an oxymoron of "chimera and reason," "deconstruction and doctrine," and "infinite and finite" and "reinlessness and scrupulousness." To term it as a whole, *Fantasticism* represents the poetics of fantastic literature. Moreover, to elucidate the true spirit of the genre, we will further explore the Eucharist or alchemy of language. The notion of *Eucharist of language* is inspired from Tolkien's sub-creation of fantasy and philological ideal in unison with his faith in Catholicism, and Jean-Luc Marion's philosophy of hermeneutic metaphysics. The term *alchemy of language* is employed on the basis of a Daoist vision of purification and metamorphosis to extend to the purification of language back into the state of both linguistic and imaginary *unus mundus*. Such reading of the fantastic would unveil the mirage of postmodern niches of fragmentary Sign to

---

[17] The conception of chôra will be explored in detail in the light of Chinese Daoism and Yi Jing philosophy in a later section: "Chôra as the Archetype of the Bourgeoning Metamorphosis of the Unknown."

reclaim the sanctuary of Word with semantic unity. While the approach of the literary imaginary with mythopoeic and metaphysical revision will crystallize the unconscious and conscious meanings underlying fantastic creation and will offer a universal vision of the genre in terms of historical evolution, thematic and style of recovery, the poetic analysis of fantastic works from different cultures by synthetic and textual comparisons will illustrate the heterogeneity in fantastic narrative rhetoric, repartitioned into three types of discourses: the dream-discourse, the mirror-discourse and the magician's hat-discourse.

Part One
The Imaginary Mimesis of Fantastic Literature:
Mythopoeia, Metaphysics, Metamorphosis and Musicality

Fantasia: The Voyage of Zephyrus in the Cave

Once there was a sage who, gaining a certain kind of magic, unbound himself and scouted out of the imprisoned cave where only candles illuminated an authentic projection of the world outside. This freed man relished the truth and beauty of the real world. Overwhelmed by the wonder of this new but true world, he rejoiced in ecstasy and couldn't wait to return to the cave to announce this bliss and truth to his fellows. However, to his great frustration, the sage was judged insane since none of his fellows were endowed with the magic to unchain themselves to move towards the entrance of the cave to glance at the wonderland. This sagacious man thenceforward spent his whole life to persuade his people to believe in his vision and to have faith in a brave true world out there. Viewing his sincerity in all his discourses, the people of the cave withdrew the epithet of "insane" and began to name him "saint." The saint established an academy to profess the invisible wisdom. One fine day, Aeolus coughed near the cave outside; some air puffed in and snuffed certain candles and buffed the projection system. The light waned, and interfered with the vision of the cave people. One curious man, who had poor vision anyway, found the source of the wind, and the whizzing and whistling beguiled him with unrestrained melody and rhythm. He chanted with the waft of music and danced with its rhythm, his hearing keener and vision cleaner. His mind's eye heard simultaneously with his ears. He painted various colours of winds; he frowned at the choppy wind; he lamented with the moan; he bellowed with the gale; he gaped at the flurry. The murky world was chanted and narrated by this man gone with the wind. The cave people appreciated his imaginary creation and thus named him "fantastic minstrel." No one, including the minstrel, could testify to the existence of Aeolus; neither could anyone prove Aeolus to be unreal. Thus spake Zephyrus: Hearken, thou shall waken!

Introduction

Before engaging in the studies of the imaginary of fantastic literature, I first need to clarify the term "poetics." The object of the present book is a thorough exploration and elucidation of the poetics of fantastic literature, in terms of the poetics received in Antiquity, viz. from Plato and Aristotle to Classicism. Poetics consists in the following phases: *inventio, dipositio* and *elocutio*. Accordingly, in the studies of fantastic literature, we explore the poetics in three perspectives: imaginary, rhetoric and style. With the imaginary, we delve into the universal roots of fantastic imagination, grounded in the consciousness and collective unconscious of creation and meaning. On the basis of the above poetic elements, fantastic poetics is characterized by the mimesis of primary imagination and storytelling with rhetorical and stylistic virtuosity that brings humans back in touch with the mystery of the unknown. The present section is a thorough investigation of mimesis and the imaginary in fantastic creation, the quintessence of myth as a door into the realm of collective unconscious and thus the unknown archetype of Platonic chôra.

While Kathryn Hume highlights fantasy as the other literary mode opposite to mimesis, I follow the perspective of Aristotle who treats epic (fantastic in essence) and tragedy as two principal types of mimesis in his *Poetics*. With this postulate, the poetics consists in three phases: mimesis and *inventio*, mimesis and *dipositio*, mimesis and *elocutio*. Bachelard, viewing poetics as the power to create imaginary worlds, indeed as phenomenological tool, defines it on the basis of the reverie on the four elements (earth, water, fire and air), indeed its "power of poeticization" [Bachelard 1984, 14]. This concept of poetics will be explored in the light of *inventio*. The *dispositio* refers to rhetoric, the study of which inquires into the discourse of fantastic literature as well as the situations of the author/implied author and reader/implied reader. In the dimension of *elocutio* or style, the emphasis is placed on the artistry of fantastic diction, such as archaism, musicality and visualization. With the meanings of the above poetic elements, fantastic poetics is characterized by the imitation of the primary imagination (to use Coleridge's term), the rhetorical storytelling and stylistic virtuosity that brings humans back in touch with the mystery of pristine space of the unknown.

From the perspective of the writing subject, Strada Vittorio proposes a metaphysical insight that the creation of the fantastic is being conscious of staying in the Platonic cave[18]. However, the gulf between language and metaphysics requires a linking bridge. Delving into the sources of imagination, the imaginary approach will bridge the Ideal Form outside the cave and fantastic literature by

---

[18] The philosophical theory of Vittorio is presented in *The Literary Fantastic from* Gothic *to Postmodernism* by Neil Corwell. The original is in Italian.

the creative imagination. The transcendental ideas are revealed as being mediated by rhetoric into a formalized language. This is a reminder of Barfield's association of myth and language through aesthetic imagination, and Tolkien's "language is the disease of mythology."[19] An exploration of the imaginative basis of the fantastic necessitates a review of the definitions of the term "imaginary." The imaginary of the unknown as the universal root of fantastic creation will be further investigated from the triple stratification of the unconscious: Archaic memory from the collective unconscious and *unus mundus*, the reverie of the four elements and metamorphosis, and fantastic storytelling vis-à-vis *la fantastique*.

---

[19] Please refer to the section "Style of Recovery – Fantastic Diction Returns to Myth Aspiring for Chôra" for the argument about "myth as a disease of language" and "language as a disease of myth."

The *Mise en Scène* of the Human Imaginary in Fantastic Creation
Definitions of the Imaginary

The substantive *imaginary* is translated from the French word *imaginaire*. Contemporary critics mostly adopt the translation to refer to Jacque Lacan's stage of the imaginary, the register of which comprises the images of primary narcissism and secondary narcissism. However, the imaginary here is received in the light of the translation of Wolfgang Iser's work, *The Fictive and the Imaginary*. Jean-Yves Tadié distinguishes the criticism of consciousness from that of the imaginary by clarifying that the former focuses on the subject that writes and the latter explores imagination [Tadié, 107]. Imagination is frequently associated with the fantastic, given that this literary creation is germane to the supernatural, the unreal, the invisible or the unknown. Tolkien uses fantasy as the art of storytelling to bridge imagination and sub-creation. Hence, imagination features as the hub in fantastic creation. What, then, is the imaginary? The investigation of the word's semantic evolution is a prerequisite to delving into the imaginary of the fantastic.

Since the Middle Ages, "imaginary" has been an adjective that qualifies in general what is unreal. Maine de Brian first made this word a substantive in his *Journal* in 1820 to designate the domain of imagination. French novelist Alphonse Daudet defines "an imaginary" as a man who is unable to distinguish the production of his imagination from the objective reality, a dreamer dominated by his subjectivity, an imaginative somewhat perturbed [Chelebourg, 7]. It is not until the French fantastic writer Villiers de l'Isle-Adam that the imaginary connotes the supernatural, a sacred part of the individual, a space not exterior to him but interior, and a composite of his psyche against reason. In his fantastic novel of the automaton, *L'Eve future*, the novelist endowed the imaginary with the meaning of an infinitive substance, a mysterious space or the spirit of the living that is able to meet the creatures of the beyond.

Jean-Paul Sartre's publication of *L'Imaginaire* in 1940 announced the debut of the substantive as an object of studies. In order to avoid employing the old word "image" to signify the "images" generated by imagination, Sartre offered the name "imaginaries." The imaginary is an object that is produced in image by the imagination of the imaging consciousness and thus distinct from the real object. Gaston Bachelard, grounded in the poetics of material imagination relating to the four elements of cosmogony (earth, water, fire, air), defined the imaginary as our mind's function of the unreal: "The fundamental term that corresponds to imagination is not image, but imaginary. Thanks to the imaginary, imagination is essentially open, evasive. Within the human psyche, it is the experience capable of opening, the capacity for innovation (*Le vocable fondamental qui correspond à l'imagination, ce n'est pas image, c'est imaginaire. Grâce à l'imaginaire, l'imagination est essentiellement ouverte, evasive. Elle est dans le psychisme humain l'exprérience même de l'ouverture, l'expérience même de la nouveauté)*" [Bachelard 1943, 7]. Responding to theories regarding image as a sign, anthropologist Gilbert Durand contends that the image is a symbol with an objective meaning. Viewing the process of the imagination as what operates as an eternal coming and going between the objective (the percept) and the subjective (the percipient) dimensions of reality, he defines this anthropological route the imaginary:

> Eventually, the imaginary is no other than this route in which the representation of the object lets itself be assimilated and shaped by the urging demands of the subject, and in which vice versa, as Piaget authoritatively pointed out, the subjective representations are explicated "by the previous adaptations of the subject" in the objective milieu. [Durand 1992, 38][20]

Durand further develops the imaginary as a response to our anxiety before time and death by means of space. The imaginary, repartitioned into the diurnal and the nocturnal regimes, also determines our representation of the world. German Reader-Response theorist Wolfgang Iser interprets the imaginary in two ways: "With flights of fancy it can wander off into worlds of its own, or as imagination, it can conjure up images or, through the powers of the imagination, it can summon the absent into presence" [Iser, 171].

Common to the aforementioned definitions of the imaginary are a semantic field encompassing the elements opposing objective reality and reason: the supernatural, the unreal image, and the psychic function of imagining the unreal or summoning the absent into presence. The imaginary is thus germane to fantastic creation, given that the genre in question is generally opposed to mundanely received reality. Henceforth, the approach of the imaginary is deemed befitting to explore the imaginary poetics of the fantastic as it relates to the unknown.

In general, the approach towards the literary imaginary derives from two sources: Lévi-Strauss's *paradigmatic* methodology, and Carl Gustav Jung's analytical psychology. Lévi-Strauss analyzed the deep and imbedded structures of discourse in myths, while Jung probed into the intimate relations between dreams, myths and art in terms of archetypes and the collective unconscious. The approach of the imaginary revives the concept of Jungian collective unconscious and attempts to restore meanings to language and thus claims that the content commands the form. The investigation of the *inventio* of fantastic literature as an archetypal genre goes in harmony with the stratification of the imaginary related to the unknown. From Jung's perspective, the imaginary of the col-

---

[20] *Finalement, l'imaginaire n'est rien d'autre que ce trajet dans lequel la représentation de l'objet se laisse assimiler et modeler par les impératifs pulsionnels du sujet, et dans lequel réciproquement, comme l'a magistralement montré Piaget, les représentations subjectives s'expliquent « par les accommodations antérieures du sujet » au milieu objectif.*

lective unconscious is rooted in archaic memory and dream that evoke the space of the Platonic chôra; Bachelard's imaginary hinges on material imagination and reverie that mirror the trace of the four elements departing from chôra; Durand's imaginary is determined by human reflexes in reaction to time and space. Mythic storytelling is the hub of *mythocritique* or *archetypocritique* (as Brunel appropriately terms it) that it reveals *la fantastique*.[21] The first level concentrates on the *qi* (breath or vibration) or spiritual communion and imagination (mystical orientation), the second on the semantic abundance of images and their repercussions in connection with the four elements (phenomenological orientation), the last one completes the diachronism and synchronism of myth with isotopism of meanings and restores the pristine meanings to language, the figurative as literal (archetypocritical orientation).

These three phases of the imaginary befittingly correspond to the totality of the fantastic imagination and its variation of narrative forms in literary representations. In general, the critical applications of this approach find the interwoven images in literary works or the mythemes, so as to appreciate the mythopoeia of literature. Images are thus taken as figures that amplify the meanings of works. Metaphors and symbols are vital bearers of meanings that converge to reveal the unconscious. More than other genres, fantastic literature appropriates, literally, the imaginary in the text. The figurative meanings implied in the realistic but mythopoeic works manifest themselves as core meanings of the language through fantastic storytelling. They reverse the engrained belief that language comes first with a literal or arbitrary meaning. This idiosyncrasy of fantastic literature harks back to Todorov's structuralist theory of the discourse, the enunciated of the fantastic is usually taken *au pied de la letter*.

Archaic Memory and Dream from the Collective Unconscious and Unus Mundus

Jung's analytical psychology brings to light a feasible way to unite the physical and the psychic to transcend to the status of one-as-whole or *unus mundus* (one unitary world." Though mainly stressing spiritual transcendence in harmony with the material world, Jung touched upon the root of archaic memory and dream (according to Jung's conception, not Freud's) in the creative imagination.

---

[21] Durand defines the mythocritical reading (*la lecture mythocirtique*) as "to discover behind the story what a text is, oral or written, a mythological core, or better still, a mythic pattern (*déceler derrière le récit qu'est un texte, oral ou écrit, un noyau mythologique, ou mieux un partron mythique*)" [Durand 1992, 184]. Given that Durand's *mythocritique* is grounded in workings on the content of archetypal images and symbols, as opposed to the studies of formal mythemes, Brunel terms Durand's mythocritique as archetypocritique to distinguish it from his mythocritique based on the traditional definitions of myth.

He described this as an eclectic way to make the unknown truth accessible, after the conflict between matter and mind. This creative imagination, grounded on myth and story, predominates in the fantastic imagination. Exploring the imaginary sources of the unknown in fantastic creation entails a resort to Jung's psychic theory of the collective unconscious and archetype. Different from the anthropological perspective, pivoting more on human culture and imagination of the consciousness, or the individual unconscious at best, Jung distinguished his archetype and the collective unconscious from others by characterizing them as predispositions or inherited forms, rather than inherited idea or patterns of thought. David L. Hart clearly delineates this idea, "Jung insists, however, that we do not begin life as a *tabula rasa*, a clean slate to be written on by what is outside us" [Hart, 90-1]. Jung's conception of archetype can be grasped by envisaging the picture of or intuiting the spirit of his collective unconscious. The collective unconscious, innate and organized in human depth, serves to oppose Freud's "repressed unconscious." Jung applied the archetypes to expound the concept of the collective unconscious as primary *imagos* or inborn images that organize the latter. However, he later revised archetypes' attribute of images into innate releasing mechanisms that form coherent images, around which developed psychological complexes. Hence, Jung at times viewed archetypes as something analogous to Plato's Ideal Form and sometimes regarded them as representable images and ideas. Jung's readings of and commentaries on *I-Ching* (*Yi Jing*) and the Daoist alchemical book *The Secret of Golden Flower* (both translated by Jung's friend Richard Wilhelm) and his dedication to the researches of alchemy facilitate the prehension of Jung's collective unconscious as the psyche extending to Plato's concept of chôra, which can be described as the archetype of the unknown. In this light, Jung's archetype is more irrepresentable than presentable images.

The anthropologists following the footsteps of Jung, in order to fit the logical tradition of research, often diminish Jung's theory by exhausting his archetypal images to more seizable layers of the unconscious. This orientation of interpreting Jung's theory ironically falls into the contradiction against the Jungian principle "that the rational mind may easily attempt to control and dictate meaning and thereby lose it" [Hart, 97]. In fact, Jung's theory tends to bring us near the untouchable Ideal Form presumed by Plato, since the collective unconscious that nourishes creative fantasy offers a solution to bridge the perpetual irreconcilableness between the material and the spiritual. This creative fantasy inherits myriads of images from the realm of the unknown, such as the imaginary figures of fairies, sorcerers, devils and sundry gods, drawn from the archaic memory of humans.

In the course of his researches in the archetypes, abstract or concrete, Jung affirms the biological origin of the archetypes; viz. archetypes are like the instincts that bear a genetic heritage. I would propose to parallel this genetic heritage of imagination with Leibniz's concept of monad, since it is an indestructible nonspatial unit. This genetic concept could also be described by the metaphor of "the DNA of imagination." The monad of imagination connects us with the ultimate archetypes proposed to enter into the realm of the unknown such as the shadow, the anima, the animus and the Self. The imaginary of the unknown envisaged by this DNA concept constructs a continuation in the mystic participation that appears innate in primitive people. The mystic participation (or Barfield's original participation[22]) enables these people to view the world with a symbolic thought, or rather a perception taken both symbolically and literally. Wherefore, the thunder is heard as the voice from a furious god, water is normally the habitat of water sprites; the caves belong to monsters and the forests are saturated with fairies and other spirits; all these supernatural figures are indeed the creation in communion with our collective unconscious. Jung explained these primitive beliefs by the phenomenon of projection, one from the contents of man's unconscious into nature. This projection is extended to define myths as "the symbolic expression of this interior drama and the unconscious of soul, which becomes knowable to human consciousness by way of projection" [Jung 1971 *Racines*, 16-7].

Different from representing symbols as in the spatial composition of art, myths express meanings through a story. Fantastic literature succeeds to this storytelling about the unknown in communion with the collective unconscious. The myths as metaphorical stories unify images and meanings. This communion between consciousness and the unconscious joins the physical and psychical worlds, hence a union of the unknown and the known reality. Jung portrayed this wholeness by the term of *unus mundus*:

> Undoubtedly the idea of the *unus mundus* is founded on the assumption that the multiplicity of the empirical world rest on an underlying unity, and not that two or more fundamentally different worlds exist side by side or are mingled with one another. Rather, everything divided and different belongs to one and the same world, which is not the world of sense but a postulate whose probability is vouched for by the fact that until now no one has been able to discover a world in which the known laws of nature are invalid. That even the psychic world, which is so extraordinarily different from the physical world, does not have its roots outside the one cosmos is evident from the undeniable fact that causal connections exist between the psyche and the body which point to their underlying unitary nature... The background of our empirical world thus appears to be in fact a *unus mundus*. [Jung 1977, 537-8]

---

[22] In his *Saving the Appearances*, Owen Barfield divides the evolution of human consciousness into three stages: the original participation, the intellectual stage and the final participation. His original participation corresponds to Jung's mystic participation where the contradiction of antithesis is absent.

Borrowed from the medieval philosophy, *unus mundus* means "one unitary world" that comprehends both the physical and psychical world. The universal symbol for this unitary nature is the magic circle mandala or a globe of circle and square or the *Taiji* circle of *Yi Jing*. With this nature of oneness in our psyche, Jung penetrated a psychic reality through a third way (between nominalism and realism; deconstruction and universalism) of imagining, creative imagination being the real Ground of the psyche.

Jung wrote in a letter of January 1929, "I am indeed convinced that creative imagination is the only primordial phenomenon accessible to us, the real Ground of the psyche, the only immediate reality" [qtd. Kugler, 79]. The fantastic imaginary corresponds to Jung's concept of fantasy: "The psyche creates reality every day. The only expression I can use for this activity is fantasy... Fantasy, therefore, seems to me the clearest expression of the specific activity of the psyche.... Fantasy it was and ever is which fashions the bridge between the irreconcilable claims of subject and object" [Jung 1971 *Psychological*, 51-2]. In psychic images, the inner and outer worlds of an individual come together. The Jungian psychic creative activity or fantasy, grounded on primitive creative imagination, underlies the artistic rendering of fantastic literature that tends to represent an image of *unus mundus* through openness to the unknown. This process, through a connection between the consciousness and the unconscious into the perfect oneness, is termed by Jung as the *individuation* of the ego into the Self. When one integrates into the collective unconscious, the wonder of synchronicity, like the secret of the golden flower, will manifest itself. The opposites will completely reconcile and transcend to a third energy as the transformation of the alchemy. Hart elucidates that the classical Jungian principle of exploring the inner world is "respect for what is *encountered*; respect for what is *unknown*, for what is *unexpected*, for what is *unheard of*" [my emphasis, Hart, 89]. The underscored elements deemed to be respected are also the essential qualities of fantastic literature.

From the age of original or mystic participation, an unknown devil-like creature seems recurrent in the human imagination. Jung anatomized the emergence of the devil image on three levels: the first and the deepest level features the archetypal image of the devil as ancient as the conception of God; the second level originates with the magician type in the primitive tribe that is gifted in magic power; the third level presents the recurrent image in the personal unconscious [Jung 1993, 168]. Deriving from the archetypal devil are myriads of symbols like transformers of psychic energy that speak the language of the archetype. All these elements from the collective unconscious eventually rise to the surface by the creation of literature.

Jung distinguished two forms of literary creation: psychological and visionary. Despite being a psychologist, he was little interested in the psychological literature. His attitude effectively explains the nexus between fantastic literature and the imaginary of the collective unconscious. Not all fantastic works are visionary; nevertheless, more fantastic works than realistic works are visionary, since the urge of creation comes from the unknown that vibrates the collective unconscious. Jung adduced Dante and Wagner, both great writers and composers of the fantastic, to illustrate that their visionary literature plunges into the collective unconscious by eliciting the archaic roots of creative imagination. Though both poets draw on myths (one Christian, the other Germanic) to fashion their masterpieces, Jung clarified that the real literary creation lies in the writer's original experience that meets the imaginary of the unknown, the corollary of which is the amalgam with mythological elements. In this manner, the artistic work is treated not as a personal creation but as a "super-personal production." The *Faust* of Goethe, another example of fantastic literature drawn from the aforementioned archetypal devil, further explains the willingly mythological nature in excellent artistic creation.

> It's not Goethe who 'made' Faust; it's the psychical component of Faust that made Goethe. Moreover, what is Faust? Faust is more than a semiotic indication and more than the allegory of one thing known for a long time; Faust is a symbol, the expression of an active and alive datum, for always, in the German soul, which Goethe, in this respect, only brought forth.
> Nothing would be more false than supposing that the poet draws from traditional material: he draws indeed rather from the original experience, whose obscure nature necessitates the mythological figures; that is the reason why it lures them greedily to express themselves thanks to them. [my translation, Jung 1995, 219-20]

Jung divulged this archaic dimension of literary creation that connects the artist with the archaic soul into a one-as-whole creation process.

Such visionary creation abounds in fantastic literature; Tolkien is a visionary writer par excellence of our times. This process of visionary creation is akin to what Plato assumed in *Ion* as he attributed the divine inspiration that controls the poet. Moreover, Tolkien revealed his writing experience as being inspired and dominated by the divine power. This particular experience of fantastic creation can also be testified by Hoffmann's hero Nathanael in "The Sandman," who claims that "the inspiration in which alone any true artistic work could be done [...] was the result of the operation directed inward of some Higher Principle existing without and beyond ourselves" [Calvino, 52]. Such perceptual analogy in fantastic creation can be construed to mean that the fantastic mimesis is a representation pertinent to the unknown, linked to the collective unconscious. This creation process can be further assimilated with the dreamlike status. Jung's concept of the dream is similar to that in oriental mysticism, Daoism, Hinduism and Buddhism, which regard the dream as a mediating space to commune with time and "ultra-space."[23] In view of modern man's lack of symbols as a result of the progressive triumph of rationality, mystic participation is only possible through dreaming. Dreams possess an important key to bridge the consciousness and the collective unconscious. Archetypal symbols are released in dreams that also inspire writers to tell fantastic stories about unknown space. Most romantic writers of the genre recalled archetypal images and symbols from their dreams. Nodier, though ignorant of the unconscious and an espouser of Neo-Platonism, acclaimed the imaginative power cradled in dreams [Castex].

Jung's theory touches upon the most profound dimension that the human psyche is capable of communicating with. Writers with the imaginary *inventio* from this layer are visionary fantastic masters. Those who create from the imaginary incorporated with *unus mundus* are prophetic artists unbounded from the limited known reality, mainly constructed by alpha-thinking[24] or logical thinking. The narrative representations grounded in this prophetic imaginary are classified as the fantastic literature with dream-discourse (to be elaborated in Part Two), the ideal of Tolkien's sub-creation. Therefore, the fantastic works of grand style hold a similar teleological view as Jung. The individualization from ego to Self takes place in the fantastic as a process of alchemical transformation of language to discover that the ancient and long obsolete idea of man as a microcosm contains an ultimate psychological truth. In the former times of mystic participation (Jung) or original participation (Barfield), this truth was projected upon the body, just as alchemy projected the unconscious psyche upon chemical substances. Hence an exploration of the substances will help trace back to the truth of the collective unconscious. Inspired by Jung, Bachelard launched a theory of the imaginary, which focuses on the material imagination based on phenomenological poetics.

The Reverie of the Four Elements and Metamorphosis

Drawing on Jung's insightful psychology, Gaston Bachelard proposed to complete the theory by a more representable method. If Jung focused on the process of individuation and imagination, Bachelard accentuated the significance of literary images inspired by the predominating elements of fire, water, earth and air. He began with the reverie, as opposed to dream, and proceeded through the

---

[23] The oriental mysticism of Hinduism, Daoism and Buddhism envisions the existence of an "ultra-space" that is accessible through meditation, alchemy and dream. Dream is believed to represent a space that goes beyond our sensible vision of the three-dimensional space and thus connecting with time.

[24] The term is borrowed from Barfield to designate the logical, abstract and rational thinking mode. Different from alpha-thinking, beta-thinking refers to "thinking about thinking" or "reflection."

preconscious to trace back to the deep collective unconscious. The imaginary of the substantial elements corresponds to the trace left by the manifestations of the four elements departing from the space of Platonic chôra. Bachelard's imaginary of the material is *the sublimation of the unconscious* [Tadié], which hinges on the metaphors of animation and metamorphosis. This imaginary of animation and metamorphosis is indeed the core momentum of fantastic storytelling.

To emphasize the poetic reverberation in images, Bachelard further distinguished formal imagination from material imagination in his work *L'Eau et les rêves* (*Water and the Dreams*). Material imagination is more significant in the dynamic of creation than formal imagination. The latter is distinguished from the former by its search for the beauty of forms and colours and the variety of languages, centring on the rhetoric to attract readers. The material imagination, in search of profundity, the primitive and the eternal, is essentially open. It invokes new metaphors that converge on the unity of substance. Bachelard regarded the profound imaginary of substance as being linked with our first intuitions that are constantly born from our sensible contact with matter. In the process of this sensible contact, the material arouses in us the will that activates gestures; for example, the molding of clay, plunging into water, the consummation by fire and flight in the air. These gestures, with the attribute of animating movements, are the indices for us to identify the reveries. With this dynamic power, Bachelard declared that the material commands the form. While recognizing the immediate impression that formal imagination appears first to readers, he maintained that the material imagination is the core source of writers' *inventio*.

With a keen insight into a long history of errors in science, except for mathematics, Bachelard developed his epistemology that delves into the functioning of the scientific spirit. His theory is initially built on studying the obstacles that imagination erects in the way of scientific knowledge, thus the concept of *epistemological obstacle* is the core of Bachelardian imaginary philosophy. He presumed that "premier intuition" is the first cause of these obstacles, which hinder the formulation and solution of scientific problems. However, he affirmed at the same time that these very obstacles function in alchemy as well as in literature. The departing point of his philosophy entails that such an epistemology develops in parallel with the analysis of imagination. He traced far back into the pre-Socratic philosophy to question the source of the errors in primitive science so as to analyze the four elements that exert fascination and imagination in human psychology. Inspired by the philosophy of four elements, initially introduced by Empedocles (493?-433? BC), Bachelard's theory is a succession to Jung's theory inasmuch as the latter extends into the realm of the irrepresentable collective unconscious akin to the Platonic chôra, while Bachelard centred on the diurnal reverie of thinking man (instead of unconscious activity) leading to the materials as manifestations of the arcane chôra. With his debut of the imaginary in *La Psychanalyse du feu* (*Psychoanalysis of Fire*) in 1938, Bachelard offered a new concept of psychoanalysis different from the Freudian definition. It is by no means an examination of repressed desires in dreams, but rather an exploration of naïf thought, the reverie vibrating with the four elements, an exploration focusing more on the imaginary than on the unconscious. Following the postulate of Greek philosophers Empedocles and Plato that all matters are composed of elemental particles of fire, water, earth and air and that all changes are caused by motion, Bachelard centred his investigation by grouping the *complexes* (consisting of primitive images) round the four elements, viz. the unknown realm traced by the materials.

The Bachelardian complex, like his psychoanalysis, reroutes Freud's complex (deriving from the unconscious and universal origin) but follows the examples of Jung (isotopic complexes serving to seize certain archetypes). He thus displayed the nuances of complexes begotten from the reveries on fire: the Prometheus complex, the Empedocles complex, the Novalis complex and the Hoffmann complex. The Prometheus complex, with the urge to know, often breeds the imaginary that tells stories of mad scientists, such as *Frankenstein* and *The Island of Dr Moreau*. The complex of Empedocles "where love and the respect of fire, instinct of living and dying, unite together" [Bachelard 1985, 35], inspires the fantastic literature of transcendental love and alchemical transformation. Paulo Coelho's *The Alchemist* also illustrates the imaginary of such a complex. While the Novalis complex represents the imaginary of romantic poetry, the Hoffmann complex opens the way to a complete phantasmagoria that launches the romantic bloom of fantastic literature.

It is clear that Bachelard's theory centres on a cultural base, different from Jung's more spiritually oriented approach but akin to anthropologists'; he developed the conception of cultural complexes, for example the above mentioned complexes of Novalis and Hoffmann and the complex of Ophelia deriving from the reveries on water. This complex unites water with women and desire of death [Bachelard 1942, 26]. The literary work adduced by Bachelard to demonstrate his theory on the psychoanalysis of fire is a romantic fantastic work in verse written by Lautréamont, *Les Chants de Maldoror*. He set forth the significance of bestiary images related to fire by analyzing approximately four hundred terms of animals [Tadié, 110]. Out of the imaginary of fire, one of the four composing elements of all beings, the complex of aggressive and animal life marks one essential source of fantastic creation, an ambivalence of fear and cruelty. Bachelard termed it the "Lautréamont complex" which characterizes an urge towards animating in our imagination. This complex is vital to the fantastic creation drawn from the imaginary of deformation of the animate and the animation of the inanimate. While Bachelard centred on the groups of metaphors and assimilated them with metamorphoses by their nature of the deformations of images, I will focus on the imaginary of animation and metamorphosis deriving from the elements underlying the fantastic creation. The two important prede-cessors from Antiquity of fantastic literature, Ovid and Apuleius, portrayed their imagination of metamorphosis and animation by poeticizing into their fantastic narratives, *Metamorphoses* and *The Golden Ass or Metamorphoses*, the phi-losophies of Pythagoras and Empedocles underlying the former and Platonism, especially the love philosophy in *Phaedrus,* underlying the latter.

From the reveries of materials to material imagination, albeit an inception with diurnal reveries of the consciousness, we touch back upon the collective or personal unconscious. In this manner, Bachelardian imagination gets connected with Jungian imagination. Once in contact with the unconscious, imagination invents not only plots and images but also a new life with a new spirit. It opens our eyes with new visions. Vision, different from the simply perceived "view," often refers to the invisible. This elaboration of reveries on materials is one of the inventive sources of fantastic literature, rendering the invisible visible. This conception of material imagination vis-à-vis vision echoes with Jung's view-point on the imaginary predominated by the collective unconscious and the vi-sionary writers.

The concretization of the fantastic imaginary into stories is like the alchemic transformation of language attaching the unconscious to the four elements. The central motor of the image deformation proposed by Bachelard is extended and incarnated through the temporality of storytelling. Bachelard imagined in the material imagination a law of the four elements that predominates the imagina-tion transforming into a specific poetics. This specific poetics lies in the func-tioning of imagination that deforms and forms images. The deforming of images here sends us back to Aristotle's idea of strangeness in the diction of poetics. Bachelard found the essence of the strangeness in the deformation of images. The decisive mechanism for this is the imaginary, the psychic function of the unreal, or deformation of the real, that governs our imagination. The imaginary allows for escape from the ordinary perception of reality and the deformation of perceived images into what he called imagined images. These imagined images are akin to literary images. Bachelard defines the poetic image as one able to make readers dream by its bridge of reverie between the author and the reader. It signifies other things and makes them dream otherwise. Eventually we have to resort to language that manifests in itself an imagining power or demiurgic power begetting the poetic image. Bachelard elaborated his theory into the law of literary creation, in particular the coherence of poetic images converging to the unique material element.

Bachelard further studied the function of deformed images by juxtaposing them with perceived images of reality to construct his core approach of analysis, namely *rythmanalysis*. To rythmanalyse literature means to realize the profound rhythm of the vibrations that animate the poetics of an author. This rhythm comes from the weaving of the real and the unreal, which enacts the literary language by a double signification. Accordingly, metaphors are the quintessence of poetic images. This rhythm of ambivalence from opposites returns us to Jung's ideal of the reconciliation of the opposites, the ideal of *unus mundus*. However, Bachelardian rhythm and dynamics generated from the imaginary focus on the ambivalence in the dialectic of the perceived and imagined images, a kind of dynamic or rhythm created from spatial contrast, or specialization of temporality. He centred on the reconciliation of opposites on a smaller scale, viz. mainly the opposites of images. Poe is adduced to illustrate this rhythm by his poetic temperament,[25] water being the reigning material that begets myriads of images. The rhythm takes place when the initially perceived water attributed with quality of limpidity is destined towards a deformation of darkening [Bachelard 1942, 16-7]. Nonetheless, this analysis falls short of the very essence of Poe's art of storytelling. According to Poe's *Philosophy of Composition*, musicality and narrative temporality are important techniques in writing. Besides the demonstration with the rhyme schemes and metres of the poem *The Raven*, his stories like "William Wilson" can illustrate these musical elements in fantastic narration. Poe created his idiosyncratic tension by the consummately poeticized prose, for example, the plentiful various rhymes and alliteration. Thus the archetype of water should also encompass the imaginary of musicality and storytelling.

Bachelard's visual focus derives from the employment of the word "verbal," disregarding the meaning of verb, to expound the importance of language in rendering imaginary images, like most other theorists that mainly focus on verbal spatiality, namely the visual images. The case of Poe extends the verbal significance to the realm of verbs, and thus to the temporality of the imaginary. The formation of the four elements resides in the permanent dynamic movement from the unknown space of chôra, as Plato expounds. Because of this, readers can not be led into the profundity of dreams through imagined images warding off thought, referent or sensation of the author through language. Refining the quality of dynamic movement in chôra, Kristeva, in her somewhat limited interpretation of this Platonic term, attributes an important feature of this unknown space – namely rhythm. This attribute of rhythm extends to the four elements and can thus explain the abounding rhythmic musicality and chanting storytelling in fantastic creation from Antiquity. Therefore, the musical narration from the "material imagination" coupled with deformed or strange or unfamiliar images underpins the creation of the fantastic.

---

[25] Bachelardian theory of the imaginary is based on the principle that the origin of imagining powers attached to the premier intuitions is related to material. Writers can portray imaginary traces by one or many elements; nevertheless, each personal imagination is predisposed to one dominating element that determines the course of reveries. This material orientation that characterizes literary representations forms the author's *poetic temperament*.

Bachelard contributed a concrete methodology to the literary imaginary. It substantializes Jung's irrepresentable archetypes by the Platonic seizable manifestations of the four elements, and grounds the demiurgic power of the imaginary in language. The perspective from the imaginary of the four elements and the reverberation of images facilitates the exploration of the *inventio* of the fantastic in terms of reverie and metamorphosis. This stratification of the collective unconscious aroused by the pure reverie of consciousness can be traced by the material imagination. From the collective unconscious or dream to the preconscious or reverie, the dissection of the psychic imagination moves from the abyss to an upper layer. This ascendant movement in the imaginary researches corresponds to the fashioning movement by the Platonic Demiurge from the state of chôra to the manifestations of particles of the four elements, exactly the four elements predominating in Bachelard's imaginary. The variations of fantastic creation through the diachronism (for example the dialectic of ego and shadow) and synchronism (universal images of the unknown) in the fantastic creation will be further illuminated by the semantic isotopism proposed by Gilbert Durand's theory.

Fantastic Storytelling and la Fantastique

As stated before, the Jungian archaic memory and dream underlying fantastic creation stresses the spiritual imagination as human genetic heritage, which is described by the metaphor of the DNA of imagination, a correlative of the archetype of the unknown or chôra. Bachelardian imaginary sheds light on the sources of the fantastic metamorphosis, literal transformation or figurative transformation of narration. Durand's imaginary is grounded in the human confrontation with time. It further probes into the physiognomy of unknown creatures, such as sorceress and monster, deriving from the imaginary of the visage of time. Not content with staying with the analysis of immobile images, Durand highlights the semantic significance of story driven by the dynamism of converging images. The storytelling is essentially a mediation of the fantastic imagination or *la fantastique*. Espousing Jung's theory, Durand defines imagination as "*la racine de toute pensée*" (the root of all thought) [Durand, 27]. Like Kant and Bachelard who saw the cognitive function in imaging and imagination, Durand proclaims that imagination is the origin of all reasoning. Through imagination, the known comes from the unknown, a similar vision being illustrated in Daoist philosophy where all beings coming from nothingness. By the same token, literary history shows that the literature of the fantastic comes prior to the literature of realism. From Durand's perspective, imagination is neither a phenomenon of consciousness nor the enemy of reason. It is in reality the foundation of all consciousness, origin of all reasoning. Durand holds physical objects and the images in high regard by asserting that "*les choses avant les mots* (things before words)." This is the very opposite of the modern semiotic conception of words. Speaking against the reigning postmodern assumption, Durand tries to find a solution to link words and things. The linkage can be possible by imagination, but not through reason. This assumption of imagination evokes the revolutionary view of Kant. He proclaimed the process of imaging (*Einbildungskraft*) to be the condition of all knowledge. The process of imaging is productive as well as reproductive, and the process of imaging transcendent to reason, the knowing subject [Kugler, 78-79]. In his conservative age governed by alpha-thinking, Kant did not go too far to rank imaging as the source of knowledge. Durand, in our times of alpha-thinking exhaustion and of consciousness of beta-thinking, affirms the supremacy of imagination.

Durand opts for a phenomenology of the imaginary against the ontological *psychologism* of the reflexive type, given that the imaging consciousness and the concrete images that semantically constitute this consciousness are inseparable. He conducts his classification of three groups of schemas (symbolized by the archetypes borrowed from Tarot symbols) by the three dominating reflexes: postural, digestive and copulative. Durand means by this schema the driving force that decides imaginary types. It refers to verbs, for example, to ascend or to fall. Archetypes constitute the substantification of schemas or the incarnation of the schemas in the objects. Different from archetypes with universality, symbols are confined to a specific culture and thus naturally ambivalent and polysemic. Firstly, the verticalizing and *diaïretical*[26] schemas are symbolized by the archetypes of the sceptre and the glaive, isotopic of a process of symbols. Then, the schemas of the descent and the interiorization are symbolized by the archetype of the goblet with its symbolic components. Lastly, the rhythmic schemas, with the cyclic or progressive nuance, are symbolized by the archetypes of the denier and the burgeoning staff, the tree. This tripartition is grouped into two systems: one is diurnal, that of antithesis; the other nocturnal, that of the euphemism strictly speaking. All these archetypal classes determine the following structural genres of the imaginary: the schizomorphic or heroic structures, the mystical or antiphrastic structures, and the synthetic or dramatic structures.

Out of his archetypology of the imaginary, Durand further sketches a philosophy of the imaginary by coining the neologism '*une fantastique transcendantale*' in the attempt to corroborate an identical and universal reality of the imaginary.

---

[26] Durand coins the neologism by forming with the prefix "di-" that means separation and "aireisis" that means the choice or preference. The *diaïretical* symbols signify the symbols of power and purity consisting in images relating to weapons and victories, such as swords and arrows.

> In this fantastic function resides this "supplementary soul" that the contemporary anguish anachronically looks for among the ruins of determinism, for this is the fantastic function that adds to dead objectivity the interest assimilative to unity, that adds to unity the satisfaction of the agreeable, that adds to the agreeable the luxury of the aesthetic emotion, which at last in a supreme assimilation, after having semantically denied the negative destiny, installs thinking in the absolute euphemism of the negative destiny, installs thinking in the absolute euphemism of serenity as of the philosophical or religious revolt. [ibid., 500][27]

The "supplementary soul" mirrors Jung's archaic soul to dilate to the illumination of the rhetoric of euphemism. The fantastic imagination or *la fantastique* will also be mediated by the imaginary language to reunite with the ideal of unity or one-as-whole.

This archetypology of symbols promises to elicit the meanings of the invented images in fantastic creation, at the level of diachronism and synchronism. Parallel to Bachelard's classification of images centring on the material archetypes, Durand proposes an approach to categorize the images of isomorphism or polarization clustering around the archetypes deriving from the diurnal and nocturnal regimes. This perspective exposes the imaginary representations in fantastic creation and the variations in narrative rhetoric. While Bachelard emphasized gestures in response to the four elements, Durand puts the accent on gestures in reaction to time and space. From Jung to Bachelard to Durand, the imaginary hence pivots on human behaviours grounded in infancy. Durand avails himself of the reflexology of psychological stages to establish the connection among corporeal gestures, nerve centres and symbolic representation. This allows him to deduce a regulation of various symbols converging on specific archetypes, a process that allows him to crystallize the intrinsic signification (which determines our world representation) of the imaginary products. He integrates the original three reflexes of position, nutrition and copulation into two imaginary systems (diurnal and nocturnal regimes) by combining the last two reflexes into the system related to darkness, stomach and sex. Though Durand's symbols are determined by the gestures vis-à-vis space, time is the animating factor that drives the gestures to ascend or descend. The two systems of day and night are thus divided according to the attitude towards time, resistance and rebellion vs.

---

[27] *En cette fonction fantastique réside ce « supplément d'âme » que l'angoisse contemporaine cherche anarchiquement sur les ruines des déterminismes, car c'est la fonction fantastique qui ajoute à l'objectivité morte l'intérêt assimilateur de l'utilité, qui ajoute à l'utilité la satisfaction de l'agréable, qui ajoute à l'agréable le luxe de l'émotion esthétique, qui enfin dans une assimilation suprême, après savoir sémantiquement nié le négatif destin, installe la pensée dans l'euphémisme total de la négatif destin, installe la pensée dans l'euphémisme total de la sérénité comme de la révolte philosophique ou religieuse.*

intimacy and submission. This insight into the diurnal and nocturnal regimes of the human imaginary predominated by time not only illustrates the production of the universal invisible images but also elucidates the difference in fantastic storytelling from different cultures, for example, the antithetic and *schizomorphic* rhetoric in French fantastic tales against the synthetic and euphoriant rhetoric in Oriental tales.

The diurnal regime is fundamentally antithetical, against bestiality, darkness or dark semantics and falling. It is characterized by verticality, transcendence, purification, light and the quest for immortality. The attitude represented under this system is the heroic will to conquer or surpass. Since the diurnal regime is a rebellion against temporality, including mortality, the first isomorphic group of archetypes is the visage of time. The human imaginary, before relentless and ineluctable time, engenders three constellations of symbols: (1) theriomorphic symbols (images of animals), (2) nyctomorphic symbols (images of night or darkness) and (3) catamorphic symbols (images of falling or heaviness). In response to the animated visage of time, the imaginary functions to create the archetypes of sceptre and glaive, which signify the escape from time or victory over death or destiny. The principal constellations of symbols converging to the archetypes are (1) ascensional or elevatory symbols, (2) spectacular symbols and (3) diaïretical symbols (neologism of Durand to mean isomorphism of weapons and ascendant archetypes). The isomorphism of the images of the diurnal regime extends to construct the schizomorphic or heroic structures of the imaginary undergirded by the schizophrenic symptom and the fight against time and death. The structures are further partitioned into four categories: (1) the pragmatic deficit or autism or excessive retreat, such as the hero in *Melmoth Réconcilié*, (2) *Spaltung* or abstraction or split *Weltanschauung*, e.g. the mental status of Dr Jekyll, (3) morbid geometrism or gigantism, the narrator's hyperbolic expressions of the Gothic surroundings in "William Wilson," (4) the antithesis, the conflict with time, morbid planning or immobility and petrification, for example, the loitering knight from "The Autumn Sorcery." The symbols of the above diurnal regime hinge on the dominating reflex of the postural, the essential dynamic schemas being vertical and *diaïretical*. The central structure activated by the isomorphic symbols underpins the rhetoric of hyperbole in language. The analysis of meaning to this point is able to explain the syntactical variation in the fantastic narration. For example, the abundant expressions of hyperbole and pleonasm in fantastic storytelling at the age of skepticism can be traced back to the imaginary of the diurnal regime.

In fact, most fantastic tales, myths and legends are couched in the imaginary of the nocturnal regime. This imaginary orientation also discloses the ignorance of hyperbolic expressions with doubt in the fantastic narration in Antiquity or in other cultures. Confronting inescapable devouring time, the digestive and copulative reflexes dominate the imaginary to opt for (1) euphemism or antiphrasis or

(2) harmony, cycle, rebirth or progress, the dominating archetypes of the first being the descent and the goblet, and the second the denier and the staff. The nocturnal regime of symbols is thus established against the diurnal regime. Contrary to the fight against time, the archetypes of the descent and the goblet aim at submitting to time to gain rest and tranquility. The antidote of time does not exist in superhuman or transcendent means but in reconciling to the reassuring, warm and intimate substance. Denying time on the mode of antiphrasis, symbols reduce its danger by euphemizing, denying and reversing. The symbols corresponding to the archetypes of the descent and the goblet are divided into two categories: symbols of inversion and symbols of intimacy. The symbols of inversion, with the idiosyncrasy of expression of euphemism and antiphrasis, encompass the isomorphism of symbols consisting in feminine figures, aquatic and telluric depth, nutrition, plurality, richness and fecundity:

> It is, as Bachelard writes, an 'involutive' process that commences all exploratory movement of the secrets of future, and Desoille in his second work studies the dreams of descent that are the dreams of return as well as an acclamation or consent to temporal condition. It is a question of 'forgetting fear" [my translation, ibid., 227].

The symbols of inversion are subdivided into four groups: (1) Inversion and double negation or the descending into the depth of the earth or water, for example, Jules Verne's *Twenty Thousand Leagues under the Sea* and Andersen's "The Little Mermaid"; (2) embedding and reduplication, the most famous example being Jonah in the whale's belly that reverses the fear before the devouring time. Durand claims that mythology and the legends are rich in this swallowing symbolism. The epic *Kalevala* illustrates a refinement of successive embeddings of the swallowing fishes; (3) hymn to the night – the images offer a divine, melodious and colourful night, related to substantial femininity, which is opposed to the *femme fatale* from the diurnal regime, such as the heroine in "Arria Marcella"; and (4) mother and material – with frequent images of the Great Mother or aquatic or telluric mother, Lady Galadriel from *The Lord of the Rings* exemplifies this par excellence. Different from antiphrasis in symbols of inversion, the imaginary of rest and intimacy orients towards the symbols of intimacy. This constellation of symbols comprises (1) the tomb and the rest, where death is imaged as sleep, for example, the representation in the Grimm's "Rose-Bud"; (2) the dwelling place and the goblet or the container that refers to enclosed and sacred space, e.g. nave, cup, chalice, grail, vase and sack; and (3) nutrition and substance often presents images of fluidity as milk, honey, divine wine and alchemical quintessence.

The interplay of both symbols of inversion and intimacy produces the mystic or antiphrastic structures of the imaginary under the nocturnal regime. (1) Replication and perseveration or the refuge structure often portrays an action or

interpretation of preservation towards different objects, especially the refuge related to obsession with intimacy, to primitive, gynecological and digestive tranquility. *Twenty Thousand Leagues under the Sea* offers a perfect refuge example.
(2) Viscosity of representative elements or attachment is a structure that depicts
an individual attached to the world and thus leading him to a genuine fusion
with it. The structure is characterized by words such as tie/link, viscose, sticky,
confusion and agglutination. It aims at deleting differences and cleavage between things and beings by detail precision. In *The Alchemist*, the boy's communion with Nature exposes such an attachment. (3) Sensoriality of representations or sensorial realism demonstrates an overemphasis on the depiction of
sensations, for example, the colours are stronger than the form, feeling things
closely so as to animate their substance from the interior. For example, the sensitive coloration in the backdrop of the night in Gautier's "Arria Marcella," and
"La Morte amoureuse" (The Dead Woman in Love or The Beautiful Vampire),
and Wilde's elaborate style (the former in fact exerting great influence on him)
of sensations in *The Picture of Dorian Gray*. (4) The last mystic structure features minuteness and miniaturization or gulliverization in contrast to the diurnal
regime's mad geometrism or gigantization, for example, the miniature universe
in Charles Nodier's "La Fée aux miettes" (The Fairy of Crumbs) and the
Grimms' "Tom Thumb." This structure is connected with meticulous description
of details so as to lose sight of the whole, thus delving into an experience of intimate eternity as a reality of microcosm. For example, one sole cypress is sufficient for Van Gogh to represent a cosmology; or just one bamboo or one pine
tree suffices for a Zen painter to show his cosmology through a microcosmic
imagination [ibid., 318]. Fantastic literature, like Gulliver's travel and the
aforementioned tales, represents the microcosm through the myriad miniature
worlds of faeries or gnomes. It does so concretely, going beyond metaphoric
language. If poetry, as the hymn to the night, chants the imaginary images
through metaphoric language or rhetoric of euphemism, then fantastic literature
stages the figures literally to restore the pristine visage to language through the
imaginary poeticization. It is a return from formalization to *la fantastique*.

The symbols that depend upon the diurnal and nocturnal regimes are the
images and motifs of the literary imaginary linked to the great memory of the
human unconscious, in an anthropological sense. Studies of these imagined
symbolic images centring on the polar systems reveal the significant images and
concrete creatures recurrent in fantastic literature. It is not fortuitous that most
examples adduced by Durand are fantastic stories, myths, legends and folkloric
tales. The departing point being the gestures dominated by reflexes in reaction to
time and space (the very source of the unknown), most symbols abound in the
imaginary of the fantastic, whether it is in the diurnal regime or nocturnal regime. Nevertheless, the essential function of *la fantastique* will be mediated
only through the mythic story.

Jung's proposal of the creative imagination as the third way leading to the amalgamation of the psychic and the physical is enhanced by Durand's mythic story as the third way beyond the dialectic of the diurnal and the nocturnal. Born from the nocturnal regime, the archetypes of the denier and the staff (bolstered up by the reflex of copulation) feature the cyclic and progressive symbols. The cyclic symbols are subdivided into the lunar cycle, the agro-lunar drama, the bestiary of the moon and the technology of cycle, all converging to the archetype of the denier (in the sense of any of several former European coins). The rhythmic schema also drives the imaginary into producing the progressive symbols, including the cross, fire and tree, constellating the archetype of the staff, or the burgeoning staff. With the clustering of these nocturnal symbols driven by the rhythmic schema, Durand presents the synthetic structures of the imaginary and the styles of story. The first structure is harmonization of contraries with the musical imagination, ideal as a victory against time. Bach's music composed with a harmonious system demonstrates this musical imagination. The second structure centres on the dialectic which corresponds to the law of musical contrast. Beethoven's music, especially his symphonies, illustrates the relations between drama and music of this structure. In addition to the musical structures, the rhythmic schema impels the symbols to a structure of history and fable. Durand uses the rhetoric of hypotyposis[28] of the past and the presence of narration to characterize the structure's styles of story. The last structure is termed that of progress, the rhetoric being the hypotyposis of the future, a prosperous future by the mastering of time and technical acceleration of history through messianism and alchemy. Durand's third structures bring to light the quintessence of mythic story apart from the symbols rich in meanings: the often ignored imaginary of music and the rhythm of storytelling. Durand associates music and myth (diachronism and synchronism) to illustrate the semantic form of myth (isotopism).

Underscoring the untranslatable quality of myths and analysis of their semantic structure simply for meaning's sake, Durand criticizes Barthes's semiotic interpretation of myth and Lévi-Strauss's linguistic interpretation of the synchronicity of myths as establishing a mathematic of myth. He affirms the inventive power of *la fantastique* in the imaginary, the transcendental sources of the imaginary symbols whose fantastic space, different from physician space, is Euclidian and imaginary (the unknown space) that transforms into the communion with time, and thus spatializing time. It is exactly this fantastic in the feminine (*la* instead of *le*) that constructs the *inventio* part of the mimesis of the fan-

---

[28] Pierre Fontanier characterized *hypotyposis* as a figure of style by imitation: "The Hypotyposis paints the things in so lively and energetic a manner that it presents them right before the eyes, and turns a narrative or a description into an image, a painting or even a live scene (*L'Hypotypose peint les choses d'une manière si vive et si énergique, qu'elle les met en quelque sorte sous les yeux, et fait d'un récit ou d'une description, une image, un tableau, ou même une scène vivante)*" [390].

tastic. With the *épaisseur sémantique* of Durand's theory of the mythic imaginary, fantastic literature recovers its semantic substance and deviates from the
semiotic interpretation of the fantastic as a mere system of signifiers and from
the dialectic exegesis of the fantastic as mere abstract logic. The formalization of
language indeed results from the mediation of the rhetoric, such as hyperbole,
euphemism or hypotyposis. Fantastic literature, as myths – the imaginary –
purges language back to *la fantastique*, the very source of its imaginary.

The approach of the imaginary offers an anatomy of the *inventio* of the fantastic mimesis from the deepest archaic soul of the human imagination linked
with the arcane and unknown space of chôra, through the material imagination
vibrating with the universal elements of fire, water, earth and air (departing from
chôra). Though the literary imaginary is usually employed to reveal the underlying images and symbols in all literary creation, we deem fantastic literature the
very genre that vividly stages as flesh and blood, a sheer *mise en scène* of these
archetypal and symbolic images that are often considered unreal or supernatural.
Through the mediation of storytelling, an artistic process combining figures and
abstract logic (temporal formalization of connecting images), fantastic literature
succeeds the tradition of myth, both engrained in the archaic soul, as it were the
DNA of imagination released from chôra. This soul enacts either literal or figurative metamorphosis, from the isomorphic figures rooted in the imaginary
space of *la fantastique* that transforms into stories from intrinsic semantism to
extrinsic momentum. The theories of the imaginary that delve into the unknown
dimension of imagination eventually converge on the significance of meanings
and the creative power of myth and language, the quintessence of the fantastic
narration. Vittorio's definition of the fantastic as the aestheticization of the supernatural further reinforces this poetic quality of the fantastic. Jung examined
the spiritual power of mythic symbols in the human psyche; Bachelard penetrated the reverberation of myths and complexes in poetic language open to semantic substance. Durand restores myths to their imaginative throne by complementing the diachronism and synchronism in the traditional mythic analysis
with the isotopism of images to demonstrate that myths are untranslatable.

The investigation of the fantastic *inventio* helps recover the universal roots
of the fantastic imagination beyond cultural boundaries. Moreover, the differences in the representation of the imaginary from different cultures can further
shed light on the differences in the narrative rhetoric of the fantastic; for example, the narrative variations in telling ghost stories by the Irish Stoker, the
French Maupassant and the Chinese Pu Songling. From the perspective of Durand's theory, the Todorovian hesitation in the fantastic discourse is indeed one
of the corollaries of the *schizomorphic* structures from the diurnal regime. Contrary to the structuralist or semiotic perspective that the form decides the content,
the imaginary exploration of fantastic literature orients towards the hypothesis
that the content predominates over the form. Nevertheless, the form of rhetoric

and style in the fantastic narration are significant, given that they conversely and artistically aestheticize the imaginary content to make a literary ideal of *unus mundus*.

The imaginary images rich in meanings through archetypes and symbols are awaiting a scrupulous study from the perspective of the imaginary. As Durand observes, man tends to formalize the fantastic imagination or *la fantastique* and thus merely retains the formalized language, which is taken as literal today. Storytelling offers the third way to formalize or rather poeticize in an imaginary manner, as a countercurrent against the logical formalization to keep the unity of the form and content of *la fantastique*. To explore the true visage of fantastic literature, we have to trace back to the true meanings and narrative art of myth, the pristine nature of mythopoeia. The rhetorical function of storytelling in relation to myth, mimesis and chôra merits exploration. The enigma of myth vis-à-vis logos and the arcane unknown space of chôra will be decoded in the light of Daoist and *Yi Jing* philosophy.

Mythopoeia – The Heritage of Human Imagination
Crystallization of Mythos and Logos

The studies of the imaginary of the fantastic in relation to the significance of narrative or story entail the mythopoeic storytelling as the third way, the mystic and creative imagination. While in the English language, *story* is well distinguished from *history*, the former connoting fictive and the latter real, French encompasses the pair of polar meanings, history and story in one word: *histoire*, which casts a certain light on the true meanings of the two apparently conflicting terms. In Chinese, *xiaoshuo* (tale, short story and novel) literally means minor relation, initially coined by the Daoist philosopher Zhuang Zi, who availed himself of fantastic *xiaoshuo* to discourse on his philosophy. A later term *gushi* (story) is employed that literally means the events in the past, while *lishi* (history) signifies rather chronicles of the past (dynasties). Nevertheless, the Chinese *xiaoshuo* eventually ceded its right to novel and *gushi* came to mean an orally told story. The semantic field of the word "story" already offers a perspective of the fact in the fictive, or the fictive in the fact. This paradox raises a similar situation in the etymology of "myth" or "mythos" and "logos." Storytelling indeed connects mythos and logos, if we consider Daoist philosophers Zhuang Zi and Lie Zi's storytelling and Plato's myth-telling through a myth teller. To understand the true meaning of storytelling, it is necessary to explore its origin in human imagination and its mediation and function.

Given that mimesis is the first concept of poetics, we would shed light on its significance in terms of mythic storytelling. Plato dismissed poets by criticizing the substance of mimesis as a false imitation of another imitation, our world. Therefore, a metaphysical exploration of the spirit or soul of myth, viz. the human imaginary in relation to chôra is requisite. Pondering upon the metaphysics of poetics by using the limited logic of the intellect appears contradictory, since we are in the fathomless realm of the imaginary, fundamentally beyond man's logic. Therefore, we will resort to Chinese Daoism and *Yi Jing* to decode the arcane concept of chôra, indeed a space of oxymoron as "a third kind" from Plato's cosmogony.

At the outset, connecting myth, mimesis and chôra appears paradoxical. By the term mimesis, we mean imitation as well as representation. Plato deemed poets dangerous because they imitate the secondary imitation without knowing the truth and elicit the irrational part of our psyche through experiencing the emotions vicariously. Aristotle, in order to defend poets, interpreted mimesis by the representation of what is likely to be. For later poeticians, mimesis can also be imitation of what ancient people believed and imitation of good writings from the ancient poets. Although in the historical tradition of Western literature, mimesis is regarded as the principle of realism, we reinterpret here the meaning of mimesis by reconsidering the significance and historicity of fantastic storytelling, given that the concept of "real" is *per se* precarious.[29]

To penetrate into the spirit of storytelling, it is necessary to crystallize and demystify the meaning of myth, which should adopt here the least obscure conception of the term. A review of the etymology of myth will expound the significance of storytelling in myth. The word myth derives from Greek *mythos* or *muthos*, designating "fictitious narrative usually involving supernatural things. XIX (c.1830). Formerly also mythe (cf. French *mythe*); modern Latin mȳthus, used in English context (from Coleridge), beside mythos (from XVIII) – late Latin mythos – Greek mûthos" [Onions, 601] or "speech, thought, story, plot of unknown origin" [Harper]. Aristotle often referred to the significance of *muthos* (taken as story) that is used in mimesis. For ancient people (or those from the epoch of original participation in terms of Owen Barfield's theory of conscious evolution), the unknown origin refers to gods, goddesses and other supernatural beings, to apply Plato's words, the process of fashioning the imitations. For example, Hesiod's *Theogony* and Homer's *Iliad* and *Odyssey* tell the stories and images of gods, goddesses and supernatural beings. Hesiod claimed that what matters in myth is "how the founding myths were invented to explain how the world came to be and how we came to be in it" [Kearney, 3]. In this manner, myths are also stories that relate the unknown past. The Chinese term of myth is already endowed with a double meaning from the two characters "shen" (god(s)) and "hua" (speech(es)). Different from Barthes's "speech" in an average or earthly way, Chinese myth refers to "speech of god." While *shen* or god means immortality and eternity, "the speech of god" represents the principle of ultimate truth. From this perspective, it corresponds to logos and the Word in Christianity, which will be investigated later.

Therefore, myth is not taken as a popularly believed personal legend, for example, the myth of Bill Gates. Nor is it in the light of Roland Barthes's definition: "*le mythe est une parole*" (myth is a speech) [Barthes 1970, 193]. This interpretation is in fact an extension of his dilating *écriture* (writing) into replacing *poétique* (poetics) or *littérarité* (literariness). Durand criticizes the lapse of Barthes's interpretation of myth by terming it the semiotic error that subordinates myth to a "secondary semiotics" in relation to language. He argues, "nothing, absolutely nothing, permits one to say that the literal meaning chronologically prevails over, and all the more reason to say, ontologically, the figurative meaning" (*Rien, absolument rien, ne permet de dire que le sens proper prime chronologiquement, et à plus forte raison ontologiquement, le sens figure*) [Durand 1992, 457]. In addition, Durand proposes that myth should be:

---

[29] Please refer to the aforementioned Daoist theories and critiques of the fantastic in the section of theorization.

all that is marked out on one hand by the stasis of symbols, on the other hand by archeological verifications. In this manner the term "myth," for us, also covers well the actual myth, that is to say the story legitimizing such-and-such faith, religious or magic, the legend and its explicative intimations, the folktale or the novel. [ibid., 411][30]

Durand gives myth an amplified definition that encompasses various narratives. Yet, he highlights the significance of symbols in myth and its colour of truth in history.

Pierre Brunel criticizes the word "myth" as being very damaged today, rich in a pejorative and mean content, and has taken the meaning of *"tromperie collecetive ou non"* (deception collective or not) [Brunel, 35]. He also criticizes the semiotic interpretation of myth by Barthes, who transforms the culture of petite-bourgeois into universal nature [ibid., 35]. He adopts Mircea Eliade's definition of myth to expound his comparative approach of *mythocritique* (mythocriticism): "Myth tells a sacred story; it relates an event that takes place in the primordial times, the fabulous times of the 'beginnings'" (*Le myth raconte une histoire sacrée ; il relate un événement qui a lieu dans le temps primordial, le temps fabuleux des 'commencements'*) [ibid., 59]. Lamenting in our times over the meagerness of myth, Michel Butor states that the speech of myth has become "silent in this world deserted by the gods" (*silencieuse dans ce monde déserté par les dieux*) [qtd. Chevrel, 5]. Myth can also be defined as "stories told as symbols of fundamental truths within societies having a strong oral tradition" [Long, 699]. Speaking of society and myth, we would further refer to Jung's theory of myth: "Myths are original revelations of the preconscious psyche, involuntary statements about unconscious psychic happenings, and anything but allegories of physical processes" [Jung 1968, 154]. Theorists of myth endeavour to bring to light the subject matter, the origin and the function of myth [Segal, 3]. For example, Jung proposed that the subject matter is the human mind at a symbolic level, the origin and function being to satisfy the human psychological need for contact with the collective unconscious.

All the aforementioned definitions of myth feature an important attribute of story. From the different phases of myth, storytelling is brought to the fore as the artistic dynamism that effectuates the contact. Wellek and Warren take the word myth as the strictly Aristotelian *muthos* or story, and thus deeming all narrative as myth. The later separation of mythos from logos elucidates the separation of story or informal logic of imaginary language [Durand] from the formal logic of dialectic discourse. Hence, an exploration of the meaning of logos will illumi-

---

[30] *tout ce qui est balisé d'un côté par le statisme de symboles, de l'autre par les vérifications archéologiques. Ainsi le terme « mythe » recouvre pour nous aussi bien le mythe proprement dit, c'est-à-dire le récit légitimant telle ou telle foi religieuse ou magique, la légende et ses intimations explicatives, le conte populaire ou le récit romanesque.*

nate the relations between mimesis and myth and their quintessential connection with chôra.

In dictionaries of etymology, "logos" is defined as "'the Word' of John i I. XVI. Greek *lógos* account, ration, reason, argument, discourse, saying, (rarely) word, related to *Légein* gather, choose, recount, say" [Onions, 535] or "words, speech and discourse" [Harper]. According to F. E. Peters, Greeks perceived logos as "speech, account, reason, definition, rational faculty and proportion" [Peters, 110]. It is, for the Pre-Socratic Heraclitus, "an underlying organizational principle of the universe" [ibid., 111]. In the Pre-Socratic period, the dichotomy of mythos/logos was not yet polarized. Effectively, mythos, with its original meaning of "something one says," remained a synonym of logos [Naddaf, viii]. With Plato, a distinction between *muthos* as a "legendary" account and *logos* as a "true" account emerges [ibid., vii]. In the broad and derivative sense of myth, Plato assumed that myth "designates a discourse that transmits unfalsifiable information and that gives rise not to certainty but to belief" [Brisson, 10-1]. Aristotle even further delimited the meaning of logos as equivalent to reason. The Christian conception of logos combines logos, God and Word, which harks back to the essence of mythos and logos: "In the beginning was the Word, and the Word was with God, and the Word was God. The same was in the beginning with God. All things were made by him; and without him was not any thing made that was made" [*King James Bible*, The Gospel According to Saint John 1:1-1:3].

With the imaginary storytelling, a secondary reunion of myth and logos will take place, especially in our times of fantastic creation. This return to mythic storytelling and its connection with the logos taken as its very original meanings is further developed by philologists and writers. Barfield called for caution in interpreting the words like νοῦς (*nous*) and λόγος (*logos*). He warned that "if we are content to translate, and to *think*, 'mind' for νοῦς and 'reason' or 'word' for λόγος, we are in continual danger of surreptitiously substituting our own phenomena for those which they were in fact dealing with" [Barfield 1988, 45]. For Barfield, logos names the "faint awareness of creative activity alike in nature and man" which remains after the decline of original participation [ibid., 185]. He called it "the depth of all theology," whereas Coleridge called the logos "the evolver." In this light, Coleridge's conception is quite close to the *Yi Jing* philosophy. Dao takes on the natural momentum to evolve the Universe. This is represented by the perpetual changes of *Yi Jing* from *Taiji* to the myriad of outgrowths.

In Greek, the word logos means both "word" and "the creative faculty" in human beings or "reason." In Lao Zi's *Dao De Jing*, Dao is announced as the first principle of all becoming. This principle is charged with mystery and divinity. The concept of Dao is much close to logos and mythos as well. Stressing the significance of imaginary semantism, Durand proclaims the supremacy of myth:

"Whether we want it or not, mythology is the first in comparison with not only metaphysics but also all objective thought, and it is metaphysics and science that are produced by the repression of mythic lyricism" (*Qu'on le veuille ou non, la mythologie est première par rapport non seulement à toute métaphysique, mais à toute pensée objective, et c'est la métaphysique et la science qui sont produites par le refoulement du lyrisme mythique*) [Durand 1992, 458]. Holding an eclectic view, Arnaud Villani argues that both *mythos* and *logos* are the wells of truth, the well of abolition and the well of immemorial constitution. He sees in *mythos* ancestral speech telling truth. With the illumination of myth vis-à-vis logos jointed up by the storytelling of hypotyposis, we will now delve into the deepest part of the truth in the collective unconscious, the obscure Platonic chôra. This is the truth that Lao Zi took pains to expound in his *Dao De Jing* and that Zhuang Zi and Lie Zi endeavoured to tell stories to illustrate. Likewise, Plato employed dialogues to explain the unfathomable concept and yet through the voice of a "myth teller," Socrates.

Chôra as the Archetype of the Bourgeoning Metamorphosis of the Unknown

In theories of the imaginary, including Jung (psychologist), Bachelard (phenomenologist), Durand (anthropologist) and Barfield (philological philosopher), a third way is often proposed to bridge the gap between the material and the spiritual worlds or between the abstract and the concrete meanings of language to return to the status of *unus mundus*. This third way is nothing but the creative or aesthetic imagination. The fantastic creation, defined as the poeticized storytelling appertaining to the unknown, is an artistic representation fermented by imagination that serves as a third way to return to the unknown origin. Jung termed this unknown realm as the collective unconscious, which can be reached through the creative imagination. Bachelard proposed the material imagination of the four elements to trace back to the original unknown space. Durand enhances the mythic imagination with the isotopism of symbols that send us back to the pristine state of the figurative language of *la fantastique* or the transcendental fantastic imagination. Barfield deemed the poetic imagination as the only access to the final participation of human consciousness. These theories of the imaginary help bring to light the universal roots of human imagination of the invisible or the unknown images. Imaginary creatures such as dragons, fairies and devils feature in literary works of different cultures. Homer's *Odyssey* and *Iliad*, Ovid's *Metamorphoses* and the Chinese *Shanhai Jing* (*The Classic of Mountains and Seas*) coincidentally disclose a universal momentum of metamorphosis. This essence of the spirit of Becoming through perpetual transforming is being represented by fantastic stories in our times, for example, Tolkien's *Silmarillion* and

The Lord of the Rings, Kafka's *Metamorphosis* and Cortázar's "Axolotl." This universal idiosyncrasy of the fantastic also grounds the rhythmic motion of storytelling, a temporal representation of the unknown space.

In the history of fantastic literature, from the primitive to the contemporary imagination, metaphysics remains a substratum of creation. Pythagorean philosophy permeates Ovid's epic. Zhuang Zi and Lie Zi and later Chinese writers illustrated Daoist metaphysics by telling numerous fantastic tales. Dante, Milton and Goethe touched upon the ideal of religion and metaphysics by means of poeticizing the fantastic. The return of fantastic narration as the *"renaissance de l'irrationnel"* during the Romantic Movement was mainly inspired by Neo-Platonism and Christian Illuminism [Castex]. Most fantastic writers from this period are espousers of Neo-Platonism. Coleridge, influenced by German idealist philosopher Schelling, proclaimed primary and secondary imagination against fancy in composing good poems. His fantastic ballads invite readers into the unknown realm of dream and mystic land. Coleridge's fantastic ballad of "The Rime of the Ancient Mariner" chants the perilous voyage into the realm of the collective unconscious of myth. As explicated and proclaimed by Wordsworth, Coleridge's primary imagination refers to divine inspiration. This vision can be further elucidated by Tolkien's concept of imagination and Marion's Eucharistic hermeneutics, which will be expounded later. In France, Nodier even clearly depicts the Neo-Platonic ideal after death in his tales, such as "Lydie ou la résurrection" (Lydie or the resurrection). Contemporary writers continue to portray an imaginary ideal of metaphysics through fantastic storytelling. As regard the writers of present day, Tolkien once confirmed in a letter to Robert Murray that *"The Lord of the Rings* is of course a fundamentally religious and Catholic work; unconsciously so at first, but consciously in the revision" [Tolkien 1995, 172]. His use of "unconsciously" and "consciously" effectively demonstrates the real creative process of the fantastic that "unconsciously" links to the collective unconscious. In the Latin American culture, Oriental mysticism influences some important fantastic writers, such as Borges and Cortázar. Inspired by Daoist metaphysics, Cortázar created his unique style of non-dualistic fantastic stories.

Engrained in metaphysics, fantastic literature is paradoxically becoming popular in our times, being dominated by deconstruction and semiotics. The paradox resides in the semiotic interpretation of the fantastic as the representation of the signifiers without the signified (e.g., a ghost only exists as a mere sign) and the fact that fantastic literature emerges as literature's rebellion against meaninglessness. This contradiction of the sensible and the intelligible in the fantastic imagination makes it a third way connecting the material and spiritual or the concrete and abstract. Such a concept of "the third way" harks back to "the third kind" proposed by Plato to describe chôra, the matrix or space of the unknown beginning to stir and transmute. Given that the concept of chôra has eluded philosophers' grasp since Antiquity, we would employ the term according to its cosmogonical and metaphysical significance in relation to the human imaginary and with reference to Daoist metaphysics grounded in *Yi Jing*.

Chôra as the third kind (*triton genos*), is the archetype of the bourgeoning metamorphosis of the unknown that makes possible imagination as the third way. This bourgeoning state can be apprehended by the initial change of *Taiji* of *Yi Jing*, viz. the first appearance of yin after *Taiji*, which is termed as *Liangyi* (two bearings or the first coming of yin to yang). The evolution of *Yi Jing* parallels the fashioning described by Plato. After the state of *Liangyi*, the four elements will be generated into *Sixiang* (four phenomena). The movement in *Yi Jing* and the metamorphosis from chôra or *Liangyi* to *Sixiang* or the four elements or the four di-grams are best expounded and illustrated by a Chinese philosopher in the Song dynasty, Zhou Dunyi. In *Taiji tu shuo* (*Annotation of Taiji Diagram*), he offered a comprehensive insight into the cosmogony portrayed by the wisdom of *Yi Jing*. He answered the question of how *Taiji* generates *Liangyi*. This had never been solved before [Wu, 97]. According to his interpretation, *Taiji* stirs to generate yang and the extreme motion generates motionlessness. The motionlessness generates yin and the extreme motionlessness motions again, in a circular manner. This establishment of yin and yang is called *Liangyi*. With the transformation of yang harmonized by yin, the five elements of water, fire, wood, gold and earth are born and the four seasons rotate.[31] In light of Zhou, the kinetic power that motions and stills comes from the interaction of yin and yang. The paradox of the coexistence of motion and motionlessness presents *Liangyi*'s principle of dualism and de-dualism through harmonization, which evokes chôra. The quintessence of both statuses of chôra and *Liangyi* resides in the amalgamation and harmonization of antithesis, in a rhetorical sense, the space of oxymoron in harmony. Since the fantastic imagination incorporates the extremes and transcends dualism, the arcane space of chôra and *Liangyi* can only be imagined and comprehended by fantastic storytelling.

The four seasons are often assimilated with the four elements. Confucius also embraced a similar view: "Yi begins with *Taiji*, *Taiji* is divided into two, therefore the sky and earth are born; the sky and earth have four seasons; since the four seasons are different in the portions of yang and yin, therefore the

---

[31] Chinese alchemists normally develop the rudimentary four elements into five elements. The element gold is derived from the element earth, which is related to the alchemy to refine gold. The element wood in Chinese traditional medicine is regarded as the element air, for wood generates air. In fact, Chinese medicine attributes the quality of wood to the organ liver, which belongs to the direction of East, with colour green; therefore, wood can generate wind or air (*Nei Jing* [*Internal Scripture of Chinese Medecine*]). Or according to the historical record about the "Chinese Adam" Fuxi, it is said that he chooses "wind" (element air) to be his family name because of his title Mu De Wang [King of the Virtue of Wood], for wood can generate wind (*Dengshi xingshu* [*Deng's Book on Family Names*]).

octa-trigrams (*Bagua*) are generated" [ibid., 26]. In compliance with the combination of "grams" in *Yi Jing*, the four elements are represented by the four di-grams: yang-yang (also called old-yang, fire), yang-yin (juvenile-yang, air), yin-yang (juvenile-yin, earth) and yin-yin (old-yin, water). Concerning the conception of *Sixiang* or the four elements or di-grams, Shang Binghe clearly expounds in his *Zhouyi shangshixuei*: "*Sixiang* are the four seasons. Spring is juvenile-yang, summer is old-yang; autumn is juvenile-yin and winter is old-yin. [...] So if *Sixiang* are settled, *Bagua* (octa-grams) are naturally born." We have so far explained the route of transmutation from *Taiji* to *Bagua* (octa-grams). The concept of adding a "yin-gram" to the first yang of *Taiji* is crucial to the understanding of chôra by Plato's metaphorical image of "a mother together with a father." However, a feminine element can not completely represent this arcane kind, since other metaphors are also offered to explicate it. Before we explore further into Lao Zi and Lie Zi's Daoist philosophy to illuminate Plato's chôra vis-à-vis the Ideal Form and the manifestations of the phenomenon, a review of Plato's explanation of this third kind will help comprehend our comparison.

At present, it is important to examine the mysterious term chôra first, often obscured by the annotations of sophistries. *Encyclopedia Britannica* proposes the following definition of the term:

> Plato's central inspiration, which unifies his metaphysics, his cosmology, his theory of man, and his doctrine of the soul, was basically dualistic (in the sense of dialectical dualism) with two irreducible principles: the Idea and the chôra (or material "receptacle") in which the Idea impresses itself. All of this world is conditioned by materiality and necessity; and because of this, the descent of souls into bodies is said to be rendered necessary as well. [CD Rom]

The quoted definition appears all the more mysterious as it mentions "dualistic" and "two irreducible principles." It is necessary to return to the Greek etymology and Plato's description of the concept to better delineate the arcane term. Chôra in Greek means "space" or "site." Plato defined it as "receptacle of becoming": a space for creation or fashioning. It is attached to the quality of void, since everything passes through it but nothing is retained. Plato recognized the difficulty in explaining the concept of this third kind, which is often characterized with the attribute of ineffable or irrepresentable. Though numerous philosophers have essayed to circumscribe the concept, it is becoming all the more obscure. The term chôra appears in Plato's *Timaeus* to elucidate the transitional kind between Being and Becoming. He presented as the receptacle as a "third kind" mediating between Forms and their imitations. Many metaphors are offered by Plato to illustrate the concept of chôra: a lump of gold, a mother that together with a father produces offspring, a plastic, impressionable stuff, and an ointment that serves as a neutral base for various fragrances [Zeyl].

Due to its image of a mother and connotation of womb, Kristeva regards chôra as a pre-symbolic instance, a rhythmic space, the psychosomatic origin of meaning. It is the pure semiotic stage prior to Lacan's mirror stage. Derrida insisted that the term must be apprehended without any definite article. It comes from nowhere, having no beginning, no essence and no nature. He rather interpreted chôra as a space that includes both Being and Becoming or the intelligible and the sensible. However, we can not apprehend Plato's chôra under this limited scope of semiotics. Some other consistent features undeniably amplify the meaning beyond a "female receptacle": malleability, formlessness, dynamism, temporality, permanent changeability, space, matters, and material substratum. By the same token, chôra cannot be so great as to include the Ideal Form.

In summary, Plato's clear delineation of chôra is that it is the third kind between the Ideal Form and the manifestations of the physical world. If the Ideal Form, like Lao Zi's Dao, is absolutely beyond our language to catch a glimpse of, chôra at least can be traced by the manifestations generated from the four elements. It is compared to the situation where ointment emits fragrance and malleable gold extends. If *Liangyi* of *Yi Jing* illustrates the temporality of chôra, the permanent kinetic metamorphosis, Lao Zi's *De* or Lie Zi's *Wu* (Nil) can be compared to its spatial nature. In *Dao De Jing*, Lao Zi kept reminding readers that Dao indeed eludes earthly language and perception; however, he availed himself of *De*'s manifestations to shed light on Dao. While we use *De* to explain Plato's chôra, his concept of chôra can conversely help grasp *De* and thus further Dao. The very common element between Lao Zi and Plato's philosophy is the existence of a Being as the Causality – Lao Zi's Dao and Plato's Ideal Form – and the "third kind" that connects this Being and the Becoming, the former being *De* and the latter being chôra. Another Daoist, Lie Zi, also portrayed a similar cosmogony and philosophy concerning such a conception. In the chapter Tianrei of *Lie Zi*, he raised the concept of *Taiyi*, *Taichu*, *Taishi* and *Taisu* to illuminate the naissance of the unintelligible Universe. His *Taiyi* is like the concept of the Ideal Form and Dao that exists before the Universe as a non-phenomenon. *Taichu* equals the concept of chôra or *De* that represents the dawn of first appearance from the non-phenomenon Nil to the emergence of phenomenon. *Taishi* refers to the manifestations of the basic four elements. The last concept of *Taisu* signifies the phenomenon of our physical world. According to Zhuang Wanshou's interpretation, Lie Zi's concept of the aforementioned four steps can be understood in the light of Lao Zi's "Dao [*Taiyi*] generates one, one generates two [*Taichu*], two generate three [*Taishi*] and three generate all things [*Taisu*]" [Lao Zi, Chapter 42].

The images that Plato tried to compare to chôra as "a lump of gold, a plastic, impressionable stuff, and an ointment that serves as a neutral base for various fragrances" and chôra's general attributes of "receptacle" evoke the nature of

Lao Zi's *De*. Lao Zi used the images of receptacle and water (as malleable and plastic as Plato's metaphors) to illustrate *De* in relation to Dao. He first used the metaphor of water to characterize *De*: "Those who are with high *De* are like water. Water can nurture all beings but does not compete against them. Abasing itself at the despicable place makes it very close to Dao" [ibid., Chapter 8]. Lao Zi often referred to water to illustrate the characteristic of malleability, humbleness and vacancy in *De* to show the spirit of Dao. He further explained that "Dao creates all beings; *De* contains and receives all beings. Manifestations take shape; circumstances accomplish the growth of all beings" [ibid., Chapter 51]. Here we have the image of "receptacle" that characterizes *De*. Chôra's feature of oxymoron as antithetic harmony and its nature of spatial vacancy (*Wu*) are further illustrated by Lao Zi in chapter 40: "Opposition is the kinetic power of Dao; malleability and vacancy are its manifestation. All beings are born from the known; the known is born from the unknown." The perpetual changes and movement portrayed in *Yi Jing* are also emphasized by Lao Zi through the conception of yin and yang after he enunciated the generation of all beings from Dao: "All beings embrace the duo of yin and yang. Yin and yang conflict each other yet harmonize each other" [ibid., Chapter 42]. This intercourse between yin and yang further mirrors Plato's metaphor of "a mother that together with a father produces offspring." The surface and contradictory polar antithesis of chôra harmoniously coexist at the same time. This conception exceeds "rational logic" of present human consciousness. Therefore, the only third way to get access to the logic of chôra is mystic or fantastic imagination.

Lastly, the idea concerning chôra's irrepresentable nature (it is unperceivable but it is still there) is also demonstrated by Lie Zi's philosophy. His focus is placed more on the seemingly non-existing space of an infinite receptacle. He begins by claiming the existence of a creating power with Nature's law of yin-yang interaction: "Therefore, when there is life, there is something that begets the life; when there is a figure, there is something that shapes the figure; when there is sound, there is something that makes the sound; when there is colour, there is something that produces the colour; when there is smell, there is something that emits the smell" [Lie Zi, Chapter Tianren (Auspice of Universe) 3]. If the above statement comes from direct reasoning of a creator out there, the following enunciation by Huangdi (the Emperor Huang) will prove the existence of the non-existence chôra or *Wu* (Nil) from a converse perspective: "When a body moves, it does not produce a body but produces a shadow; when a sound moves, it does not produce a sound but an echo; when *Wu* or Nil moves, it does not produce *Wu* but produces all manifestations" [ibid., Chapter Tianren 6]. Lie Zi's conception of *Wu* is similar to chôra; both are irrepresentable and yet offering the infinite space for all Becoming. According to Lie Zi's explanation, we may better grasp the arcane space of chôra. In addition, given that the concept of *Wu* against manifestations corresponds to the concept of the unknown against the known, the present statement further illustrates the general Daoist conception of "the known deriving from the unknown."

If we consider the further illumination of chôra in the section of Physics, we may conclude that it is the initial state of a perpetually unstable space of silence with spastic motions that produce manifestations of the inarticulate traces of the four basic elements, a pre-cosmic beginning before the fashioning of the basic corpuscles (*sômata*). These four elements are the same elements presumed by Empedocles: fire, air, water and earth. The inarticulate traces of the elements are nonetheless articulated here with mythic figures, respectively: Zeus, Hera, Nestis and Hades [Kingsley]. This representation by mythic names of the ineffable forms of the elements is significant to mythic storytelling as a spiritual imitation of chôra. Bachelard's theory of material imagination also derives from Empedocles's philosophy of the four elements. His works on the poetics of the four elements delve deep into the unconscious. In the light of Bachelard's phenomenological reading of the human imagination of the unreal, the imaginary of the unreal functioned in our mind is thus linked with the imaginary of chôra via imagining the four elements submerging in our collective unconscious.

Here we merge with Jungian archetypes and are *synchronically* in communion with myth. In fact, Bachelard's theory is developed from Jung's to extend to appreciating literary images and metaphors. Thanks to Bachelard, we link the supernatural or unreal images to the four elements and thus to the deeper tier of Jung's collective unconscious, the arcane space of chôra. Though based on an anthropological viewpoint to analyze our behaviour through the imaginary route, Durand attributes a transcendental function to *la fantastique*. Myth, as the collective dream of man, or human collective memory, can also be regarded as the DNA of human imagination. We may also apprehend chôra as a certain mathematic formula of the Universe, invisible and inarticulate but remaining the origin of something like the void for the ointment vaporizing fragrances. If Plato disdained poets for their imitating the secondary imitation, he should have valued the poet-philosopher who *imitates* the "invisible truth" (like the truth outside his mythic cave). From this perspective, we interpret fantastic mimesis as the poetic imitation linked with the original light (as Tolkien perceived it). Therefore, myth is the source of fantastic mimesis, mediated by storytelling, the art bridging our known world with the unknown dimension. Attracted by the magnetism of chôra, *Liangyi* or *De*, the fantastic imagination transcends to the metaphysical imagination, which links back to Durand's transcendental function of *la fantastique*. Fantastic literature explores the mysterious unknown realm through language and stories.

From the theories of the imaginary, through investigation of myth and chôra and eventually the evaluation of storytelling, the realm of the unknown that triggers the fantastic poeticization manifests itself as an imaginary space of stratification. Here is a proposed table of the synthetic analysis of chôra, the collective unconscious, the four elements, myth and fantastic literature with reference to *Yi Jing* and Daoism, to illustrate the irrepresentable space of the unknown vis-à-vis the realm of the known:

The unknown realm	The transitional realm between the unknown and the known	The known realm
The unknown realm of *la fantastque* Accessible through dream, death and sublime sex or love (according to Daoist and Yoga Hinduism).	Myth Fantastic literature Inspired by the imaginary of *la fantastique* 2^3: The basic *Bagua* or octa-trigrams of *Yi Jing*, the known with names or definitions after the third transmutation from the unknown. The individual unconscious (the unknown out of the known)	The known realm 2^6: The complete myriads of hexagrams of *Yi Jing*, the known after the fourth transmutation, the interactions of the known.
The collective unconscious and the four elements: earth, water, air, fire 2^2: The primeval tetra-couples *Sixiang* of *Yi Jing*: old-yang, juvenile-yang, old-yin, juvenile-yin		
The collective unconscious and chôra or *De* 2^1: The forming of *Liangyi* by the first appearance of yin, the bourgeoning metamorphosis of the unknown		
The collective unconscious and the Ideal Form or Being, Archetype, Brahma, Dao, or God or the Universal Consciousness, the Demiurge *Taiji* 2^0: The Cause of all Becoming		

A reviewing summary of key concepts will help further understanding of the present study of fantastic literature. Depicting directly the invisible or the inaudible, the imaginary in literary creation extends to different levels of the unknown. The most irrepresentable depth or infinite is at the deepest tier in our table, different philosophies and religions essaying to describe it by makeshift epithets such as Lao Zi's Dao, Plato's Ideal Form or Archetype, Jung's irrepresentable Archetype and Hinduism's Brahma. Jung's collective unconscious reaches deep into the level of the Ideal Form, and also encompasses the levels of chôra and rudimental elements. Since it is hard to portray the arcane space the collective unconscious connects to, Jung resorted to archetypal images to expound the irrepresentable archetype. The Platonic concept of chôra corresponds to the *Liangyi* status of *Yi Jing* philosophy and the *De* of Lao Zi, in that chôra or *Liangyi* and *De* can still be uttered, unlike the almighty unknown Demiurge or the Ideal Form or Dao. Or we may use Lao Zi's *De* to help understand. Dao can't be said, whereas *De* can be talked about since it manifests through non-existence and is sensible. Chôra can be termed as the archetype of the unknown or the very initial traceable state of the collective unconscious. In the light of Lao Zi's *Dao De Jing*, all beings are begotten from nothingness, the Mother of all existence. According to Plato, the primal elements are generated from this space of nothingness. This happens with perpetual movement from traces to particles to the perceived manifestations. This pre-Socratic philosophy of the four elements has its counterpart in Hinduism and Buddhism, whose practice centres on the emptiness of the four principles: earth, water, fire and wind or air. In *Yi Jing*, the four elements are formed at the stage of the forming of yang-yang, yin-yin, yang-yin and yin-yang, which we demonstrate by binary digital of mathematics: 2^2 or the primeval tetra-couples of *Yi Jing*. Hinging on the changes and transformation of the elements, the material imagination exposes the metamorphoses of the elements through animation to substantialize or concretize the mystic unknown.

The tier of the individual unconscious refers to the projection of libido (as defined by Jung), which also includes Freud's repressed desires. According to Daoist, Hindu or Zen interpretations of dream, the individual unconscious floats at the shallow tier of dream. We reckon this realm to be the unknown coming out of the known realm. The dream at deeper tiers is here apprehended in compliance with its universal significance. As illustrated in the above table, the dream features as one of the three means to get access to the mystic unknown. Death and sex are more difficult than the dream to enter the collective unconscious, since they are concerned with arcane alchemical and religious practices believed in mysticism. Jung only touched upon the means of sex spiritually and symbolically, by adding a feminine element to the traditional Occidental trinity. His main focus is still placed on dream and synchronicity. Accordingly, we conceive the dream as the crucial fantastic space that forces us with the figure of litotes that we cannot assert that another dreamlike reality does not exist. Durand envisions the abounding meanings of imaginary symbols in the human collective dream of the mythic imagination, which forms a Euclidean space of *la fantastique*. Myth (we have to be cautious about certain false myths), as a collective dream of humans, is effectively created from the inspiration of "the monad of imagination" that connects with its principal cause or Archetype. We are obviously far from the pristine times of original participation; nonetheless, fantastic literature continues to arouse in readers the primary imagination to explore the realm of the unknown. The function of fantastic literature should be to inspire the exploration of the unknown universe. This exploration indeed takes place in scientific researches. If mathematics can reach space far beyond three dimensions by abstract symbols, fantastic literature may ascend to such ultra-dimensional space by the poetic language of the imaginary.

The above table also serves to explain the problems encountered in the course of metaphysical and epistemological developments. Philosophy is forced into an impasse by being sundered from science. The philosophical methodology established by Aristotle orients Western civilization into an analytical and logical but dialectical epistemology, a vital furtherance of the contemporary accomplishment of science. This thriving scientific development later exerted its influence worldwide. Barfield regarded the evolution of this phenomenon as one of our consciousness arriving at the culmination of intellectual or scientific stage, which is the polar difference from the stage of original participation. Likewise, we see a divergence from synthetic apprehension to analytic deduction which results in the tendency to research narrowly isolated fields. Nevertheless, science improves human life to a great extent and thus incrementally divulges the secret of Nature.

Also inspired by the unknown realm, science explores truth through logical deduction and laboratory experiments. By the same token, fantastic literature explores truth through storytelling as an experiment on the unknown. Storytelling, with its magic rhythm and temporality, connects the fantastic space of the unknown and the known. Fantastic literature, as illustrated above, does not fall completely into the realm of the unknown, but is a mediator between. It is a poetic creation oscillating between what Lao Zi proclaimed as the key to truth: "Discard desire to intuit mystery of the Universe (this refers to wisdom in the unknown realm); regard desire to deduce knowledge of the Universe (this refers to the knowledge and science gained in the known realm). This can also explicate why, following the wheel of Virgil, epics were considered as the grand style (*style élévé*) in contradistinction to the mean style (*style tempéré ou moyen*) of didactic poetry and plain style (*style simple*) of pastoral or lyric poetry. Roman rhetoricians developed a complex schema called the wheel of Virgil. This clearly illustrates how different styles are employed by the same poet. The repartition of the stylistic typology is based on three of Virgil's works: *The Aeneid* with grand style, *The Georgics* with mean style and *The Bucolics* with plain style [Dessons, 143]. Epic is considered as the grand style because it is the very art form that represents the soul from the original participation and arouses our imagination to dream into the collective unconscious. In like manner, Aristotle's highly estimating story in the poetics of mimesis reinforced this poetic assumption. Either didactic poetry or lyric poetry is literary creation for moral or graceful reasons, grounded firmly in the realm of the known.

Mythopoeia, Rhetoric and Poetic Paradox – From Poetry to Fantastic Storytelling

In light of the critics of *mythocritique*, such as Pierre Brunel, mythic language is mostly portrayed in poetry, especially when we consider the meaning of *mythopoeia* on the basis of *poïesis*. Most critics highly esteem the aesthetic achievement of poetry and value it as the lofty form of mythopoeia. However, if we look at the genre closely, we will find that the poetic creations centring on myths are narrative verses. Since verse was the major poetic form in Antiquity and was a very useful aid to memory, it was normal to tell stories through verses. Moreover, the above exploration of the meanings of myth entails attributing storytelling as the dynamic essence of mythopoeia. In fact, the original etymological meaning of *poïèn* is to fabricate or create instead of composing a poem. The true nature of mythopoeia is myth-making through storytelling, according to Aristotle's perspective on the rhetorical function of story. Aristotle emphasized the unique feature of the invented story striding across both real history and the imaginary realm. In addition, the thriving creation of free verse in poems swerves poetry from musical harmonization and rather falls into a certain collage of images as a manifestation of poetry's visualization. This phenomenon in poetry makes it deviate from genuine mythopoeia.

According to Durand's theory, the isotopism of the nocturnal images activate the synthetic structures, comprising the structure of harmonization of the contraries (musical imagination), the structure of dialectic (law of musical contrast), the structure of history (history as fable and history as epic) and the structure of progress. The archetypal or symbolic images of the nocturnal regime are linked by an extrinsic dynamism one with another to form a story, haunted by the style of history and dramatic structures. This style is called *myth* [Durand 1992, 410]. The elements of musical harmonization, musical contrast and dynamism are to be highlighted here. Remembering the aforementioned idea of rhythm and dynamism of chôra, the dynamism of idiosyncratic storytelling of myth parallels the permanent motions of chôra, both characterizing temporality through immense space.

The nature of temporality in storytelling further reminds us of the musicality of metres and rhymes. In Western literature, Homer's *Iliad* and *Odyssey* or Ovid's *Metamorphoses* are considered as origins of fantastic writing. As to Chinese literature, *Shanhai Jing*, *Chu ci* and *Mutianzi zhuan* are writings of myths and considered as origins of Chinese fantastic tales *zhiguai*. In fact, almost all ancient mythic writings are in verse. As Aristotle emphasized, story is vital to the poetics of mimesis. The homogeneity of verse and story in epics (such as the Babylonian *Gilgamesh*, the Indian *Mahabharata*, the Greek *Odyssey* and *Iliad*, the Viking *Elder Edda* and the Finnish *Kalevala*) manifests itself as the quintessence of mythopoeia. Therefore, the cardinal factor of mythmaking is storytelling in a musical style, rather than poetry or verse. Storytelling inherits the disposition of chôra to render words fragrant like the ointment and malleable like gold and thus bringing the known to the unknown and *vice versa*. The unknown can be as remote as the unknown past of human origin and cosmogony and as immense as the ultra-dimension and the future. Richard Kearney emphasizes the importance of stories:

> Hesiod tells us how the founding myths (mythos in Greek means "story") were invented to explain how the world came to be and how we came to be in it. Myths were stories people told themselves in order to explain themselves to themselves and to others. But it was Aristotle who first developed this insight into a philosophical position when he argued, in his *Poetics*, that the art of storytelling—defined as the dramatic imitating and plotting of human action—is what gives us a shareable world. [Kearney, 3]

The principal power of storytelling is its mediating between the unknown and the known realm. Through its musical quality such as rhythm and rhyme grounded in the fluid movement of the plot, storytelling echoes with the great dynamic vibration of *la fantastique* which, across the realm of the collective unconscious, links us to chôra and thus not far from the Ideal Form or Dao.

Storytelling, besides its imaginary function in the mythopoeia of mimesis that bridges the gap between our world and chôra of the collective unconscious, is qualified by the attribute of rhetoric and style. In his *Poetics*, Aristotle considered the story as a form to be of "superior quality" as a version of the poetic art, viz. *muthos*, which is further valued by Roman poeticians in the illustration of the aforementioned Virgil's wheel of style. The French poeticians from Renaissance evaluated the epic poem at the level of "grand style," pastoral poem as "mean style" and didactic poem as "plain style." This hierarchical classification of poetry spotlights the value of story. By distinguishing the art of orator (field of rhetoric) and the art of actor from the art of representation or mimesis, Aristotle emphasized that the poet should be considered the creator of stories rather than of metres. Since the object of *Poetics* is mimesis not genres, viz. representation of stories not versification, the two principal target genres chosen by Aristotle are only versified genres that represent actions – tragedy and epic with the exclusion of didactical and lyrical poems. The importance of story in Aristotle's poetics can be exposed from two perspectives: myth and rhetoric. In the first case, myth bears in its definition a dimension of narrative, though usually defined as narrative of the unreal or imaginary. In the other case, in terms of discourse, the rhetoric of Aristotle is not treated as propositional logic but what is likely produced in an ordinary manner. The "likely" thus defined appears as indissociable from linguistic practice. Contrary to truth, the "likely" implies a notion related to representation, in fact a product of *mimesis*. The connection between rhetoric and poetics resides in fictional creation inasmuch as fiction belongs to the literary dimension. Aristotle recommended the employment of narratives in the rhetoric, in that narratives have "the good aspect that it is difficult to give an account of facts from the past, while inventing stories is an effortless work, for we have to imagine them, also like the parables, by attending to what we could catch in the analogy" (*ce bon côté que, trouver des faits analogues à puiser dans le passé est chose difficile, tandis qu'inventer des histoires est chose facile; car il faut les imaginer, comme aussi les paraboles, en veillant à ce que l'on puisse saisir l'analogie*) [Dessons, 106].

The value of story, brought to the fore by the Aristotelian perspective of poetics in terms of *muthos* and rhetoric, can be further enhanced by the imaginary poetics of Durand in terms of the synthetic structure. He sees in myth a double character of music and history, for myth tells (*raconter*) and repeats (*répéter*) [Durand 1992, 418], which is also the essential attribute of storytelling, a combination of synchronism and diachronism with a synthetic and rhythmic nature. Apart from this natural dynamism generated from the constellation of symbols that entails the role of story, story also manifests itself as a rhetorical function in discriminating myth from ritual. Story serves as the rhetorical stratagem that fills in the hiatus between the simplicity of ritual and the temporal complication of myth (both treasures of symbolic richness) by providing certain logic, or rather pre-logic (Durand's term), to depict the cause-effect of the events. It is this interplay of storytelling that metamorphoses the fantastic imagination into various rhetorical discourses. Storytelling joins the fantastic imagination with the magic of incantation (this quality of incantation is also attributed to the musical rhythm and refrain, and narration in mythic story by Durand) to bridge the unknown and the known realms and presents various forms that help reach the elusive visage of chôra. Therefore, storytelling is considered as a pre-logical rhetoric that renders *la fantastique* into *le fantastique*, fantastic literature through perpetual metamorphosis into a different manner of storytelling: the dream-discourse as idealistic sub-creation, the mirror-discourse as ambiguity and the magician's hat-discourse as a vivid hypotyposis of the unknown phenomena.[32]

---

[32] Please refer to "Rhetoric of Fantastic Literature" in Part Two.

This feature of forever retelling stories of the fantastic is explicitly demonstrated by a fantastic author himself from Antiquity, Ovid. Espousing Pythagorean philosophy, Ovid proposed his own interpretation of human existence as perpetual metamorphosis vis-à-vis the Universe. He did so through his epochal chef-d'oeuvre of fantastic literature *Metamorphoses*. This fantastic philosophy is completely represented by his sequential storytelling of the metamorphoses of the Universe, nature, gods and eventually heroes, ending with Caesar's death and transformation into the celestial star. The fantastic imagination of transformation as the essential momentum of storytelling mirrors Chinese *Yi Jing*'s philosophy of changes (Yi means changes in Chinese). The pivotal principle of *Yi Jing* lies in the unending changes of becoming beings and objects in Nature and the dynamic power generated from the dialectic of yin and yang. All vibration and transformation of the Becoming are derived from the primeval appearance of yin in combination with yang.

Penetrating the core spirit of fantastic creation, we may conclude that this special genre is an imitation or rather emulation of fantastic masters' works or the imaginary vision of the people from the epoch of original participation, in the light of the Renaissance's interpretation of mimesis (to imitate great works of the predecessors or what our ancestors believe). It is not a completely capricious fancy that pretends to reach the unknown but rather the fantastic imagination grounded in repetition or imitation of the past forms, a forever storytelling. Therefore, fantastic literature is in essence not original, but re-creation with the imaginary rooted in the collective unconscious and form of narrative models. Similar to Ovid, who portrayed pre-Socratic philosophy through fantastic storytelling, Apuleius, centring on Platonism, elaborated his fantastic epic *The Golden Ass* with saturated satire to further characterize the consistency of metamorphosis in the most capricious creation of literature. Thus fantastic creation originates with the collective unconscious as well as the model forms. With a second title of *Metamorphoses* to his *The Golden Ass*, Apuleius succeeded Ovid in delineating their imagination of the unknown by means of the essential spirit of all rhetoric: metamorphosis of storytelling. As stated before, perpetual metamorphosis and changes in the philosophy of *Yi Jing* underlies the imaginary of Chinese fantastic creation. Most writers tell myriad stories, which demonstrate a metamorphosis of forms. Since all things are merely products of the interaction of yin and yang, they are all considered as a whole throughout transmutation in Nature. Men can eventually metamorphose into gods, as Lu Xixing portrayed in his *Fengshen Yanyi* (*The Investiture of the Gods*) and an individual can metamorphose into myriads of forms, like the monkey king or Sun Wuking penned by Wu Cheng'en in his novel *Xiyou Ji* (*Journey to the West*). Metamorphosis connotes on the one hand the spirit of *Yi Jing* and Dao on the level of content and on the other, the telling and retelling of fantastic stories on the level of form.

From the perspective of rhetoric as a totality of fantastic storytelling, meta-morphoses represent the human desire for the freedom of being unbound by time and space. If Durand's reflexology confronting diurnal and nocturnal regimes predominates over the isotopic symbols, which are also conditioned by time and space, the pristine desire for freedom underlying the schema of metamorphosis forms the central rhetoric of fantastic storytelling. The significance of storytelling in his theory of symbol constellations is thus emphasized:

> [The] nocturnal regime of the imaginary tends to organize the symbolism into a dramatic or historical story. In other words, in the nocturnal regime, especially its synthetic structures, the archetypal or symbolic images, are not satisfied with their intrinsic dynamism any more, but extrinsic dynamism links them under the form of a story. It is this story – haunted by the styles of history and the dramatic structures – that we call "myth." [Durand 1992, 410][33]

Homer, the predecessor of Ovid and Apuleius, also brought into play the hypotyposis of metamorphosis to depict the unknown world related to the known world. Like the principle of alchemy, metamorphosis (external practice and internal practice) offers the key to the sublime state, i.e., the highest realm of the unknown. In literature, the storytelling of metamorphosis serves as writers' rhetoric to invite readers to completely observe and explore the unknown space and time. It is a key to enter the realm of the unknown. For example, Stevenson manipulates storytelling to explore Dr Jekyll's unknown conscious through metamorphosing into Mr Hyde by means of chemicals. Although pathetic, the storytelling of the metamorphosis of Kafka's Gregor opens the door to the investigation of the unknown human relations between a person and other(s). Metamorphosis thus has a double attribute as rhetoric, a fantastic element from the imaginary as it itself belongs to the unknown, and a perpetual form intermediating the imaginary. And through the art of storytelling, fantastic creation metamorphoses into sundry generic forms or sub-genres and styles: epic, tragedy, ballad, episodic prose novel and romance that generate fantastic epic, fairy-story or fantasy, fantastic tragedy, Gothic or horror fiction, French fantastic or low fantasy or *le fantastique* in a strict sense, fantastic ballad, fable, *le merveilleux* or fairy tale and science-fiction.

Storytelling, lastly, functions as the ineluctable poetic paradox for sages. They espouse silence and true wisdom beyond the scope of language; however, they often resort to telling stories to illustrate the unintelligible truth. Plato was

---

[33] *[Le]* Régime Nocturne *de l'imaginaire inclinait le symbolisme à s'organiser en un récit dramatique ou historique. Autrement dit, dans le* Régime Nocturne *et spécialement ses structures synthétiques, les images archétypales ou symboliques ne se suffisent plus à elles-mêmes en leur dynamisme intrinsèque, mais par un dynamisme extrinsèque se relient les unes aux autres sous forme d'un récit. C'est ce récit – hanté par les styles de l'histoire et les structures dramatiques – que nous appelons « mythe ».*

wary of poets and their inclination in telling lies or false invention. Paradoxically, he staged a myth teller to teach his philosophy. Zhuang Zi enunciated all his philosophical discourses by telling stories. He can be deemed as the father of Chinese fantastic literature. Given that metaphysical ideas are arcane and abstract, fantastic storytelling, a third way striding across the known and the unknown, can tell in a concrete manner

Barfield's comparison between Plato and Aristotle may shed light on the corollary of poets' significance in the human history of conscious evolution. Plato maintained that "all matter is but an imperfect copy of spiritual 'types' or 'ideas' – eternal principles which, so far from being abstractions, are the only real Beings, which were in their place before matter came into existence, and which will remain after it has passed away. The other assumption concerned the attainment by man of immortality" [Barfield 1967, 103]. On the contrary, Aristotle imagined that "the two worlds, outer and inner, met and came into contact in quite a new way. The mind was, as it were, put at the absolute disposal of matter; it ceased to brood on what arose from within, and turned its attention outward" [ibid., 105]. If Plato's ideal state had been realized, poets might and could have been excluded since the philosophers of the first rank were at the same time visionary poets and wise rhetoricians. This paradox about philosophers is found in Plato since he himself appropriated the artistry of poetry and rhetoric and called his fictional Socrates a myth teller. This analogous paradox is also felt by oriental philosophers. In China, the Daoist master Lao Zi pronounced at the start of his *Dao De Jing* that "Dao or logos (logos is here understood as the first principle) of the Universe can be enunciated, but it is not the commonly enunciated logos. The phenomenon of the Universe can be defined, but it is not the commonly defined phenomenon" [Lao Zi, Chapter 1]. He clearly denounced the enunciation of Dao, which is a negation of philosophy. However, he still wrote down or uttered about five thousand Chinese characters to illuminate the truth that Dao cannot be enunciated. A parallel paradox is present in Buddhism. Buddha kept exhorting his disciples that wisdom of Nirvana is beyond discourse, while preaching ceaselessly. This is even paradoxical in Zen Buddhism. The masters radically rebuked the attachment to written scriptures in practicing Buddhism. Ironically, they wrote scriptures and told numerous stories to annihilate the words. This paradox of a clamorous requisite in silence is ubiquitous.

Though the words have never been rejected, Plato's ideal state was unfortunately not realized and the world swerved to, ever since Aristotle, the acquisition of knowledge about the outer world that can be apprehended through sensation and cerebration. This is a faithful investigation of the world of imitation, the world inside Plato's allegorical cave, or the wisdom gained through "regarding desire to deduce knowledge of the Universe," presumed by Lao Zi. In an age of rationalism, the art of mimesis scorned by Plato proves to be vital to human imagination able to bridge the gulf between the Ideal Form (the Being) and our world (the Becoming). However, a mimesis of our known world, that is, the world empirically received, is not sufficient. Therefore, a *sur*-mimesis or *transcendental* mimesis or *fantastic* mimesis remains an important mediation between the subject and the world, viz. a connection between the known and the unknown. This entails that the banished poets must return to elicit our dream-like emotion to arouse our aesthetic imagination. The fantastic and mythic imagination of the unknown eventually proves to be germane to chôra. In order to ward off this paradox, most great philosophers or religious masters resort to storytelling to illuminate the abstract wisdom. Therefore, the Daoist philosophers like Zhuang Zi and Lie Zi, paradoxically disobeying the teaching of Lao Zi of "non-discourse," told myriads of tales, mostly fantastic, to explain Dao. Likewise, Plato himself, scorning poets, ironically appropriated tales to illuminate his philosophy, especially obscure concepts. The function of storytelling in bridging the limited known world and the unknown realm, such as Dao and Platonic Ideal Form, parallels to the function of Eucharist that unite the concrete form and God.

Periodization of Fantastic Literature and the Evolution of Human Consciousness

Contemporary theorization of fantastic literature, among others, theories along the lines of Todorovian approach, often refuses to identify related genres such as fairy tales or supernatural stories to be a part of it. Most French critics, for example Todorov and Bessière, assert that the fantastic is born only in an age of disbelief or rationalism. They embrace the thesis that the fantastic and the fairy tale manifest a historical rupture. For Todorov, the fantastic is only reserved for the 19th century, more exactly for the French fantastic fiction. On the contrary, critics and writers with a historical vision, mostly Anglophonic, often relate the fantastic to works from Antiquity by referring to classical epic writers such as Homer (900-800 BC), the author of *Beowulf* (?), and Dante (1265-1321). These references are often mentioned as the fantastic sources or historical background.

A thorough investigation and historical analysis of the evolution of fantastic literature is awaiting accomplishment. We attempt to delineate the history and evolution of fantastic literature from a general and comparative perspective in relation to the evolution of human consciousness. Critics and authors of the fantastic who have a historical vision of the genre will be examined to commence a historical reflection. The exploration of Barfield's theory of the conscious evolution enhanced by Goethe's viewpoint on the evolution of the human mind underlies the proposed periodization of fantastic literature. Grounded in the evolution of human consciousness, the fantastic creation as a universal phenomenon is divided into four historical stages.[34]

Critiques with Historical Vision of Fantastic Creation

Mathews claims that "nearly all of the surviving literature of the ancient world, from *The Epic of Gilgamesh* to *The Odyssey*, is rooted in fantasy, though at the time each work was composed much of it was believed by those who heard or read it to be true" [Mathews, 5-6]. He undertakes a survey of the deemed sources to modern fantasy, from the foundations of fantasy in the ancient world, through medieval fantasy, Victorian revelation of Antiquity, the dark fantasy, the shaping of modern fantasy up to the fantasy of our times as global experiments and innovations. Although he intends to be universal in his chronological survey, Mathews sometimes confuses psychological works with fantastic literature, for

---

[34] The rudimentary theory on the periodization of fantastic literature was first developed in my article "Essay at a New Periodization of Fantastic Literature from Owen Barfield's Evolution of Human Consciousness and Language," published in *Arcadia: Internationale Zeitschrift für Literaturwissenschaft / International Journal for Literary Studies*, 2007.

example, Jung's *Psychology of the Unconscious* is included. In contrast, most Chinese fantastic tales are ignored (since he adopts a universal definition for fantasy) despite of his including Wu Cheng-en's (1500?-1582) *Journey to the West* (1592). Nevertheless, his contribution to scrupulous studies of English fantasy with a historical vision of the genre is excellent and provides a good starting point for further work.

Concentrating on the fantasy of England, Manlove traces its origins back to the classic English fairy tales,

> since whenever they reached England, their analogues are to be found as far back in time as stories have been told. By whatever route they arrived, via Neolithic wanderers, Roman legions, the invading galleys of Hengist and Horsa, the longships of the Vikings, or Norman *jongleurs*, we hear nothing of their existence till Chaucer begins to use them; and it is not till George Peele's *The Old Wives' Tale* (1595) that we find the clearest evidence for the existence of a body of English popular narrative, nor till the seventeenth century that we see their first appearance in chapbooks. [Manlove 1999, 10]

With an inquiry into the inception of fairy tales, Manlove brings to light that England is "one of the most impoverished nations so far as indigenous fairy-tales are concerned" [ibid., 10]. He explains the absence of a storytelling tradition in England, commencing with the repression of Saxon culture by the Normans, through ages of Christian bias and condemnation of fairies to the neoclassic age of disdaining for vulgar culture. Among the rare surviving fantasies from the whole period 450-1050 in England, Manlove adduces *Beowulf* (c.700-1000) and *Dream of the Rood* (c. 8th century). In fact, this scantiness in fantasies of the past is exactly the momentum of Tolkien's mythopoeia of *Silmarillion* and the ring trilogy, as he regretted that England lacks its own mythology in dismissing Arthurian legend as an English one [Tolkien 1995, 131]. Nonetheless, Tolkien affirmed the historical lineage from myth, legend to "fairy-story." This observation of the history of fantasy can be reinforced by the examination of the history of fantastic literature by French writers.

Nodier highly estimated the power of the fantastic imagination and storytelling. Different from that of Todorov's structuralist vision that dismisses historicity, he associated the fantastic with the long tradition of western myths. He had hopes of a future for fantastic literature; meanwhile he lamented the insufficiency of fantastic writing in French when compared to German. Different from later French writers, Nodier maintained a historical vision on fantastic creation by connecting the fantastic with great classics such as *The Odyssey* (c. 700 BC) and *The Iliad* (c. 750 BC), *The Golden Ass* (Apuleius, c. 2nd century), *The Divine Comedy* (Dante 1308-1321) and *Faust* (Goethe 1808 & 1842). His assumption that the first literature comes from the mythic creation corresponds to the imaginary of the fantastic. He termed it as the naïve expression of sensation: "If we look for how the imagination of man had to proceed in the choice of its first delights, we naturally come to believe that the first literature, aesthetic because it had no choice, has long been contained in the naïve expression of sensation" [Nodier 1989, 9].[35] This naïve expression of sensation mirrors Barfield's original participation and Jung's mystic participation. Similar to Jung's perspective on the creative imagination, Nodier regarded myth, dream and reverie as the inexhaustible sources of fantastic literature. His counterpart in the 20th century, Tolkien, created his English mythology in the middle of a time bereft of myth and imagination. He also traced the origin of fairy-stories back to myths and legends and emphasized the significance of historicity in fantastic creation.

Nodier, raving over the advent of the fantastic creation (inspired by German literature) related fantastic literature to myth. In *Du Fantastique en littérature*, he referred to Antiquity as offering the freest writings with the imaginary inventiveness and traced the fantastic back to myths, the marvellous, Christian fables and the 18th century fairy tales of Charles Perrault. He further joined the fantastic to the world *superstant* (Nodier's neologism), on which the science of God makes sense and superstitions offer witnesses. In order to render legitimate the coming of the fantastic in his times, Nodier established its affiliations with fantastic predecessors: Homer, Virgil (70-19 BC), Dante, Shakespeare (1564-1616) and Goethe (1749-1832). Therefore, the evolution of the fantastic is, based on his argument, closely tied with civilization, where thought can be broken down into three successive phases: "that of the inexplicable intelligence who has founded the material world, that of divinely inspired genius who has guessed the spiritual world, and that of the imagination which has created the fantastic world" (*celle de l'intelligence inexplicable qui avait fondé le monde materiel, celle du génie divinement inspiré qui avait deviné le monde spirituel, celle de l'imagination qui avait créé le monde fantastique*) [Nodier 1989, 18]. Nodier saw in his epoch new favorable dispositions for a new inception of the imaginary operations of purely poetic fantasies. Therefore, the romantic fantastic belongs to the times when the civilization is undergoing its obsolescence. He enhanced his theory of the fantastic by the assumption that madness, drowsiness or dreams are the imaginative force called "creative naivety" (*naïveté créatrice*) of children's state. Viewing purely poetic and imaginary works through the centuries, we are led to contemplate a way of eternal return to aestheticize the *superstant* world, which echoes with Strada Vittorio's viewpoint of the fantastic creation. Like Tolkien who lamented over meagerness of mythology and fairytale tradition in England, Nodier regretted that French writers are not sensitive to true imagination, which, on the contrary, was innate in German writers. He pro-

---

[35] *Si l'on cherche comment dut procéder l'imagination de l'homme dans le choix de ses premières jouissances, on arrivent naturellement à croire que la première littérature, esthétique par nécessité plutôt que par choix, se renferma longtemps dans l'expression naïve de la sensation.*

claimed the imaginary power and artistic value of German people and made the assumption why German writers were better at telling fantastic tales than French people:

> Germany has been rich in this genre of creation, the richest in the world, without excluding these happy Levantines, the eternal suzerains of our treasures, in the opinion of the antiquarians. This is that Germany, favored with a particular system of moral organization, bears in their beliefs fervor of imagination, vivacity of sentiment, mysticism of doctrines, a universal counterpart of idealism, which are essentially proper to the fantastic poetry; [...]. [ibid., 31-2][36]

Among the few French critics who accept a historical heritage in the fantastic is the anthropologist Pierre Maxime Schuhl. He interpreted the marvellous and the fantastic as the production of a literature attached to "primitive mentality." Although human civilization evolves and develops, the primitive mentality as a subjacent structure of modern civilization never stops inspiring artistic creation. The imaginary literature, the marvellous and the fantastic, for example, blossoms in drawing from this primitive mentality. The essence of this mentality drives Schuhl to assume that a historical connection exists between the marvellous and the fantastic. Though differentiating the fantastic from the marvellous as distinct genres, Caillois claimed that passage of the fairy to the fantastic and then to science fiction is a continuity of the tradition of unreal fictions. These three types of fiction fulfil in literature an equivalent function, historically immutable:

> On the one hand, they [these functions] prolong in the imaginary the present state of power and of knowledge of a being whose ambition is boundless. On the other hand, as this same being is laborious and fatigable, they beguile him with the eternal mirage of magic, whose instantaneous and total efficacy simply costs him the making of a master sign or the uttering of a master word. [Caillois, 23-4][37]

---

[36] *L'Allemagne a été riche dans ce genre de créations, plus riche qu'aucune autre contrée du monde, sans en excepter ces heureux Levantins, les suzerains éternels de nos trésors, à l'avis des antiquaires. C'est que l'Allemagne, favorisée d'un système particulier d'organisation morale, porte dans ses croyances une ferveur d'imagination, une vivacité de sentiments, une mysticité de doctrines, un pendant universel à l'idéalisme, qui sont essentiellement propres à la poésie fantastique; [...].*

[37] *D'une part, elles prolongent dans l'imaginaire l'état présent de la puissance et de la connaissance d'un être dont l'ambition est sans bornes. De l'autre, comme ce même être est besogneux et fatigable, elles le bercent de l'éternel mirage de l'efficacité magique, instantanée, totale, qui ne lui coûterait que de faire un maître signe ou de prononcer un maître mot.*

This historical vision appears less problematic when applied to German fantastic literature. Zondergeld and Wiedenstried define fantastic literature with a historical and universal attribute:

> Phantastische Literatur hat es zu allen Zeiten und in allen Epochen gegeben. Geschichten über den Einbruch unerklärlicher, wunderbarer, bedrohlicher oder heilbringender Dinge in unsere sichtbare und leidlich geordnete Welt hat man sich schon an den Lagerfeuern der urvölker erzält, und diese mündliche Tradition hat sich bis zu den Märchen und Gespenstergeschichten an den Herdfeuern der Spinnstuben der Neuzeit erhalten. Seit es Tontafeln gibt, hat man "Berichte" über phantastische Begebenheiten in sie geritzt, mit der Erfindung des Buchdrucks bekamen diese Geschichten eine feste Form, und es gelangte der Autor gegenüber den wechselnden Erzählern in den Vordergrund.

Fantastic literature is thus defined as a universal literary manifestation of all epochs. This historicity of the fantastic is easier for German scholars to penetrate. Given the long storytelling tradition of *Märchen* with underlying myths and legends, German writers draw on their cultural heritage to enrich their fantastic creation. For example, the Faust myth sees its artistic variations in history dating from 1587 to 1947, and even the present day; or the Grail Romances metamorphose from Wolfram von Eschenbach (c.1170-1230) to the theme of *Tannhäuser* in our modern times.

Likewise, Chinese literature sees no controversy in the historicity of fantastic creation. The fantastic narrative or *zhiguai* has a long history, originating with Zhuang Zi's (c. 370-280 BC) storytelling, until the end of the last dynasty Qing (1911). Both the terms *zhiguai* and *xiaoshuo* derive from Zhuang Zi's discourses. According to Fang Zhengyao, Chinese fantastic literature is created along the lines of the fantastic mimesis contrary to the realistic mimesis. The former is espoused by Daoist writers, such as Lie Zi (?), Ge Hong (284-364), Hong Mai (1123-1202) and Lu Xixing (1567-1620).

Grounded in the investigation of theories and the preceding exploration of the imaginary or fantastic *inventio*, we assume that fantastic literature, from a universal and imaginary perspective, can trace its origin back to the earliest epic of human civilization, *The Epic of Gilgamesh* (2700 BC). This historical vision could be exemplified by re-reading the story from our prelude. If we only focus on the fact that the mind is stirring, we tend to delimit fantastic literature as a genre begotten within an age of rationalism and skepticism. In this manner, all fantastic literary works will be examined under the microscope of psychoanalysis. On the other hand, persistence on the stirring of the banner would incline scholars to circumscribe fantastic literature a game of sign, thus hinging on a vision of ambiguity and hesitation, which also excludes a historical vision of fantastic creation. Likewise, the predilection for the mysterious power as insisting on the fact that the wind is stirring would generalize unlimitedly fantastic literature into all possible records of supernatural phenomena.

Although the aforementioned critics embrace a historical view on the fantastic genre, a pertinent periodization of the genre is still to happen. Thanks to Barfield's theory of the evolution of human consciousness, the historicity of the fantastic will be analyzed systematically in terms of how the imaginary is represented throughout the evolution. Early in the nineteenth century, Goethe had already postulated the evolutionary stages of the human mind in terms of literary creation. Inspired by Goethe and other progenitors such as Rudolf Steiner, Barfield developed a thorough historical map of human evolution of consciousness vis-à-vis the history of language. With the significance of human consciousness and language, we accept Barfield's theory as appropriate for the periodization of the fantastic genre.

On the Evolution of Human Consciousness

Barfield developed his philosophy of imagination, language and human consciousness in the light of Austrian occult philosopher Rudolf Steiner's anthroposophy. According to the teaching of anthroposophy, human beings evolve from the original participation, through the age of the intellectual soul, to the final participation and the imaginative soul. Observing the history of phenomena, Barfield defined participation as "the extra-sensory relation between man and the phenomena" [Barfield 1988, 40]. The existence of phenomena indeed depends on the participation. We, as well as the primitive men, are under this participation without being aware of it. The evolution of consciousness has its inception in Antiquity, which Barfield named original participation. In the process of original participation, the percipient is a part of the percept. This stage of participation corresponds to Jung's observation of the mystic participation among primitive people and to Goethe's stage of poetry with primitive faith. In the course of development of alpha-thinking and beta-thinking, we depart gradually from the without and perceive the world with thought (not thinking). "For medieval man, then, the universe was a kind of theophany, in which he participated at different levels, in being, in thinking, in speaking or naming, and in knowing. And then – the evolutionary change began" [ibid., 92]. Accordingly, "the Graeco-Roman period is seen as extending, practically unbroken, to the end of the Middle Ages" [ibid., 98].

Barfield contended that human evolution can never become completed without the evolution of consciousness. Biologically determined evolution is only demonstrated through alpha-thinking. He insisted that "the actual evolution of the earth we know [...] must have been at the same time an evolution of consciousness" [ibid., 65]. Our understanding of Darwinian evolution is a fallacy resulting from idolatry, a corollary of the dilatation of alpha-thinking. Both Jung and Barfield made the critical comment that modern men are undermining their souls through the abstraction of idolatry. Men's creating idols resembles their thinking the thought:

> The soul is in a manner all things, and the idols we create are built into the souls of our children; who learn more and more to think of themselves as objects among objects; who grow hollower and hollower. In the long run we shall not be able to save souls without saving the appearances, it is an error fraught with the most terrible consequences to imagine that we shall. [ibid., 161]

French philosopher Jean-Luc Marion discriminates the idol from the icon. This is parallel to Barfield's and Jung's distinction between the idol and the soul or truth. Marion interprets the idol as purporting to be a visible representation of the divine, and thus offering knowledge with reference to the invisible. Like the evolution of human consciousness where alpha-thinking turns out to be the thought as content, the visible representation of the idol eventually supersedes the invisible truth "visible" through iconic gaze in communion [Marion, 125-36]. Therefore, idolatry manifests as a pure sign system bereft of the original meanings. This idolatrous conception of evolution presents us only with half-truths: "The biological evolution of the human race is, in fact, only one half of the story; the other has still to be told" [Barfield 1988, 184]. The final participation is the culminating stage in the evolution of consciousness; it is not attainable simply through imitation of the original participation. Barfield proposed imagination as a key to the final participation. He was confident that "the world of final participation will one day sparkle in the light of the eye as it never yet sparkled early one morning in the original light of the sun" [ibid., 161]. However, this stage is looming beyond the horizon in the far distant future. Final participation

> is indeed the mystery of the kingdom – of the kingdom that is to come on earth, as it is in heaven – and we are still only on the verge of its outer threshold. Two thousand years is a trifle of time compared with the ages which preceded the incarnation. More than a thousand years had to pass before the Western Church reached even that premonitory inkling of final participation which it expressed by adding the Filloque to the Creed, and acknowledged that the Holy Spirit proceeds from the Son as well as, originally, from the Father. [ibid., 182]

While Barfield viewed the original participation from Antiquity until the Middle Ages, Goethe discriminated the robust stage of the primitive faith from the sacred stage of the rising to the Ideal. He divided the evolution of the human mind into the four stages illustrated as follows:

Basic Origins			
Considered in depth, appropriately defined			
Poetry	Primitive Faith	Robust	Imagination
Theology	Rising to the Ideal	Sacred	Reason
Philosophy	Intellectual Doubting	Sensible	Intellect
Prose	Dissolution into the Ordinary	Common	Sensuality
Intermingling, Hostility, Dissolution			

[Goethe 1994, 204]

The gist of Barfield's evolutionary theory is that the only key to attain the final participation of conscious evolution is imagination. Since we are still under the participation process, aware or unaware of it, imagination keeps on playing an important role. The creation of fantastic literature signifies the importance of imagining *the unknown* since alpha-thinking deals with pure science based on the known, and beta-thinking speculates on the perceivable phenomena. The only door that opens to the possibility of *extra-sensory experience* will be the diction of fantastic literature, given that contemporary poetry is much influenced by the above two thinking modes and severs language into splinters. The quality of strangeness vital to the lexis in poetics is taken to an extreme interpretation. To elucidate the true meaning of Recovery and Escape in the creation of fairy-stories, Tolkien highlighted the fantastic elements' function of "cleaning our windows" and disclosed the biased conception of strangeness in poetics:

> But the true road of escape from such weariness is not to be found in the willfully awkward, clumsy, or misshapen, not in making all things dark or unremittingly violent; nor in the mixing of colours on through subtlety to drabness, and the fantastical complication of shapes to the point of silliness and on towards delirium. [Tolkien 1997, 146]

The incremental fragmentation in language and refusal of meaning in our times inhibit a possible reconciliation between our world of deduction and the original unity of induction.

Considering the universal imaginary of the fantastic kind of storytelling in different cultures, the historical vision on the genre proposed by the aforementioned writers, Barfield's evolution of human consciousness and Goethe's of the human mind, we extrapolate that fantastic literature undergoes an evolution in history. The variations in their forms hinge on the changes of human consciousness. As an imaginary genre appertaining to the unknown or the alleged unreal, the fantastic evolves with our consciousness. By the same token, the mimesis in

Aristotle's times applied to epic and tragedy (often with fantastic elements) evolves in the intellectual age as the poetics of realism. Under this postulate, the fantastic genre manifests four stages of evolution: (1) primitive conception, (2) myth as the fabrication of truth, (3) intellectual skepticism and (4) truth in mirage.

Primitive Conception

The first stage of fantastic creation corresponds to the period of primitive mentality (proposed by Lucien Lévy-Bruhl) that primitives perceive with different minds from ours, albeit we see with the same eyes. This first fantastic stage also corresponds to Goethe's primitive stage and Jung's stage of mystic participation, but slightly differs from Barfield's period of the original participation. We esteem that the primitive conception of fantastic literature starts to wither as the domination of monarchy or monotheism reigns. In the first stage, poets or fantastic storytellers like Homer and Ovid (1 AD?) were inspired by the Muses to create by *imitating* the truth of the universe and human fate. This explains why Aristotle also considered Homer's epics as the subject matter of his poetics of mimesis.

The creation from this stage is a natural combination of fantastic perception with literary artistry. Writers, in the original participation of the conscious evolution, told fantastic stories in harmony with Nature and depicted the imaginary of the unknown realm by the mediation of hypotyposis based on the known. The fantastic stories of the first stage feature a vision of *unus mundus* that connects men with gods by an informal logic. The scope of the narratives spans cosmology, mythology, metaphysics and human fate. The musical harmonization is manifested in fantastic storytelling conceived by primitive mentality through verse form. *The Epic of Gilgamesh* stages the earliest literary rendering of the human imaginary faced with death and the quest for immortality. The Babylonian epic *Enuma Elish* (1000 BC) chants the story of cosmology, the war among the gods and the creation of heavens and the Underworld and mankind out of the fallen body of the god Tiamat. In the Chinese mythic sources of *The Classic of Mountains and Seas* (1600 BC – 771-221 BC), we learn about the mythic history of the emperors and heroes in relation to the gods until the Xia dynasty as well as the myriad of deities of Nature. Zhuang Zi and Lie Zi, like Plato's myth teller, told fantastic tales to illustrate Daoism. *The Mahabharata* (400 BC – 400 AD), the most copious epic ever composed, depicts the Hindu concept of dharma or sacred duty by interweaving mankind's wars (between two groups of cousins of a ruling family), gods' interference, and the quest for perpetual bliss in Indra's heaven.

The interaction between gods or God and men and the concept of sacred duty are also represented in the Western fantastic works such as *The Odyssey* and *The Iliad*, *Book of Genesis* (440 BC) and *The Aeneid* (Virgil 1ˢᵗ century BC). The imaginary of cosmology related to life and death as perpetual transformation of gods and men is rendered in *Metamorphoses* (Ovid 1 AD?). *The Golden Ass* initiates the episodic picaresque novel by telling the misadventure of the hero Lucius, metamorphosed by a sorceress into an ass and cured by a priest of the Goddess Isis. *Soushen ji* or *In Search of Gods and Spirits* (Gan Bao ?-336) is a collection of Chinese fantastic tales, mostly Daoist stories, whereas *Fengshen Yanyi* or *The Investiture of the Gods* (Lu Xixing 1601) is a Chinese typical epic novel telling the "sacred duty" of the heroes by the assistance and obstruction of gods.[38] *Elder Edda* (Vikings, Iceland, composed 800-1100, written down 1150-1250) and *Nibelungenlied* (German myth, ca. 1200) vividly chant the creation myth and the fall of gods in the Germanic musical imagination.

Fantastic storytelling from a primitive conception opens a door into the unknown realm that is beyond the control of monarchs or religious leaders closely combined with politics. The true fantastic literature is by no means woven by political language; it is genuinely poeticized by imaginative language. At this first creation period, fantastic writers projected themselves into Nature, both known and unknown to them, and counted as *natural* what modern men consider as *supernatural* events. Primitive people's vision is very different from that constructed by a deductive methodology. We may conclude that most fantastic literature created from the stage of primitive conception offers a universe of sub-creation which mirrors our perceived world and dreams about the unknown space of chôra that our collective unconscious is attached to.

Myth as the Fabrication of Truth

The second stage, "myth as the fabrication of truth," refers to the period where the world is dominated by monarchy and political religion, which needs to create myth to control people. In order to consolidate the monarchic authority, the fabrication of fantastic stories proves to be effective as the means to intimidation and propaganda. The years of the advent of this epoch can vary in different cultures. The proliferation of Christian fantastic tales in medieval literature manifests the supremacy of Christian monarchy. Many remnants of fantastic litera-

---

[38] Though written in 1601, a period amidst the stage of myth as truth fabrication in Chinese literature, *The Investiture of the Gods*, along with other Daoist fantastic stories, is counted as the fantastic creation from the stage of primitive perception in that Daoist writers and practitioners often led a life beyond the control of the Confucian monarchic system. Their vision of the world retained them in the state of original participation with the primitive perception.

ture from primitive perception remain by their conversion into Christianity. *Beowulf* of English literature and *Kalevala* (Elias Lönnrott 1835) of Finnish literature are examples of such fantastic narratives after the slight modification with a Christian touch on the original pagan epics. In French literature, Perrout de Saint Cloude's *Le Roman de Renart* (c. 1175), rooted in folklores, serves as an excellent example that illustrates how a cunning politician (Renart the fox) can profit from his good relationship with the sovereign. Besides the fabulous depiction of animals, vegetation also intrigues writers' imagination. Guillaume de Lorris's (1200-1238) *Roman de la rose* (c. 1230) represents a fantastic narration based on the dream vision. This theme of dream in fantastic creation reminds us of *Dream of the Rood* in Old English literature.

In the hub of Christianity, Italy, Dante created his religious fantastic epic of *The Divine Comedy*. Likewise, the emergence of French *chanson de geste* (*La Chanson de Roland*, c. 1080) was related to the French monarchy of the Charlemagne dynasty. The most popular Arthurian legend or Romance of the Grail is surmised to be an imaginary product of both monarchy and Christianity. The legend could at the same time secure the English king's reign (Henri II Plantagenet as a Norman descendant) [Berthelot 37-38] and reinforce the connection between the monarchy and the religion. This may be why the tales centering on Arthur the king are more important in England, though *Sir Gawain and the Green Knight* (c. 1400) appeared earlier as an example of Arthurian legend that emphasizes knights' valor and loyalty, essentially based on the motif of "severed head" in Celtic myth. Malory's (c. 1405-1471) *Le Morte d'Arthur* (1485) established the narrative tradition about King Arthur. The appropriation of Arthurian legend to consolidate the monarchic power and Christianity is explicitly manifest by Edmund Spencer (1552-1599) in his *The Faerie Queene* (1590, 1596). The poet, amidst the religious conflict of the time, unashamedly supported Queen Elizabeth, whom was depicted to have connection with King Arthur. In contrast, in France and Germany, we notice the emphasis on telling stories of knights, especially the romance of the grail. The series of Arthurian romances of Chrétien de Troyes (ca. 12th century AD) and *Parzival* (13th century AD) of Wolfram von Eschenbach are important literary models of Arthurian knights, and the romance of the grail. Though Christianity and monarchy predominated in the creation of Arthurian legend, authors' stories revolving around the legend demonstrated their narrative artistry and extent of imagining the unknown. The monotheism in Europe was consolidated, which left the only space for the unknown imagination mainly to the pious and mysterious communion between men and God.

Doctor Faustus's tragic and horrible death depicted by Christopher Marlowe (1564-1593), "limbs all torn asunder by the hand of death" [Marlowe, 82], illustrates how the political and religious milieu constructed this German legend. The moral of eternal condemnation for signing a pact with the devil is all the more explicit by the scholars' ending discourses of the play. This espousing of paramount Christianity culminates in Milton's (1608-1674) epic *Paradise Lost* (1667). In Spain, we learn about the lamentation for the fading of medieval chivalry from Cervantes's (1547-1616) *Don Quixote de la Mancha* (1605), an imaginary creation of the unknown past in the author's contemporaneous environment where monarchic centralization reigned. In Arab literature, *Thousand and One Nights* (9th century), later an important influence on European romantic fantastic literature, reveals the cruelty of the king. The storytelling of the Arabian tales manifests itself as a protest against dictatorship. This also indicates why monarchs or politicians do not encourage people to be imaginative.

In Chinese literature, the stages of primitive perception and myth as the fabrication of truth indeed coexisted after the monarchic unification of the Qin dynasty (221BC-207AD). The writers along the lines of primitive Daoism continued the fantastic writing from the imaginary of primitive perception, albeit Confucianism and Buddhism were the predominating ethics and religion. Thereby, the most productive period of the Chinese fantastic creation was the Six dynasties (265-589), when the centralized monarchy collapsed into scattered kingdoms. On the contrary, the literati's writing of the fantastic tales from the Tang dynasty (618-907) purported to show the narrative skill to the jury prior to the imperial examination, the act of which was called *wenjuan* ("warm-up of examination").[39] Fantastic literature regained its niche in Chinese literature during the interval between the collapse of the Tang dynasty and the establishment of the Song dynasty (960-1279). Episodic novels thrived with the trend of popular literature in the Ming dynasty (1368-1644). This fashion of employing vernacular narration resulted in the re-creation of some fantastic tales and novels. Among the abundant moral tales of Buddhism, Confucianism and religious Daoism (Daoist religion is different from philosophy), *Journey to the West* features as a paradigmatic religious fantastic novel. The imagined adventures of the novel cater to all the teachings of Buddhism. Fantastic literature with such a narrative style fits our assumption of myth as the fabrication of truth. The last dynasty, Qing (1644-1911), boasted a great fantastic writer, counted probably as the greatest in Chinese literature, Pu Songling (1640-1715). His fantastic opus is considered as representative of fantastic creation at the second stage, instead of primitive perception. Grounded in Confucianism, his impulse to write fantastic tales indeed came from his repeated failure in the imperial examination. Most writers poeticized by following the styles and mimesis of their predecessors. Because of the Confucian oriented monarchic system in China, the stage of

---

[39] The criteria for the examination during the Tang dynasty were repartitioned into three perspectives: poetry, narration and commentary. The candidates of the examination viewed writing fantastic tales as a pertinent practice to show the three required skills. The fantastic tale is *per se* a narrative form. The convention of embedding poems and a commentary at the end of the tale makes the fantastic genre an ideal form of practice for the examination.

myth as the fabrication of truth, actually overshadowing the creation of primitive perception, lasted until the collapse of the last dynasty at the beginning of the twentieth century.

This historical stage in fantastic literature was hostile to genuine fantastic imagination, especially the primary imagination that divulges truth. Sometimes such imaginary connected to *la fantastique* was condemned as heresy. Sixteenth-century hermetic philosopher, Bruno Giordano, revised the traditional view of image by proclaiming that the source of thought is human imaging, which precedes and creates reason. At his times, this was considered heretic since such theory challenges the supreme power of the Church. In this opinion, the creative force could be generated from human beings instead of the Demiurge, which was still mediated by the Church. His cutting edge theory, unfortunately an anachronistic lapse, condemned him to be burnt at the stake [Kugler, 75-6]. Likewise, fantastic creation at the present stage is predominated by the Christian imagination.

Therefore, this stage is the very inception of disdaining and sundering mythic or folkloric storytelling. Fairies, trolls, gnomes, devils and sorcerers have become taboo under the Christian tenet. However, the Germany of the Holy Roman Empire was by no means a centralized sovereignty as England, France or China. The sundry kingdoms diluted the reigning power of monarchic Christianity and reserved free space for people and writers to continue their imaginary storytelling. Consequently, Germany's long fragmentation may clearly explain why the tradition of fairy storytelling and myths remained in Germanic literature. This is indeed what French and English Romantic writers highly esteemed in German literature. They at the same time lamented their meagerness of such unique imaginary tradition. Nodier's and Carlyle's admiration for German fantastic tales was explicitly expressed in their works. Sir Walter Scott, in addition to his personal appreciation of the fantastic and the Grimm's fairy tales, himself scoured the borders in search of ballads. By the same token, in the history of Chinese literature, the period before the centralized sovereign of the Qin dynasty (221BC-207AD) and the disunited periods of the six dynasties (265-589) and the five dynasties (907-960) featured the richest works of the fantastic.

Intellectual Skepticism

The third evolutionary stage of fantastic literature is termed as intellectual skepticism. This urge to dissipate the mirage of the false belief in the unknown, especially the supernatural, is a product of an age of rationalism and science. We could avail ourselves of Barfield's stage of the intellectual soul to expound the essential spirit of this period of fantastic literature. As intellect predominates over the imaginative mode, skepticism is a central attitude towards all the phenomena of the unknown. In Europe, this period may roughly be circumscribed as ranging from the late humanism of renaissance to the 20th century. This period approximately coincides with Barfield's intellectual age of idolatry, from the commencement of scientific exploration to its culmination towards the end of the 19th century, which is comparable to Goethe's intellectual and prosaic stage. This deviation from participation with Nature is also criticized by Bachelard: "We understand Nature by resisting it (*Nous comprenons la Nature en lui resistant*)." The waning of participation throughout this stage entails a scanty production of fantastic literature, which is considered germane to the irrational and the imaginary. Though the period extends over three centuries, we have to wait until the end of the 18th century to behold the burgeoning of fantastic literature again: from Gothic novel, the romantic fantastic to the realistic fantastic.

The 17th and 18th centuries were preoccupied with knowledge deduced from the known realm and thinking the thought, to employ Barfield's concept. Intellectuals, especially scientists, endeavour to dissipate the mirage of superstition or the false presumption of unknown phenomena. In the European Renaissance, we only find literary canons of fantastic literature in Christian writing. With the increasing concern about humanism and the emergence of the baroque and classicism, fantastic literature was abased into paraliterature, except for La Fontaine's (1621-1695) *Fables* (1668-78), considered as classic. Many scholars disagree on including fables into the realm of fantastic literature. However, according to our premised definition grounded on the unknown and the approach of imaginary theories, in particular Durand's theriomorphic symbols of the imaginary, bestiaries as well as religious allegories can be considered as narratives appertaining to the unknown. In this case, the unknown touches the imaginary of the animals and gods. Fantastic literature can be didactic or non-didactic; the essential effect lies in arousing readers' aesthetic imagination of the unknown realm, or in other words, drawing readers closer to the dreamy land of the collective unconscious.

In France, much earlier than the Grimm's publication of fairy tales, *Les Contes* of Perrault (1628-1703) presented in 1697 an early version of European fairy tales such as "The Red Riding Hood." Moral teaching embedded in the tales is one of the disguises for fantastic tales to be retained in such an intellectual age. Tolkien also accepted the use of satire in the writing of fairy-stories with a proviso: "if there is any satire present in the tale, one thing must not be made fun of, the magic itself" [Tolkien 1997, 114]. With writing on philosophy proliferating during the 18th Century, the space for fantastic literature shrank even further. Nevertheless, England boasted its great fantastic novel in 1726, *Gulliver's Travels* by Jonathan Swift (1667-1745). It is noticeable that most fantastic works of this period were satire par excellence. Besides Swift's novel, we can also adduce earlier works from the French Renaissance such as Rabelais's (c. 1494-1553) *Pantagruel* (1533) and *Gargantua* (1542) as an inception of the fantastic satire during the skeptical epoch. Both writers poeticized their diurnal and nocturnal imaginary of mad geometrism and miniaturization into their famous novels. Durand even coined the latter imaginary structure as *gulliverization*. Satires do not hinder the identification of fantastic creation, since writers avail themselves of imagining the unknown: trolls, giants, gnomes and dwarves long inhabiting the fantastic space of the collective unconscious.

The century of enlightenment with reason and science even pushed faith to the precipice. Monotheism started to be interpreted as natural God; faith in the divine almighty was questioned by philosophers. Humans became far more important than at the age of Renaissance. Goethe saw it as a separation from the sacred stage. Towards the end of the century, fantastic literature was paradoxically reborn as a *renaissance of the irrational* [Castex] to counterbalance the rationalist and scientific mainstream. The long existing sparkles of mysticism or occultism (for example, the French literature of colportage features novels about lives of the saints that echo the mysteries: *Robert le Diable* (*Rober the Devil*)) illuminated with the popularity of Swedenborg, Martines de Paqually and Luis Claude de Saint-Martin. Swedenborg furthermore exerted great influence on many important writers such as Blake and Nodier. In addition, the renaissance of Neo-Platonism during the Romantic period is an important factor to fantastic writing. This resurrection of fantastic literature commences with the Gothic novels. The first Gothic novel is *The Castle of Otranto*, written by Walpole (1717-1797) in 1765. Thereafter England featured a series of Gothic novels: Beckford's (1760-1844) *Vathek* (originally written in French in 1786), and in the 1790s, we see the heyday of the English Gothic: Ann Radcliffe's (1764-1823) *The Mystery of Udolpho* (1794) and *The Italian* (1797), and Matthew Lewis's (1775-1818) *The Monk* (1796). The Gothic novels metamorphosed in the 19th century by combining the ancient faith with modern incredulity, the Gothic setting remaining a distinct feature of the narration. Mary Shelley (1797-1851) created the first modern Gothic science-fiction on the theme of artificial man: robot or automaton in 1818, the renowned *Frankenstein*. With the renaissance of the fantastic, writers also turned to folklore to tap inspiration. John Polidori (1795-1821) wrote the first English literary vampire story in 1819, *The Vampyre*. Maturin (1782-1824) resumed the ancient alchemical theme of immortality and the elixir of long life to create his *Melmoth the Wanderer* (1820).

The English Gothic novels are considered by French scholars as the first influence on French fantastic literature. German fantastic literature, including ballads, fairy tales and Hoffmannian tales, exerted its vital influence on the boom of French fantastic literature. German fantastic creation was grounded in the storytelling tradition of *Märchen*, comprising *Volksmärchen* (folktales) and *Kunstmärchen* (artistic tales), similar to the division between folk ballads and literary ballads. Under the impact of the movement of *Sturm und Drang* (Storm and Stress), tales were reintroduced by great writers and the impact of

Neo-Platonic philosophy inspired fantastic literature. After their thorough and diligent researches throughout Germany for Teutonic mythology, philologists Jacob and Wilhelm Grimm (1785-1863; 1786-1859) published *Kinder- und Hausmärchen* (*Children's and Household Tales*) in 1812-1815 as the European landmark of researches in fairy tales and myths. Ludwig Tieck's (1773-1853) *Eckbert the Blond* (1796) and the three-volume collection *Phantastus* (1812-1817) are examples of the aforementioned *Kunstmärchen*. Goethe asserted that German authors (such as Tieck, Von Chamisso, Eichendorff, Hoffmann and Goethe) distinguish themselves in the style of fairy tales; Heine affirmed the imaginary power in the German fantastic by proclaiming that this was exactly what French writers lacked. This exuberance of fantastic tales in German literature inspires to extend into an idiosyncrasy of romantic fantastic literature.

According to French studies, 19th-Century fantastic writing started with Romantic fiction, which was also the Golden Age of the fantastic. This specific period roughly ranges from 1810 to 1850, also contemporaneous to the Napoleonic wars in Europe and the industrial revolution. The term "Romanticism" in fact derives from the medieval style Romance, which entails a resurrection of romances. Joseph von Eichendorff (1788-1857) stylized his fantastic tales by resurrecting the medieval legend of the wandering knight. His "Autumn Sorcery" (1808) represents the typical *Tannhauser's sojourn in the pagan paradise of Venus*, which later inspired Wagner. The principal motifs of the sojourning knight, the femme fatale, disquieting animals, petrification, magic and forest are recurrent elements in romantic fantastic literature. Achim von Arnim's (1781-1831) fantastic is characterized by his bizarre style that offers identifiable time and space by insinuating legendary elements, for example "Isabelle of Egypt" (1812). He also portrayed the popular theme of the doppelganger in "The Heir of Majhorat" (1820). The paradigm of depicting a doppelganger by initiating the theme of the lost of one's shadow is created by Adelbert von Chamisso (1781-1838) in *The Marvellous Story of Peter Schlemihl or The Man Who Lost his Shadow* (1814), based on a popular German theme of a pact with the devil, but not along the lines of the Faustian legend. This theme of the double was also elaborated by Goethe as the eponymous hero of *Faust* utters, "Two souls, alas, are dwelling in my breast, / And one is striving to forsake its brother. / Unto the world in grossly loving zest, / With clinging tendrils, one adheres; / The other rises forcibly in quest / Of rarefied ancestral sphere" [Goethe 1990, 145]. This chef-d'oeuvre of Goethe created a phenomenon in Europe. The French Romantic painter Eugène Delacroix dedicated illustrations for the master piece and French Romantic poet Gérard de Nerval contributed the French translation. Though *Faust* was not widely copied, this significant play inspired many musical adaptations, such as Hector Berlioz's (1803-1869) dramatic cantata *The Damnation of Faust* (1846) based on the French version and Franz Liszt's (1811-1886) *A Faust Symphony* (1854, revised in 1857-61).

Different from Goethe's epic scale of fantastic play, Hoffmann (1776-1822) rejoiced over his lithe and grotesque style of storytelling, inspired from his artistry of music. What Hoffmann portrayed is fantastic literature of sonata but not symphony. It cannot be over-exaggerated that France would not have its 19th-century fantastic literature had Hoffmann not written his *Fantasiestücke* (1814-15) and had it translated into French (1830). Before entering into the mainstream of French fantastic writers, it is necessary to mention two important fantastic pioneer figures in French literature. Jacques Cazotte's (1719-1792) *Le Diable amoureux* (1771) manifests his typical French style of fantastic narration, viz. centring on realism to narrate the fantastic. The novel fits Todorov's definition of hesitation between the supernatural (the true existence of the woman metamorphosed from a horrifying devil) and the natural (the hero's nightmare). Little noticed by scholars, Cazotte was in fact influenced by Hoffmann. Another important pioneer is the Polish writer Jean Potocki (1761-1815) who created a French fantastic novel, *Le Manuscrit trouvé à Saragosse* (1797-1807). The novel is, strictly speaking, not fantastic since its denouement explains that all the supernatural phenomena were nothing but purposely arranged temptations to test the hero. Nonetheless, considering the hypotyposis of the successive episodes of supernatural stories, though slightly undermined by the eventual natural explication, most scholars deem the novel as a great work of the romantic fantastic.

Charles Nodier (1780-1844) produced treatises on the fantastic genre and other works on dreams and reveries. He himself wrote fantastic tales, the exclusive genre that merits his lucubration despite his reputation of erudition and being bibliophile. His imaginary *inventio* is mainly drawn from myths, legends and folktales from his homeland and other European countries. Furthermore, as he brought to light the fantastic tradition in Western literature, he was greatly inspired by the works from the previous two periods of fantastic creation. "Une Heure ou la Vision" (1806), a vague kind of fantastic tale, was created under the influence of Goethe's *Werther* (1774), "Trilby ou le Lutin d'Argail" (1822) was inspired by Sir Walter Scott (1771-1832) to depict the love Jeannie feels for a Scottish sprite. The narrative skill of medieval romances (also featuring in Rabelais's *Gargantua* and *Pantagruel*) and the rich imaginary elements like mandragora and fairy makes his "La Fée aux miettes" (1832) a chef-d'oeuvre of the romantic fantastic. His tales are as rich as his theories, according to the categories of fantastic literature proposed by Nodier: false, vague and true fantastic stories [Nodier 1961, 330]. His late fantastic creation, classified as the mystic cycle by Castex, offers readers a tale drawn from the philosophy of Neo-Platonism. The eponymous heroine of "Lydie ou la résurrection" learns about the ideal love from her dead husband George who resurrects to angelic heaven and introduces to her the teachings of Plato's ideal love in *Phaedrus* and the true evolution of human beings. Nodier's stylized fantastic tales have been gradually ignored and overshadowed by the ambiguous genre of fantastic tales and other Romantic genres. His imagination makes him a visionary writer who foresaw the popularity of the fantastic in our times.

Inspired by Nodier, Théophile Gautier (1811-1872) also dedicated his literary genius (as Baudelaire appreciated him) mostly in fantastic tales in addition to his poems. Compared with his mentor Nodier, Gautier is more renowned and studied in that he is a great influence on Oscar Wilde (1856-1900) and Charles Baudelaire (1821-1867). Gautier, the first writer that proclaimed "art for art's sake," also illustrates his ideal of art in his fantastic tales. Centring on love and beauty, Gautier presented readers with a picturesque and rococo style truly *à la française*, suffice it to adduce "La Morte amoureuse" (1836) (one of the very first vampire literatures) and "Arria Marcella" (1852). Different from Nodier, who espoused the Platonic ideal love, Gautier quested for his ideal love featuring supernatural women, sensual but sincere in his tales. His ornate style especially influenced Wilde's fantastic writings, such as *The Picture of Dorian Gray* (1891) and "The Canterville Ghost" (1887). Gérard de Nerval (1808-1855), more renowned as a poet, searched for his ideal love in the yonder and created his fantastic *Aurelia* (1853). Under the inspiration of *The Arabian Tales*, he rendered his own *Le Voyage en Orient* (1851).

In the American literature of Romanticism, Washington Irving (1772-1834), inspired by the witchcraft remnants, the legends of his European ancestors and of the indigenous Indians, created numerous fantastic tales such as "The Legend of Sleepy Hollow" (1820), "Rip Van Winkle" (1820), "The Spectre Bridegroom" (1820), and "The Adventure of the German Student" (1824). The employment of a German hero in the fantastic evokes some French writers' narrative technique such as Pétrus Borel's (1809-1859) "Gottfried Wolfgang" (1843). This narrative strategy shows the German influence on the romantic fantastic. Another American master of the romantic fantastic, Nathaniel Hawthorne (1804-1864) created an ambiguous style of fantastic tales by incorporating the persecution of witchcraft and relentless Puritanism, for example, his famous "Young Goodman Brown" (1835).

Lilian R. Furst elucidates, "The English excel at lyric poetry, the French concentrate on drama, and the Germans find their most appropriate vehicle in the Märchen-like narrative with their transcendental yearnings" [Furst, 82]. In this light, the scantiness of English fantastic fiction, though with the abounding predecessors of Gothic novels, can be explained by their lyrical predilection. Nonetheless, English poets dedicated an important form of fantastic literature, the literary ballad, the genre of narrative poem that serves as a perfect form for Romantic poets to tell stories. Coleridge (1771-1834) can be entitled as a fantastic poet given that he wrote mostly fantastic ballads. Furthermore, his theory of primary and secondary imagination by excluding the false imagination of fancy is only realized by fantastic creation. This theory of imagination was indeed derived from German idealist philosophy, the writers of influence being mainly

Goethe and Schelling (1775-1854). Goethe himself also wrote numerous fantastic ballads such as "Erlkönig" (1782), "Der Zauberlehrling" (1797) and *Die Braut von Korinth* (1797). His *Faust*, a fantastic epic play in verse *per se*, also embeds many ballads. Coleridge's (1772-1834) famous "The Rime of the Ancient Mariner" (1797-1799) is a classic fantastic ballad that impels readers' imagination back into connection with the collective unconscious of the unknown mysterious power. The primary imagination is illustrated by man's relationship with the divine power, which is the key concept to Coleridge's ideal of primary imagination, as Wordsworth interpreted, only possible through a communion with God.

The aforementioned story of the wandering knight from "Autumn Sorcery" by Eichendorff evokes the fantastic ballad of John Keats (1795-1821), "La Belle Dame sans Merci" (1819). Both stories feature a loitering knight in the enchanting faerie land as a continual loss. Sir Walter Scott, attached to Scottish history and legend, composed a series of fantastic ballads or verse romances, for example, "The Lady of the Lake" (1810) and "The Vision of Don Roderick" (1811). Besides his ballads, Scott may be regarded as the sole English (rather Scottish) storyteller that succeeded the fantastic creation emerging in continental Europe, German tales having been his main influence. He may also be considered as a precursor of mixing the supernatural in religious legends with the art of the historical novel. His "Wandering Willie's Tale" (1832) presents a quasi-detective story mixed with a fantastic monkey, a popular Renaissance element of fantastic literature. Like Scott, most English writers interested in the fantastic genre elaborated the fantastic artistry as a form of fairy tales and folktales, which can also explain the boom of a later development of the specific genre *fantasy* in England. George MacDonald (1824-1905) is one of the great influences on Tolkien (1892-1973) by his fairy tales of mystery such as "The Golden Key" (1867), which further inspired Tolkien to create his story of "Smith of Wootton Major" (1967), and by other children's books such as *The Princess and the Goblin* (1872) and *The Princess and Curdie* (1883), which led to Tolkien's depiction of goblins in *The Hobbit* (1937).

In Finland, influenced by the zeal for searching and resurrecting native treasures of myths, legends and tales burgeoning in Germany, Elias Lönnrott collected and compiled their great epic *Kalevala* in 1835. Though written and published during the Romantic period, we would place *Kalevala* as an imaginary production from the primitive conception period amalgamated with modern Romantic diction and style. In about the same time, Russia boasted a great fantastic storyteller, Nicolaï Gogol (1809-1852), who foresaw the Kafkaesque fantastic with his unique style of absurdity and realism. It would be more appropriate to place Gogol in the generation of the realistic fantastic, the time roughly ranging from 1850 to 1900.

Gogol's fantastic writing appears anachronistic in the sense of foreseeing the narrative of his next century. From the aspect of narration, his fantastic falls into the category of realistic fantastic or even the category of later generation as the fantastic of absurdity. The realistic fantastic focuses on the inner processes of the character and the alienation of his vision confronting inexplicable phenomena on a daily basis. While German literature reached its culmination of fantastic creation by the perfect form of Wagner's operas of Germanic mythology, French literature looked for its model in the realistic fantastic from the American writer Poe (1809-1849), thanks to Baudelaire's translation. It is pertinent to say that the French romantic fantastic is oriented by Hoffmann's style and that the French realistic fantastic is under the influence of Poe's weird tales. Prosper Mérimée (1803-1870) told many fantastic tales rich in local colours that completely followed the law of realism without the romantic traits of the hero's melancholic frame of mind. His "Lokis" (1869) tells a Ukrainian folktale of a count who is suspected to be begotten from a bear. "La Vénus d'Ille" (1837), often considered as the perfect fantastic tale according to Todorov's definition, presents a horrible story in which the enchanted hero seems to be murdered by the wicked statue of Venus at his wedding night. Similar to Poe's effect of the fantastic, readers are more driven into the realm of the detective story, encountering an unsolvable mystery of the supernatural interference. Mérimée's story of "La Chambre bleue" falls in the category of detective story due to the denouement with a natural explication of all the earlier inexplicable events taking place in the blue room at the hotel.

Dedicated to spiritism, Villiers de l'Isle-Adam (1838-1889) showed his predilection for mysticism and created all his "cruel" tales (*contes cruels*) revolving around the imaginary of the unknown world, especially the beyond. He interpreted the imaginary as something related to the supernatural. Nonetheless, his fantastic narration is rooted in the realistic depiction under an ambiguous atmosphere of the mysterious and seemingly supernatural events, such as "Véra" (1874) (the falling of the key from the tomb reminds one of the returning of the spirit of the hero's beloved Véra) and "L'Intersigne" (1867) (under a dreamy atmosphere the hero realizes that the spirit of the priest lends him the coat), "L'Inconnue" (1876) (the appearance of the uninvited guest remains unknown) and "Le Secret de l'ancienne musique" (1876) that uncovers the knowledge of ancient music by a mysterious man who disappears to remain unknown.

Guy de Maupassant (1850-1893), besides his tales about the legends of Normandy, which are full of local and superstitious colours (such as "La Légende du mont Saint-Michel" (1882) and "La Mère aux monstres" (1883)), created his idiosyncratic style of realistic or naturalistic fantastic tales. "Le Horla" (1887), "Sur l'eau" (1876), and "Un fou?" (1884) are fantastic tales that focus more on the psychological fantastic narration than on the fantastic as external intrusion into daily life. Castex regards Maupassant as the last fantastic writer of the romantic spirit since Nodier. After Maupassant, fantastic literature enters the epoch of the fin-de-siècle, where the fantastic narration makes a paradigm shift to extreme interiority.

The absence of fantastic creation in the period of Romanticism in English literature was complemented in the second half of the nineteenth century. Fairytale writing after George MacDonald featured Andrew Lang (1844-1912) who also exerted great influence on Tolkien's fantastic creation. Lewis Carroll's (1832-1898) publication of *Alice's Adventures in Wonderland* (1865) and later of *Through the Looking-Glass and What Alice Found There* (1871) distinguishes the English style of fantastic literature from the continental fantastic which appears more gloomy and dark. Besides the marvellous kind of fantastic writing in English literature, ghost and vampire stories were featured, differentiating it from continental European's ambiguous narration. English writer and medieval scholar, Montague Rhodes James (1862-1936) was noted for his ghost stories of an antiquary. His style of supernaturalist short fiction influenced American writer Lovecraft (1890-1937). Irish writers were more apt at depicting supernatural beings in a vivid and blunt way. Suffice it to adduce the following Irish writers: Joseph Sheridan Le Fanu (1814-1873, who also contributed a great vampire story: *Camilla* (1872)), Fitz James O'Brien (1828-1862), Bram Stoker (1847-1912, the author of the vampire novel paradigm *Dracula* (1897)), Oscar Wilde and Lord Dunsany (1878-1957).

Fantastic writing during the Romantic period and later may still have elements from Antiquity such as the devil, goblin or fairy as a concrete figure. However, these turn out to be man's own double. It is the evil within but not without. This is the visage of the fantastic of decadence. Under the shadow of the abstract evil inside the human soul at the turning epoch of decadence, three main figures of such fantastic narration appeared in French literature. Jules Barbey d'Aurevilly (1808-1889) wove in his tales fantastic phenomena merely by the complication of narration (foreseeing the *Nouveau Roman* narrative technique) interplayed with human interior evil spirit; Jean Lorrain (1855-1906) represented his unique fantastic narration by the horror behind the hole of the mask; Marcel Schwob (1867-1905) proclaimed horror against grace in human nature and created a fantastic mode centring on the double nature of humans, where man's evil soul is the most horrible devil instead of a concrete figure of devil with horns and cloven hooves. The double theme of split personality initiated by Schwob further influenced Stevenson's (1850-1894) creation of *Dr Jekyll and Mr Hyde* (1886). Likewise, under the influence of Poe's fantastic, Arthur Conan Doyle (1859-1930) integrated the unknown with science and reason. He has become an archetype of detective creation, for example, in the Japanese manga Conan series. The fashion of portraying split personality grounded in human psychology, in addition, encouraged by the popularity of psychology at the times, reigned over the fantastic creation of the fin-de-siècle.

Oscar Wilde's *The Picture of Dorian Gray* can be evaluated as the chef-d'oeuvre of the epoch that delves into the human soul by means of an art work. American writer Henry James (1843-1916), inclined for European culture, depicted a tale (*The Turn of the Screw*, 1898) based on the ambiguity between the heroine's personality split deriving from the repressed desire and the supernatural existence of the ghost that deprives the life of the boy under her care. The extreme development of psychology in fact made fantasy unpopular and Western literature oriented towards the literature of modernism, the narrative stream of consciousness being the main artistry. Although French literature developed a new method of narrating dreams, the alleged auto-writing of surrealism, yet we hold a skeptical perspective on surrealist literature as fantastic literature since this is an extreme illustration of strangeness in language and the art of storytelling becomes abstract and fragmentary. Furthermore, Tolkien excluded this genre of writing as fantasy or artistic creation of the fantastic:

> Many people dislike being 'arrested' [by the strangeness of Fantasy]. They dislike any meddling with the Primary World, or such small glimpses of it as are familiar to them. They, therefore, stupidly and even maliciously confound Fantasy with Dreaming, in which there is no Art; and with mental disorders, in which there is not even control: with delusion and hallucination. [Tolkien 1997, 139]

He further expounded the distinction between Fantasy and Dream by noting that "Fantasy is a rational not an irrational activity" [ibid., 139, n. 2].

At the turning of the century, fantastic literature, though undermined by the development of psychology, derived a new variation that came to nearly dominate the contemporary fantastic creation: science-fiction. The only branch of fantastic literature that keeps the fire may be science-fiction, the English *fantasy* and horror stories. As we mentioned earlier, the fantasy tradition in English literature affirmed by the landmark of Carroll's Alice's stories was under continual development into the twentieth century. The resurrection of Arthurian legends is burgeoning in English literature, initiated by the poet laureate Alfred Lord Tennyson's (1809-1892) *Idylls of the King* (1856-1885). The Arthurian legend inspired American writers, such as Mark Twain (1835-1910) who dedicated a fantastic romance about travelling into the past to the times of King Arthur in *A Connecticut Yankee in King Arthur's Court* (1889) and Howard Pyle (1853-1911) who, both writer and illustrator, contributed a thorough version of stories stressing more on King Arthur than his knights in *The Story of King Arthur and his Knights* (1903). This idealization of the Middle Ages in the imaginary of English literature reached its climax in the fantastic novels of William Morris (1834-1896), Pre-Raphaelite artisan, poet and socialist, who is considered as the initiator of the genre *heroic fantasy* or *fantastic epic* [Bozzetto 2002]. His creation of fantastic epics is mainly inspired from the Greek mythology such as *The*

Life and Death of Jason (1867) and Nordic and Germanic legends such as *The Story of Sigurd the Volsung* and *The Fall of the Niblungens* (1877). Morris depicted his fantastic epic by a dreamer travelling into the past of 1381 in *A Dream of John Ball* (1888) and into the future of the 21st century in *News from Nowhere* (1891). His *The Well at the World's End* (1896) follows the Western tradition of initiation by love in the fantastic since the antique work of *The Golden Ass*. Richard Mathews terms this fantastic epic as fantasy, a unique Anglo-Saxon narrative mode established by Morris, who helps shape the mode with "materials from saga literature, Arthurian legend, Old French romances, Anglo-Saxon philology, utopian visions, and vigorous medieval and Gothic scholarship rapidly evolved in the first few decades of the twentieth century" [Mathews, 21]. Contemporaneous to this emergence of fantastic epic in English literature, a new dimension of the imaginary of anticipation is under development, viz. the Wellsian style of science-fiction or "scientific romance" as Bozzetto terms it. Because of its modernity in crafting the unique narrative, science-fiction is often considered as a separate genre discriminated from other neighbouring genres such as fantasy. Orson Scott Card distinguishes science-fiction from fantasy by the setting: "If the story is set in a universe that follows the same rules as ours, it's science fiction. If it's set in a universe that doesn't follow our rules, it's fantasy" [Card, 22]. In his chapter of "The Fantastic and Genre Criticism," Rabkin perceives science-fiction (e.g. Asimov's *I, Robot*) and fantasy (e.g. Lindsay's *A Voyage to Arcturus*) as two ends of continuum with blurred boundaries in the middle [Rabkin, 136]. Bozzetto sees science-fiction as a narrative genre that is not presently real but could be real in the future. Despite the above distinction between science-fiction and other approximate sub-genres, science-fiction is yet considered as a variation of fantastic literature in light of its inventive imagination that appertains to the unknown, albeit rooted in scientific knowledge. Asimov's (1920-1992) viewpoint may throw light on the above idea: good science fiction has exactly one assumption that differs from currently accepted scientific knowledge. This scientific imaginary incorporated into fantastic artistry effectively took off after the industrial revolution and the thriving development of science after the period of skepticism.

The emergence of modern science-fiction can be traced back to Mary Shelley's *Frankenstein*, through the development of Poe's realistic and detective genre of fantastic tales and Stevenson's *Dr Jekyll and Mr Hyde*, until the settled visage of the sub-genre created by the French writer Jules Verne (1828-1905) and English writer H. G. Wells (1866-1946). Both writers were specialists in science-fiction, though in a more imaginary fantastic writing. Most of Jules Verne's science-fiction deals with fantastic voyages, ranging from the moon to the centre of the Earth, for example, *Voyage au centre de la terre* (1864), *Autour de la lune* (1869), *Vingt mille lieues sous les mers* (1869) and *Le Tour du monde en quatre-vingts jours* (1873). His science-fiction is often characterized as science-fantasy. Verne's English counterpart Wells wrote fantastic fiction, mostly science-fiction, to espouse his ideal of ethics guided by great scientists. Nonetheless, he created many stories of dystopia to reveal the danger triggered by an unethical and mad scientist, for example, *The Time Machine* (1895), *The Island of Dr Moreau* (1896), *The Invisible Man* (1897) and *The War of the Worlds* (1898). With the advent of their science-fiction, the imaginary of the unknown in fantastic creation opened to the realm of science, which further became a mainstream of the fantastic genre. After the literature of modernism, with the trend of postmodernism, the fantastic will recuperate its niche in artistic creation, among others, in the field of cinema.

Unlike the West, Chinese people stayed in the state of original participation for about three more centuries. This phenomenon resulted in a fixed narrative style of Chinese fantastic fiction until the moment of westernization. Because of the periodization of Chinese fantastic creation, as discussed previously, the stages of primitive perception and myth as the fabrication of truth lasted from Antiquity to the collapse of Qing dynasty. Contrary to the long duration of the Western stage of skepticism with a later countercurrent of romantic fantastic creation and the eventual renaissance of the genre, Chinese literature experienced this stage in the twentieth century with an unprecedented meagerness of fantastic creation, overshadowed by the trend of realism and science under Western influence.

Truth in Mirage

The twentieth century can be barely regarded as the dawn of the fourth stage of fantastic literature, since we are still under the stream of antithesis and the unending discourse of "-isms." In light of Barfield's insight into the evolution of human consciousness, we start to be conscious of the participation but not yet reach the stage of the final participation. This fourth stage of fantastic creation is the dialectic obscurity of mirage and truth or of negation and affirmation. In the period of skepticism, science and rationalism influenced the narrative art of fantastic literature as well as the world vision underlying the imaginary of creation. The collapse of many conventional and central values in the Western culture evolves into postmodernism, which questions everything and even the semantism of language. In the skeptical period, philosophy viewed God as a natural God instead of an almighty demiurge or a religious God. In the twentieth century, after God's being claimed dead by Nietzsche, existentialism saw absurdity in human existence and extreme phenomenology deconstructed the meanings constructed by language, thus bringing about all possible emancipation. It seems that everything is possible and can not be denied by any clear-cut standard. This reasoning fosters the popularity of fantastic literature, an ideal of literary creation called forth by Charles Nodier almost two centuries ago.

German literature regains its important position in fantastic creation by the Kafkaesque style of fantastic, the metamorphosis deriving from the absurdity of daily life with a solemn sense of religiosity. Kafka's (1883-1925) writing is in fact indebted to Gustav Meyrink (1868-1932) in the aspect of mysticism and the seemingly magical realistic style. Meyrink's *Golem* (1914) uses a dreamy and magical narrative technique to tell a story based on the mysticism of kabala and the hero's eventual realization of hermaphroditism. German fantastic writing orients more in the direction of spiritual initiation. Hermann Hesse's (1877-1962) fantastic and spiritual novel *Siddhartha* (1922) and other fantastic tales illustrate an oriental spirit of mysticism, for example his story of "The Poet" (1913) is exactly like the Chinese *zhiguai* story mixed with Daoist and Zen philosophy. Inclined to the fantastic that blends realism, absurdity and irony, Günter Grass's (1927-) *Die Blechtrommel* (*The Tin Drum*, 1959) incorporates fantastic imagination of the protagonist of Peter Pan figure archetype into his mainstream work. Michael Ende's (1929-) *Momo* (1973) harks back to the eternal theme of "shadow" and "time." Considered as the German counterpart of J. K. Rowling (1965-), Cornelia Funke (1958-) continues the tradition of German *Märchen* and creates a unique intertextual style of fairy storytelling in *Inkheart* (2003).

Following the movement of surrealism and the *Nouveau Roman*, French writers have been more concerned with crafting the narrative revolution and leave little space for fantastic storytelling. Among a few writers, we may adduce Gaston Leroux (1868-1927), Marcel Aymé (1902-1967), Claude Seignolle (1917-) and Michel Tournier (1924-). Nevertheless, contemporary female writers start to demonstrate their art of fantastic storytelling. For example, Marguerite Yourcenar (1903-1987) was among the first writers delving into the mysterious past of the Renaissance. Her *L'Oeuvre au noir* (1968) brings readers back to the unknown secret of alchemy and Roman church. The so-called supernatural and the natural have already started their dialogue in her novel replete with historical, alchemical and mythological references. Lea Silhol (1967-) creates her mythic fantastic tales or hard fantasy in *La Tisseuse: Contes de fées, contes de failles* (2004) and *La Sève et le Givre* (2002). Marie Darrieussecq (1969), resorting to the realistic narrative mode of the fantastic, makes a lady metamorphose into a pig in her novel *Truisme* (1998). In Belgium, Jean Ray (1887-1964) continued the tradition of the fantastic. Russian writer Mikhail Bulgakov (1891-1940) wrote a bestiary science-fiction of *Heart of a Dog* (1925) by blending the theriomorphic imagination with molecular biology. The famous Romanian mythologist Mircea Eliade (1907-1986) also created his own fantastic stories apart from his erudite researches in mythology.

Popular fantastic literature became popular in America at the turn of the century: Henry Rider Haggard (1856-1925), Howard Phillips Lovecraft

(1890-1937), Robert Erwin Howard (1906-1936), American magazine of *Weird Tales* (1923-1954), L. Frank Baum (1856-1919) and John Dendrick Bangs (1862-1992). The world centre of contemporary fantastic creation still remains in England and America, spanning North America and Latin America. Hispanic literature takes pride in its unique style of *realismo mágico* or magical realism. In 1948, Arturo Uslar-Pietri considered that the contemporary Venezuelan tale was dominated by "a poetic divination [...] of reality" [qtd. Rozas, 21]. He further characterized this new approach of the real as *realismo mágico*. Later, with the creations of the Cuban writer Alejo Carpentier (1904-1980) and the novel of Garcia Márquez (1928-), *One Hundred Years of Solitude* (1967), the aesthetics of the strange, the magic and the marvellous characterized the literature of magical realism. This new narrative technique refreshed fantastic creation as an amalgam of European fantastic and Latin American Indian magic. Jorge Luis Borges (1899-1986) and Julio Cortázar (1914-1984) are representatives of this cultural combination in contemporary fantastic literature under the influence of continental literature (among others, Kafka) and indigenous legends and oriental mysticism. Other writers from Latin America also distinguish themselves by the style of magical realism with a harmonious atmosphere of mystery, for example, Octavio Paz's (1914-1998) "The Blue Bouquet" (1949) and Paulo Coelho's (1947-) *The Alchemist* (1988), *The Pilgrimage* (1987) and other novels of spiritual journey. The popularity of Coelho's writing also marks a return to the alchemical and spiritual quest.

The fantastic impulse continues to urge writers throughout the world. In English literature, the disillusionment with modern values and science ferments the creation of utopian literature, such as Aldous Huxley's (1894-1963) *Brave New World* (1932) and George Orwell's (1903-1950) *Animal Farm* (1954) and *Nineteen Eighty-Four* (1949). The Arthurian legend continues to beget its variation and resurrection in contemporary literature. T. H. White (1906-1964), profoundly affected by Sir Thomas Malory's *Le Morte d'Arthur*, made a major contribution to Arthurian literature by his humorous retelling of the legend from *The Sword in the Stone* (1938), *The Once and Future King* (1958) to *The Book of Merlyn* (1977). Roger Zelazny (1937-1995), writer of science-fiction, also contributed a contemporary version of Arthurian legend, focusing on Merlin and the immortal Lancelot in "The Last Defender of Camelot" (1980). According to Richard Mathews, the Anglo-Saxon mode of fantasy was established by the start of the twentieth century "as a fully distinct genre" in England and the United States, because literary realism was so dominant there [Mathews, 20]. This land of advanced science paradoxically gestates the popular imagination starved for fantasy:

> In many ways, science absorbed supernatural power; it evoked awe and wonder with its apparent magic. These factors, coupled with the relative absence of universal folkloric and mythic traditions in England and America, contributed

to the formation of modern fantasy as a distinct literary form in theses countries where the popular imagination was nearly starved for fantasy. [ibid., 20]

This perspective on the proliferation of Anglo-Saxon fantasy is also the very
reason for the emergence of the last period of fantastic literature. Daoist philosophy views as an eternal truth that the extremity always rebounds; by the
same token, the extreme skepticism of the third period will generate a counter-
balancing momentum of a thirst for the fantastic imagination in spite of the scientific world vision.

Besides Morris's dedication to a fantastic mode incorporating traditional
narrative forms, the Irish writer Lord Dunsany, as a major successor to the former, created a phenomenon of mythmaking in fantastic literature, in particular
mapping an imaginary land with the publication of *The Gods of Pagana* in 1905.
This invention of mythology refined with a unique archaic style of Celtic lyricism and King James Bible cadences remains an artistic model to his fantastic
posterity, the main master of the genre along the lines of Dunsany's art being
Tolkien. G. K. Chesterton (1874-1936) also features among the main influences
on Tolkien's fantastic creation, though the latter criticized his allegorical and religious colours. For example, *The Everlasting Man* (1925) inspired Tolkien's
depiction of the character as the everlasting man in many of his fairy-stories,
such as "Farmer Giles of Ham" (1949). Harold Bloom regarded David Lindsay's
(1876-1945) *A Voyage to Arcturus* (1920) as the most eminent of modern fantasy
narratives. The universal and alchemical spirit circulating in E. R. Eddison's
(1882-1945) fantastic novel, *The Worm Ouroboros* (1922) manifests itself as another example, like many works of magical realism, of a cultural mixture of the
East and the West. The ouroboros, also a Jungian archetypal image, associates
with the cycle of the four elements and the archetypal circle of *Yi Jing Taiji* of
yin and yang. The ensuing development of Anglo-Saxon fantasy, in the direction
of a theological fantasy, thrived with the contribution of the Oxford dons, especially the writers of "the Inklings." Following the fantastic art of the Oxford
group of "the Inklings," J. R. R. Tolkien, C. S. Lewis (1898-1963) and Charles
Williams (1886-1945), British literature saw a new emergence of fantastic novelists. Terry Pratchett (1948-) continues the epic-style fantastic narration and
creates his myth of Discworld in a very humorous tone. J. K. Rowling and Neil
Gaiman (1964-), one concentrating on fairy-story, the Harry Potter series, the
other essaying in various forms encompassing dark fantasy (*Neverwhere*, 1997),
fantastic comics (*The Sandman*, 1988-1996) and fairy-story (*Stardust*, 1998).

With the help of prosperity in cinema, technology and multiculturalism,
American literature manifests itself as the great centre of fantastic creation,
mostly orienting towards popular literature. Vampire writing attracts the American market, works ranging from Richard Matheson's (1926-) *I am Legend* (1954)
to Anne Rice's vampire chronicles. Stephen King (1947-) succeeds in the tradi-

tion of American writers Poe and Lovecraft and creates his Gothic horror in a contemporary style, often connected with science. Isaac Asimov, the creator of *Encyclopedia Galactica* and science fiction epics, integrated science with religion, myth and prophecy in his *Foundation Trilogy* (1951, 1952, 1953). His science fiction represents the eternal return of human civilization. Ray Bradbury (1920-) distinguishes himself by science-fiction, the most famous being *The Martian Chronicles* (1950). Under the influence of Tolkien's ring trilogy and art of language, Ursula K. Le Guin (1929-) was inspired to create her own legend of the Earthsea, by incorporating her understanding of Daoism. In our times of computer technology, the imaginary of the unknown drives writers to create a new genre of fiction, the so-called Cyberpunk, the American novelist William Gibson (1948-) being the representative writer. His fiction, such as *Neuromancer* (1984) and *Idoru* (1996), deals with the close interaction of men and electronic machinery in an overpopulated and decadent future. Recently, the success of Dan Brown's (1964-) novels indicates that readers are intrigued by the fantastic intertextual writing interwoven with mystery, cryptic code, mystic religion and advanced science. In his *Angels and Demons* (2000), indeed the fantastic explained, scientists even discover the connection between religion and science, past and present. The fantastic genre seems to lead the trend worldwide in the cinema. We find continual adaptation of fantastic novels and cinematic creations of the fantastic, especially in Asia where ghost and horror films proliferate. Nonetheless, Asian literature does not produce any great chef-d'oeuvre of the fantastic genre, except for, if we admit its position in Chinese fantastic renaissance, the Nobel laureate Gao Xingjian's (1940-) *The Soul Mountain* (1989) and *Shanhaijing zhuan* (*Tales of The Classic of Mountains and Seas*, 1990). The former is an intertextual writing of Chinese traditional fantastic stories (*zhiguai*) and folklores interwoven with postmodern narrative technique and the French dramatic style of absurdity. The latter is a rewriting of Chinese myths from *The Classic of Mountains and Seas* into a satirical play.

Along with the popular trend of fantastic creation, the literary and fantastic ideal of Nodier's true fantastic literature and Tolkien's fairy-stories will hopefully be realized and perfected in the future, a real period of crystallizing truth out of mirage. The fantastic characteristic in contemporary literature stresses a quest for the third way leading to the universal harmonization or the ultimate truth. The aforementioned contemporary fantastic tales and novels mostly feature a general theme on religious faith, magic, mysticism and alchemy, which evokes the "modern man in search of a soul." This post-postmodern fantastic trend echoes with the creative imagination as a third way back to the primitive participation (Jung), with the aesthetic imagination aroused by poetic diction as a third way to reach the final participation (Barfield) and the fantastic imagination or *la fantastique* that returns the true visage of figure to language (Durand). Long ago, this imaginary third way was proposed by the Chinese Daoist Zhuang

Zi who first resorted to fantastic tales to bridge the gap between material phenomena and metaphysics, the arcane space of Plato's chôra or *Yi Jing*'s first metamorphosis of *Taiji: Liangyi*.

The whole scale of the evolution of fantastic literature can be lastly apprehended in terms of Zen and Daoist three stages of perception and realization. The antique and medieval times of fantastic creation corresponds to the stage of "seeing mountains as mountains, waters as waters," since the modern times of skepticism sees mountains that are not mountains and waters that are not waters, and eventually, post-postmodern times will see mountains that are still mountains and waters that are still waters. With the fantastic epic created by Tolkien, author of the century [Shippey], we may expect more emulation with refined style and genuine imagination to continue the fire of fantastic creation that corresponds with the divulgement of mirage and brings about the Eucharistic creation of Coleridge's primary imagination. Barfield, like Tolkien, brings to light the universal features in myth and language. The historicity of fantastic creation in chorus with the evolution of human consciousness further exposes a universal fact: human impulsion to poeticize to explore the unknown realm. This invites a thematic revision of mythopoeia and the imaginary.

Metamorphosis of the Fantastic Imaginary –
The Universal Themes

Existing theories and critiques on the fantastic genre, especially the approaches grounded in structuralism or dualism, are inclined to contradict the fact that fantastic literature represents the universal imaginary of the unknown realm. Critics along the lines of Todorov's poetics, such as Irène Bessière and Christine Brooke-Rose, stress the idiosyncratic discourse of the fantastic and thus ignore the universal roots of the fantastic imagination across linguistic barriers. Todorov's theory of the fantastic in fact emphasizes only the *dispositio* or narrative discourse of poetics in that he focused on the figurative as literal expressions at the enunciated level and the significance of the narrator at the enunciation level. The rest of the poetic tripartition proposed by Horace, *inventio* and *elocutio* are often overshadowed by the renaissance of the new rhetoric. The former encompasses the imagination and the creation, whereas the latter touches upon the stylistics such as lexicons, sentence patterns and sonority. An exploration of the poetic *inventio* makes the comparative criticism of fantastic literature feasible.

The literary imaginary approach sheds light on the universal roots underlying fantastic creation, from the mystic participation with the collective unconscious proposed by Jung, and through the metamorphosis of the four elements theorized by Gaston Bachelard to the isomorphic images produced from the temporal-spatial imaginary postulated by Gilbert Durand. The perpetual mythopoeia as the true mimesis related to the metaphysical space of chôra continues the creation of the unknown images. The history of fantastic literature presents recurrent themes and motifs both in the West and East. Therefore, the approach of thematic studies, appearing "archaic," is yet vital to comparative researches into the fantastic. It is necessary to delve into the universal imagination of the fantastic before comparing and paralleling the rhetoric and style of fantastic literatures from different linguistic cultures. We propose a universal thematic scheme of fantastic literature that spans culture and language.

In response to the disparate and discrepant categorization of fantastic themes, Jean-Luc Steinmetz proposed a more comprehensive thematic study of the genre. His fantastic thematology can be deemed the most reasonable and universal. The axis of his classification is to distribute the themes into three perspectives: Beings and Forms, Actions, and Causative Principle. Under the category of Beings and Forms are included ghost, vampire, double, automaton (golem, android, mannequin), mandragora, shattered parts of the body and monster. Actions comprise apparition, possession, destruction and metamorphosis. Finally, Causative Principle refers to reasonable explication, dream, magic or occult, drug, telekinesis, telepathy, hypnosis, animism or magnetism. However sensible it seems, this repartition of themes still reveals an insufficiency. For example, the action of metamorphosis can include possession and apparition and destruction. In the category of Beings, we may question the distinction between monster and automaton as well as the ignorance of benevolent beings. Furthermore, his inclination of orienting fantastic literature to conform to Todorov's definition renders the themes inapplicable to the present research. Nevertheless, Steinmez's themes offer a systematic scope and solve the recurrent problems of mixing being and action or causality in categorizing the themes in other critical works or anthologies.

Inspired by Durand's studies of human imagination, we propose a new standpoint of thematizing fantastic creation: the basic triangle of subject-object (I – human – nonhuman, this is formed as 1 and 2) relations plus a tripartite (3) *Weltanschauung* background of nocturnal kingdom, diurnal kingdom and diurnal-nocturnal kingdom. This scheme of the universal thematic structure of the fantastic forms a Pythagorean perfect triangle and the Platonic equilateral triangle that composes the basic corpuscles (*sômata*) transforming from the burgeoning change of chôra. Moreover, the numbers three and six are significant in Daoism. In *Dao De Jing*, the number three is the very number that generates all things and beings. The cerebration or imagination of number three in the aforementioned Greek philosophers and Daoists converges at the number's quality of proliferation to myriads. This imaginary scheme of subject-object triangle can be regarded as a revision of Todorov's thematic theory combined with Durand's diurnal and nocturnal regimes of the imaginary. It combines the relations between the subject and the object with the relations between the subject and time-space. Besides his influential definition of hesitation, Todorov developed a simplified taxonomy by inducing common denominators. He eventually proposed the theme of *I* and the theme of *you*. The former consists of all the subjective perception and formation of the fantastic, while the latter embraces the objective fantastic phenomena. This over-simplification could be a flaw to a serious thematic analysis. The philosophy of the triangle thematic scheme set forth in this book can solve the perennial paradox and discordance in the taxonomy of the fantastic.

The proposed imaginary thematic classification is by no means exclusive, since many fantastic works, especially among those masterpieces, embrace more than one theme in their storytelling to depict the imaginary that bridges the known and the unknown. Consciousness is in fact the momentum of all imagination formed by the percipient. Being conscious of relentless time and immense space, the subject imagines the unknown related to time and space. The Durandian visage of time is represented by symbols of bestiality, darkness and fall. All three isomorphic groups together represent the visage of hell. Durand highlights the fear confronting the imaginary of heaviness and gravity of falling into the abyss of darkness, which can be reinforced by Plato's depiction of dynamism of chôra as separating and sieving lighter particles upward and heavier particles downward. This can be further testified by Daoist philosophy as lighter above and heavier below. All this conception of spatial vision explains the homogeneity in the human imaginary of a paradise upward and hell downward. In what follows, the Buddhist interpretation of human desires (eat, sleep, sex and security) will serve as the substratum for the thematic study of the imaginary.

Sujbect "I" Confronted with Time and Space

The inmost fear and insecurity felt by man is irrevocable death. This is also the unsuccessful quest of the mighty and never-defeated Gilgamesh, the hero of the earliest found epic. Derived from this kernel are related themes of revenants, such as ghost stories (the examples are numerous in different cultures: Stoker's "The Judge's House," Wilde's "The Canterville Ghost," Irving's "The Legend of Sleepy Hollow," Wells's "The Inexperienced Ghost," and the abundant Chinese ghost stories such as Cao Pi's "Zong Dingbuo Catches a Ghost" and "Literatus Tan" or Pu Songling's "Nie Xiaochian"), the immortality from dreamy resurrection (Dunsany's "The Sword of Welleran" and Gautier's "Arria Marcella") and the immortality with transgression of vampirism (Gautier's "La Morte amoureuse" or "The Beautiful Vampire," Stoker's *Dracula*, and Rice's *Vampires Chronicles*) and occultism or alchemy to ascend time and space (the pact with the devil or the Faustian pact such as Goethe' *Faust*, Marlowe's *Doctor Faustus* or Mann's *Doctor Faustus*; sorcery in Arthurian legend, Meyrink's *Golem*, Coelho's *The Alchemist* or Le Guin's *Earthsea* legend; and the scientific imagination in Shelley's *Frankenstein* and Wells's *The Time Machine*).

The imaginary of space, inspired from the insecurity faced with relentless time and death, arouses writers to create a space of death, escapism and immortality. The universal creation is paradise, purgatory and inferno, which can be found in Western literature such as Dante's *The Divine Comedy* and Milton's *Paradise Lost* and in Eastern literature such as *Fengshen Yanyi* (*The Investiture of the Gods*) and Pu Songling's "Siwenlang" (The Public Servant of Literatus in Inferno). This imaginary of a Euclidean space (Durand's fantastic space) beyond our physical space abounds in fantastic creation. The dream is often depicted as an access to such imaginary space. Hoffmann's "The Nutcracker" presents readers with such a possible space in the dream. Turgenev's "The Dream" confuses readers with the blurred boundary between the conscious space and the dream. Carroll's *Alice's Adventure in Wonderland* invites readers into the dreamy world and *Through the Looking-Glass* divulges the space behind the mirror. The imaginary space can be Faerie as is often portrayed by Tolkien and writers of fairy tales. Gaiman's *Stardust* deploys Faerie on the other side of the Wall. Or Faerie can be an alchemical land of ultimate truth, the Atlantis, as in Hoffmann's "The Golden Pot," which is only accessible to the elites with artistic imagination. The spatial imagination can be sensible, not supernatural, as in Wells's "The

Country of the Blind" where the man with vision is eventually considered faulty, a retelling of the Platonic myth. Cortázar contrived a metamorphosis of space merely by craftily shifting the narration into the other side of the Möbius strip, such as in "Continuity of Parks." Andersen's "The Marsh King's Daughter" should be considered a complex representation of imaginary space that comprises dream, Faerie, exotic realm and metamorphosis of time into strange space.

Subject "I" Confronted with Humans

Besides this imagination conjured up by the insecurity confronting time and space, the percipient's next cause of insecurity will be found in people, including himself. This is the imaginary of the first person subject *I* confronted with human beings of the first person *I*, the second person *you*, and the third person *he/she/they*: themes of first person against first person, themes of first person against second person and themes of first person against third person. Since all humans are dominated by time and space, the following relations between the subject and the object will often interplay with the imaginary of time and space. The intimate living percept that places the percipient into insecurity is the percipient's very own image, which can be extrapolated respectively as the principal theme of Doppelganger, including the redoubled identity of the subject *I* (Poe's "William Wilson"), the split personality (Stevenson's *The Strange Case of Dr Jekyll and Mr Hyde*) and the parted parts of the body such as the shadow (Chamisso's *Peter Schlemihl* and Andersen's "The Shadow"), reflection (Hoffmann's "A New Year's Eve Adventure"), portrait (Wilde's *The Picture of Dorian Gray*) or corporal parts (Gogol's "The Nose," Maupassant's "La Main" (The Hand) or Nerval's *La Main enchantée* (*The Enchanted Hand*)).

The theme of *I* vis-à-vis *you* derives from the Jungian archetype of anima and animus, i.e. the amalgamation of *I* with *you* as a second oneness. The most common motif under this thematic scale is fantastic love. William Morris's novel *Well at the World's End* succeeds along the lines of Platonic philosophy of love that initiates the ultimate truth, the model of this imaginary of love is Apuleius's *The Golden Ass*. Espousing Neo-Platonism, Nodier's "Lydie ou la résurrection" (Lydie or the Resurrection) offers a fantastic trip into the intermediate space between the human world and paradise guided by the heroine's beloved dead husband. Another of Nodier's tales, "La Fée aux miettes" (The Fairy of Crumbs) tells how the naïve hero attains absolute happiness in the realm of Faerie by the fairy's initiation. Similar examples of fantastic love are numerous in fairy tales, for example Andersen's "The Snow Queen," and other fantastic romances in Arthurian legend. If woman as spiritual initiator appears rarely in the fantastic tales of Christian culture, Chinese fantastic tales abound with this motif of supernatural love to the point of saturation. The deceased woman in "Li

Zhangwu zhuan," the divine women in "Liu Chen and Ran Zhao" and "Pei Hang," the plant fairies in "Pianpian," the fox-women in "Qing Feng" and other numerous tales on fox-women by Pu Songling, all depict how love can initiate the hero to a higher accomplishment of spiritual wisdom and secular richness. This kind of works presents the resurrection of the beloved from the other world. Examples are Villiers de l'Isle-Adam's "Véra," Gautier's "Arria Marcella" and Dumas's "Le Bracelet de cheveux" (The Bracelet of Hair).

This *I-you* theme of the fantastic is often suited to psychoanalytical application or rather diagnosis, since the repressed desire is intimately related to phantasm. The images of ghosts or other supernatural beings are often interpreted as beings projected by the repressed desire; suffice it to adduce the following tales: James's *The Turn of the Screw*, Potocki's "The Story of the Demoniac Pacheco," Cazotte's *Le Diable amoureux* (*The Devil in Love*), Gautier's "Omphale, histoire rococo," "Arria Marcella" and "La Morte amoureuse." A central motif coupled with this fantastic love is the interference of the Father figure. Gautier excels in arranging such figures in his stories. The woman from the tapestry of "Omphale" is obstructed forever, since the hero's uncle sells the tapestry; Arria Marcella is exorcized by the father from her times and the vampire Clarimonde is eventually annihilated by the priest Sérapion. Dominated by Durand's diurnal regime of the imaginary, this *you* as desired object can be accompanied by the three visages of time (theriomorphic, nyctomorphic and catamorphic) and deformed into the recurrent theme of *la femme fatale*, for example, the fatal woman in Goethe's *Die Braut von Korinth* (*The Bride of Corinth*) the enchanting damsel in Keats's "La Belle Dame sans Mercy" and in Eichendorff's "Autumn Sorcery" or the medusa and serpentine figure in Coleridge's "The Rime of the Ancient Mariner."

Deviating from the intimate relations between *I* and *you*, the individual imaginary vis-à-vis the distant others of the third person is more coloured with insecurity that arouses a strong feeling of disquietude. Poe's paranoiac narrator of "The Tell-Tale Heart" madly kills the old man just because his vulture-like eye that unnerves him. This uncanny feeling originates from the insecurity and the fear towards the unfamiliar and strange others. Once combined with Durand's diurnal visage of time, the insecurity is driven to hyperbolic tyranny. Hoffmann's "The Sandman" also creates the uncanny feeling from this fear towards others, in the present case, a mysterious and sinister master of the hero's father. This fear is connected with the theriomorphic image of the sandman and haunts the hero's life until his tragic end. The disillusion of the hero in Hawthorne's "Young Goodman Brown" from the nocturnal journey into the unknown forest (can be partially regarded as the imaginary of the inanimate object) may originate with his insecurity towards others in his village, who are in reality devilish. Kafka's fantastic tales place absurdity and pathos in the centre of this human relationship in the family and society which deforms the reality, such as *Metamorphosis* and "The Country Doctor."

Subject "I" Confronted with the Nonhuman

The last angle of the fantastic thematic triangle schema is the imaginary concerning the nonhuman, which is further divided into the animate and the inanimate. The former includes the imaginary of animals, monsters, extra-terrestrials, devils, fairies, gods, etc.; the latter involves the imaginary of vegetation, objects and concrete space. Durand's theory of theriomorphic symbols from the diurnal regime will be extended by the Daoist, Hindu visions, Buddhist reincarnation. American Indian myth on the genesis of man corresponds to the theriomorphic imagination that is integrated into the nocturnal regime. The First Nations of Canada, human beings were originally animals that metamorphosed into human form at night. But one day, one tribe decided to assume human form forever and thus started the race of man [Bridge, 16-25]. Here we have a combination of theriomorphic and nocturnal imagination. This universality in imagining the relations between man and the nonhuman is further analyzed by Jung in terms of the unconscious. Besides, his interpretation of the archetypal images of animals as the representation of our libido (different from Freudian libido) is similar to the Hindu or Daoist conceptions of animal spirits.

Animals are attributed with temporality, dynamism, primitive spirit and bestiality. With this semantic richness in the imaginary of animals, fantastic literature features most tales revolving around animal behaviour and its relations with human beings. Animal fables or bestiaries depict the unknown world, including language, behaviours and thought, of animals, for example, the Greek Aesop's fables, French medieval animal romance of *Le Roman de Renart* and French writer La Fontaine's *Fables*. Numerous examples of the metamorphosis between man and animal can be found in fairy tales. In the Grimms' tales, a frog can turn into a prince ("The Frog-Prince") and a pretty girl is changed into a frog ("Cherry, or the Frog-Bride") or a boy metamorphoses into a fawn after drinking the spellbound water ("Hansel and Grettel"). Under the pen of Andersen, animals are not only anthropomorphic but also attributed with virtue to sacrifice for love, "The Little Mermaid" remaining a fresh memory to readers. Richard Adams' *Watership Down* and several other books are examples of human imagination of animals. The Chinese imaginary of animals is an identical projection of human nature underpinned by the belief of reincarnation and Daoist vision of eternal equilibrium through metamorphosis. This mystic and escapist world vision concerning unknown animals has generated myriads of fantastic tales about metamorphosis between men and animals and interactions between them. Suffice it to adduce examples of the old man Hao transforming into a tiger in "Hao

Huahu" (Hao Paints the Tiger), the monkey that hoaxes man in "Qiuxin lu" (Quest for a Heart), the eponymic hero transforming into a fish in "Xue Wei," the eponymic hero metamorphosing into a tiger and eating his neighbours in "Zhang Feng" and the numerous fox-women stories by Pu Songling. All kinds of animals have their role to play in Chinese fantastic tales and they are exactly as human as the animals in Western fables.

One ambiguous animal or imaginary beast should be clarified here. While the mysterious beast or monster of dragon is the very concretization and symbol of evil in Western culture (Tolkien deemed dragons as the perfect creature of evil), the Chinese dragon is a divine creature mediating between men and gods. The Chinese imaginary also creates dragon kings (the gods of seas) that govern the dragon palace underwater. Therefore, it is not surprising to read a fantastic tale ("Liu Yi chuan shu" (Liu Yi Sends the Message)) about the love and marriage between a general Liu Yi and the stray daughter of the dragon king. In contrast, the dragon figure is more vividly depicted in the Western fantastic literature with ambiguous colours. The first storytelling about the naissance of the creature dragon comes from the Nordic myth that presents the dragon transformed from a wicked dwarf who kills his own family out of greed for the gold ring. Readers may refer to the retelling of "The Story of Sigurd" by Andrew Lang to learn about the wicked nature of the dragon. The most famous dragon in European literature is Grendel from the English medieval *Beowulf*, which stages a wicked dragon with a paradoxical complex of its ineluctable fall. In "The Reluctant Dragon," Kenneth Grahame depicts a pacific dragon that is immersed in literature and refuses to fight with Saint Geroge. E. Nesbit, specialist of telling dragon stories, describes a dragon fooled by human beings in "The Dragon Tamers." This interesting tale evokes Tolkien's dragon Chrysophylax Dives in "Farmer Giles of Ham" where he portrays in a humorous manner the dragon as stupid and somewhat naïf creature. However, in his mythology *Silmarillion* and the ring trilogy, Tolkien pens the dragons as the genuine devil that incarnates Shadow. Dragons are minions of Melkor in Angband. Glaurung features the first of the Uruloki, the fire-drakes (fire-serpent or dragon) of the North, who are the perpetual enemy to Elves.

Besides the dragon, the snake, with a similar form to the dragon, is a symbol of evil in Western culture, especially under the reign of Christianity. Milton presented a vivid picture of snakes as devilish animals and minions of Satan in *Paradise Lost*. Nevertheless, romantic fantastic tales retrieve the pristine primeval imagination of the snake and salamander that is attributed as possessing wisdom with symbolic fire. Hoffmann's "The Golden Pot" portrays Serpentina (snake-girl) as the student Anselmus's ideal love that initiates him and opens his eyes to an ultimate truth. With his unique artistic vision and taste of love, he enters the realm of the unknown: Atlantis. While snakes are absolutely the evil symbol in the Christian world, they are endowed with a double meaning for the

Chinese. On the one hand, they can be evil spirits that harm the human soul and body, such as the snake-woman in "Baishe ji" (The White Snake) that lures the hero and eats him. On the other hand, snakes are considered as a lower rank incarnation of divine dragons and can reach the divine state of dragon by means of Daoist practice. This ambiguous trait in snakes is portrayed in the story of *Baishe zhuang* (*Biography of the White Snake*), in which a white snake-woman falls in love with a literatus Xu Xian and is eventually exorcized by a Buddhist monk. The story has thus become a beautiful and romantic tragedy of the heroine snake-woman. This story takes place on the day of the dragon boat festival and thus becomes the token of the festival that also reminds people to hang talismans on that day to ward off evil spirits.

Besides the dragon and the snake, the cat is a mysterious and sinister animal in the West as well as in the East. In Chinese superstition, cats can die nine times and are capable of taking revenge; they are generally considered ominous. The Japanese writer Kurahashi Yumiko's "The House of the Black Cat" tells a weird tale about a video photographer and his family that are suspected to be cats. In Western culture, this negative impression of the imaginary of cats is represented in fantastic tales such as Poe's "The Black Cat." Parallel to the contrast between the horror and marvellous style of fantastic tales, cats can be beneficial to men such as the cat in Brothers Grimm's "The Poor Miller's Boy and the Cat" that can be a princess and Perrault's "The Puss in Boots" that can help men improve material life.

Many kinds of animals feature in fantastic literature, such as axolotls in Cortázar's "Axolotl" and beasts in "House Taken Over"; the disquieting insects like the mob in Susanna Clarke's "Mrs Mabb" and the bug in Kafka's *The Metamorphosis*. Gregor's metamorphosis into a bug forces him to find meanings of his existence related to his family and society; however, as a bug, his being denied a voice makes his death more pathetic. The disquieting insects may deny discourses; on the contrary, more often than annihilating the *parole*, fantastic literature imagines animals such as storks, nightingales and lions as *spokespersons* that regain men's lost words and enunciate *the meanings*. They not only are personified but also animate the metaphorical meanings. The storks tell the story as intradiegetic narrators of Andersen's "The Marsh King's Daughter" and divulge the cruel deeds of the heroine's sisters, the very true visage of human wickedness. Wilde confers the discourse to the Linnet with his audiences the Duck and the Water-rat to tell the story of the poor Little Hans in "The Devoted Friend," which uncovers human relentlessness and selfishness. Birds are often considered benevolent and near-divine in fantastic creation. The speaker of "The Rime of the Ancient Mariner" kills the albatross, to be punished by the ensuing sinister adventures. The bird in "The Story of Sigurd" reminds Sigurd to eat the slain dragon's heart and to kill his real enemy. The affectionate nightingales in

Wilde's "The Nightingale and the Rose" and Andersen's "The Nightingale" are portrayed as a romantic dreamer and a faithful friend and artist respectively.

The extreme deformation of animal imagination predominated by the iso-topic symbols of time visages from the diurnal imaginary regime incarnates the devil and monster. Devils can be seen as the modification of dragon and snake images incorporated with the imaginary of Satan. Victor Hugo, though a realistic novelist and playwright, still pictured a devil tricked by two saints and eventu-ally becoming crippled in his "Le Diable chiffonnier" (The Rag-and-Bone Devil). In the Faust legend, Lucifer (the prince of devils) and Mephistopheles represent a vivid picture of the Western devils. Sara Douglass envisages in "The Evil Within" gargoyles to be hybrids from devils and hounds of Hades and that the evil within human beings can never stop chasing such monsters. Maupassant told another story about the devil tricked by a saint in "La Légende du Mont Saint-Michel," Nerval created a special kind of monster begotten from the ab-stract devil and human in "Le Monstre vert" (The Green Monster).

This imaginary of hybridism between the devil and human finds its coun-terpart in the hybridism between the beast and human. The Chinese fantastic tale of "Bujiangzong baiyuan zhuan" (The White Monkey) implies that the heroine is abducted by a big white monkey and later gives birth to its hybrid. Mérimée's "Lokis" tells an ambiguous story about the mysterious birth of the count whose mother is alleged to be kidnapped and raped by a bear. The end of the story is a bloody scene of the count's fiancée ferociously murdered (as if by a beast) on the wedding bed, and this further drives to confirm such an implication.

The imaginary of monsters connected with science and the future creates the most popular creatures of contemporary science-fiction, the extra-terrestrials or aliens. The aliens from Mars under the pen of Wells in *The War of the Worlds* disquiet readers by the hybrid form of human and animal, especially insect. The theriomorphic images of the diurnal regime of the imaginary extend to outer space and are incorporated with the imaginary of disquieting animals to form a general image of the aliens in fantastic literature. This kind of creation makes visible the imaginary of animated nonhuman images from the isotopism of time visages. These devouring bestial images are heroic and antithetic structures of the fantastic. However, the imaginary of the nonhuman can also lead to a tran-scendental euphemism in literary creation, and thus represent the image of light in the fantastic, such as fairies, deities and gods or God. As to fairies and deities, examples are ubiquitous in the Western fairy tales, mythic tales and Christian tales or allegories.

Chinese fantastic tales show more interest in depicting the divinities, in-cluding the original gods and the gods reincarnated or transformed from humans. The Daoist novel *Fengshen Yanyi* (*The Investiture of the Gods*) centres on the respective stories of gods, alchemists, immortals and men and how gods have been nominated. The imaginary of God is unique as its position in Chinese literature; Yuhuang Dadi (The Emperor God) is the Chinese counterpart of the Western monotheistic God. More fantastic works from the first two periods of creation take pains to delineate the visages of the divinity. In Western Antiquity, Ovid's *Metamorphoses* centred on gods, and on heroes ascending to the rank of gods. Apuleius's *The Golden Ass* also depicts fairies and gods blended with human stories. Dante and Milton portrayed the grace and power of the almighty God. In the prologue of Goethe's *Faust*, readers or audiences are presented with a conversation, rather a bet, and interaction between God and Mephistopheles. Tolkien incarnated the spirit of God by his sub-creation of *Silmarillion* and the ring trilogy into his mythological Eru the One or God and Ainur the Holy Ones or gods, including the lower degree maiar, and elves, dwarfs and other related creatures from the imaginary of light. This human imaginary of antithesis between the devouring theriomorphic images and the ascending glistening images of time or the unknown principle perpetuates the poeticization of the fantastic imagination.

Rooted in the primitive mentality with a vision of pantheism or natural gods, the imaginary of inanimate percepts inspires to tell fantastic stories about the actions of metamorphosis, inclusive of enchantment and animation. This inanimate imaginary can be further divided into objects, vegetation and physical space (different from the universal or abstract space mentioned in the imaginary of subject confronted with time-space). The history of the theme of the inanimate animating is as long as fantastic literature. Early in Chinese literature *Lie Zi* tells a tale about an automaton dancer that acts like a real woman. This very fact makes the king meditate the difference between man as creator and the Demiurge as creator. This story may feature as the earliest record of an automaton in literary history. In Latin literature, Ovid's *Metamorphoses* shows that the Universe and Nature perpetually animate. The episode of Pygmalion features the first Western story of automation. The sculptor Pygmalion marries his animated sculpture with the help of Venus. This story has served ever since as a fantastic model to later writings grounded on such a theme. The theme of an artist who loves his own creation and espouses it/her is universal in fantastic literature. Tales of such themes also abound in Chinese fantastic literature; for example, the story of "Zhenzhen" tells about a painter who conjures up the painted figure (in reality a fairy) to come out of his painting so as to establish a family with him. However, the woman eventually returns with their son to the painting because the painter suspects that she is an evil spirit.

This animation theme may combine with the theme of doppelganger to make a horrible story like *The Picture of Dorian Gray* where the picture animates with flesh and soul, while the model Gray never ages. Mérimée integrates the goddess that animates Pygmalion's sculpture into a wicked bronze statue to create a femme fatale that takes revenge in "The Venus of Illes." The statue remains in the whole story as an unnerving object with indications of slight animation and eventually animates, walks and kills the bridegroom. Though many statues depicted in fantastic literature are menacing, they can be benedictional as Pygmalion's wife, for example, the statue in Wilde's "The Happy Prince." In this story, the animated statue (in the eyes of readers and the Swallow) serves as a piercing contrast to men's being ingrate and realistic.

The superstition that antiques often bear magic powers, even cursed and ominous, is a recurrent theme in fantastic tales. Gautier's "Le Pied de momie" (The Foot of the Mummy) presents an antique of the foot of an Egyptian princess that animates and forces the hero who has purchased the object to go back to the times of ancient Egypt. Another story of Gautier's, "La Cafetière" (The Coffeepot) also centres on the animation of an object, here a coffeepot metamorphosing into a girl and holding a party with the hero. Besides the animation of a statue, Mérimée elaborated a story that the paintings and tapestries animate to divulge a murderous future before the eyes of the king in "Vision de Charles XI."

The malicious judge in the portrait of "The Judge's House" (Stoker) starts the animation by wicked smiles and evil eyes and eventually comes out of the portrait to hang the poor student. In this case, objects are haunted by evil spirits or ghosts. The imaginary of a microcosm existing in miniature objects forms many fantastic tales, especially fairy tales. Hoffmann depicted an animated universe of toys and household decorations in "The Nutcracker," where the figure from the nutcracker animates and becomes a real charming prince. In the aforementioned tale of "The Golden Pot," the golden pot is a magic object that links the realm of the known and the unknown. In both Alice's books of Carroll, the figures of pokers and of chess animate and speak and interact with Alice. Gaiman, a contemporary writer, even imagines the star, distant in the sky, into a fallen fairy in his novel *Stardust*.

Under the influence of a Daoist world vision, Chinese fantastic offers a variety of animation stories, such as "Xiangyang laosou" (The Old Man from Xiangyang) where sculptures animate, "Wuse bi" (Brush of Five Colours) that presents a magic brush to create paintings able to animate, "Yuan Wuyou" where the eponymic literatus witnesses four poets improvise poems in the middle of the night and discovers that they are nothing but a pestle, a candleholder, a bucket and a broken stove the following morning. Lives in the objects from this Chinese tale evoke tales from Andersen: the conversation between the pen and the inkwell in "Pen and Inkwell" and the monologue of the teapot in "The Teapot." The humble teapot is further reminiscent of Wilde's self-deceived rocket in "The Remarkable Rocket." Near the end of the nineteenth century, Maupassant appeared more scientific in depicting the phenomenon of animation. His tales reflect the popularity of magnetism in his times, for example, in "Un fou?" (A Madman) and "Magnétisme," the character is able to make the objects on the table move. Mauppasant was rather skeptical about the ability and pushed it to the natural explication of magnetism, a future science.

Just as the objects are imagined to animate in literary creation, vegetation is even more apt to animate since it is alive. According to Daoist cosmogony, the world is a permanent bio-chemical metamorphosis, a man can transform into a tree or an animal. The Buddhist vision offers the concept of karma with an eternal return of reincarnation in all beings, including vegetation. Greek pantheism underlies the imaginary metamorphosis in Western literature, for example, Daphne changes into a laurel to escape Apollo's chase. In the primitive conception, man was a part of nature and saw nature as himself. Rivers, mountains, trees, animals and all other elements were anthropomorphic. Nodier's "La Fée aux Miettes" (The Fairy of Crumbs) presents a mandragora that chants and the country of the plants inhabited by the fairy, where the hero George eventually joins her. Daudet's "Wood'stown" indicates a critical viewpoint on men's invading natural space and tells a horrible story about how trees revenge themselves on the inhabitants of the town who wantonly clear the woods and destroy nature. The end of the story is open as the woods invade the town and reclaim their territory. From the nineteenth-century focus on space intrusion to the twentieth-century environmental destruction and pollution, Tolkien's vivid portrayal of the hostile willows and the friendly Ents is a twentieth century idiosyncratic fantasy of vegetation that reflects the traditional imagination of the fantastic (The forest has its own life) and the modern eco-critical perspective (the industrial destruction of nature drives them to fight back). The imaginary of vegetation in fantastic literature is further developed in contemporary eco-critical writing.

The traditional imaginary of an enchanting forest as a pagan world is a typical motif in the knight's tale. Eichendorff's hero from "Autumn Sorcery" is lost in the forest and is never able to escape the haunting spider web of this pagan space. The same enchanting space plays a menacing role in Keats's "La Belle Dame sans Mercy" where a knight loiters in the wilderness under the enchantment of a beautiful damsel. Forests are also intimately related to animals; therefore many tales with motifs of man-animal metamorphosis take place in the forest, for example, the above mentioned "Loki" and "Zhang Feng."

Besides the insecurity that generates the fantastic imagination from the land, water is another principal element that composes disquieting space. As already mentioned, many of Maupasant's fantastic tales take place by the waters, especially the river Seine ("Sur l'eau" and "La Nuit") and the Atlantic ocean by Normandy ("La Légende du mont Saint-Michel"). The dreadful image of the marshes in Tolkien's *The Two Towers* also demonstrates the imaginary of water-space with the connotation of peril and death. Frankenstein dies and his monster disappears in the immense Nordic sea. In Chinese literature, the hero of "Liu Yi" encounters the daughter of the dragon king by the lake Dongting and starts his adventure in the dragon king palace under waters. In the story "Lihun ji" (The Soul Separates from the Body), the heroine's soul is parted from her body to join her cousin in a boat by the waters.

If water gives the image of vertical extension downward, as Bachelard analyzes in his material imagination, then the mountain extends the imaginary upward. Chinese imaginary of mountains is rather spiritual and divine. A Daoist who succeeds in the practice to reach the absolute state or to gain Dao or simply to be immortal, is entitled *Xian* – immortal man in the mountains. Thus the hero in "Qiuxin lu" (Quest of a Heart) lets himself be fooled without doubt by a monkey who pretends to be a Daoist master recluse in the remote mountains. In "L'Orgue du Titan" (The Organ of Titan), one of George Sand's tales from her collection of *Contes de Grand Mère* (*Grandmother's Tales*), the mountains are occupied by the spirits of Titans who metamorphose before the eyes of the hero and initiate him into the power of musical creation.

The imaginary of geographical space imbued with antiquity plays an important role in the contrivance of fantastic plot, for example, Rome in W. Jensens's *Gradiva* and Pompeii in Gautier's "Arria Marcella." The haunted house is the main universal location for fantastic literature, especially ghost stories: the sinister Gothic house and school in Poe's "The Fall of the House Usher" and "William Wilson," the mysterious and haunted mansion Bells in Edith Wharton's "Mr. Jones," the famous haunted mansion of Wilde's "The Canterville Ghost," the haunted old house of Stoker's "The Judge's House," the haunted cellar in Nerval's "Le Monstre vert" (The Green Monster), the haunted castle in Nodier's "Inès de las Sierras," and various places related to death. Among all haunted places, the most dreadful should be the space of the dead, tombs, cemeteries or guillotines. The horrible guillotines brood in many French authors' imagination to depict beheaded ghosts such as Borel's "Gottfried Wolfgang" or the slaughterman haunted by nemesis in "L'Enfant de la punition" (The Child of the Punishment) by Paul Feval. The story of E. F. Benson's "The Confession of Charles Linkworth" develops around the haunted prison by the executed prisoner. Dumas's "Les Tombeaux de Saint-Denis" (The Tombs of Saint-Denis) stages the apparition of the spectre of the French king Henri IV around the royal cemetery. The hero in Maupassant's "La Morte" (The Dead Woman) witnesses a supernatural scene of the dead coming out of their tombs to write down the deeds of their past lives. In Asian literature, Chinese, Japanese or Korean, this fear towards the places and times of death is a predominating imaginary drive in many ghost stories, for example the mansion haunted by fox-women in "Qing Feng" of Pu Songling and the haunted house in "Ci Tuinu" where the ferocious ghost murders the heroine. The old battle field from Antiquity resurrects in "Huazhou canjun" as the hero travels and stays at a hotel there. The heroine in "Lujiang Feng'ao zhuan" encounters a ghost-woman in the approximation of the tomb. The narrator of "Qinmeng ji" (Dream of the Qin Kingdom) dreams of marrying a princess of the Qin kingdom and is informed the next morning that the hotel he stays is the very spot of the tomb of the king Qin Mugong.

As Durand's theory demonstrates, human imagination, based on the axis of diurnal and nocturnal regimes, is always dualistical. Therefore, men can imagine religious sanctuaries as both benevolent and malevolent. This is a space that creates insecurity and security at the same time. Dracula moves from his castle in Transylvania to a chapel in London, which should have been a sanctuary to protect people from devils. Mérimée's "Les Âmes du purgatoire" (The Souls of Purgatory) presents the apparition of Don Juan's future tortured soul in Purgatory before his eyes in a church. Balzac's "L'Église" (The Church) depicts the church as a space of disquietude to the hero and projects chilling images of the dead coming from Purgatory. Abel Hugo's "L'Heure de la mort" (The Hour of Death) tells that the hero undergoes a dreamy experience in a church that is also pagan. Just as churches are related to divinity but also to time and death, temples in Chinese literature manifest themselves as places frequented by ghosts and spirits or devils. Pu Songling's "Xiaoqian" features attractive fox-women who seduce the hero in a temple. Another tale of Pu, "Huabi" (Paint the Wall), concerns a mysterious story that invites us to reflect on the meaning of reality since the hero seemingly experiences an adventure with the woman that figures in the painting attached to the wall of a Buddhist temple. This character of oxymoron underlying the aforementioned places illustrates again the very nature of the combination of yin and yang. This is a manifestation of the oxymoron of chôra as space embracing antithesis and hypothesis.

The proposed triangle thematic schema (I / human / nonhuman) reflects the imaginary system of the fantastic at an ostensive level. The subject *I* at the centre of the relation and at the top of the triangle echoes with Jung's process of individuation of the ego. The Jungian mystic participation offers a third way, the creative imagination related to the individual projection in communion with the collective unconscious. The archetypes of anima, animus, shadow, the wise old man and others are concretized in the imaginary conducted under the scheme of the thematic triangle. Under the scope of Bachelard's material poetics, the universal roots of the rudimentary elements also project and fashion the metaphors and metamorphosis of the fantastic. Durand's imaginary of the diurnal and nocturnal regimes constructs the basic formation of the themes deriving from the subject faced with time and space.

As Durand observed, the isotopism of the unknown images rich in semantism will metamorphose by the extrinsic dynamism from the intrinsic semantic attachment. The fashioning process of images in transformation parallels the transformation and manifestation of the particles out of the mysterious space of chôra. This third way is exactly fantastic storytelling, the primitive mimesis of mythopoeia. We have so far delved into the imaginary in relation to mythopoeia, mimesis, metaphysics and metamorphosis. Bachelard's insight into the origin of metaphor with metamorphosis and its correlation with poetic language that vibrates with metaphysic is embodied in fantastic storytelling. The embodiment of the aforementioned thematic imagination further demonstrates the matter of figures in metaphors. Grounded in metamorphosis, metaphor is a composite of oratory and ordinary discourse as well as of literary discourse. However, in the course of linguistic evolution, metaphor eventually finds itself to be a selective place of poetry. Its abasement into the alleged "figurative" can only be raised and purified by the musicality of hypotyposis of fantastic storytelling. To retrieve the golden visage of myth and language, we have to recover the magic power of metaphors. H. Werner connected metaphors with magic world vision. Metaphors imply primitive imagination of the fantastic. Cassirer stated that antique rhetoric of metonymy and synecdoche comes from a mythic mind. Metaphor is not a substitution, a mere rhetoric rewriting; it is a genuine direct identification in a mythic thinking mode. Roman rhetorician Quintilian remarked that men speak mostly by figures. The alchemical refinement of metaphors or figures of language will be possible through the poeticization of fantastic storytelling. Lastly, we have to return to Nature and its musical harmonism to go through the process of the Eucharistic alchemy of language.

Unus Mundus of Harmonism –
Music and the Eucharistic Alchemy of Language

The exploration of the imaginary brings to light the depth of the unknown realm related to the *inventio* of the fantastic *mimesis* underlying the rhetoric and style of the narrative creation. The mythopoeia of fantastic literature harmonizes the severance from semantic unity in language and meanings, entailed throughout the evolution of human consciousness. This imaginary harmonization harks back to the mutating space of Platonic chôra or *Liangyi* (first change that makes antithesis of yin and yang) through the mystic participation of creative imagination into the Jungian collective unconscious, the vibration between the poetic images and the four elements (*Sixiang* (the four elements of yang-yang, yang-yin, yin-yang and yin-yin)) and the purification of the fantastic imagination from the semantism of images (the phenomenological manifestations of *Bagua* (the octa-trigrams)) derived from the diurnal and nocturnal regimes of human reflexes. This profound realm of the unknown human imagination is apt to touch upon remains of primitive people's consciousness in original participation. The acquisition of the known is from the unknown. The mysterious origin of *myth* may lie in the pristine drive of *muthos* (story) about the arcane and impalpable secret of *logos* (the first Causality, God or Principal). Myth is thus the *muthos* of *logos*, albeit both terms suffer from semantic degeneration along the evolution of human consciousness. In this light, mythopoeia bears the DNA of human imagination that incessantly arouses our fantastic creation. This creation mirrors the aesthetics of metamorphosis proposed by Ovid as the perpetual poetic creation and the permanent transformation from Plato's chôra and the perpetual changes of *Yi Jing*. The essence of metamorphosis in fantastic storytelling is in the aesthetics of strangeness.

The aesthetics of strangeness essentially lies in language itself, hence fantastic diction, since the fantastic bears in itself a connotation of strangeness. Barfield defined strangeness in a stylistic way and distinguished it from wonder. This strangeness that arouses wonder can be connected with the function of recovery among the four requisite elements in Tolkien's theory of fairy-story creation. He claimed that a fairy-story should encompass the artistry of Fantasy, the function of Recovery and freedom of Escape and the turn of Consolation. Gaining recovery through the artistry of fantasy (the link between imagination and the final result of sub-creation) illustrates the significance of both psychological reception and stylistic creation. The concept and aesthetics of strangeness will be extended and refined under this scope: the musical style of fantastic diction. Barfield used strangeness to denote a wide variety of effects (archaism is one of the stylistic uses), all of which produce in a reader a sense of the unexpected or unusual:

for wonder is our reaction to things which we are conscious of not quite understanding, or at any rate of understanding less than we thought. The element of
strangeness in beauty has the contrary effect. It arises from contact with a different kind of consciousness from our own, different, yet not so remote that we
cannot partly share it, as indeed, in such a connection, the mere word "contact"
implies. Strangeness, in fact arouses wonder when we do not understand; aesthetic imagination when we do. [Barfield 1973, 177]

The notion of strangeness, in fact, derives from Aristotle's comments on *lexis* in
his *Poetics*. The core function of strangeness lies in its differentiating poetic
language from ordinary or vulgar language, and later from prosaic language.
This kernel concept is effectively the departing point of style, grounded in the
myth of the language of poetry, built on the instauration of lexicons. These
unique lexicons compose a realm of literary language as opposed to ordinary
language. Nonetheless, the term "strangeness" has its variations from the same
semantic field. It is thus necessary to clarify the meaning of strangeness with an
investigation of the scope of lexis and later of style.

The French translation of Aristotle's concept is *écart* or difference. Aristotle's *lexis* concerns the valorization of the foreign (*étranger*) words to ordinary
usage. These words introduce the differences (*écarts*) by their unusual character.
By foreign words, Aristotle meant: "(1) rare words, (2) words with transferred
meanings, (3) lengthened words, and (4) everything which is opposite to the ordinary." And these strange words remove the stately used diction from the
common idiom. As Aristotle postulated, "The function of diction is (1) to make
clear what is said and (2) to lift it above the level of the ordinary" [Aristotle
1970, 45], the style of fantastic literature focuses on the lucidity and purity of
diction and its aesthetic strangeness.

In fact, French poetician Bergez also highlighted the character of strangeness. The gist of his argument on the studies of style lies in the form of *difference* of the text, based on the notion of different stylisticians, "the fact of style
results from a difference (*écart*) of expression in comparison with a standard"
(*le fait de style résulte d'un écart de l'expression par rapport à une norme*)
[Bergez, 62]. The essential feature of difference reminds us of the above review
of strangeness in poetics. This difference and strangeness then hinge on the form
of language in the text.

Strange but familiar language of harmonism refers to both content and form.
Quintilian exposed an expressive theory of style, predominating over French
classicism, often stylistics: "All discourses are composed of what is expressed or
of what expresses, that is to say of content and of form" [qtd. Dessons, 148].
From this angle, style is linked with thought by an analogous relation of imitation, viz. the mimesis is not confined to the content, and the form takes on the
visage of mimesis. This insight of connecting the content of thought and the
form of diction is crucial to the appreciation of fantastic diction. It further indi-

cates that certain words or metric forms correspond to certain imaginary or rhetoric of fantastic stories. By the same token, fantastic literature may manifest an idiosyncratic style of diction as a whole. This is in fact the figure of harmonism, proposed by Fontanier:

> *Harmonism*, where onomatopoeia and alliteration can enter as elements, consists in a choice and a combination of words, in a texture and a layout of the sentence or of the period, so that by the tone, the sounds, the numbers, the cadences, the pauses, and all the other physical qualities, the expression is in harmony with thought or with sentiment. [my translation, Fontanier, 392][40]

"In harmony with" is translated from "s'accorde avec." The word "accord" refers to "imitation." This universality of imitation in thought and style evokes the philosophy of Ernst Cassirer who claimed that symbolic forms of representation articulate truth in different cultures. These forms are further divided into the form of expression (Art), presentation (Myth) and representation (Science) [Cassirer 1955, 24]. The onomatopoeic forms of language characterized by Cassirer as the "symbolic pregnancy" of expression shed light on the imitative harmonism of style. In the expression, the felt life is unified with external object to express human feeling. This expression yields to presentation, as the storytelling of the unknown truth. This vision of unity corresponds to the entirety of imitation. The harmonism in language, appearances and myth evokes the musical harmonization in the creation of primitive imagination that perceives a semantic unity of language. The quintessence of the fantastic as a third way lies in this reunification of form and content in language. The secret of making the alchemy of language possible is: hearken to Nature.

Grounded in the imaginary space of chôra and the four elements, fantastic literature defends the literary synthetic and harmonious Sanctuary against sundered and antithetic Niches by its diction of fantastic style. Every author has his own style, as Barthes and Goethe defined the term.[41] However, fantastic literature has its unique style as an organic entity. A further exploration of myth and language will illustrate fantastic diction, characterized by the style of recovery

---

[40] *L'Harmonisme, où peuvent entrer comme éléments l'Onomatopée et l'Allitération, consiste dans un choix et une combinaison de mots, dans une contexture et une ordonnance de la phrase ou de la période, telles que par le ton, les sons, les nombres, les chutes, les repos, et toutes les autres qualités physiques, l'expressions s'accorde avec la pensée ou avec le sentiment.*

[41] Roland Barthes brought into play the opposition between style and writing to expound his theory in *Degré zero de l'écriture* and defined that style as related to psychological and biological life of the author and by which the thought of literariness is taken from. According to Goethe's definition of manner and style, though mainly for artists, what he deemed as manner mirrors what Barthes defined as style, both are attributed with the author's characteristic performance.

(in terms of Tolkien's fairy-story element) returning to myth. This recovery through the purification of language back into myth with the semantic unity is the communion of Eucharist or alchemy of language. This process of linguistic purification brings us back to hearken to the birds after the epic hero slays the evil dragon. We will be lastly enchanted by the chanting of perpetual musical metamorphosis of fantastic stories. This is the primary music of the Universe as *unus mundus*.

From Sundered Niches to Sanctuary – Fission and Fusion

Fantastic diction should fall in the realm of Sanctuary instead of Niche. I mean by Sanctuary that the fantastic imaginary and diction defend the last stronghold of imagination and poetic language. The meaning of diction is defined according to Aristotle's assumption: "expression [of thought] by means of language – a power which is the same in both metrical and non-metrical language" [Aristotle 1970, 15]. The signification of the compound word – fantastic diction – is an extension of Owen Barfield's definition of poetic diction: "When words are selected and arranged in such a way that their meaning either arouses, or is obviously intended to arouse, aesthetic imagination, the result may be described as *poetic diction*" [ibid., 41]. The aesthetic imagination refers to the key to enter the final participation of human consciousness as proposed by Barfield. It can be associated with Jung's proposal of a third way as creative imagination that conduces to the accomplishment of individuation, the communion and integration between the consciousness and the collective unconscious through synchronicity. This aesthetic imagination extends to metaphysical imagination as the key to come in and go out of the real and the unreal space as promulgated by Daoism. It also brings into play a Eucharist of words that bridges and harmonizes the split meanings through Faerie the perilous realm as proclaimed by Tolkien. Fantastic literature relays poetry by amplifying poetic diction with fantastic diction in that literature in verse centring on lyric poetry is tarnished to a certain extent by dialectical and obscure discourses of fragmentation. For example, in Chinese literature, the prose poems often sacrifice versification for visual images or speculative language. In this manner, the very pristine feature of poetic diction, musical harmony, is waning and the semantic severance waxing. Genuine fantastic diction brings to life the harmonism of the imaginary, semantic richness and sonority. The nature of fluidity in fantastic storytelling echoes with musical harmony, Tolkien's fantastic diction being the example par excellence.

In our times of fragmentation, a phenomenon constructed by the philosophy of deconstruction and by the over-dilation of the alleged semiotic poetics, signs replace literariness or poetics along the lines of Plato's and Aristotle's legacy. The myriad of *écritures* or writings (as Roland Barthes claimed to replace the traditional poetics) accounts for the ubiquitous segments of niches. We are now rather in the vortex of "Discourse for Discourse's sake" or "Sign for Sign's sake" but recollecting from afar the ideal of "Art for art's sake," not to mention the ideal of the unity of form and content. Everyone prays for his own idol of discipline or theory in one's niche, everyone's discourse celebrates the polyphonic ideal. This sundering spirit inhabiting each niche will irremediably jeopardize the poeticity of language and thus mislead literature into a cul-de-sac. It is important not to include all works dealing with the supernatural or the impossible as fantastic literature. Niche implies a meaning of superstition and crudeness without distillation; while Sanctuary – undergirded by human ideal, belief, faith, literary legacy – scintillates with pristine and genuine imagination that intuits the universal value and with conscious and poetic diction that creates the beauty of literariness.

The spirit of *Fantasticism* in the twenty-first century is in essence homogenous to the *Romanticism* in 19th century Europe inasmuch as imagination coupled with language is the pivotal aesthetics of literary creation. The connection between the Romantic and the fantastic is manifested in Western Romanticism and Chinese "Romanticism"[42] in that fantastic literature was resurrected in the Romantic period. In Chinese literature, the *zhiguai* or fantastic tales, with the catalyst of Daoism, thrived in the Six and Tang dynasties. In European literature, Germany, England and France offer an unprecedented corpus of the fantastic. The Romanic period is thus also considered as a time of *"renaissance de l'irrationnel* or renaissance of irrational" (coined by French scholar of fantastic literature, Castex). This notion of renaissance is pertinent to Chinese literature because the "Romantic" writers resorted to the writing – the fantastic that Confucius refused to discourse – against Confucian thought, the rational tradition in Chinese culture. This defiance of Confucianism derives from Daoism that praises metaphysical and mystic imagination with freedom. In Europe, the "renaissance" resurrected among others poetic diction and mythic imagination. In Germany, Goethe proposed systematic imagination; in England, Coleridge highlighted primary or secondary imagination in contrast to fancy; in France, Nodier evaluated the fantastic imagination or reverie. Coleridge's caution of the perilous and false imagination, termed as fancy, is all the more relevant to our times in which contemporary writers are inclined to unlimitedly roam through the lexicons of fancy. The stylistic feature of unfamiliarity or strangeness in literary language espoused by poeticians swerves into a new interpretation of obscurity

---

[42] The term Romanticism or Romantic Movement finds no equivalent in the history of Chinese Literature. Nevertheless, many Chinese literary scholars and writers, such as Lu Xun and Huang Renyu, employed the term Romanticism to characterize literature of the Six dynasties and Tang dynasty because the poets and literati of these dynasties distinguished themselves by the writing style related to imagination, freedom, aesthetic language and nature.

and insignificance. This is absolutely an interpretive fallacy deriving from the exhaustion of imagination and discordance between "foreign words" and "familiar words." Moreover, Aristotle reminded his readers to be wary of the excessive use of "foreign words." The corollary of this fallacy will be the death of literature deluged by linguistic signs; by the same token, the deluge of splintering Niches tolls the bell for Sanctuary.

The pivotal difference between Sanctuary and Niche is the aesthetics and metaphysics of unity. A general slanted notion has reigned over the evolution of human consciousness: logical deduction means continuous fission, and complication means profundity. In Daoist thinking, there is a long tradition of reduction and deduction functioning in harmony with mystic imagination. The principle of the generation of the Universe from Dao, through one, two and three changes to the myriad of things, reveals that the spirit of Dao also resides in the myriad grains. However, it is of import to ward off the discourse of Zen that all is Zen. The manifestation of Dao in the embodiments of fission is only possible through the philosophy of *Yi Jing*, a perpetual fusion from the unending fission into antithesis. This fusion coupled with natural harmony insists upon the principle of unity, be it of psyche or language. Daoist writers retained semantic unity in the practice of alchemy and the fantastic writing, originated with Zhuang Zi's definition of the genre *zhiguai* (fantastic tales), which even precedes shenhua (myth). The unity derives from the word Dao. Zhuang Zi's and Lie Zi's fantastic storytelling are teleological in connecting the mystic imagination with metaphysics. Their narrative art of plot unity mirrors the unity of Dao. This notion of unity is also embraced by some Occidental philosophers from Antiquity to the present day.

Aristotle's poetics portrays unity as the principle of mimesis, albeit he was the forefather of the evolution of Western philosophy oriented towards rational logic, the very cause of today's fission. He counted a unified plot as a requisite for good writing of epic and tragedy. Certain confusion needs to be clarified here. A plot dealing with a single individual does not necessary mean unity of plot. "Therefore, those poets who write a Heracleid, a Thesiad, and poems of that kind appear to be following a wrong principle; for they think that since Heracles was a single individual any plot dealing with him must of necessity have unity" [ibid., 17]. A virtuoso like Homer would compose an epic by not including an account of everything which happened to the hero. According to Aristotle, "Homer has made both the *Iliad* and the *Odyssey* centre around an action which is unified" [ibid., 18], which conforms to Aristotle's poetic demand. This ideal of unity in plot is by no means fortuitous. Mircea Eliade argued that all beings come from a unified totality. Eliade coined this origin *coincidentia oppositorum* (the coincidence of contraries or the primordial totality), the dense and homogeneous chaos containing originally all vitality. He assumed that in the course of cosmogonic evolution, the world is created from the fragmentation of the unitary mass [Eliade 1995, 166]. Accordingly, Eliade's viewpoint, along with the aforementioned Daoist vision, reinforces the conception of holding an ideal of unity in the poetics postulated by Aristotle. The formal unity of poetics converges with the unity of the imaginary and cosmogony. In addition, this nostalgia for the lost paradise of unity is illustrated in Plato's *Banquet* where he adduced Aristophanes's evocation of the original unity of androgyny to presume that man and woman must be united. This imaginary of unity is similar to the Daoist unity of yin and yang. Already in the studies of the imaginary, fantastic creation functions as a third way that bridges the known and the unknown realm and further sublimates transcendentally to the arcane space of chôra understood as the first change of *Yi Jing*'s *Taiji*. Fantastic diction undergoes the process of alchemical language for the sublimation of unity, the fusion from fission, albeit disdained or misunderstood as the writing of the irrational or unreal.

As regards the historical evolution of fission, the three epochs proposed by Goethe serve to expound the scattering of niches. In light of his observation, the last stage of man's mind – a prosaic epoch – is effectively at its prime in our times, where the Romantic master's prognostication is completely fulfilled:

> Qualities that formerly diverged naturally in their development now interfere with each other as hostile elements. And so, chaos has returned – not the original that was fertile and life-bearing, but a chaos of death and decay which even the Spirit of God could not use as material to create another worthy of Him. [Goethe 1994, 204]

The above chaos is fundamentally different from the original chaos of cosmogony. This "chaos of death and decay" characterizes the fission of niches deviating from the original unity. Goethe's prosaic stage indicates the corollary of Barfield's intellectual stage, the convergence of alpha-thinking and beta-thinking. However visionary he was, Goethe failed in warning his contemporaries to rein their rhapsody of desire and dissipation. From the extreme Romanticism of decadent symbolism, through pessimistic modernism with a crepuscular epiphany, to the complete dissolution of postmodernism, the dialectical discourses have been thriving at the detriment of the artistry of literary language.

By comparing two different German works based on the Faustian myth – Goethe's *Faust* (1808 & 1832) and Thomas Mann's *Doctor Faustus* (1947), we can grasp the depravation and exhaustion in the 20th century in contrast with the idealism and exuberance of Goethe's times. The visual images representing the niches through perpetual splitting of language and thought, such as the splinters of Tolkien's silmarils and the pieces of the Sampo in the epic Kalevala, are further illustrated by the synesthesia through musicality of Mann's bedevilled musician Adrian Leverkühn's twelve-tone piece or dodecaphony. This new and horrifying music laments for the impossibility of the "Ode to Joy" ending Beethoven's symphonies. Music is the best medium to measure the disharmony while it is out of tune. In thinking and language, our mind is in fact splitting and abstracting with the process. In music, even white noise is able to bother us. Accordingly, the writing of Mann brings to light this discordant fact in our times by bringing Mephistopheles into play. The dodecaphonic music, though minced into more complicated tones, proves to be inharmoniously tearing instead of solemn profundity. Therefore, music is the pristine sensor to our sundering consciousness. Tolkien also used the devilish image to refer to the corruption of language. The central satanic figure in his mythology *The Silmarillion*, Melkor, wields his devilish power by his evil tongue. He lies to instigate and beguile the Maiar, Elves, Dwarves and Men into severance and strife. Like the severing power accompanying the evolution of human consciousness, the seeds of lies that Melkor "sowed in the hearts of Elves and Men are a seed that does not die and cannot be destroyed; and ever and anon it sprouts anew, and will bear dark fruit even unto the last day" [Tolkien 1999, 310]. Though Melkor is shut beyond the world in the Void, his evil power is still reigning like the lingering shadow and destroys the musical harmony and good will of the Valar:

> But Manwë put forth Morgoth and shut him beyond the World in the Void that is without; and is without; and he cannot himself return again into the World, present and visible, while the Lords of the West are still enthroned. Yet the seeds that he had planted still grew and sprouted, bearing evil fruit, if any would tend them. For his will remained and guided his servants, moving them ever to thwart the will of the Valar and to destroy those that obey them. [ibid., 310]

Durand stressed the significant musical imagination in his synthetic structure of the imaginary. He accorded the synthetic structure of musical harmonization more important than other structures. In light of his argument concerning the imaginary in relation to mythic story, the musical imagination encompasses holistic musical harmonization and secondary harmony from dialectic contrast. To save the original visage of language, it is thus necessary to save its musicality from logical abstraction and unmusical visualization. Therefore, Aristotle's unity of plot echoes with the musical composition of unity, whereas the musical and temporal fluidity of storytelling resonates with the musical kinetic rhythm and movement.

The unprecedented polyphony of theoretical discourses through the postmodern age offers a deconstructed space for brewing fantastic creation. In our idolatrous age, deconstruction renders the fantastic possible. Since the essence in the imaginary of the fantastic lies in storytelling and searching for truth in the unknown, the method of deconstruction serves for the reconstruction of meanings. For example, the romantic fantastic appears as the effect resulting from the cause of deconstructing Rationalism. Despite deconstruction, the central momentum of storytelling and the mythopoeic imagination integrated the fission into re-fusion. Hoffmann wrote against the current of classicism for a literary possibility, apart from music, to arrive at the unknown realm or another "reality" through his musical language. Certainly, sound and vision are encoded through language as inner music and vision that are harmonized through the fantastic imagination to delve into the universal unity. The strangeness and mutation in the fantastic conduce to an ideal space. In "The Golden Pot," Hoffmann imagines an arcadia of Atlantis inhabited by alchemists of the salamander family.

Likewise in France, Nodier first deconstructed Rationalism to reconstruct his thesis that dreams and reveries are the access to truth. He questioned the perceived reality and valued only the fantastic imagination. However, this irrational countercurrent of fantastic creation ebbs away in front of the tides of Realism, Naturalism and Symbolism. The twentieth century underwent continual deconstruction, but in the direction of permanent fission. This extreme of deconstruction as a revolt against the Father or tradition or history inspires the fantastic imagination. The philosophy of Daoism better corroborates such phenomena: the extreme will reverse. Paradoxically, most fantastic works of our times seek for the imaginary "ultimate truth" or portray nostalgia for myths and stories. Tolkien created a mythology for his England and crystallized the truth of light throughout his mythopoeia of fairy-stories. He brought back the ideal semantic unity in language through deconstructing the established worldview and the split language and mind. Latin American writer Paulo Coelho seeks sublime language through his creation of the fantastic, such as his *The Alchemist*. Under the influence of oriental mysticism, Cortázar utilized animated language to portray the mystical logic of Daoist truth in his fantastic short stories. With the fantastic mask, many fantastic authors launched their quest for meanings or more exactly, truth, a word or a sign that nowadays intellectual and rational people irremediably elude. The fantastic is created not to deconstruct, but to reconstruct, maybe by means of deconstruction, but eventually to crystallize the truth.

We witness a long irreducible contrasting force of the polar "yes" and "no" in our times or the dialectic of affirmation and negation. Just as Zen practitioners meditating on the nil of the mundane world and dismiss language, the deconstructionists depart from a method alike and fall into an unending deconstruction. The Zen masters deconstruct to question the true meanings of words to reach Nirvana; whereas the deconstructionists deconstruct to question the logocentrism into a labyrinthine space. While nowadays Zen Buddhism is popular in the West, the renaissance of traditional Buddhism, especially, Hinayan or the Little Vehicle, gradually recuperates its Sanctuary. Finally, Buddhists return to the scriptures that have recorded the words of Buddha. And the cycle repeats again. The end of deconstruction is reconstruction and after the re-establishment, the cycle repeats. This is what Buddhism terms as the cycle of "cheng – zhu – huai – kong" (accomplishment, the prime of stability, deterioration, destruction). We would hopefully expect the resurrection of God/gods (announced dead by men) to reproduce the shattered heart of the world into a living body. This requires imagination and mythic language. Barfield's insight into our severing world caused by the deviation from the original unity further illustrates the aforementioned niches, broken apart but worshiped. By the same token, disparagement of the semantic unity in the original sanctuary, paradise lost of myth and language, arises from such sundering. With a metaphorical interpretation at variance with Nietzsche's, Barfield employs mythic figures to elucidate this observation of our world: "The world, like Dionysus, is torn to pieces by pure intellect; but the poet is Zeus; he has swallowed the heart of the world; and he can reproduce it as a living body" [Barfield 1973, 88].

Style of Recovery –
Fantastic Diction Returns to Myth Aspiring for Chôra

As, in the process of historical development, languages bear within themselves a record of the evolution of human consciousness, the rise and fall of the world's fantastic literature also manifests such conscious evolution. The lacuna of the fantastic mythopoeia in the twentieth-century Chinese literature reveals the undergoing changes in Chinese people's consciousness after the impact of Western civilization, including science and rationalism. This is an epoch of logical analysis in Chinese culture that has long been in the synthetic thinking mode. Similarly, Chinese language also suffers the severing of meanings and the deviation from the poetic to the prosaic. This acceleration of the conscious evolution in Chinese culture throughout last century overshadows the fantastic impulse in that scientific thinking is the core of advancement. Nevertheless, the three thousand years of Chinese literature offer a testimony to the unity of the concrete and abstract in language. In his *Poetic Diction*, Barfield used many Chinese examples to illustrate his assumption of the semantic unity of words.

While Barfield proposed poetic diction as the third way to the reunification of the semantic unity in language as a key to reach the final participation, we would resort to the fusion of the split meanings and worldviews by the fantastic imagination, the underlying philosophy being *Yi Jing*'s perpetual changes and sundering, but throughout harmonization of yin and yang. The idea of harmonization echoes with Fontanier's *harmonism*, through which the integration of the form and the content is possible. The fantastic mythopoeia eventually arouses the musical imagination as a process of Eucharist or purge that vibrates with the nostalgia of harmony to envision a future of unity. This purge of myth hinges on the fantastic diction to retrieve the nexus between the concrete and abstract meanings as to extend to the celestial bridge between the known and the unknown realms.

Tolkien interpreted the import of recovery in creating fairy-stories as pre-requisite before we reach the states of escape:

> We should look at green again and be startled anew (but not blinded) by blue and yellow and red. We should meet the centaur and dragon, and then perhaps suddenly behold, like the ancient shepherd, sheep, and dogs, and horses – and wolves. [...]
>   Recovery [...] is a re-gaining – regaining of a clear view. I do not say 'seeing things as they are' and involve myself with the philosophers, though I might venture to say 'seeing things as we are (or were) meant to see them' [...].
> [Tolkien 1997, 146]

Tolkien used the metaphor of "to clean our windows" to regain the original vision of the things from the "familiarity" out of "appropriation." Confirming the purifying function of fairy-stories of recovery, he claimed, "It was in fairy-stories that I first divined *the potency of the words*, and *the wonder of the things*" [my emphasis, ibid., 147].

Combining things and words is the crux of various assumptions of the history of language and myth. Durand declared the significance of meanings and things in words prior to his thorough exploration and dissection of the human imaginary and the production of rich images. Tolkien's highlighting the recovery in fairy-stories mirrors Durand's retracing to *la fantastique* via the imaginary semantism and Barfield's valuing imagination as the nexus bridging figures and ideas and thus returning to the state of original unity. However, Barfield accorded poets the quality of arousing aesthetic imagination, and this can not be received without reserve. It is undeniable that contemporary poems are not completely free from the impact of alpha-thinking and beta-thinking. We may simply adduce the increasing use of discursive and abstract language in contemporary Chinese poetry. Moreover, the ignorance or disregard of musicality in poetry with the trend of poems in free verse (a Western importation into Chinese literature), reveals our distancing language from primitive harmonization. Maybe this is why Barfield more often quoted great poets from the period of original participation and Romanticism, for example, Homer, Virgil, Dante, Milton, Wordsworth and Shelley, to exemplify his theory. Among the cited poets, the most recent to our times are those from Romanticism. This is coincidentally the epoch of modern resurrection of the fantastic genre. The romantic writers wrote fantastic works mostly to question the known knowledge gained through rationalism and science. They stressed the power of dreams and reveries and quest for an ultimate truth believed along the lines of Neo-Platonism. They may have resorted to mysticism, and valued symbolic language. They searched for the limit of the unknown realm through the aesthetic imagination of freedom. Hoffmann is the paradigmatic figure that represents the combination of music and fantastic to quest for the truth concealed in the unknown realm. The aesthetic unity is embodied in his fantastic tales.

The fantastic creation, inspired from the imagination of the unknown realm, may be the third way to dissolve the split myriads of meanings to blend into a secondary harmony. Arrival at the re-harmony status necessitates the purification of the percipient's vision by means of the fantastic imagination. This first purification of vision refers to the Recovery proposed by Tolkien. His clarification of the concept of escape through recovery may explain the significant role that fantastic diction plays in our times to "clean the windows":

> But the true road of escape from such weariness is not to be found in the willfully awkward, clumsy, or misshapen, not in making all things *dark* or unremittingly *violent*; nor in the *mixing of colours* on through subtlety to drabness, and the fantastical *complication* of shapes to the point of silliness and on towards *delirium*. [my emphasis, ibid., 145-6]

The aforementioned characteristics as a fallacious means of escape, the same fallacy in highlighting strangeness to differentiate (in poetics) as pointed out earlier, frequently feature in the poetry of our times. If poets (taken as poetry composers) lose their readers nowadays, it is not because their literary taste degrades but because great poets like Tolkien resorted to composing fantastic epics. Embracing a similar view to that of Tolkienian recovery, Jacob Grimm stated that:

> The true poet is like a man who is happy anywhere, in endless measure, if he is allowed to look at leaves and grass, to see the sun rise and set. The false poet travels abroad in strange countries and hopes to be uplifted by the mountains of Switzerland, the sky and sea of Italy. He comes to them and is dissatisfied. He is not as happy as the man who stays at home and sees the apple trees flower in spring, and hears the small birds singing among the branches. [Grimm, 13]

In the light of Grimm's definition of the true poet, great fantastic writers are to be evaluated as true poets whose fantastic diction arouses our imagination into communion with the original unity. Recovery of fantastic diction entails a return to the origin of language and myth.

Under the modern scientific anatomy of language and myth, language is obscured into a sign subject to semantic and poetic constituents, whereas myth is simplified to symbolic signs or mathematic parametres that succumb to language. Like language undergoing semantic severing, myth suffers split interpretations from the sundered disciplines in our times. Semiotic poetician Barthes's assertion that myth is speech abases myth under the sign system of language. Structuralist anthropologist Lévy-Strauss assimilated myth to a mathematical language and its symbolic components to phonemes. The theories more akin to history of language and myth are deduced by philologists.

Under the influence of rational vision, many philologists postulate that there exist Roots in language, be it from the perspective of grammar (prefixes, suffixes, inflexions) or of semantics (naissance of metaphor). For example, the inflexions of verbs derive from a root word; metaphor is dependent on prior plain speech. Similarly, German philologist Max Müller surmised that a metaphorical period existed in the history of language: "a wonderful age when a race of anonymous and mighty poets took hold of a bald inventory and saturated it with poetic values" [Barfield 1973, 84]. His assumption of the naissance of metaphor leads to the corollary that myths undergo a similar process of a mysterious "metaphorical period." His postulation of the root of meaning extending to metaphor and myth implies that "the myth is a kind of disease of language" [ibid., 89]. This "distorted" (epithet offered by Barfield) vision on myth and language was also deprecated by Tolkien who retorted that "European languages are a disease of mythology" [Tolkien 1997, 122]. Theorists and scholars of modern times are inclined to submit literature and myth to scientific study. They may be deceiving themselves by taking the studies of literature and myth farther and farther from the core spirit of the subject – Imagination. This rational orientation in literary and mythological researches may be questioned again in our times as fantastic literature gradually recovers its poetic significance.

The countercurrent to the above rational and scientific approach to the history of myth and language proposes both aesthetic and philological judgment. Imagination plays a crucial role in the observation of the evolution of myth and language. Durand's theory on myth enhances this revision of myth and language. Refuting Barthes's poststructuralist interpretation of myth and literary language and Lévy-Strauss's mathematical simplification of myth, Durand's postulate hinges on the mythic or fantastic imagination (*la fantastique*) as the original source of what we gain as knowledge and logical language through the mediation of formalization. Durand contended that "myth is always primary in all the meanings of the term and that is definitely far from the product of repression or of some derivation, it is the figurative meaning that prevails over the literal meaning" (*le mythe est toujours premier dans tous les sens du terme et que, bien loin d'être le produit d'un refoulement ou d'une quelconque dérivation, c'est le sens figuré qui prime le sens proper*) [Durand 1992, 458]. His presumption that the figurative meanings of language are *de facto* the important ones echoes Barfield's philological supposition. Interestingly, both theorists used Chinese thought and language in important examples. The former introduces the Daoist notion of yin and yang to elucidate his synthetic structure of myth; the latter refers to the semantic unity in Chinese language.[43] This also explains the bias in

---

[43] Though Barfield adduced Chinese language as evidence to prove his hypothesis of a semantic unity in language, he did not offer any Chinese words to illustrate his theory. We

defining fantastic literature in the East and the West. For Chinese writers, fantastic themes are meaningful and decisive in defining the uniqueness of the genre. For example, the word ghost is taken in the reference system. "Ghost" means those who come back after death and the mourning family members wait for their dead beloved to come back to the house seven days after his/her death. In contrast, modern Western reception of the unknown tends to treat fantastic writing as a play on words. The word "ghost" is abased and abstracted to the level of signifying without signification and reference. This discrepancy in the meanings of fantastic characters or phenomena illustrates the differences in the evolution of human consciousness and language.

The above perspective on myth and language mirrors the studies conducted by Ernst Cassirer. Like Barfield and Tolkien who held that myth is the pristine language, Cassirer found the clue to the understanding of the genesis of language in the conception of myth. He claimed that it "is in intuitive creative form of myth, and not in the formation of our discursive theoretical concepts, that we must look for the key that may unlock the secrets of the original conceptions of language" [Cassirer 1946, 34]. He differentiated formal logic from mythical language. The former demonstrates a feature of extension, the nature of quantity; the latter an interior contraction focusing on lighting and meanings, the nature of quality. This conception corresponds to Durand's distinction between formal logic and the fantastic imagination or myth. The fantastic imagination appertains to the quality of meaning and lighting. Throughout human communication, the core quality requires extension of mediation by means of formal logic. The transformation and abstraction from mythical language to split and abstract language and formal logic again shows the evolution of human consciousness and language. Cassirer took Usener as example to support his theory of mythical language. Usener considered that truth, myth and language take place synchronically with the concept of *Augenblicksgötter* (Moment God) that is "the creation

---

would, on this occasion, complement his assumption by giving examples of Chinese words. The word *fengshui* signifies specific *qi* (breath or vibration) of the location and bearing of a person's house and ancestral grave, supposed to have an influence on the fortune and health of the person, the family and his offspring. The above definition is grounded in a formalized language, rather as an explanation to foreigners. However, we can just define *fengshui* as the vibration and circulation of *feng* (wind or air) and *shui* (water). The figures of air and water signify that a house of good *fengshui* is able to conserve the air and *qi* and stop at the limit of water. If the house is of bad *fengshui*, the air won't breathe and water is either stagnant or flooding. The semantic unity remains in *fengshui*. Another example to be adduced is related to phrenologic divination. The word *jiangutou* means a despicable or ignoble person. According to phrenologic divination, a person's milieu and moral character can be read through his bones. By means of feeling or just observing a person's bones (with naked eyes not x-ray), the seer can tell the life of his client. The word *jiangutou* encompasses both figure and abstract meaning, the character *jian* means despicable, *gutou* means bone(s). Myriads of such examples can be found in Chinese language.

of a moment [and the god] becomes an independent being, which henceforth lives on by a law of his own" [ibid., 35]. For Cassirer, primitive words are assimilated with the image of gods. However, "language itself is what initiates [the] articulations [the analysis of reality], and develops them in its own sphere" [ibid., 12]. Language and mythic thinking split out of an original unity. Language gradually gains its logical power by lagging behind art and myth. Literature is attributed with a double quality of art and myth, as against language.

Usener's concept of Moment God reminds us of Tolkien's exemplification of the Norse Thunder God, Thórr, to illustrate his belief that "legends and myths are largely made of 'truth.'" He brought to light Thórr's idiosyncratic features, which have nothing to do with thunder or lightning such as red beard, loud voice and violent temper and raises the following question:

> Which came first, nature-allegories about personalized thunder in the mountains, splitting rocks and trees; or stories about an irascible, not very clever, red-beard farmer, of a strength beyond common measure, a person (in all but mere stature) very like the Northern farmers, the boendr by whom Thórr was chiefly beloved? [Tolkien 1997, 124]

Here is the answer Tolkien proposed for readers: "It is more reasonable to suppose that the farmer popped up in the very moment when Thunder got a voice and face; that there was a distant growl of thunder in the hills every time a story-teller heard a farmer in a rage" [ibid., 124]. The notion of the semantic unity in myth mirrors the picturesque reality in the age of original participation. His story of "Farmer Giles of Ham" can better illustrate such an assumption of unity.

As regards mythology and religion, we could accordingly surmise that the unity should have existed before the sundering of language and the human mind, given that the Moment God can be further perceived and received as a religious God. Chinese Daoism portrays such a perception of gods since Daoism is the philosophy of nature. Andrew Lang viewed mythology and religion as two distinct things that have become entangled, albeit he claimed that mythology shows little religious significance. Tolkien attributed the religious divinity or the mystical to one of the three faces of fairy-stories.[44] MacDonald's "The Golden Key" obviously purports that fairy tales and religion (or the mystical divinity) can be conflated into unity that leads further to the divine realm through Faerie. The religious and sublime tone of the story invites readers to reconsider the semantic unity of language, including the abstract, figure and even divinity. Fantastic literature dreams of going back to the Golden Age of *unus mundus*. This recovery of fantastic literature back to the pristine state of myth entails the return to An-

---

[44] "Mystical towards the Supernatural; the Magical towards Nature; and the Mirror of scorn and pity towards Man" [Tolkien 1997, 125].

tiquity. The very first catalyst for the refinement of language back to myth and thus into the communion with the space of the four elements and chôra will be fantastic diction of archaism that bridges the past, present and future and goes beyond spatial confinement.

Archaism – In Search of the Archaic Soul

Archaism suggests a mythic and glamorous past, a key sign of original partici-pation, a prime creator of strangeness in the poetic. According to stylistics, ar-chaism is obsolete words or syntax that an ornate and mannered style often makes use of. In poetic diction, archaism is employed to connect the gulf be-tween "the language of the age" and "the language of myth" and to characterize the differences between the language of poetry and prosaic language. The poetic diction here is taken in the light of Barfield's definition; it intrinsically refers to the result caused by the meanings of words arousing or intended to arouse aes-thetic imagination. "The language of myth" refers to the language belonging to the phase of "original participation" or the language with semantic unity. For scholars of *mythocritique* such as Pierre Brunel, Gilbert Durand and André Si-ganos, archaism refers not only to formal imagination, but also material (Bache-lard) and unconscious imagination (Jung and Durand). Archaism hence encom-passes both stylistic and mythopoeic meanings. In the course of the history of fantastic literature, archaism has been a dominating style that great fantastic writers utilized. Among them are the writers following the literary tradition of epics, ballads and Latin prose of chronicles.

From the perspective of Aristotle's poetics, the pleasure aroused in reading literary works comes from the appreciation of mimesis or representation. In this representation, the art is in how language is used, a language of strangeness or unfamiliarity that is different from the ordinary language. Barfield further de-veloped this aesthetic concept into "poetic pleasure – the stir of aesthetic imagi-nation – is caused by a change of consciousness from one level to another." Such a change can be attained by various means through language, and he deemed that "the one most constantly operative is the lapse of time" [Barfield 1973, 152]. With difference of time, language is attributed with different fea-tures. Besides the property of strangeness, this lapse of time reconnects the gap between the unconsciously created meaning and the reception in consciousness, in view of the evolution of language from poetic towards prosaic. In Aristotle's times, this temporal peculiarity in diction may not have been important in his *lexis*, since he belonged to an epoch of original participation, amidst Antiquity. However, this art of diction has poetic significance in our prosaic times. There-fore, Barfield highly esteemed the artistic operation of the lapse of time by stat-ing that "the most characteristic phenomena of poetic diction, the most typical differences between the language of poetry and prosaic language, can be grouped under the heading of Archaism" [ibid., 152].

The style of archaism has been employed by writers from the times of Antiquity. Even for writers living the original participation, resort to archaism is significant in creating fantastic literature, given that the archaic style is the key to getting communion with the realm of the unknown, including the forgotten past. Homer composed his epics by drawing from oral history and legends with his masterful poetic art that henceforth became the forever pinnacle to all the writers of posterity. As the French poeticians Du Bellay and Ronsard from the sixteenth century interpreted, the mimesis may refer to *imitating the best Greek authors and imitating what the ancients estimated as true*. Imitation of the ancient literature is significant in poetics, thus archaism plays an important role in the poetics of mimesis. Du Bellay depicted the Romans "imitating the best Greek authors, transforming themselves into them, devouring them and after having digested them, converting them into blood and nutrition" (*imitant les meilleurs auteurs grecs, se transformant en eux, les dévorant, et après les avoir bien digérés, les convertissant en sang et nourriture*) [Du Bellay, 214].

Homer is evidently the very archetypal poet for imitation. In fantastic literature (in fact, all literature comes from the fantastic, just as what we already proclaimed, all the known comes from the unknown), the authors following Homer imitate or emulate his epic form. Roman writers such Virgil, Ovid and Apuleius imitated the epic style of Homer and created their masterpieces: *The Aeneid*, *Metamorphoses* and *The Golden Ass*. The style of Virgil and Ovid is that of the Augustan poets but with a certain originality. The use of archaic language in the epic *Aeneid* further affirms the connection between Homer's and Virgil's poetics. In *Metamorphoses*, Ovid employed an archaic variation of inflection of verbs (-_re) that fit into the dactylic metre to his mythological writing. Besides the archaic inflection, Ovid also used obsolete words in his prose. When referring to a sword, the word *ensis* m. (sword, glaive) is almost exclusively found in poetry. Ovid showed an archaic taste in his work and Virgil also used the word sixty-four times in *The Aeneid*. This taste for archaism may even trace back to the Indo-European languages, for *ensis* derives from Sanskrit *asis*, while the other word form, *gladius,* belongs to a more recent level of vocabulary [Sandoz]. This predilection for archaism implies a pedantic style of the author. Apuleius, like his predecessors, exposed his pretentious and pedantic style by "search[ing] for archaism, the terms of jurisprudence, the alliances of strange words; he strove to highlight himself and particularly to make people admire his descriptive talent" [my translation, *Dictionnaire*]. The employment of archaism in fantastic literature is even more frequent in modern writing.

If Germanic and Nordic myths and languages are a cardinal influence on the Anglo-Saxon *fantasy* writers such as Lord Dunsany and J. R. R. Tolkien, Greco-Roman myths and languages are the imaginary and linguistic cradle to the French *fantastique* writers, among others, Charles Nodier, Theophile Gautier, Prosper Mérimée and Guy de Maupassant. The archaic style in Samuel Taylor Coleridge's, John Keats's and Edgar Allan Poe's fantastic ballads is reminiscent of classic and medieval imagination and poetic diction. A close reading of Oscar Wilde's and Edgar Allan Poe's tales (both writers' symbiotic style of archaism and pedantry, especially their embedding French diction in their writing) will expound the transference of archaism to English via French.

In French fantastic literature, the use of Greek and Latin is often a specific style to tell the fantastic story in connection with the past time and space. For example, Gautier's style of archaism in "Arria Marcella" enhances the narration of the inexplicable experience undergone by Octavion. Before the plot unfolds the travel into the times of antiquity, the archaic diction of Latin already saturates the narration to cradle the ensuing quasi-supernatural incident. Occasionally decorating Greek words also enhances the effect of visual animation. The narrator's enunciation that "Octavian started upon hearing this dead language articulated by a living tongue" [Kessler, 133] mirrors the resurrection of Latin language to the resurrection of the dead city. From realistic narration to the supernatural intrusion until the eventual exorcism of the supernatural and back to reality, the archaic diction of Latin permeates the whole narration to enhance the rococo ornate style as well as to create the strange atmosphere that prepares for the impending supernatural incident. Nodier also occasionally employed archaic French words to conjure up the fantastic atmosphere in his tales.

The style of archaism joints the imaginary gap between the present and the past and thus arouses readers to enter the realm of the unknown past. If Latin and Greek feature more often in the archaic diction of French writers, old English words and French (from the heritage of the Norman Conquest) are the most inserted language of archaism by English writers of the fantastic. Archaism features a narrative tradition of telling stories revolving around the Arthurain legend. Fantastic masters such as Poe, Dunsany, Wilde and Tolkien distinguished themselves in the style of archaism. All these writers preferred using poetic diction such as the second person, verb-endings in -eth and old strong aorists like clomb, spake, etc. Likewise, in Chinese literature, the style of archaism predominates in fantastic creation from all dynasties (until the establishment of the republic at the beginning of the 20th century). Most writers tended to use *pianwen* (tetra-character set of phrase) and embed antique poems or ballads in their prose. For example, the most famous writer Pu Songling (from the Qing dynasty) still used *pianwen* and archaic, even arcane, words to tell his fantastic tales. In fact, the writing of the Chinese fantastic manifests a complete mimesis of existing works traced back to the classic of myths *Shanhai Jing* (*The Classic of Mountains and Seas*). The title of this earliest book of the Chinese myths brings to light the significance of the archaic images of mountains and seas. The images of mountains and seas also occupy an important position in the Occidental fantastic, such as Tolkien's and Maupassant's mythopoeia.

French scholars of *mythocritique* or the imaginary emphasize not only the archaic diction in the literary creation but also the archaic images. This nostalgia of myth permeates in the works with "emergence, flexibility and irradiation" [Brunel] of myths or we may term it as a sort of nostalgic intertextuality. If the archaic lexicons beguile readers by the lapse of time into the past of the semantic unity, the archaic images charm readers by awakening their archaic soul to glimpse again Nature "perceived as immediate realities."

The effect of employing archaic images in fantastic writing lies in what Jung termed as *archetypal amplification*. Commenting on Jung's creative and symbolic use of unconscious material, Sherry Salman expounded the significance of the mythopoetic language of the unconscious: "When unconscious material is surfacing, the *specificity of the image* is the informing principle in working with it, i.e. a river is a river, not a censored sexual image. The unconscious has its own mythopoetic language and point of view on things, albeit foreign, not derived from verbal language" [Salman, 65]. Among the two kinds of thinking postulated by Jung, rational and non-rational, he highlighted the latter mode that orients the symbolizing, imagistic part of the mind working by analogy and correspondence. This non-rational thinking mode also operates as the bridge connecting the physical and psychic worlds or the concrete and the abstract realms. For example, the magic object or talisman bridges the rational and the mystic. This can be illustrated by the Sampo (a magic mill that endlessly grinds out salt, meal and gold for its possessor) in the epic *Kalevala*. The image of gold is recurrent in many fantastic tales such as *The Golden Ass*, *The Golden Pot*, "The Golden Key" and the Daoist arcane book *The Golden Flower*. Jung's method of *archetypal amplification* thus interprets modern dreams and phantasies in the light of archaic mythological motifs. The aforementioned archaic lexicons and images converge into a temporal structure by the extrinsic momentum, according to Durand's isotopism of images. The archaic words and images as the catalyst of the third way echo with the archaic music that rhymes with the alchemical refinement of language through fantastic stylish storytelling. The archaism of the fantastic as the imaginary catalyst will conduce to Eucharistic alchemy of language, given that it reverses time and chants the music in oblivion.

Eucharistic Alchemy of Language

The discussion of divinity or God in regard to language and myth necessitates an examination of the concept of the Eucharist, alluded to by Tolkien in terms of the creation of fairy-stories and proposed by Marion in terms of his solution for metaphysics on theology, both being catholic. The Greek root of the word is ευχαριστω, Latin word as eucharisto, bearing the meaning of "to give thanks or to rejoice." In Christian tradition, Eucharist refers to the process of communion and sanctification. *Encarta Encyclopedia Deluxe* thus defines Eucharist:

> Eucharist or Lord's Supper, central rite of the Christian religion, in which bread and wine are consecrated by an ordained minister and consumed by the minister and members of the congregation in obedience to Jesus' command at the Last Supper, "Do this in remembrance of me." In the Orthodox and Roman Catholic churches, and in the Anglican, Lutheran, and many other Protestant churches, it is regarded as a sacrament, which both symbolizes and effects the union of Christ with the faithful. Baptists and others refer to Holy Communion as an "institution," rather than a sacrament, emphasizing obedience to a commandment. [CD Rom]

The central idea of Eucharist in fact assimilates the spirit of alchemy, external or internal. The Daoist practice of alchemy is to refine the purest essence from impure materials. The tenet lies in the quest for eternity, like the quest for the Emerald Table or the Philosopher's Stone. The element gold is the very image that represents eternity since it is the purest of all and never deteriorates. External alchemy invokes help from Nature or gods or the collective unconscious. The alchemist accomplishes the refinement through the communion with gods, similar to the concept of Holy Communion. Internal alchemy also depends on the process of communion but in a spiritual way. The alchemist himself is the furnace to refine the impure elements inside his own body. The status of achieving Nirvana is the vision of "golden flower," as represented in the Daoist scripture that Jung annotated – *The Secret of Golden Flower*. The principle in alchemy resembles the Catholic Eucharist, the transubstantiation. Therefore, the process of purification of language can be termed as Eucharist or alchemy, given that the semantic unity embraces the material and the spiritual or the concrete and the abstract. And language is *per se* substantial (writing and sound) and abstract.

French phenomenologist Jean-Luc Marion developed his philosophy by the Eucharistic contemplation on hermeneutic metaphysics to find a solution to contemporary metaphysics in impasse. He sheds light on the distinction between the idol and the icon to raise his proposal and argumentation of a third way as Eucharistic hermeneutic beyond Heidegger's theology (science of faith) and theiology (metaphysics of "God"). Concerning idolatry, we may parallel Barfield's criticism on the idol produced throughout the intellectual age in comparison with Marion's clarification of the confusion between the idol and the icon. Barfield criticized the modern severance of semantic unity in language away from the original participation, which entails the worship of idols constructed by our alpha-thinking and beta-thinking. Language has idled into idols. In compliance with Durand's theory, things and meanings come prior to linguistic signs. The fantastic imagination manifests as pre-logical generation of knowledge, including language. In the process of communication, the formalization of language severs the original unity and thus abases the meanings and thrones the idol of language. Marion's definition of idol is also assimilated with the aforementioned writers' conception, except for his inclination towards theology. Both the idol and the icon are germane to envisaging the divine. Marion refutes the possibilities of the idol's representing the divine. Man's gaze in front of the idol never conduces to the agape with conveyance of the divine intention. He deems that any philosophical thinking on and expressing a part of the concept of "God" functions as the idol [Marion, 90-98]. Therefore, he proposes a Eucharistic image, the icon, not resulting from a vision of the divine but rather agape. Like the phenomenon of idolatry in language that regards signifiers as they are, the visible and invisible that a gazer can grasp revolves around the sign as it is. In the light of Marion's Eucharistic theory, the gazer before the icon is *de facto* passive. The icon provokes a divine vision by convoking sight through the saturation of the invisible into the visible. Through the icon, the gazer passively receives the divine intention [Ibid., 142-143].

Barfield also raised the issue of idolatry and iconoclasm in relation to the evolution of human consciousness. In his *Poetic Diction,* he proposed the power of imagination as the secret of regaining the semantic unity of language and reaching the final participation. We would count the process as the alchemy of language or Eucharist. He criticized modern man for seeing the idols of signs or language as the substance and gradually ignoring the true meanings and essence of the unity in the phenomenological world and our language. From the perspective of language, linguistic idolatry refers to the worship of words as signs, taking the literal meanings as literal, whereas the significance in the icon of words is abandoned. Barfield thus commented on the way of iconoclasm:

> the life of the image is to be drawn from within. The life of the image is to be none other than the life of imagination. And it is of the very nature of imagination that it cannot be *inculcated*. There must be first of all the voluntary stirring from within. It must be, not indeed self-created, but certainly self-willed, or else – it is not imagination at all; and is therefore incapable of iconoclasm. Iconoclasm is made possible by the seed of the Word stirring within us, as imagination [Barfield 1988, 179].

The emphasis of the quoted "within" and "imagination" reminds us of Marion's vision of Eucharist in terms of icon, a passive experience of agape.

Consequently, the hermeneutics of Scripture is possible in this light. Marion proposed that the only solution to be *granted* the comprehension of Scripture is, like the passive reception of the divine intention, the communion of Eucharist where Christ, the Word, the Living Reference, speaks the words. Accordingly, the fallibility in decoding the meanings of languages or scriptures (can be applied to other religious scriptures) is no evidence of emptiness or meaninglessness. In reply to Derrida's understanding of "negative theology," which is indeed a paradoxical misconception, Marion resorts to the third way (*la troisième voie*), the Eucharistic hermeneutic of theology [Marion 162]. Deconstructionists tend to push the reproductive theory of language to extreme so as to deny the centre of meaning or transcendent entity. In fact, Derrida's concern is more on the linguistic level of metonymy than referentiality, given that a sign comprising both signifier and signified refers to a referent. Durand, from linguistic perspective, criticized that Derrida shifted the attention to the unending indeterminacy in the relation between words. Marion's Eucharistic hermeneutics can thus serve to solve the language problem that easily falls into deconstructive nihilism. He also pointed out that the biggest paradox of contemporary philosophers is their being abominators of wisdom instead of the etymological meaning of the term as wisdom lovers.

Marion's Eucharistic metaphysics can conduce to the elucidation of mythopoeic quintessence by referring to Plato's notion of mimesis and Lao Zi's Dao as well as *Yi Jing*. If the world is a genuine imitation of the Ideal Form, the divine unity in theology will also have its counterparts in the imitation of Beings. The enigma of the origin of language further arouses our imagination of the divine intention in language. As maintained by *Yi Jing*, the myriads of things and beings manifest the perpetual spirit of yin and yang deriving from *Taiji*, the state of oneness before the first catalysis of the ensuing changes. The unending changes of fission are, in harmony with *Yi Jing* philosophy, coupled with consecutive fusion. The microcosm of a grain is able to refract the light from the macrocosm. In similar fashion, language and myth can be treated as the *mise en abyme* of theology and metaphysics. Although Lao Zi was alert in employing the word "Dao" to represent the ultimate truth or the referent of "Dao" that eludes any signifiers, he still resorted to language to write about Dao by means of the manifestations of *De* or chôra. Throughout *Dao De Jing*, Lao Zi elaborated the quintessential concept of transcending beyond the polar antithesis or a return to monism of non-dualism. He endeavoured to illuminate the logic of Dao (the unknown Causality or God or Plato's Ideal Form), higher than *De* as the coexistence of antithesis and nonexistence of antithesis.

Such logic of Dao echoes with Marion's idea of God's "indifference of the ontic difference of being and nonbeing." The metaphysical language employed by Lao Zi appears contradictory to human logic, since man is unable to think beyond dualism. Therefore, his followers, such as Zhuang Zi and Lie Zi and other fantastic writers, told stories to reflect Dao through the language of Daoist aesthetics. In Christian theology, Scripture of words features as the object of hermeneutics, whereas in Chinese Daoism, Dao or the Word or the Living Reference is embodied in nature, fantastic stories, alchemy and the sundry gods. Different from the slight derogation of "unreal" and "untrue" in the Western definition of myth, myth in Chinese means "the words of gods/God" that implies a quality of divine scriptures and can be counted truer than man's words since gods are considered superior and "real." As a result, Chinese fantastic literature, as a variation of myth, continues the fantastic mimesis, based on the words of God, to represent the wisdom and beauty of the realm unknown to man. Therefore, gods, immortals, monsters, spirits and ghosts are taken as the unknown "real," for Chinese worldview believes that they may become known reality in the future. The semantic unity is in this manner preserved in the human imaginary, manifest in its embodiment in language and the ubiquitous divinity in Dao.

Marion's Eucharistic hermeneutic is a process of transubstantiation. This process makes the comprehension of Scripture as a communion between the exegete and the texts, Christ, or the Word, or the Living Referent. This transubstantiative communion leads to *unus mundus*. The Eucharistic hermeneutics mirrors the experience of the original participation, the perceiving man, at the same time being a part of the perceived world, has undergone a quasi-eucharistic process in the primitive consciousness. There is a parallel between the passive reception of the divine vision through the gaze at the icon in relation to the illumination by the Living Referent through Eucharist in the hermeneutic metaphysics and the "icon" inspiration in relation to the "Eucharist" in myth and language. Therefore, we would regard the "icon" in language as characterizing genuine fantastic literature, and the "Eucharist" as the process of purification of language or the alchemy of language. The Living Referent represents the ultimate meanings couched in the collective unconscious that leads further to the arcane chôra.

In different cultures, the communion of Eucharist (taken as communion between the material and the spiritual) can be effectuated through language, cult and meditation. Several oriental religions have practices that are similar to the Eucharist, although not called the same name. Through such a cult, the core spirit being to unite the concrete with the transcendental and metaphysical realm, the individual is thus purged to make the realm of the unknown or collective unconscious accessible. For example, the practice of Hindu yoga centres on a process of purging that rids of the five poisons: greed, anger, ignorance, arrogance and doubt. In Daoist alchemical practice, the cult of Eucharist refers to the harmonious amalgamation of material and spirit, which leads to a transcendental communion. Jung's theory of the collective unconscious could be apprehended in the light of this Daoist spirit, in view of his annotation and intimate researches of the Daoist writings. In philosophy connected with theology, Eucharist is the key to the hermeneutic of cryptic scriptures. This is a process of communion that links the gap between the two apparently diverse fields. When it comes to the Eucharist of language or literature as implied by Tolkien and Barfield, literature as Eucharist purges language of pollution to its pristine mythic status, even prior to the thinking state, the separation between mythos and logos. The art of fantastic storytelling is what is common to these views. Fantastic storytelling makes abstract and disembodied philosophy accessible; it makes the disconnected images connected fluidly through musical and temporal transformation; it also makes the ego better understand and integrate into his society and his own universe. The functioning of fantastic storytelling eventually leads to the psychological issue of Jungian individualization, a harmonious amalgamation of the ego into the collective unconscious to attain the Self.

Jung's proposition of the third position, beyond the binary conflict between the deconstruction and universalism or essentialism, and nominalism and realism, is *esse in anima* by placing imaging as the mediator between subject and object or inner world and outer world: "Living reality is the product neither of the actual, objective behaviour of things nor of the formulated idea exclusively, but rather of the combination of both in the living psychological process, through *esse in anima* [Jung 1978, 78]. This solution of a third way, as we can also find in Daoist philosophy and Marion's philosophy, serves as a bridge to the sublime. The communion between our consciousness and the unconscious connects the physical with the psychical worlds, hence a union of the unknown and the known reality. In language and literature, storytelling assumes the role of nexus. Its rhetorical artistry bridging the physical known realm with the unknown through a Eucharistic communion will be lastly reinforced by the result of intimate researches by anthropologists like Lévi-Strauss and Mircea Eliade: "one of the earliest roles of the shaman or sage was to tell stories which provide symbolic solutions to contradictions which could not be solved empirically. In the process, reality itself would find itself miraculously transformed" [Kearney, 6]. Storytelling takes on a magic and psychological function, an impalpable dimension. Its third way is imaginary language as Eucharist or transcendental communion, to attain the above status. The archetypal images in tales analyzed by psychologists and anthropologists should be taken as the materials to be constructed under the magic creation of storytelling.

Many critics of fantastic literature embrace the view that it brings the unreal into play. For example, Bessière analyzed the fantastic as the representation of words at the signifying level without referent. This arbitrary assessment of fantastic diction is indeed analogous to the philosophers holding negative theology. The alchemy of amalgamation of language referring to the known and the unknown through the catalysis of primary imagination (to employ Coleridge's term) elucidates Tolkien's Eucharist of Fantasy.

Tolkien viewed a unique aesthetic process of Eucharist in the creation and reading of fairy-stories poeticized through fantasy storytelling. He uncovered the ineffable feature of language, or more precisely, rational language, a language awaiting purification. With his erudite and philological background, Tolkien claimed that "it would be more near the truth to say that languages, especially modern European languages, are a disease of mythology." Likewise, Tolkien paralleled the assumption with "thinking is a disease of mind" [Tolkien 1997,

121-2]. A Catholic, Tolkien implemented the Eucharistic theory of language by telling stories of *Silmarillion* mythology. His conception of myth and language is analogous to Durand's theory, which presumes that the figurative language substantially bears the literal meaning. In fact, this actual inversion of the figurative and the literal has evolved from the logical formalization of fantastic imagination rich in transcendental semantism [Durand 1992, 483]. Storytelling then plays an important role in this process of purification. The aforementioned paradox (the limitation of dialectic language faced with the immensity of wisdom) that philosophers suffer from makes them resort to fantastic storytelling to shed light on the impalpable truth by language. In terms of Jungian individuation or spiritual quest, Tolkien's fantasy as Eucharist can be associated with Jung's process of individuation that connects consciousness with the collective unconscious. This parallels the process from the known realm (our world) to the unknown perilous realm (Tolkien's Faerie). Like Tolkien who clearly depicted the power of shadow throughout his novels, Jung saw the shadow as the darker side of our unconscious self with the metaphor that "the shadow is the invisible saurian tail that man still drags behind him" [Jung 1978, 217]. The "saurian tail" evokes Tolkien's evil figure "Sauron". If Jung used the quest of fire and light to purge human consciousness so as to meet *synchronically* the collective unconscious, then Tolkien purified his language through artistic storytelling to purge myth and language, through the process akin to the Catholic Eucharist.

Tolkien's philosophy on myth and language in terms of Eucharist is best illustrated in his poem:

> Man, sub-creator, *the refracted Light*
> through whom is splintered from *a single White*
> to many hues, and endlessly combined
> in living shapes and that move from mind to mind.
> Though all the crannies of the world we filled
> with Elves and Goblins, though we dared to build
> Gods and their houses out of dark and light,
> and sowed the seed of dragons – 'twas our right
> (used or misused). That right has not decayed:
> *we make still by the law in which we're made.'* [my emphasis, Tolkien 1997, 144]

The images presented by Tolkien in the quoted poem on mythopoeia will further shed light on the Eucharist of language through myth and the fantastic. The semantic severing taking place in the evolution of language as "disease of mythology" can return to the sources of light, the status of unity through the purification of "the refracted Light." The notion of microcosm related to macrocosm mirrors the metaphor of "the refracted Light" vis-à-vis "a single White." As Tolkien revealed, "we make still by the law in which we're made," myth and language are accordingly made by the same law of the Word, the Living Referent. Tolkien's Eucharist of words is better comprehended in this light. Human mythopoeia manifests our impulse of imitating the truth in the single White. This impulse of sub-creation is eventually a reflection of the individual's re-fracted aspiration for communion with the origin of light. Tolkien's sub-creation, as opposed to the primitive epics, is significant in our times since we are now in the age of conscious soul with the remnants from the intellectual age.

From myth to language, Tolkien preserved the life of words with semantic unity throughout his mythopoeic creation. His love of language inspired him to penetrate into the original semantic unity in myth and language. His scrupulous selection of names for his characters and other words in his fantastic writing de-rived from his unique insight into myth:

> The seed [of the myth] is linguistic, of course. I'm a linguist and everything is linguistic – that's why I take such pains with names. The real seed was starting when I was quite a child by inventing languages, largely to try to capture the esthetic mode of the languages I was learning, and I eventually made the dis-covery that language can't exist in a void and if you invent a language yourself you can't cut it in half. It has to come alive – so really the languages came first and the country after. [qtd. Birzer, 28]

From mythopoeia to *linguopoeia*[45], Tolkien reifies the single light and the splin-tered light in his literary creation of myth and language. As he criticized critics as monsters, critical language will surely undermine the harmonious unity of language. Instead of theorization, he embodied his fantastic imagination into the Silmarillion mythology, the ring trilogy and fairy-stories through a Eucharist of words.

Tolkien once mentioned that many members from the Inklings, including "a solicitor," appreciated *The Lord of the Rings* [Tolkien 1995, 122]. The solicitor here refers undoubtedly to Barfield, the philologist embracing the belief of a semantic unity in language. Furthermore, Tolkien even explicitly indicated that the philological meanings in *The Hobbits* "will be missed by any who have not read Owen Barfield" [ibid., 22]. The work of Barfield here refers to his *Poetic Diction*, first published in 1928. Barfield did not adduce Tolkien's works in his theory of poetic diction and the evolution of human consciousness. However, Tolkien's mythopoeia can be considered as the manifestation par excellence of Barfield's ideal theory of myth and language and the significance of aesthetic imagination aroused by poetic diction. As mentioned earlier, the poetic diction as defined by Barfield is rather in fantastic literature to arouse aesthetic imagi-nation. Fantastic diction is more likely to harmonize split meanings into a se-mantic unity, for the essence of its language is the style of recovery that will

---

[45] The term is coined here to signify Tolkien's language making.

undergo the process of Eucharist to return to the pristine purity of myth in communion with the space that combines and transcends antithesis – chôra.

After Slaying the Dragon, Hearken to the Birds!

Fantastic diction offers us a rich reservoir of imagined knowledge. As we mention in the chapter on the imaginary, human imagining can derive sensible knowledge. Jung, Bachelard and Durand all valued supposedly erroneous knowledge that was derived from imagination of the human psyche. Combining the arguments of Cassirer, Barfield and Tolkien that myth is more of an original language with the aforementioned theories on the fantastic imagination, we extrapolate that the secret of the genesis of language could be hidden in myth itself.

In Nordic and Germanic mythologies, a common motif occurs as the hero accomplishes his challenge of slaying the evil dragon; he begins to understand birds' language to learn about the ensuing dangers and be advised to kill the true enemy. For example, in the story of Sigurd the Volsung (from *Elder Edda* or *Poetic Edda*), understanding birds' language is a gift after his slaying the dragon. Fascinated by the dragon, Tolkien regarded the creature as a monster of import that embodies all evil natures of human beings and plays an important role in the writing of fairy-stories. He depicts dragons as one of the minions of Melkor in his mythology. They are the fire-drakes from Angband that continually raid the stronghold of the Elves. Another race of dragons, the Angband Balrogs, menace the lives of the Elves in the great wars of Middle-earth. Fëanor, the mightiest of the Noldor, is eventually smitten by Gothmog, Lord of Balrogs. Further in the ring trilogy, the wizard Gandalf is once annihilated by this darkest evil creature of fire Balrog "Demon-of-Power" into the abyss under the bridge of Khazad-Dûm. Corrupted language is represented by the name of Wormtongue given to Théodon's counsel Gríma. Dragons' trunk bears the physical traits of snakes and their wings resemble those of the fallen angel. The deed of dragon slaying can be compared to the aforementioned process of Eucharist. Annihilation of the dragon equals the purification of language and thus proceeding to the comprehension of Nature's language, represented by birds. We may clean the windows of our perception and perceive with extra-sensation to purge langue so as to apprehend birds' or other animals' languages through "slaying the dragon."

Understanding animals' language signifies understanding Nature's language. This desire for language as for being integrated in Nature is portrayed through myths and tales in different regions of the world. In the European culture, the dragon as monster symbolizes greed, fury and foolishness. It appears as a sheer figure that reifies the abstract attributes of man as elicited by Buddhism in the tripartite human frailty: "tan, chen, chi" (greed, wrath, ignorant). For Buddhist practice, the riddance of these three defects, the very human nature, is the principal tenet.

In Chinese culture, the imaginary dragon is on the contrary considered as a divine beast, which is tightly related to Daoist imagination. As the figure of Satan and the space of Hell do not exist in primitive Daoism along with the thinking of *Yi Jing*,[46] evil can be embodied by any beings, including Daoist xian, the immortals or gods. The Chinese imagination envisions an unknown or "supernatural" divine creature called *Long*, translated as dragon. The foremost significant feature in this fantastic imagination is the theriomorphic form of the god-like Cang Jie who created Chinese written words. This word creator is depicted in many mythic and historical stories as having a dragon-like head with four eyes. It is told that while Cang Jie was creating words, the spirits and ghosts howled in the night to disturb the calling of their names and the delineating of their shapes [Zhu, 62]. This compelling word-creating process foretells the perpetual fantastic creation by language. Writing makes the supernatural or the invisible inescapable. However, the creation of words is celebrated by gods from heaven by sending grain rain. What is in common about the dragon figure in the East and West is its association with linguistic secret. Yet, the Chinese dragon is quite different from Western dragons, though sometimes they are described as speaking with a wheedling tone of voice. For example, it is told in the astrological tale (the twelve animals as the cycle of years) that the cock originally had a pair of horns but was coaxed by the dragon into lending them to him. The dragon ate the words and appropriated the horns. In this regard, Chinese dragons resemble the European ones gifted with coaxing and hoaxing. Nevertheless, Chinese dragons are highly esteemed as celestial beings that belong to the class of birds since they fly. In sum, the imagination of the dragon from the East and the West thus find their influx in the secret of language, albeit the ethical stances are different.

In Europe, the hero needs to slay the dragon to get the secret of language and wisdom through the language of birds, whereas in China, the dragon helps give the words to man to complement the speech of the bird, the signs with the musical sounds. The homogeneity found in birds from different cultures lies in the revelation of wisdom and luck. Birds are a crucial motif in myths and fantastic literature, whether in the East or West. In Chinese myth, birds, like dragons, are regarded as divine animals and messengers. The turquoise bird of the Goddess Mother of the West (Xiwangmu) governing the paradise of the West is a divine messenger competent in different languages. It can bridge men with gods. In Daoist practice, attaining the state of Nirvana or obtaining Dao is also termed

---

[46] According to Xiao Dengfu's historical studies of Daoism, Chinese people borrowed the image and conception of hell from Indian Buddhism. The complete vision of a Daoist hell image was completed in the Tang dynasty. We would here complement this fact with an imaginary explication.

as bird-metamorphosing into the immortal (*yu* (plume) *hua* (metamorphose) *cheng* (become) *xian* (immortal)). The archetype of "the ascending wing" deriving from the diurnal imaginary regime of Durand is represented by the bird. The ascending image corresponds to the air element described in the cosmogony and thus endowed with the meaning of messenger and communication. Appertaining to the air element and celestial image, birds are germane to wisdom. In the Old Testament, Solomon is said to be wise to understand birds' language. In Confucius's renowned dialogue *Lun Yu*, his disciple Gong Ye Chang saves his life because he understands birds' language. Under the pen of Chinese great fantastic author of *Liaozhai zhiyi*, Pu Songling, a Daoist master wards off the impending dangers with the help of birds' language. Accordingly, we may read the stories concerning birds and languages both literally and metaphorically.

From the viewpoint of Barfield, Cassirer and Tolkien on myth and language, language is begotten with myth and a semantic unity, viz. endowed with the literal meanings and metaphors as well as abstract and concrete interpretations. Tolkien's assumption that truth resides in myth and legend as a semantic unity may come close to scientific truth, which reinforces the vision of myth as logos and truth. We have developed this extrapolation in the studies of myth and mimesis. Appearing paradoxical in connecting scientific researches with fantastic imagination, our hypothesis of human imagination of language related to birds and dragon, especially to birds, may converge with future science. In this manner, the Daoist vision that what is known comes from the unknown bears a profound truth and the fantastic imagination could be the caldron of truth. According to recent scientific researches, birds, whales, dolphins and humans are the animals capable of learning languages by imitation. Birds are especially akin to men in the nature of language. German scientists have decoded the same gene of language FoxP2 in men and birds. Like birds, men's difficulty in learning language may derive from the mutation of this gene.[47] Another research on nightingales' language is quite interesting. The laboratory analyzes that the nightingale's sound contains five syllables in a pico-second, which is beyond the grasp of human hearing. The trills of birds' language are similar to the alliteration in epics. This traditional musical art frequently appears in Tolkien's works. That more and more scientists and linguists associate human language with birds' language seems to echo with the myths about the secret of language.

Based on Barfield's and Tolkien's conceptions of myth and language as well as recent scientific researches, a hypothesis on the evolution of language may be imagined. The men in the stage of original participation were faced with natural phenomena that they perceived. The innate genes of language commence to operate as men are feared and touched by sublime and divine nature. They want to utter some voice in harmony with their emotion and nature. Usener proposed the

---

[47] The related information is reported in *Guoji xianchu baodao* or *International Herald Leader* on April 8, 2004.

concept of "Moment God," whereas Cassirer brought to light the natural imitation of onomatopoeia. If we connect the Chinese meaning of myth as "the speech of gods" and the Daoist alchemical language without signs (similar to telepathy) with Jung's conception of the human collective unconscious, there probably is a universal memory of meanings endowed by the Ideal Form or God that will be triggered and synchronized to combine with the outer world of nature and form the sound system of language. We may refer to Tolkien's *Silmarillion*, where Elves are depicted as being endowed with telepathy: "Now the Eldar were beyond all other peoples skilled in tongues; and Felagund discovered also that he could read in the minds of Men such thoughts as they wished to reveal in speech, so that their words were easily interpreted" [Tolkien 1999, 163].

The idea that there exists a silent language rich in symbols or meanings can be found both in the East and the West. Swedenborg (1688-1772), Swedish scientist and theologian, described his vision of the spiritual world and revealed that symbolic language is used in the beyond. Communication is possible through hearing melodies and seeing images. In our earthly world, animals such as birds and beasts emit sounds when they are hungry or scared. Humans are likely to imitate the sounds of nature, such as birds, beasts, mountains and seas. The change of mood or form from nature offers an acoustic model of imitation for men. For example, the collapse of mountains models as a kind of vowel sound. The change of power or dynamics stirs a human impulse to utter.

In the fantastic tales mentioned earlier concerning the imaginary of man relating to the nonhuman, men are originally able to communicate with animals, even with inanimate nature. Maybe the first process of formalization of language deprives men of such magical power. Linguists often elicit the unique function of recursion in human language to distinguish it from animals' language and reject the hypothesis of a common genesis between men's and birds' or other possible animals' language. We would rather surmise that this recursion may be the cause of losing communication with nature. Naturally, the aforementioned recursion is involved in the formation of human language. However, children still need to learn language like the newborn birds and dolphins who imitate their parents to learn their language. In a similar manner, men have to learn language by imitating their parents and other people in their environment. Eventually, the evolution of human language resides in the perpetual deduction and induction of formalization. Then men need myth to purge their perception and conception of nature, as the theories of the imaginary propose, for we still need to slay the dragon to hearken to the bird.

As a last point, we emphasize that by applying Durand's imaginary system, we can see the significance of birds as archetypal images. They are universally symbols both in the West and in the East. This is illustrated by the examples of dragons and birds previously discussed. Birds fly, and this is involved in the wing archetype, which involves meanings of ascension, angels and air. Birds, coming from the sky, are ranked with deities. The archetype of flying and ascending manifests birds' attribute of lightness and nimbleness that floats and trills with the element of air. The Myth of birds eventually flies back to the archetypal unknown realm of God, the Word or Logos. The recursion in human language often elicited as uniqueness to man takes place in the fantastic imagination of language: recursion as reversion to semantic unity.

Harmonism in the Footsteps of Nature
Fantastic Storytelling as Enchanting Chanting

As stated before, the singing of birds is encoded into the chanting of words in fantastic storytelling. Music first launched the storytelling of the primitive imagination. Herder maintained that all languages and concepts bear mythical characteristics. Nature is a sound-emitting system. Naming is closely related to sound and voice. Fantastic literature brings into play such mythical characteristics and narrates with musical fluidity. Like Cassirer, who placed the sound elements as the pristine parts in harmony with Nature, Barfield analyzed the sounds of consonants and vowels in terms of their relations with our world and mind:

> Those who have any feeling for sound-symbolism, and who wish to develop it, will be advised to ponder [word-roots]. They may find, in the consonantal element in language vestiges of those forces which brought into being the external structure of nature, including the body of man; and in the original vowel-sounds, the expression of that inner life of feeling and memory which constitutes his soul. It is the two together which have made possible, by first physically and then verbally embodying it, his personal intelligence. [Barfield 1988, 124]

Barfield's special insight into the relation between the world and the sounds of words, the real connection between the physical and the spiritual, further expounds the style of *harmonism* proposed by Pierre Fontanier. The phonetic elements in incantation of oriental religions that consist in the repetition of vowel sounds also echoes with Barfield's analysis of the relationship of vowel sounds to inner life and soul.

Likewise, Durand's theory of the imaginary proposes the best musical analysis with reference to literary writing and mythic creation. His thorough investigation of the pivotal role of the diurnal and nocturnal regimes in mankind's imaginary production is relevant here. It converges with a second line of logic, concerning the role of semantics in myths when examining the synthetic structures of imaginary creation, and the transcendental function of the fantastic imagination or *la fantastique*. Among synthetic structures, the musical harmonization of the contraries and musical synthesis from dialectic or contrasting theses are the primary ones. Durand highly estimates the untranslatable art of myths, and highlights their musical and storytelling features by the idiosyncrasy of repetition as incantation and telling of stories. He even claims that "myth has the same structure as music" (*le mythe a la même structure que la musique*) [Durand 1992, 417].

We would further clarify this parallelism between myth and music by the core structure of music, viz. a discreetly stipulated and set of rules of music theory for composition. It is this musical feature in fantastic literature that defines it by the most scrupulous language with unlimited imagination, which is actually the quintessence of music. The creation of fantastic literature exactly rocks with the primeval imagination of music and storytelling. This is the very insight that Tolkien held on the creation of fairy-stories and the process of Eucharist. The true meaning of Eucharist in fantastic creation and appreciation is the process of purging language of corruption and abstraction. This purification of language through the fantastic imagination crystallizes musical melody and rhyme, and the semantic unity in language and myth. The musicality in fantastic literature from the stages of primitive conception and myth as the fabrication of truth not only predominates over formal presentation, but also often features as the theme of the story.

The recurrence of archaic musical power as magic can enchant and metamorphose the world, as told in the epic *Kalevala*. With his singing, Väinämöinen (one of the three heroes) defeats his foe by causing him (Joukahainen) to sink into a swamp. Another hero, Lemminkäinen, bewitches the people of Pohjola with his singing in order to woo the maiden of Pohjola, the daughter of Louhi (the mistress of Pohjola as well as a sorceress). In the attempts to win the magic Sampo, Väinämöinen spellbinds all living things of Pohjola to sleep by playing his Kantele, a magic instrument made out of the jawbone of a giant pike. In the escape after the three heroes steal the Sampo, hindered by Louhi's conjuring, they lose the Kantele in the sea and the Sampo is eventually smashed and falls into the sea. A second kantele is made by Väinämöinen from birchwood. The playing of this instrument once again makes the whole of creation rejoice. The perennial imagination through musicality of writing is predicted in the closure of the epic by the same hero who departs in a copper boat. He knows he will need to play new songs (besides to make a new Sampo and bring new light). The Finnish epic is an enduring enchantment of storytelling through musical movement. And this prediction proves to be true especially at the present day. We need new songs in literature. Tolkien, the great fantasy writer of the last century continues to play the magic instrument to chant for us and enchant us into the experience of Eucharist.

The fluidity of Tolkien's fantastic storytelling is the foremost manifestation of the music of Nature. The embedment of ballads, lays and songs in the development of the plot enhances the musical art of the author. His espousal of the ideal semantic unity in language is thoroughly illustrated by his euphoriant musical narration. This exuberance of the musical imagination is in fact first settled and uttered in *The Silmarillion* through the narration of his creation myth: "And he (Eru, the One, who in Arda is called Illuvatar) spoke to them (the Ainur, the Holy Ones, the offspring of his thought), propounding to them themes of music; and they sang before him, and he was glad" [Tolkien 1999, 3]. The explicit portrayal of music taking part in the cosmogony of the Universe contrasts with the style of *The Silmarillion* that appears less poetic and musical than *The Hobbits* and *The Lord of the Rings*. The style of Tolkien's mythology appears stern and neutral with a historian's tone. Readers have the impression of reading a mythic history. Nevertheless, the purposely enunciated themes of music functioning in the creation of the Universe are shown to be saturated in the created world. The musicality in the ring trilogy embodies this musical spirit throughout his fantastic diction, the genuine mediation of the sub-creation, a living demonstration of Eucharist or alchemy of language. The *harmonism* in the footsteps of Nature presents the resonance of the mountains and the seas and the whispering of natural sound in the air. The very first phenomenological music in Nature, the vowel and the consonant, reverberates with chanting and enchanting in the storytelling. Now that the Universe is created simultaneously throughout the chorus of the Ainur the Holy Ones, the harmony of the Great Music continues to harmonize the unfolding of the Becoming.

The semantic unity, effectively unified by the Great Music, will be regained through the linguistic purification of Eucharist. The language closer to the sources of creation manifests itself as the fossil of the oblivious past that shows a unity in sounds, meanings and souls. For example, Tolkien's creation of the Ents manifests such unity. The language of Treebeard illustrates the reminiscence of the language of music and nature. The telling of the story of Fangorn following the chapter of the Uruk-hai makes a sheer contrast between the language of the Orcs and the Ents. As the former are distorted lives fabricated by Saruman, their unnatural existence is radiated by their language. Normally, Orcs snarl, growl, mutter and hiss, "'Don't draw attention to yourself, or I may forget my orders. Curse the Isengarders! *Ugluk u bagronk sha pushdug Saruman-glob bubhosh skai*': he passed into a long angry speech in his own tongue that slowly died away into muttering and snarling" [Tolkien 2001, 47]. They are apt to utter guttural sounds that are disagreeable to hear. The cacophony of the vowel sounds such as "a, o, u" makes the orcs' tongue all the more ferocious.

Similarly, the animal traits surrounding Gollum are vividly staged by its actions and sounds like animals. The disagreeable sound of gutturals first appears as Frodo and Sam pass the "gully" and then is reinforced by the depiction on "Gollum." After the thunder "growled" and "rumbled," we hear later Gollum "growl" and "snarl." Besides the traits analogous to the Orcs, Gollum is also characterized as a somewhat slimy snake, "Snakes and adders!" [ibid., 268] with a "venomous look" [ibid., 274] He speaks exactly like snakes:

> 'Ach, sss! Cautious, my precious! More haste less speed. We musstn't risk our neck, must we, precious? No, precious – *gollum!*' He lifted his head again, blinked at the moon, and quickly shut his eyes. 'We hate it,' he hissed. 'Nassty, nasty shivery light it is – sss – it spies on us, precious – it hurts our eyes' [ibid., 269]

These sibilant sounds correspond to Gollum's identity, both physical and mental. The sibilant sounds also characterize his being like insects such as "spider" and "grasshopper." The variety of onomatopoeic verbs makes the diction of unity even perfect. Gollum "cackles," "gobbles," "hisses," "whines," "chuckles," "croaks" and "splutters.". Like a snake he "crawls," "grovels," "whispers" and "writhes." Like a dog he "whines," "growls," "snarls," "paws," and "fawns." And he can "caper" like a grasshopper. Tolkien's painting and chanting of Gollum is a genuine life illustration of what semantic unity is. Cacophony and hypotyposis concretely represent the foul images of monstrosity.

The embodiment of the Durandian theriomorphic images in the fantastic imagination is further perfected by Tolkien's virtuosity in phonology. The devouring power of the dark evil is represented in both the theriomorphic figures and sounds. After the snarling and growling of the Orcs, the audible harmony in Fangorn evokes a past of sheer musical imagination and the *unus mundus* communion status.

Contrary to the coarse guttural sounds forming a totality of dissonance growled by the Orcs, the wood of Fangorn is saturated with sounds of euphony based on onomatopoeia. The fricatives and aspirates vibrate with the air element and the low and solemn /um/ sound resonates with the deep soul of Nature. The name of Fangorn can be decoded by partial anagram into "organ" and "f[a]n" and both referring to air and music. The clustering of /f/ sounds in the chapter such as "fragrance, fan, fair, fern, forest and fountain" makes readers breathe with the wood. Resuming Barfield's assumption that consonants reflect the outer world and vowels the inner spirit, we can better comprehend Tolkien's disposition of the sonority in relation to the meanings in the chapter. The outer world of the Ents is the wood Fangorn that emits scents and fragrances of the natural forest along with the rustles of the leaves. This phonic effect of Nature echoes with the Entish. On the other hand, the lowest-pitch vocalic sound of "boom" in Entish impresses readers with the fact of their being *slow* and *old*, echoes with their *soul* deep from their *bole*. The resonance with soul illustrates Barfield's assumption of the relation between vowel sound and inner soul. The acoustic effect of Entish is represented in the word "ENT" itself: Ear, Nose and Throat. In addition, the aforementioned sound of soul is also further manifested by the name of Ent, for "ent- or ento-" is the prefix that means "inside or within." In harmony with the nature of wood, Tolkien employed vivid words with aspirated sounds to mirror the physical reality of the forest.

The dialogue throughout the Entmoot is depicted like antiphony that animates the old wood: "The Ents began to murmur slowly: first one joined and then another, until they were all chanting together in a long rising and falling rhythm, now louder on one side of the ring, now dying away there and rising to a great boom on the other side" [ibid., 94]. This musical idiosyncrasy also abounds in the narration on the Ents' action. The narration on the gait of the old Ent carrying the hobbits is rich in /h/ sounds, which in addition resurrects the epic style of alliteration: "so they rode proudly at the head of the singing company with beating hearts and heads held high" [ibid., 101]. The *harmonism* highlighted by Fontanier is thoroughly illustrated by Tolkien's art of semantic unity appertaining to ecological ideas. Tolkien's eco-critical writing is a sheer poeticization grounded in semantic unity, as opposed to the ideological writings that only espouse the idea. The contrast between Tolkien's penning the Elves and the Dwarves further reinforces the significance of *harmonism*. That the Elves love nature as it is and are attached to its beauty and harmony explains the nature of their music, language, temperament and art. On the contrary, the Dwarves, first retained in the darkness under stone under the will of Eru, are born to love caves and metals. As inborn smiths, the Dwarves enjoy shaping the world to realize their ideals. They would fell trees to make charcoals for their forges. Their interaction with Nature embodies their language. Gimli seldom sings songs or recites poems and his discourse is permeated with sarcasm. The scarce occasion for Gimli to be poetic may be his praises of caves [ibid., 181-3]. In contrast, Elves' language resembles air and water, fluid like water and flying like air.

Literature comes from music, the pervasive invisible art. Storytelling also derives from the impulse of unity in musical creation. If we refer to literary history, the more influence visual art exerts on literary creation the less unity the works contain. The spatiality of fine arts slows down the narrative pace into a frozen spot of pictorial depiction. Likewise, psychological description of the characters' inner world parallels the above visualization. A dilation of spatial pause in literary works, especially narratives, often makes the plot fragmentary. For fantastic literature, fluidity and temporality are the core in storytelling, especially to tell stories related to the realm of the unknown. In the style of hypotyposis, musical fluidity in storytelling predominates over fantastic diction, whereas in antithesis, visualization reigns over the deployment of a plot of doubt. In a word, storytelling is a vital element in fantastic art, which essentially mediates the imaginary by means of magical logic, different from rational formalization.

Archaic Music – Narrating through Poems and Embedding Poems in Prose

From the perspective of form, the poem or even the verse is a kind of archaism. Barfield stated that "to the average person, the phrase 'poetic diction' is probably almost synonymous with what the literary mean by 'Archaism'" [Barfield 1973, 153]. The fact that most literary works from the stage of original participation are in verse endows verse-form with certain archaic flavour. By the same token, the classic writing in Chinese literature of *guwen* appears archaic in comparison to the modern prose writing *baihuawen* (a revolutionary writing influenced by Western culture). Although *guwen* is divided into prose and poetry, to modern Chinese readers, reading the arcane *guwen* in prose often requires translation. We may count all the Chinese fantastic stories of *zhiguai* as emulation of fantastic archaism, given that the same storyline was retold by different writers until the Qing dynasty. Many writers of *zhiguai* were themselves poets and couched their fantastic writing in the style of *gushi* (antique poetry, often freer in versification) and *pianwen* (ornate style with sets of four and six characters and vigorous versification). *Guwen* may appear "poetic" (with concrete images, metaphors, ellipsis and archaic lexicons, to certain extent, they may be termed as "free verse") to modern readers; however, classic writers still availed themselves of implanting poems in their stories in "prose" to make it more "poetic." The repetitive imitation and emulation of writing fantastic tales demonstrates the musical quality of storytelling. The repetition echoes with musical refrain and the fluid storytelling imitates musical melody.

Some modern writers of the fantastic resort to poetry to tell stories, especially stories with archaic cultural memory based on myth and legend. Goethe was apt to tell fantastic tales in ballads ("Erlkönig" or *Die Braut von Korinth*) and tragedy of epic poem (*Faust*). Many Romantic poets, such as French Nerval and Lautréamont and English Coleridge and Keats, resorted to ballads to tell fantastic stories. Along the lines of the creation of Arthurian legend, to emulate the medieval romance in verse, Tennyson retold the legend of Arthur and his knights in poetic form – *Idylls of the King*. This thorough rendering of musical archaism in verse-form notwithstanding, requests narrative connivance in modern readers. Just as Barfield pointed out, the human mind is distanced from concrete perception and sundered into the abstract. Alpha-thinking thus tends to obstruct the original perception of storytelling in verse. Therefore, an eclectic employment of verse-form turns to embedding poems amidst fantastic storytelling in prose. In the course of literary evolution, Western and Eastern alike, the development of alpha-thinking entailed the waning of poetry and the waxing of prose. Therefore, the use of verse is the most conspicuous way of indicating the lapse of time. In Western narrative, the enrichment of fantastic prose with poems enhances numerous fairy tales, Romantic, realistic and contemporary works. Instead of deviating from the plot, this embedment of poems rather reminds readers of an archaic memory of Nature's music. The more we are in the intellectual and conscious stages, the farther we are from a predilection for verse. This can be further illustrated by Goethe's observation of his times as prosaic. Tolkien is the unusual author of our times who has resurrected the epic form by embedding verse (mostly in the tetrametre of ballad and Germanic epic) in his prose storytelling.

The fact that Chinese literature stays much longer than its Western counterpart in the original participation can be further corroborated by its abundant fantastic tales embedded with poems. Being a tone language[48], Chinese is endowed with a unique musical feature. This may complement the simplicity of Chinese music that only contains the five whole tones. The meagerness in musical creation entails the prosperity of poetic creation by musical language. The basic qualification to be Chinese literati is composing poems. The prose form seems to be left for didactic essayists. However, as mentioned earlier, the classic Chinese or *guwen* is by itself poetic with its terseness, archaic diction and tones. The predilection for versification in Chinese literature does not elude the fantastic writers, most of whom are poets, for example Cao Pi, Shen Yazhi, Cui Hu, Pei Xing, Niu Sengru and Pu Songling. The poems embedded in the fantastic tales, in the Western tales alike, are presented as, instead of lyrics, a narrative unity endowed with functions and indices (*fonctions* and *indices* to employ Barthes's terms). Some of the inserted poems are composed by earlier poets or from the folk ballads; some are composed by the writers themselves.

As stated previously, every being is anthropomorphized in the Chinese worldview. Animals can not only metamorphose into human beings but also behave like men such as composing or reciting poems. Pei Xing's (the Tang dynasty) story "Shen Tucheng" embeds poems recited by the hero and the heroine (supernatural character). The inception of the story stages the hero who, menaced by the blizzard, asks for shelter at the heroine's house. They reveal their liking for each other by exchanging the poems or songs from *Shi Jing* or *The Book of Songs or Poetry*.[49] The hero incites the heroine to reply by reciting "厭厭夜飲 / 不醉無歸 or *yan yan ye yin / bu zui wu gui*" (Mirth and revel we drink the night / Until drunk will we return); the heroine antiphonally recites "風雨如晦 / 雞鳴不已 or *feng yu ru hui / ji ming bu yi*" (Murk as night blot wind and rain / Without cease crow the restless cocks). Pei's ellipsis of the next two lines in the poem is in fact left to readers to make up. If readers do not fill in the

---

[48] The four tones in Chinese Mandarin are distinctive features. For example, the same pronunciation of "dao" can be written in many different forms according to its different homophones with four possible tones. The word of Dao from Daoism (generally transcribed as Tao in the West) is in the fourth tone.

[49] *Shijing* or *The Book of Songs or Poetry* contains some of the oldest songs or ballads of Chinese literature. It is surmised to have been compiled by Confucius, who has chosen some 300 poems out of 3000.

blank ("既見君子 / 云胡不喜 or *ji jian jun zi / yun hu bu xi*" (Seeing my ideal man arrive / How can I not be merry?)), they will certainly not understand why the hero deems that the heroine likes him. The heroine's real identity will be uncovered as a tigress at the end of the story. Before the revelation of her meta-morphosis, she has already recited a poem that implies her animal nature: "琴瑟 情雖重 / 山林志自深 / 常憂時節變 / 辜負百年心 or *qin se qing sui zhong / shan lin zhi zi shen / chang you shi jie bian / gu fu bai nian xin*" (Despite the at-tached conjugal love / The passion for the mountains and woods is profound / Fear often the changes of seasons / Disappoint the hundred-year heart[50]).

Another example is Cui Hu (the Tang dynasty) whose poem is well known today, albeit most readers are not familiar with the original fantastic tale. The tale "Cui Hu Ye Jiang" (Cui Hu visits for drink) is collected in *Benshi Shi* (*Sto-ries of Poems*) that tells the story about the context of composing the poem: "去 年今日此門中, / 人面桃花相映紅. / 人面不知何處去? / 桃花依舊笑春風. or *qu nian jin ri ci men zhong, / ren mian tao hua xiang ying hong. / ren mian bu zhi he chu qu? / tao hua yi jiu xiao chun feng*" (Exact today from last year inside this door, / Her charming face blushed with the red peach blossoms. / Where is now the beautiful face? / Only the peach blossoms laugh with/at spring breeze). The hero (normally taken as the poet himself) one day comes to the heroine's house for a drink. After he returns home, he can not rid himself of the sweet memory of the charming girl. Next year, on the same day, he goes to visit the girl but finds the door locked. He leaves the above poem on the door and leaves. The girl comes home to see the poem and dies of heartbreak some days later. Overcome by the passion for her, the poet goes to the girl's house again but learns from her father that she is dead from reading his poem. The poet cannot help but wail and thus resurrects the dead girl. Readers mostly enjoy the beauty of the poems in the tale, albeit the story appears obviously simple. This simplic-ity permeates Chinese fantastic short stories. The writers are more interested in portraying their art of poetic language than polishing a complicated and uncon-ventional technique of enunciation. The central aesthetics of telling fantastic sto-ries is closer to the repetition of playing music.

Similar presentation of poems that serve narrative functions in fantastic tales is frequently found in the conventional narrative style, such as fairy tales. The employment of verses is even arranged as the musical refrain. Such examples abound in Brother Grimms' tales. The narrative form of "The Fisherman and his Wife" adopts the musical repetition or refrains in the storytelling. The fisher-man's insatiable wife step by step forces her husband to ask for more and more boons from the fish or the enchanted prince of the sea. Her greed is intensified

---

[50] The expression of the hundred-year heart means the heart for life. However, Chinese read-ers understand the expression by both meanings, literal and figurative. According to Chi-nese Daoist belief, it takes one hundred years of Daoist practice for the destined spouses to get married and live together in the present reincarnation.

and growing in gradation with the rhythm of the poems as refrains of the story. The poem seems to chant a forever story of mankind's insatiability.

In the beginning, the fisherman lives with his wife in a ditch, close by the sea-side. The fisherman goes to the sea six times to recite the same poem to ask for boons from the fish:

> 'O man of the sea!
> Come listen to me,
> For Alice my wife,
>
> The plague of my life,
> Hath sent me to beg a boon of thee!' [Grimm, 36-41]

Through the repetitive recitation of the poem, the fish, who is the enchanted prince, grants the fisherman consecutive boons enunciated with the same sentence pattern (Go home... she is ... already) that echoes with the poem as refrain: from "'Go home, then,' said the fish, 'she is in the cottage already,'" through "she is standing at the door of it [a stone castle] already,'" "'she is king already,'" "'she is emperor already,'" and "'she is pope already.'" Eventually, the fisherman's wife asks to be lord of the sun and moon and the fish replies, "'Go home,' said the fish, 'to your ditch again!' And there they live to this very day" [ibid., 41]. This repetition as musical refrain in fantastic writing enhances the telling of the synchronism in human imagination and nature.

Such examples of embedding refrains in fairy tales are numerous. Examples are the famous tale of "Snow-Drop" (or "Snow White") and "The Frog-Prince." In the first tale, readers are refreshed by the refrain of the enquiry of the queen and the glass's answer:

> 'Tell me, glass, tell me true!
> Of all the ladies in the land,
> Who is the fairest? Tell me who?' [ibid., 93-8]

The glass answers, like the variation of the fixed pattern of the above fish's reply, in gradation to the queen:

> 'Thou, queen, art fairest in the land.' [ibid., 93]
> 'Thou, queen, may'st fair and beauteous be,
> But Snow-drop is lovelier far than thee!' [ibid., 93]
> 'Thou, queen, art the fairest in all this land;
> But over the hills, in the greenwood shade,
> Where the seven dwarfs their dwelling have made,
> There snow-drop is hiding her head, and she
> Is lovelier far, O queen! than thee.' [ibid., 95]
> 'Thou, queen, art the fairest in all this land;
> But over the hills, in the greenwood shade,

> Where the seven dwarfs their dwelling have made,
> There snow-drop is hiding her head; and she
> Is lovelier far, O queen! than thee.' [ibid., 96]

At last, after the queen poisons Snow-drop, she gets the reply she expects, "Thou, queen, art the fairest of all the fair" [ibid., 97]. Then the story closes with the last answer of the glass, "Thou, lady, art loveliest *here*, I ween; / But lovelier far is the new-made queen" [ibid., 99]. Likewise, in "The Frog-Prince," the frog comes to the door of the princess to ask her to keep her promise by the refrains of poem: "Open the door, my princess dear, / Open the door to thy true love here! / And mind the words that thou and I said / By the fountain cool in the green-wood shade" [ibid., 137-8].

In French literature, fond of traditional myths, legends and fairy tales, Nodier applied the musical art of fairy tales in his tale of "La fée aux miettes" (The Fairy of Crumbs) to smooth the proceeding of his narration. Here is the refrain that resounds and penetrates the whole story:

> It's me, it's me, it's me,
> I am the mandragora,
> The daughter of the summer time that wakes up at dawn,
> And that chants for you! [Nodier 1961, 180, 210, 216, 304, 316][51]

The implantation of poems in fantastic prose writing is common to writers under the influence of romance and literary ballad. Eichendorff's "Autumn Sorcery" serves as a good example. Different from the fantastic ballad of Keats who depicted the unfortunate loitering knight enchanted by the belle dame sans mercy, Eichendorff embedded poems into his fantastic tale to enhance the musical art of the romantic work. The enchantment in the story thus reverberates throughout the tale by the initial prayer song and the ensuing enchanting songs. From the last stanza of the song, we, as well as the hero Ubaldo, learn about the agony and suffering of the hermit, later known as Raimundo:

> Oh break my chains too!
> To save all men
> You suffered a bitter death.
> I am lost at the gates of Hell.
> How forsaken I am!
> Jesus, help me in my anguish! [Calvino, 20]

Then the intradiegetic narration enunciated by the hermit echoes the extra-diegetic by the connection of the enchanting songs seemingly sung by the beau-

---

[51] *C'est moi, c'est moi, c'est moi, / Je suis la mandragore, / La fille des beaux jours qui s'éveille à l'aurore, / Et qui chante pour toi !*

tiful damsel or femme fatale that weaves the spiderweb to ensnare the poor knight Raimundo as prey. This Romantic version of the medieval legend of *Tannhäuser's sojourn in the pagan paradise of Venus* (the world of seduction and sin) is perfected by the play of music in the storytelling, the forever chanting of the melody carried by the wind that also closes the story:

> The further he advanced, the more the song transformed into the old melody of the hunting horns, which in another time had seduced him.
>> My golden curls wave
>> And my young body sweetly flowers,
> He heard, as if were an echo in the distance:
>> And the streams that in the silent valley
>> Go their way whispering...
> His castle, the mountains, and the entire world all sank behind him.
>> And the warm greeting of love,
>> The echo of the hunting horns offers you.
>> Come sweet love, before they fall silent!...
> resounded once again.
>> Overcome by madness, poor Raimundo followed after the melody through the depth of the forest. From that day on, he was never seen again. [ibid., 31-2]

This archaic form of inserting poems in fantastic prose writing is not only reserved for Romantic writers. Examples can also be found in the realistic fantastic. Poe, the master of fantastic short stories working on the art of tension as the total effect, embedded the verses in some of his tales such as "The Fall of the House of Usher," not only for the sake of poetic and musical effect but also for the sake of the *mise en abyme*. The title of the verse, "The Haunted Palace" resounds with the gruesome house of Usher:

> I
> In the greenest of our valleys,
> By good angels tenanted,
> Once a fair and stately palace –
> Radiant palace – reared its head.
> In the monarch Thought's dominion –
> It stood there!
> Never seraph spread a pinion
> Over fabric half so fair. [Poe 1994, 155]
> VI [last stanza]
> And travelers now within that valley,
> Through the red-litten windows, see
> Vast forms that move fantastically
> To a discordant melody;
> While, like a rapid ghastly river,
> Through the pale door,

A hideous throng rush out for ever,
And laugh – but smile no more. [ibid., 156]

Poe's employment of poems in prose writing of the fantastic strengthens the effect of the insecure and strange atmosphere and prepares for the eventual inexplicable denouement of the story. The embedment of verse form in Poe's fantastic tales endows them with an archaic musicality that echoes with a verse line from his "Ligeia": "the orchestra breathes fitfully the music of the spheres" [ibid., 231].

The embedment of poems in fantastic tales gradually lost its attraction with the ebb of the Romantic Movement. The twentieth century was at its prosaic prime. However, readers are refreshed again by the musical and poetic storytelling of Tolkien. Throughout *The Lord of the Rings*, readers encounter many embedded poems. Though many readers disapprove of this musical measure by its hindering them from following the plot, the poetic forms, mostly ballads and lays, are indeed significant components that enhance Tolkien's narrative art of fantasy as a musical organism. The complete work of Tolkien can be appreciated as a symphony of euphoria, similar to the delightful style of Mozart. This integration of poems into prose writing is, however, not employed in his mythology *The Silmarillion*, with the exception of the Song of Parting made by Beren in praise of Luthien and the lights of heaven [Tolkien 1999, 209-10]. We can guess the reason for this lack of poems in the mythology. It is this very reason that sheds light on Tolkien's exuberance of poetic forms in the ring trilogy. Since the Silmarillion mythology manifests itself as the origin of all, the very original visage of archaism, music of Nature, it is explicitly narrated throughout the creation of the world. In contrast, the time of Frodo is a later stage far from the mythological times, similar to our idolatrous times. People disbelieve in supernatural beings, having only dim memory from ballads and songs.

Theoden's reflective response to Gandalf's explanation of tales concerning the origin of the Ents raises the significance of songs ("Songs we have that tell of these things") highlights their poetic importance in fantastic storytelling. They are the form and the content of universal music that tell tales in tune with Nature. The poems, like the above quoted examples, play the part of telling stories; they are not independently added to the prose but amalgamated with it. The embedded poetry is the reminiscence of the past, light or shadow. Minstrels keep on reciting the poems to keep the fire of memory and creation. All characters are endowed with different style of poems, for example, the Hobbits' songs are closer to folk songs and portray a vernacular nature. In the first chapter of the trilogy, the first song sung by Bilbo before his departure, which harks back to the song towards the end of his journey in *The Hobbit* [Tolkien 1995, 276], serves as a prelude for Frodo's quest:

> The Road goes ever on and on
>> Down from the door where it began.
> Now far ahead the Road has gone,
>> And I must follow, if I can,
> Pursuing it with eager feet,
>> Until it joins some larger way
> Where many paths and errands meet.
>> And whither then? I cannot say. [Tolkien 1999 *Fellowship*, 47]

And this same song rejoins with the last poem of Bilbo towards the end of the trilogy with a variation of the second quatrain:

> ……………………………………....
> Let them a journey new begin,
>> But I at last with weary feet
> Will turn towards the lighted inn,
>> My evening-rest and sleep to meet. [Tolkien 2003, 321]

This musical echo in the trilogy repeats of nuance of the first and last songs sung by Frodo. The first song is in fact sung by the three hobbits, Frodo, Sam and Pippin as they walk in the lands of the Water-valley and talk about Adventure. Bilbo made the words to a tune that was as old as the hills.

> ……………………………………..
> Still round the corner there may wait
> A new road or a secret gate,
> And though we pass them by today,
> Tomorrow we may come this way
> And take the hidden paths that run
>
> Towards the Moon or to the Sun.
> …………………………………….. [Tolkien 1999 *Fellowship*, 103]

After the accomplishment of his quest, Frodo is not the same Frodo, he has become a poet and returns to the realm of Elves. His completing of personal individualization and the purge into the realm of myth manifests in the variation of the poem recomposed by him:

> Still round the corner there may wait
> A new road or a secret gate;
> And though I oft have passed them by
> A day will come at last when I
> Shall take the hidden paths that run
> West of the Moon, East of the Sun. [Tolkien 2003, 374]

The second poem is replied by the song sang by the Elven folk:

> A! Elbereth Gilthoniel!
> silivren penna miriel
> o menel aglar elenath,
> Gilthoniel, A! Elbereth!
> We still remember, we who dwell
> In this far land beneath the trees
> The starlight on the Western Seas. [ibid., 374]

The trilogy uses the Elven song as the very last poem in the story, "for the Third Age was over, and the Days of the Rings were passed, and an end was come of the story and song of those times" [ibid., 376].

Besides Bilbo and Frodo, most characters recite poems or sing songs, for joy, truth, charm, secret, sorrow, courage, etc. The scene where the hobbits relax and take a bath is depicted by their bath-song that reveals delight and joy: "Snatches of competing songs came from the bathroom mixed with sound of splashing and wallowing. The voice of Pippin was suddenly lifted up above the others in one of Bilbo's favourite bath-songs" [Tolkien 1999 *Fellowship*, 133]. The last stanza of the song echoes with the following narration:

> O! Water is fair that leaps on high
> in a fountain white beneath the sky;
> but never did fountain sound so sweet
> as splashing Hot Water with my feet!
> There was a terrific splash, and a shout of *Whoa!* from Frodo. It appeared
> that a lot of Pippin's bath had imitated a fountain and leaped on high. [ibid.,
> 134]

The bath-song and many other songs sung by the Hobbits are characterized as pristine, rustic, and above all, euphoriant.

Different form the Hobbits' poetic style, Aragorn radiates a noble disposition of a great king. Being a descendant of Men and Elves, Aragorn portrays his graceful and lofty language through the poems he recites or the songs he sings to his companions. His real identity is revealed by the solemn poem by Gandalf:

> All that is gold does not glitter,
> Not all those who wander are lost;
> The old that is strong does not wither,
> Deep roots are not reached by the frost.
> From the ashes a fire shall be woken,
> A light from the shadows shall spring,
> Renewed shall be blade that was broken,
> The crownless again shall be king. [ibid., 224]

This poem of import is composed by Gandalf and sent to Frodo with his letter to reveal the identification of Strider Aragorn. The octave composed by Gandalf, a Maiar, like those by Elves, appears solemn and lofty with wisdom. It has its part to play in the plot to foretell the future adventure of the fellowship and the return of the king.

The dirge sung by Aragorn and Legolas for Boromir is an example of poems of sorrow: Through Rohan over fen and field where the long grass grows / The West Wind comes walking, and about the walls it goes. / [...] / 'O Boromir! From the high walls westward I looked afar, / But you came not from the empty lands where no men are'" [Tolkien 2001, 11]. The missing of the East Wind in the dirge further emphasizes the fellowship's resolution to fight against the evil power even after their death, since Mordor is in the east of Middle-earth. The rhyme that Tom Bombadil teaches the hobbits to sing is a charm in case of falling into any danger by ill-luck. His songs resemble the oldest songs as the enchanting music in the Norse epic of *Kalevala*. The Ents chant while striding and chant while heading for the war to Isengard. Likewise, the riders sing the songs of Rohand for courage. Even Gollum sometimes *croaks* in a sort of song: "The cold hard lands / they bites our hands, / they gnaws our feet [...]" [ibid., 278].

These poems, whether considered by themselves or within the context of their prose setting, express the archaic musical style. They are not separated from the development of the plot. Instead, they are a motif to the whole piece of fantastic work as music. Tolkien's fantasy makes the most of poetic music and best illustrates the musical features of verse-form in fantastic prose. The poems re-chant the shadow and light of the past throughout the fantastic stories. Barfield pointed out that the verse-form itself is the most obvious manifestation of the style of archaic musicality and the very nature of archaism is its future vision. These features of archaism also appear in fantastic literature that is germane to the imaginary of the unknown. It vibrates with the reminiscence of the past music into the perpetual music of the future. The composition of fantastic poems and the embedment of verse-form in fantastic stories demonstrate a conspicuous style of *harmonism*.

Primitive Rhythm of Chôra and Tetra-Elements

The assumption that primitive literature comes from music or songs is lastly illustrated by the principle of perpetual metamorphosis from chôra to the four rudimentary elements or the tetra-elements to result in the myriad of all things. Aristotle is the first poetician who explicitly connected form with content or versification with physical manifestations. His analysis of tragedy and epic in *Poetics* is scrupulous and detailed in bringing to light the musical function in the narratives. His insight into metres vis-à-vis action and dancing helps combine the studies of language as sound and rhythm with language as semantic units that extend to the syntactic structure of story: "The iambic and the trochaic tetrametres are the metres of movement, the trochaic for dancing and the iambic for dramatic action [Aristotle 1970, 52]. The metric quality of movement is vital to the narrative imitation. Movement implies musical rhythm and fluidity in the narration, whether it is dramatic or dancing. Besides Homer's use of iambic metre to narrate his epic, other epic poets such as Milton, utilized heroic couplets to tell the story of Satan's rebellion against God in *Paradise Lost*. The iambic pentametre was also the basic English verse pattern during the Elizabethan age.

The fantastic epics from Antiquity, Virgil's *The Aeneid*, Ovid's *Metamorphoses* and Apuleius's *The Golden Ass*, are all poeticized by trochaic metre. According to Aristotle, the trochaic is the metre of movement and dance, and these three epics accentuate musical movement like dance to create the musical effect of gaiety and storytelling. The same metrical measure is applied in Finnish and Icelandic epics, *Kalevala* and *Elder Edda*. This metre of momentum can be best illustrated in the epic poem of *Kalevala*, which is written in eight-syllable trochaic verse or trochaic tetrametre. The image of dancing and music is vividly depicted through this unique metre. Since music, the reiterative enchanting singing and the playing of the magic instrument Kantele of Väinämöinen, is the core spirit of the epic, the trochaic metre of dancing movement is befitting to the epic narration.

Besides these examples that employ a specific metre in epic storytelling, modern writers of fantastic literature also avail themselves of applying metres and rhymes in their fantastic prose. Given that French literature is occupied with visualization in writing, such as symbolism and revolutionary narrative technique of *Nouveau Roman*, examples of musical writing are fewer than in English literature. English writers such as Lord Dunsany and Oscar Wilde incorporated archaic musicality into their storytelling. The narration of Dunsany's "The Sword of Welleran" is a complete rhythm and sonority of a dreamy state, which is like swinging in a remote dream, connected with the rhythm of chôra. The sentences replete with "ands" become rhythmic through the musical assonance: "O Welleran, thou wast our sun and moon and all our stars. Now is the sun fallen down and the moon broken, and all the stars are scattered as the diamonds of a necklace that is snapped off one who is slain by violence" [Silverberg 1990, 41]. Wilde excelled in rendering his fantastic narration in prose in a genuinely poetic way like musical chanting. His fairy tales already manifest such poetic musicality. He even poeticized his ghost story into a chanting melody. For example, in "The Canterville Ghost," he versifies with iambic pentametre in the course of telling this parody of a Gothic romance. This musical effect makes the parody even sharper as he versifies the scene that the Canterville ghost encounters the fake ghost planned by the naughty and nasty twin brothers: "From the eyes streamed rays of scarlet light, the mouth was a wide well of fire, and a hideous garment, like to his own, swathed with its silent snows the Titan form" [Wilde 1994 *Lord*, 55-6]. Iambic pentametre with alliteration, assonance and rhymes makes the story a classic of the fantastic par excellence.

In our times of linguistic niches, literary works seldom offer musical chanting. However, thanks to Tolkien, a philologist sensitive to words with their sonority and imagination, we may experience again the reading and hearing pleasure as experienced in the original participation. Music is ubiquitous throughout Tolkien's fantastic creation, in the embedded poems and the narration in prose. His embedded poems are mostly iambic tetrametre. Tetrametre is, as mentioned above, indeed the metre of ballad and Germanic epic, or a common metre for telling stories in verse. With the abundant use of alliteration, his intention to create a fantastic epic is quite obvious. The aforecited poems composed by Bilbo and Frodo are octave in iambic tetrametre. Apart from his predilection for tetrametre, he created a variety of verse forms, such as ballads sung by minstrels and songs of Tom Bombadil and the Ents. The older the songs are, the more alliteration is used. Even the dirge for Boromir is rich in alliteration with /f/, /g/ and /w/ (as quoted earlier). Legolas mostly sings ballads. For example, he sings the song of the maiden Nimrodel consisting in tetrametre followed by trimetre. An Elven-maid there was of old, / A shining star by day: / Her mantle white was hemmed with gold, / Her shoes of silver-grey" [Tolkien 1999 *Fellowship*, 445].

Tolkien's musical artistry and acuteness manifest not only in the poetry accompanying his novel but also in his prose writing, which is even harder to do than merely poetic writing. The following quotation may illustrate Tolkien's musical art in prose narration:

> The hosts of Isengard, swaying this way and that, turning from fear to fear. Again the horn sounded from the tower. Down through the breach of Dike charged the king's company. Down from the hills leaped Erkenbrand, lord of Westford. Down leaped Shadowfax, like a deer that runs surefooted in the mountains. [...] The Orcs reeled and screamed and cast aside both sword and spear. Like a black smoke driven by a mounting wind they fled. Wailing they passed under the waiting shadow of the trees; and from that shadow none ever came again. [Tolkien 2001, 175]

Such exuberance in alliteration, assonance, rhyme and anaphora manifests Tolkien's virtuosity in musical prose. Readers have the impression of seeing through sound. This musical artistry is also evident in his mythology *Silmirillion*, albeit appearing less musical in its entirety compared with the ring trilogy:

> Then the *s*eeds that Yavanna had *s*own began *s*wiftly to *s*prout and to burgeon, and there arose a multitude of gro*w*ing things *great* and *small*, *mosses* and *grasses* and *great* ferns, and trees *whose* tops were crowned with cloud as

they were living mountains, but *whose* feet were wrapped in a *green* twilight.
[Tolkien 1999, 27-8]

A scrupulous analysis of musical style or versification of fantastic storytelling
appears difficult when comparing works from very different linguistic cultures.
For example, Chinese language has no tradition of alliteration; it values more
the end rhyming and assonance. Moreover, being a tone language, Chinese versification does not feature the interplay of stressed and unstressed syllables. Instead, the four tones are decisive in poetic composition. Nevertheless, there is
universal rhythm in the musical imagination of mankind, to conclude our studies
of the fantastic imagination.

The homogeneity in musical beats is quadruple time. In Western literature,
tetrametre is the principal metre for ballad and Germanic epic; in Chinese literature, tetra-character is the primary metre for ballads and myths, such as *Shi
Jing* (*The Book of Songs and Poetry*). This common feature in rhythm of telling
stories from the age of original participation suggests a hypothesis that literary
musicality derives from the collective unconscious or the collective memory
connected with the tetra-elements of earth, water, fire and air, given that all
things are generated and transmuted from them. Therefore, the human collective
memory still echoes with this unknown past. In the Chinese history of versification, the basic tetra-character poetry is alleged to have been derived from the
combination of two di-characters, which is from the antique verse writings on *Yi
Jing* [Li]. Then we may trace back to *Liangyi* or the chôra state of the Universe,
where the yin and the yang form the basic musical duple time. Western literature
has undergone a similar route of rhythmic metamorphosis from dimetre, trimetre
to tetrametre. However, the manifestations of phenomena have settled with the
four elements. Therefore, tetrametre or tetra-character remains the pristine
rhythm of the musical imagination.

Chinese fantastic tales are often written in tetra-character because the four
elements echo with the fantastic imagination. Verses in hepta-character are often
employed in colloquial storytelling. The hepta-character is in fact a combination
of tetra-character and tri-character. This set of "tetra-" and "tri-" evokes a Western ballad that is formed by a tetrametre and trimetre. We can refer to the novel
Fengshen Yanyi or *The Investiture of the Gods* and other numerous *zhiguai* tales.
Pu Songling used abundant tetra-characters to write his corpus of fantastic tales,
in fact to demonstrate his consummate archaic style of *pianwen* (consisting in
tetra-character and hexa-character metre). This predilection for hexa-character
metre in *pianwen* in the Six dynasties, esteemed as ornate and florid style, is
reminiscent of the popularity of hexameter in Latin and French poetry. As to the
universality of number three, we may refer to the Daoist significant number
three (the third change generates all things), *Yi Jing*'s number three (*Taiji* (one)
plus *Liangyi* (two) equals three) and the Western Trinity. Just like in music,

where the basic beats are quadruple time and triple time, narrative poetry uses tetrametre / tetra-character and trimetre / tri-character to tell stories by chanting and reciting. The later development of poetry into pentamtre or penta-character is another common trend in Western and Chinese literature. According to such metre multiplication in poetic creation, it seems quite logical to encounter dodecaphony composed by Faustus with the help of Mephistopheles in the twentieth century.

Conclusion

The exploration of the *inventio* of fantastic literature as the universal root of fantastic creation invites us to delve into the abstract and impalpable realm of the unknown that is essentially linked to metaphysical imagination. Therefore, we make the assumption that the imaginary course in fact leads back to the pristine visage of myth and mythopoeia. The semantic unity of myth and language is regained by means of Eucharistic creation and reception of fantastic literature or alchemy of language. Through the process of linguistic and metaphysical purge, the imaginary creation is able to bridge the gap between the known world and the unknown realm. The position of myth and fantasy amidst the transitional space of octa-trigrams arouses our aesthetic imagination and enlightens our vision to commune with the space of *Sixiang* or four elements and trace back to the origin of changes, the space of *Liangyi, De* or chôra. The art of storytelling changes as human consciousness evolves throughout human history. Therefore, we propose to look at fantastic literature from a historical perspective. The historicity hinges on the evolution of human consciousness. In the light of Barfield's and Tolkien's insight into language and myth, the creation of fantastic literature also undergoes a parallel route. Out of the universal roots of human imagination connected with the Universal Consciousness or human collective unconscious, the memory of *unus mundus*, reminiscence of joy or fear, inspires authors to poeticize a great variation of fantastic stories, in form and content. We offer a new angle to look at seemingly disparate fantastic narratives in a synthetic thematic schema: the basic triangle of the interrelation among the percipient "I" and the percept "other humans and the nonhuman." While theorists of imaginative writing essay to expose the significance of the universal images generated in the processes of our psychological and psychic behaviours and embodied in human creation, our researches extend to the alchemy of language that reifies and embodies the metaphysical light and imaginary figures through the fantastic poetic diction.

As the idolatrous trend waxes in Chinese literature, we regret the waning of musical and semantic unity. A renaissance of Chinese fantastic creation, *à la chinoise*, is still waiting. In Western literature, Tolkien merits to be entitled "the modern Homer" according to our appreciation of his works. Besides alliteration, his use of ballads and lays in iambic tetrametre corresponds to the perpetual movement and rhythm of the four elements that lead us back to the arcane space of chôra. His entire poetic fantastic diction arouses readers' aesthetic imagination. Imitation and emulation modelled on Tolkien's fantasy continue to sustain the light of the style of recovery in our times. This is the quintessence of Eucharist or alchemy of language. The true meaning of *harmonism* lies in the *unus mundus* of formal imagination and material imagination. We may term this precious process of purification and refinement as the Eucharistic alchemy of language. Through the fantastic and aesthetic imagination, language as well as our six senses (five senses plus mind) will be purified into the semantic unity of the coexistence of the abstract and the concrete. This is the unity of soul, form, things and meanings, reunited by the storytelling of musicality.

Part Two
Rhetoric of Fantastic Literature:
Discourses of Dream, Mirror and the Magician's Hat

Capriccio: Zhuang Zi and Zephyrus

One day, Zhuang Zi, the father of Chinese fantastic literature, heard some songs composed by a minstrel who'd been inspired by a lunch with the family of Zephyrus. Zhuang Zi listened to the minstrel's intriguing ballads, a somewhat rococo style that sounded curious to him. He decided to have a chat with this exotic poet. In those times, there were no aircraft or ships to support inter-continental transportation. Zhuang Zi must have been the first traveler equipped with a flying shuttle. In fact, this was the stirring banner that had aroused meditation and was later called the magic banner of time travelling. He gaped at the brand new world unfolding before his eyes, for everything appeared exotic to him. The minstrel was meditating and frowning on Descartes's "*cogito ergo sum.*" He was in fact totally swallowed up by the strife between the dialectic language and the poetic language. He tried to convince Descartes that his fantastic poetry was no less true than his rationalist philosophy. But intuition appeared unconvincing as rhetoric to confront philosophy. After hearing the minstrel's lamentation, Zhuang Zi, fond of his French chanting accent, made some wise and serene coughs and told him the following story:

Two houses stood on an immense plain. One was the home of some people who went about their daily tasks. They are called percepts. The people of the other house, the percipients, however, made a study of the actions of the first lot, and built their model of reality on the basis of these observations. With their scientific methodology, formal logic and pure reason, they were confident that they had found the truth. After a while, dissension arose among them. Some of them came to doubt the truth of the previous conclusions. They proposed to deconstruct the settled rules and meanings taken to be true from the predecessors, by denying any possible truth in the world. The first house is the object of the known; the second house is the subject capable to know; the plain itself is the immense unknown.

My dear friend, imagine how gargantuan the unknown space is in comparison with the house already known and the house to know. You are entrapped in the morass of defending yes or no. If no one in the world can testify that the ultimate truth does not exist, why bother to testify for its existence? Knowledge comes from the unknown. Curiosity drives us to explore unknown space, whether to prove or disprove that unknown something.

Inspired by this wise tale, the minstrel regained his smiling countenance. He plucked his lyre and chanted again his tales about the unknown. He requited Zhuang Zi with an impromptu musical tale:

Once there was a lyre who boasted that she was so great that everyone hearkened to her music for the divine blessing. The musician bragged that he was even greater than the lyre since his technique of plucking the strings outplayed the instrument. Then a breeze wafted by, contending that he was the real source of harmonious music. However, the lyre and the musician ignored the presence of the wind and continued their competition. Furious at their nonchalance, the wind exhaled a gust, whipped the musician until he fainted, and swirled away the lyre. After the musician came to, he tried to play music for passers-by, but could not find his lyre. He tried to sing by himself, but his voice was nothing but a frog croak. He started to miss his lyre and set off to search for it. Meanwhile, wayfarers passed to and fro in an unknown forest. One wayfarer found a delicate lyre lying under a birch. The lyre woke up as he approached. She told him that she was so wonderful that she could make many beautiful melodies. Astonished by this speaking instrument, he drew back a few steps, rubbed his eyes and stared again at the lyre.

"Trust me, I can offer you the greatest music in the world!" said the lyre.

Then the wayfarer waited to appreciate beautiful music, but waited over a long period of silence. Eventually, the lyre realized that she needed fingers to pluck her strings. Then the lyre pleaded the wayfarer to pluck her strings, but he refused lest he broke the delicate instrument. The lyre regretted her haughtiness and missed her lyrist. She couldn't help but cry. Her whining and weeping resounded with the sobbing and moaning of the wind. The incremental remorse made her continue to bawl. The bewailing was so loud that the wind carried it to the hearing of the musician. He recognized the cry of his lyre and rushed to her. He held his beloved lyre and plucked the strings and started to sing. He sang the song of art between the musician and the lyre. The lyre vibrated the music of a world perfected by the couple of instrument and musician. Then all of a sudden, the song and the music were muffled. The whole world turned into a perfect mute and void, the musician's mouth still stirring, and the lyre's strings still vibrating. They then realized what sacrilege they had committed. Their hubris eventually succumbed to the universal unknown might. The musician invoked the inspiration of the Muses with humility; the lyre implored benediction to magic strings. The impasse broken, the wind whistled past the lyre and the lyrist. The chant, the music and the whiz resonated into a chorus of unending harmony and mystery, ever after.

Zhuang Zi returned an understanding smile to the minstrel and soared up with the magic banner. His words still reverberated in the air: "Unbind the ego from the known, fly the self into the unknown." The minstrel continued his trip, telling stories about the unknown. He was thus hight the minstrel of Zephyrus.

Introduction

Ever since the Hellenistic epoch (300 BC), rhetoric has influenced the theorization of literature. We learn from Horace the tripartite elements of rhetoric – *inventio, dispositio, elocutio* – to analyze the composition of poetry. Modern poetician Tzvetan Todorov interpreted the tripartitions of the old rhetoric by the following linguistic concepts: "semantic (*inventio*), syntactic (*dispositio*) and verbal (*elocutio*)." On the other hand, Russian formalists interpreted them respectively into "thematics, composition and stylistic" [Todorov 1992, 15]. Rhetoric originally referred to the art of the orator. Aristotle emphasized the importance of rhetoric in the art of mimesis and thus referred to rhetoric in the section treating *lexis* (expression, language, style or writing) in his *Poetics*. Aristotle in fact kept *Rhetoric* as a separate work from *Poetics*. However, with the evolution of literary theory hinging on poetics with the emphasis on the *lexis* section, rhetoric had gradually superseded poetics from the Renaissance to Classicism. Jacques Legrand even subsumed poetics to rhetoric by terming it "the second rhetoric" [Dessons 60]. The theory of rhetoric in its prime defined a poet as a historian, an orator and a philosopher. However, this overemphasis on rhetoric, also designated as "restricted rhetoric" (*la rhétorique restreinte*), was censured by Romantic writers and thus remained ignored until the resurrection of "the New Rhetoric" (*la nouvelle rhétorique*) in the 20th century. Gérard Genette was a leading rhetorician (or poetician) whose rhetorical theory (or narratology) is concerned with literary discourse and figure.

The term "rhetoric" is employed here to treat the discourse and figure of fantastic narration, inclusive of the enunciated (*énoncé*), enunciation (*énonciation*) and syntax (*syntaxe*). The rhetoric of the fantastic refers to informal logic (*la logique informelle*) [Chaïm Perelman] in contradistinction to formal logic. The concept of informal logic may be compared to Durand's rhetoric of the imaginary, termed as pre-logic. According to Durand, the discourse of rhetoric appears "between the pure image and the system of logico-philosophical coherence that it [image] promotes, like a middle-term constituting what we can call [...] a 'transcendental schematism'" (*entre l'image pure et le système de cohérence logico-philosophique qu'elle promeut, comme un moyen-terme constituant ce que nous pouvons appeler [...] un « schématisme transcendantal »*) [Durand, 482-3]. In this light, rhetoric assures "the passage between the semantism of symbols and the formalism of logic or the literal meaning of signs" (le passage entre le sémantisme des symbols et le formalisme de la logique ou le sens proper des signes) [ibid., 483]. However, this "transcendental schematism" is adopted by Durand not in the sense of "an *a priori* determination of time," but on the contrary, "an *a priori* determination of anti-destiny, of euphemism that will colour, in its entirety, all the process of thought formalization. Rhetoric is definitely this pre-logic, intermediary between imagination and reason" (une détermination a priori de l'anti-destin, de l'euphémisme qui va teinter, dans son ensemble, toutes les démarches de formalistion de la pensée. La rhétorique est bien cette pré-logique, intermédiaire entre l'imagination et la raison) [ibid., 483]. In his theory of the imaginary, Durand raises the issue of rhetoric, originally an intermediary bridge to assure the semantic transmission of *la fantastique*. Identifying the function of rhetoric further explains that the more we formalize, the farther we go away from the original semantism of great fantastic archetypes. The structure or syntax in the eyes of Durand is determined by semantic elements, since a pure formal structure is impossible. Therefore, throughout his classification of the diurnal and nocturnal structures of the imaginary, he keeps reminding readers that his structures should be taken semantically. Accordingly, the semantic significance also decides the rhetoric of fantastic narration that we will analyze in this section.

Furthermore, besides the semantic significance stated above, rhetoric also refers to the relationship between the author/text and the reader. In fact, apart from the discourse itself, the rudimentary meaning of rhetoric includes an art of oratory (especially deemed by Aristotle) that refers to the moral character of the orator-speaker (*ethos*) and the spirit of the auditor-receiver (*pathos*). In light of Aristotle's conception of rhetoric, fictional narration plays a vital role as a joint between rhetoric and poetics. The art of fantastic storytelling introduces fantastic imagination into readers' reception. The aesthetics of reception of fantastic literature indeed depend on cultural differences that anchor the thinking mode and imagination concerning the unknown.

The title words of *dream, mirror* and *magician's hat* refer to the tripartite pattern of the fantastic rhetoric. All three terms are to be taken as metaphors. The differences between the categorized narrative discourses can be illustrated by the image of the sea. The dream-discourse presents the whole scale of the collective unconscious as an immense sea. This type of fantastic discourse vibrates with the collective dream of man. The mirror-discourse sees the unconscious as a representation of reality perceived by humans. It is like the reflection on the surface of water, or a mirage. The magician's hat-discourse refers to splinters of the collective unconscious as the spindrifts of the immense sea.

The tripartition of fantastic discourses may be further associated with Tolkien's division of the faces in fairy-stories: "the Mystical towards the Supernatural; the Magical towards Nature; and the Mirror of scorn and pity towards Man" [Tolkien 1997, 125]. The first two faces dominate storytelling with the discourses of dream and magician's hat, whereas the last face determines the narrative rendering of the mirror-discourse.

The dream-discourse means the "mimesis" of the collective unconscious linked with the secret space of chôra. The discourse is structured by the transformation of four fundamental elements. These elements will be later joined by the purest metal, gold, termed as the fifth element. The discovery of gold is an inkling of human civilization since it is related to artificial refinement and forging of metals. The practice of alchemy is initiated from gold refining, which symbolizes eternity and wealth. Thus Chinese culture features five elements instead of four (gold, wood or air, water, fire and earth) in the fundamental elements. The fifth element, as in many fantastic tales, appears as the key that connects the known and the unknown realm. For example, gold bridges the divine and the mundane worlds in "The Golden Pot" (E. T. A. Hoffmann) and "The Golden Key" (George MacDonald). In terms of narrative structure, the four elements semantically construct the fantastic plot, whereas the element gold often symbolizes the aesthetic language or serves as the sustaining motif.

The dream-discourse includes the narrative type, being myth, epic or saga. Such a discourse abounds with great works from the first two stages of fantastic creation (primitive conception and myth as the fabrication of truth). During the period of skepticism, Goethe's *Faust* was a prototype of the dream-discourse. Tolkien's sub-creation is a fantastic prototype in our times as the emergence of the fourth stage of truth in mirage or final participation.

The mirror-discourse is characterized by the narrative structure of ambiguity or duality. The reading effect of such fantastic works is like gazing at the mirror to the point that the originally perceived reality appears to be unreal. It is as if the curtain that conceals the unknown realm is temporarily circumvented through the mirror reflection. The main rhetoric of the mirror-discourse has its variations in the style of Todorovian hesitation (e.g. Poe's "William Wilson"), ambiguity with doubt (e.g. Hoffmann's "The Sandman") and the Möbius strip[52] (e.g. Cortázar's "The Continuity of Parks"). According to Brooke-Rose's theory of fantastic narrative modes, the mode of "the real as unreal" can characterize the mirror-discourse.

The magician's hat-discourse, together with the dream-discourse, can be classified under Brooke-Rose's narrative mode of "the unreal as real." It comprises stories that portray the unknown, but on a smaller and more fragmentary scale than the dream-discourse. The magician's hat-discourse corresponds to Aristotle's "unique epic," whereas dream-discourse "the complex epic." With the rhetoric of magician's hat, it is like removing the curtain that conceals the unknown realm as a juggle with the magician's hat to let readers appreciate parts of the unknown world. Fairy tales, fantastic ballads, fables, some fantasy stories (e.g. *Harry Potter*), supernatural tales (e.g. the absurd kind like Gogol's "The Nose," *The Arabian Nights* or Chinese fantastic tales), vampire literature (e.g. *Dracula* and *Camilla*) and myriads of ghost stories are variations of the fantastic fiction that draws on the rhetoric of the magician's hat.

---

[52] The Möbius strip is a "surface that can be formed by taking a long, rectangular strip of paper, rotating the ends 180° with respect to one another, and joining the ends together to form a loop. The Möbius strip is a two-dimensional surface that has only one side" [Encarta Encyclopedia, CD Rom].

While the theory of the imaginary (developed in the first part of the present book) pivots on the paradigmatic axis, the commentary on the narrative discourse presented here depends on the syntagmatic axis. Fantastic storytelling is a kind of intermediating rhetoric that executes the *mise en scène* of fantastic imagination by the pre-logical grammatical syntax. Revolving around the *semantism* of *la fantastique*, the rhetoric of fantastic literature will be studied according to the stratifications of structures that are rooted in chôra, the mystic participation of the collective unconscious, the material imagination of four elements and the diurnal/nocturnal structures of the imaginary. The synchronism of the universal roots of the imaginary (the perpetual images and symbols remaining intact throughout time) is represented by three main categories of diachronism (the art of storytelling as the narrative rhetoric that proceeds through time). At the same time, the narrative discourse is also predetermined by the imaginary orientation and the *isotopism* of images. The three patterns of narrative discourse possess a common attribute in spite of the ostensive heterogeneity among them. This common attribute is the rhetorical syntax of strangeness as the metamorphosis related to chôra. Therefore, the quintessence of the imaginary as the *inventio* in fantastic poetics will further elucidate fantastic rhetoric. This rhetoric enables fantastic storytelling as an orator that affects readers to appreciate and rejoice over the representation of *la fantastique*, which is inspired by the Muses from the collective unconscious or chôra. To demystify this art of fantastic storytelling, we will commence with an investigation of the perpetual metamorphosis of fantastic forms. Fantastic storytelling *per se* already signifies transformation that renders unknown images in connection with the known realm by narrative temporalization, based on musical imagination. The characteristic of strangeness derived from the unknown and unfamiliar further reinforces the reading effect as the essence of fantastic mimesis. Therefore, the essential topic for rhetorical analysis is the interplay between storytelling, metamorphosis and strangeness. It is formalized into the dream-discourse, the mirror-discourse and the magician's hat-discourse.

The Essence of Strangeness in Metamorphosis

The elusive space of chôra as a third factor that links Forms and Becoming appears strange to our ordinary perception. It is hard to trace such imaginary space that welcomes the coexistence of antitheses. It is like an imaginary space that embodies the rhetoric of oxymoron in a harmonious way. As stated in the first part of the book, the concept of this arcane space finds its counterpart in Daoism. The changes departing from *Taiji* correspond to the quintessence of fantastic storytelling grounded in strangeness and metamorphosis. Fantastic literature manifests strangeness, the vital feature in poetic diction, by telling stories rooted in the imaginary of the unknown. The aesthetics of strangeness is demonstrated on two levels: rhetorical discourse and lexical style.

Poets and rhetoricians use strange diction to facilitate reception by readers and audiences. An artistic slant of strangeness impresses readers and helps to convince them to understand and receive the discourse. However, contemporary emphasis of the alleged "strangeness" in diction is pushed to extremity as "a refusal of meanings." Along the lines of the conception of "strangeness," readers are often provided with a series of arcane works that interfere with the connection between the author and the reader. This is in fact a corollary of literary development that has centred on unbound desires and realistic rationalism. This mainstream literature of realism entails modernism and postmodernism, whose extreme resort to strangeness results in obscurity that is constructed by an abstract combination of words as mere signs eluding truth and meanings. In contrast, fantastic literature resorts to imaginative strangeness (in both subject matter and diction) by fluent storytelling as formal metamorphosis to arouse aesthetic imagination to commune with the unknown world. Grotesque or weird as it may be, as Scott criticizes certain works of Hoffmann, fantastic literature never deviates from the essence of strangeness to the extremity of semantic void. Accordingly, the strangeness or difference *(l'écart)* in *lexis* extends to the fantastic discourse as a unity. As poetic diction values strangeness or difference, fantastic storytelling appropriates the strangeness of the unknown. A complete extension of strangeness from the lexical level to the whole creation is thus implemented in fantastic narration. This feature of strangeness or foreignism is also portrayed through the discourses of dream, mirror and magician's hat. The created uncanny or marvellous effects agree with what Aristotle deemed valuable and useful in rhetoric: "This difference or strangeness excites surprise" [Aristotle 1991, 36]. He further emphasized that wonder and surprise are pleasure arousing: "Whatever excites wonder and surprise is pleasant to people, as may be seen from the fact that everyone, when relating [such incidents] makes additions because he thinks they are pleasing" [Aristotle 1970, 53].

Given that its narration is related to the unknown, which refers to the unfamiliar and the strange, fantastic literature appears as the sheer representation of the rhetoric of strangeness. The evocation of the unknown touches upon the core triggers for distancing from the mediocre through the inventiveness of poetics. Fantastic discourses are *per se* the storytelling that interplays with the rendering of strangeness. In this manner, the poetical analysis of strangeness requires a double examination. The first operation of strangeness in the fantastic appears on the syntactic level or composition. The second employment of strangeness, as enhancement to the fantastic syntax, lies in the fantastic style of diction. The total effect of the syntax is manifested in three forms: dream, mirror and magician's hat. The first form presents by virtuosity a strange space as a second reality (dream reality cannot be denied, though cannot be proved); the second form reflects that the normally-perceived real images seem to be uncanny (gazing into the mirror makes one doubt the presumed reality); the third form audaciously and craftily concocts strange elements into reality as *trompe l'oeil* (the magician's hat can make the visible invisible and the invisible visible). All three metaphors of strangeness as narrative structures are adopted from the generally perceived objects of man: man dreams, man gazes at the mirror and man wonders as the magician pulls a rabbit from his hat.

Like Jung, Barfield and Marion who propose a third way for reaching the state of *unus mundus*, of the final participation with the semantic unity or the true hermeneutics of Scripture, fantastic storytelling essentially offers a third way for language to integrate the intelligible and the sensible or the spiritual and the material. With the attribute of strangeness and creative imagination, fantastic storytelling is able to return to the unknown archetype of chôra via the mystic participation with the collective unconscious. From this perspective, fantastic literature is teleological and allegorical. The rhetoric of strangeness in the dream-discourse arouses a total effect of hypnotism when it accesses the unknown realm. The quality of dream-arousing in fantastic literature is best illustrated by Bachelard's conception of the imaginary that makes man dream, and forms a bridge between the reader and the author. The connection between sub-creation of the collective unconscious and the conscious world is thus linked:

> A literary image is a meaning to the nascent state; the word – the old word – comes there to receive a new signification. But this is still not enough: the literary image must be enriched by a new fantasizing. Signifying a different matter and making dream otherwise, such is the double function of the literary image.[53] [Bachelard 1943, 283]

This quality of making readers dream depends on artistic implementation of the dream-discourse, which invites one to move backward to chôra along the traces of the manifestations of the becoming elements.

The mirror-discourse throws in uncanny elements in its storytelling to create the ambiance of strangeness. The dream depicted or appropriated in this type of discourse is more than a nightmare. The enunciated setting rooted in realism, i.e. the known realm, unfolds a weirder and weirder setting that tumbles the familiar reality into the unfamiliar realm of strangeness. This process animates the original concept of the uncanny (or *das Umheimliche*): what was originally familiar turns out to be unfamiliar. Characters from fantastic works are just like settings

---

[53] *Une image littéraire, c'est un sens à l'état naissant ; le mot – le vieux mot –vient y recevoir une signification nouvelle. Mais cela ne suffit pas encore : l'image littéraire doit s'enrichir d'un onirisme nouveau. Signifier autre chose et faire rêver autrement, telle est la double fonction de l'image littéraire.*

under the same narrative law of realism. The only fermentation that stirs the metamorphosis of the story is action. In the metaphorical reception of the mirror-discourse, actions parallel the immobile gaze at the mirror so as to paralyze and incline characters and/or readers to temporarily accept the author-created reality. The rhetoric of strangeness thus reaches its goal to animate the paralyzed figurative language and to connect readers with the unknown realm of sea through the mirage of mirror.

The magician's hat-discourse catches the fantastic undulation of the grand sea to create the vibration of strangeness. While the gaze into the mirror renders reality as the illusory reflection in the mirror, the magician's hat juggles astute storytelling to present a kaleidoscope of strange events to make the audience believe. This is exactly what bothers those theorists who cling tenaciously to the assumption that fantastic literature should be set in realism so as to exclude fairy tales or supernatural tales. However, other critics, who are mostly writers of the fantastic, regard these supernatural or faerie elements as the key to fantastic creation. According to our investigation, this third narrative rhetoric occupies an importation position in the history of fantastic literature and can not be ignored as aesthetic incarnation of the imaginary. Different from the dream-discourse that represents a complete unknown universe through a pre-logical depiction with hypotyposis of the mythic structure and from the mirror-discourse that pathologically portrays the image of reality with hyperbole, the magician's hat-discourse contents itself with telling stories related to unknown elements by means of hypotyposis or euphemism that conversely sublimates the meanings of figurative language.

By recapitulation, this inversion of rhetoric could be termed as animation and metamorphosis of rhetoric. Metaphors eventually metamorphose back into their pristine state of "semantic unity." Durand sees different governing figures (hyperbole, euphemism and hypotyposis) in the three structures (antithetic, mystic and synthetic) of the imaginary. In fantastic literature, these figures are extended and animated so as to return to language its original character: the figurative meanings were originally the literal meanings. This is presented in the fantastic by the enunciated that dissipates the metaphorical understanding. This eternal return of language mirrors the harmonious reunification of spirit and material, which Barfield considered as the semantic unity of concrete and abstract meanings. Fantastic storytelling in reality puts into practice a linguistic alchemy that, through aesthetic imagination, reverses the logical formalization process to trace back to the immense yet elusive space of the unknown. This alchemy is also associated with imagination in resonance with the four elements, the only traces left from chôra.

Strangeness through Alchemy of Language – Metamorphosis

Both Jung and Barfield embraced the view that modern men are in search of a soul to transcend to the realm of *unus mundus*. The former focused on spiritual light, the latter on the magic power of language. It is evident that our world is rather affected by idolatry. The formalization of idolatry also sprawls over the field of language. Therefore, modern language is also in need of a quest for its soul. Like Jung's proposal for our ego to go through the process of individuation, language will experience its individuation by a linguistic alchemy. This is a process of purification to return to the primeval state where semantic unity existed, as Barfield proposed. Throughout the history of fantastic literature, fantastic storytelling never stops maintaining the unity of abstract and concrete meanings. The process of rendering strangeness is at the core of the fantastic rhetoric that reverses our ordinary understanding of expressions. The central rhetoric of the three types of fantastic discourse is linguistic metamorphosis from figurative language taken as figurative to its being taken literally. Two levels of sublimating figurative language may take place: an entire animation of figurative expressions and the inclination to require a literal reading of the figurative.

In his theory of fantastic discourse, Todorov analyzed the enunciated (*énoncés*) of various French fantastic texts and reveals its characteristic of requiring a literal reading (*il demande de lire aux pieds de la lettre*). It is important not to engage a metaphorical reading of fantastic literature. However, he maintains that the supernatural is a mere production of language:

> The supernatural is born from language, this is at the same time the consequence and the evidence: not only the devil and the vampires exist in the words, but also only language allows us to conceive what is always absent: the supernatural. The latter has thus become a symbol of language, in the same way as the figures of rhetoric. And the figure is, as we have seen, the purest form of literature.[54] [Todorov 1970, 87]

According to Todorov, the figure is a pure representation of non-existence. This is a strict semiotic vision of language and its referent.

Though he insists that fantastic images only exist in the signs of language, which contradicts the imaginary perspective that sees semantic unity in language or semantic essence prior to the formal language, Todorov's insight into the inversion between the figurative and the literal in fantastic literature brings to light the special feature of fantastic discourses.

---

[54] *Le surnaturel naît du langage, il en est à la fois la conséquence et la preuve : non seulement le diable et les vampires n'existent que dans les mots, mais aussi seul le langage permet de concevoir ce qui est toujours absent : le surnaturel. Celui-ci devient donc un symbole du langage, au même titre que les figures de rhétorique, et la figure est, on l'a vu, la forme la plus pure de la littéralité.*

Durand holds an opposite view on the relation between figure and language. He disputes the non-existence of the signified. He insists that it is more pertinent to regard figurative meanings nowadays as literal meanings of language. Modern reception of language with an abstract or logical and literal meaning indeed derives from the formalization process from fantastic imagination mediated by rhetoric. Beyond the ambiguity between the literal and the figurative, the central rhetoric of fantastic literature then lies in the hypotyposis of the fixed and defunct figurative language, such as symbols and metaphors, which have retrograded into nothing but sign. On the verbal level, Bachelard presumes that *metaphors* with figurative meanings that refer to literal meanings are *metamorphoses* of words. His statement concerning the metamorphoses and metaphors of images offers a measure to poetic imagination: "We see that metaphors are naturally linked with metamorphoses and that under the reign of imagination, the metamorphosis of beings is already an adaptation to the imaged environment" (On verra que les metaphors sont naturellement liées aux métamorphoses, et que, dans le règne de l'imagination, la métamorphose de l'être est déjà une adaptation au milieu image) [Bachelard 1985, 55]. Only musicality, repetition and mimesis of the unknown can make this linguistic refinement possible. The linguistic alchemy in essence goes through the process from the storytelling of synchronism and diachronism against the predilection of rational realism into the narration of anachronism.

As T. A. Shippey, well known for his study of J. R. R. Tolkien, claims, the "dominant literary mode of the twentieth century has been the fantastic" (vii), our last century was indeed a cradle for the proliferation of the fantastic, given that a demand for stories about the unknown realm was incrementally growing. The contemporary phenomenon of the fantastic emerged as a renaissance of the art of storytelling, engrained in the imaginary of the unknown. A retrospect to the last century's development in humanities brings to light the sundered condition of literature, which may account for the meagerness of stories in our times. Ironically, literature, indeed originating with the storytelling of myths and legends, is oriented towards avoidance of stories. The very essence of literature, musicality and storytelling with poetic language, seems to be overshadowed by the formalization of logical language. Writers disregard the art of storytelling; audiences crave for stories. Shippey's analysis of the necessity for fantasy can be taken in this light: "Those authors of the twentieth century who have spoken most powerfully to and for their contemporaries have *for some reason* found it necessary to use the metaphoric mode of fantasy, to write about the worlds and creatures which we know do not exist" [Shippey, my emphasis, viii]. The above "reason" indeed harks back to the primitive imagination with a pristine language and mind that is mediated through fantastic storytelling, which bridges the gulf between the known and the unknown realms by fantastic strangeness.

Ethos: Rhetoric vis-à-vis the Author and the Reader

The intermediate status of rhetoric between *la fantastique* and the logical form implies a secondary factor for consideration: the relationship between the author and the reader. As mentioned before, Aristotle and the following poeticians and rhetoricians (up to French Classicism) emphasized the significance of the orator and the audience. Apart from the worldview that influences critics and theorists to define and theorize the fantastic genre, the stances of authors and readers with different *Weltanschauungen* play a decisive role in the art of fantastic narration. The universal definition proposed by Vittorio considers the author as a crucial factor in defining fantastic literature. In compliance with the general assumption of Vittorio, the creation of fantastic literature means the author's being conscious in the Platonic cave.

If we focus on the imagination of the subject from the metaphysical perspective, we can adopt Vittorio's cave theory of fantastic literature by embellishing and complementing it. Authors being conscious in the cave will be further categorized into four types: (1) Syntax of hesitation (Todorovian criterion) is created from the consciousness being inside the cave, but fear and insecurity impel the author/hero to prefer staying inside. (2) When fantastic narration portrays no doubt while confronting unlikely or inexplicable phenomena, authors and heroes are assumed to be not skeptical about the existence of the outside reality but have to be confined to the laws of the in-cave reality. They depict the unknown outside and try to go out but fail. (3) For certain fantastic writers and the heroes under their plumes, fantastic literature is nothing but a linguistic game. Incredibility is a beguiling rhetoric. Their reason normally denies the world outside the cave. (4) Fantastic writers who dexterously tell stories by creating a secondary and imaginary space not only are conscious of being inside the cave but also shed true light from outside to project an imaginary world of the ultimate reality. Writers endowed with such imagination are mostly visionary writers. H. G. Wells's fantastic tales clearly illustrate these differences of consciousness. The imagination of invisibility is central to his literary creation. "The country of the blind" and "The New Accelerator" reveal the problems of human limitation in vision. The first one can be regarded as an adaptation of Plato's cave allegory; the second tale is an imaginative and scientific testimony of an extra-dimension (fourth or beyond). Our senses of perception tend to betray us.

Readers' reception of fantastic literature also hinges on the cultural background of each individual. Bachelard's and Durand's theories of the imaginary highlight the reception of readers. Bachelard's phenomenological theory invites readers to imagine in communion with the author's literary images based on material imagination. This process leads to sublimation. Durand's theory is a re-education of readers by illustrating the symbols generated from the systems of day and night. His theory of the literary imaginary attempts to restore language shrunk to an abstract and logical sign to its original figurative meanings that were also the literal meanings. This theory offers a guideline of imaginary treasures for readers to appreciate fantastic literature so as to arouse their imagination to return to the realm of *la fantastique*. For Chinese Daoists, fantastic tales are the representation of Daoist metaphysics or wisdom through the art of language. The gist resides in liberating readers' relative points of view. Like Zhuang Zi, Lie Zi also told fantastic stories to deconstruct human fallacy of relative bias while illustrating the value of fantastic stories in philosophical instruction. One of Lie Zi's tales can further explain why fantastic literature is attributed with paradoxical interpretations (that keep deconstructing its imaginary entirety) by different critics.

Here is a summary of Lie Zi's story: Gumang is a country in the south of the extreme west. It is in the backwoods, and nobody knows where its borders are. Since there is no convergence between the air of yin and yang, there is no distinction between winter and summer. Lacking in the shining of the sun and the moon, this country is ignorant of the distinction between day and night. The civilians do not eat and get dressed, but hibernate. They wake up every fifty days and think that their dreams are reality, but what they perceive while awake as illusion.

In the middle of the world there is a country called the Middle country. This one follows the law of yin and yang and has winter and summer. With the discrimination of dark and light, the country sees day and night. The people demonstrate their variations in intelligence and stupidity as well as various talents. Hierarchy is thus formed and education and law are applied to govern people. They take what they do while awake as reality but what they perceive in dream as illusion.

Finally, Fuluo country is in the extreme east of the north. The climate is forever hot. The sun and the moon shine. The earth is infertile and people eat roots of grasses and fruits of trees. They never cook with fire. All the people are ferocious and advocate victory instead of benevolence and righteousness. Rarely taking a rest, they are mostly afoot, forever awake and never asleep. [My retelling of Chapter Zhoumuwang, 3-4]

The above story reminds us of Zhunag Zi's questioning of the uncertainty between the dreamer and the dreamed object and extends to spatial and temporal relativity.[55] By the same token, readers from a diurnal country who accept the conscious perception and rationalism as reality will never agree with readers coming from a nocturnal country who only accept dream as reality. Likewise, Durand's classification of isotopic symbols can be better demonstrated by the imaginary differences predetermined by the diurnal country, nocturnal country

---

[55] This refers to the famous tale of "Zhuang Zhou Dreams of a Butterfly." Zhuang Zi tells this story to question whether it is Zhuang Zhou that dreams of the butterfly or the butterfly that dreams of Zhuang Zhou.

and diurnal-nocturnal country. The relativity existing in the percipient that decides the percept is completely elucidated by Lie Zi's story. Therefore, defining fantastic literature by the reader's responding attitude and reception requires reconsideration of the relative lapse derived from different *Weltanschauungen*.

The evaluation and classification of fantastic literature into dream-discourse, mirror-discourse and magician's hat-discourse demands readers' poetic education and unique appreciation of fantastic teleology. Here we may have recourse to the German school of reader-response theory to further throw light on the requirement of literary evaluation. Wolfgan Iser developed an approach to the interpretation of literature. It derives from the philosophy of phenomenology, and emphasizes the perceiver's role in the process of perception. Parallel to the perceiver-percept relation, Iser set forth the significant role of the reader vis-à-vis the literary work. He insisted that critics should consider the text's effect on the reader instead of explaining the text as an object. Though the reader's importance is thus emphasized, Iser's proposal of an implied reader is the central spirit of the reader-response theory. Implied readers are deemed to be qualified to decode text that is grounded in literary conventions, so as to transcend them to prove the text's inexhaustibility. Likewise, in the reading process of fantastic literature, the implied reader is expected to transcend formal conventions of the work through the arousal of aesthetic imagination to commune with the collective unconscious. The implied reader of the fantastic is often expected to understand the implied author's fear, doubt or vision and thus undergoes a teleological reading.

Hans Robert Jauss's reception theory can further reinforce and expound Iser's notion of an implied reader. He proposes an implicit reading contract. The central idea of Jauss's aesthetics of reception is bridging the gulf between interpretation that tends to ignore history, and interpretation subject to social or ideological theories to the detriment of the text. His proposal of "horizons of expectations" among readers mirrors the "connivance" of a reading pact and the implied reader's special stance. These horizons of expectations are crucial to the evaluation and apprehension of fantastic literature. An implied-reader of sophistication in the imagination, rhetoric and style of fantastic literature will ascend to the transcendental realm of the fantastic and thus attain to the state of Tolkienian consolation through a linguistic Eucharist.

The reader's reception, as Iser and Jauss emphasized, is an important aesthetic element to be considered in evaluating literary works. In this light, Todorov's narrative principle of hesitation in defining fantastic literature is only reasonable to readers and critics from the Cartesian thinking tradition. As to authors, under the currently fashionable tendency to skepticism during the third period of fantastic creation, the discourse of hesitation is a common rhetoric for hinting at the unknown realm by using mirror-discourse to create an aura of ambiguity and doubt. Accordingly, the mirror-discourse, converged from Durandian diurnal images of antithesis, is a frequently employed modern rhetoric. In contrast, the magician's hat-discourse, considered as naïve and only for children in most Western countries until the popularity of the fantasy genre, is a conventional rhetoric to depict the unknown in other cultures, for example China and India. In fact, Tolkien retorted upon the assumption that fairy-stories are created for children, who have more imagination than adults. The difference, he insisted, lies in the content of knowledge in children and adults, instead of the ability of imagining. He stated that children listen to or read fairy-stories just like they do with realistic works and learning; for children, almost everything belongs to the realm of the unknown. In similar fashion, Hegel's commentary on Chinese people as always staying in the primitive age or children's stage in human civilization indeed derived from such a fallacy about children and imagination.[56] The permanent rhetoric of the magician's hat in telling fantastic stories in Chinese literature is evidence that this culture has remained in the stages of primitive conception and myth as the fabrication of truth. In addition, science was devalued during the Chinese empires, thus being sustained superstition. Authors from such a cultural background often receive the unknown as a possible reality in the future and tell stories about ghosts, monsters, gods and other unknown elements.

Despite the thriving of rationalism in Western literature, authors faithful to the imaginative consciousness from original participation are attached to the surging waves of the sea of the collective unconscious, and continue their lines of the rhetoric of the magician's hat. This was especially true when a countercurrent of rationalism, such as the Romantic Movement, took place. Nonetheless, the depiction on a small scale inspired from the splintered light of the immense sea is not able to represent a whole imaginary picture of the grand sea as sub-creation. Prophetic or visionary (in a mythopoeic sense) writers of modern times try to recapture the true spirit of their predecessors by creating a revolutionary fantastic style to resurrect the art of epic narration based on the rhetoric of dream-discourse. Such virtuosos of dream-discourse are rare in modern times after the stages of primitive conception and myth as the fabrication of truth.

This type of discourse, narration in epic style, compared with short narrative, is relatively scanty in Chinese literature, given that Confucianism and Buddhism fostered rather the didactic and pastoral styles, and Daoism oriented towards a metaphysical and fantastic discourse of philosophy. Nevertheless, the narrative tradition of historiographers has sustained the creation of epic style by using the expedient of vernacular romance form. Durand's synthetic structures explain this meagreness of epics in Chinese literature. His third structure of the style of history is common in Western culture that constructs the tradition of epics, whereas for Chinese and Indian culture (except for its epic *The Mahabharata*), the imagination of history turns into fables. The epic and historical magnitude

---

[56] Hegel is surprised by the Chinese civilization that, he claims, remains in the stage of childhood in his *Leçon sur la philosophie de l'histoire*.

shrinks into the storytelling of fables. Another possible reason is that Chinese writers, under the influence of Confucianism, regarded historical chronicles as the only narratives worthy of writing. The works we reckon to be   representative of epic style are *Fengshen Yanyi* or *The Investiture of the Gods* (1566 by Xu Zonglin or 1601 by Lu Xixing) and *Xiyou Ji* or *Journey to the West* (1590 by We Cheng'en)[57]. The former is a fantastic novel with 100 chapters that depict the interference of gods and goddesses in man's war and fate. The story concerns the destruction of the Shang dynasty (1600-1046 BC) and the rise of the Zhou dynasty (Western Zhou dynasty 1046-771 BC and Eastern Zhou dynasty 770-221 BC). Those who died in the war, including gods and men (from both good and bad sides) are rewarded to be nominated as gods. The naissance of the Universe and gods is slightly different from Ovid's *Metamorphoses*; nevertheless, metamorphosis remains the central philosophy in both works. *Journey to the West* is better known to Western readers (also known as *The Monkey King*) and remains highly popular to the present day. The journey represents a complete process of Daoist internal alchemy through the integration of Buddhism and Daoism. Similar to *The Investiture of the Gods*, men and animals' actions and fate are predetermined by gods.

The epic tradition of storytelling in our times is becoming ignored under the impact of the evolution of consciousness into the intellectual and conscious age. After Goethe dedicated a great epic play of the fantastic, *Faust*, in the nineteenth century, fantastic epic writing was ignored for almost a century. The contemporary model of dream-discourse inheriting the poetics of epic par excellence is Tolkien's sub-creation of *The Silmarillion* and *The Lord of the Rings*.

---

[57] The English title of these Chinese novels will be henceforward adopted.

The Dream-Discourse

Based on the issue raised by Todorov concerning fantastic narration being between the marvellous and the uncanny, the marvellous elements in the dream-discourse manifest the relations between gods, devils and humans. The dream-discourse in fact stages the set expression of human nature vis-à-vis divinity and devilishness. The expression of the human soul as imitation of God, and the body as imitation of Devil is here returned to the origin of language and meaning. According to Todorov, this is only a narrative technique that demonstrates pure literariness of the figure, i.e., the representation of pure language referring to the void. The God and Devil only exist through language, nothing more. In contrast, Durand, voicing the opposite to the extreme semiotic position undermining the meanings, affirmed that the figurative offers essential meanings to language. Barfield and Tolkien also embraced such a view from an aesthetic and philological perspective. The rhetoric of dream-discourse is here characterized more in the light of Barfield's, Tolkien's and Durand's visions on figures and semantics than on Todorov's pure semiotic interpretation. Nevertheless, we are still indebted to Todorov's formal analysis, which elicits the significance of figurative language in relation to fantastic discourse.

Holding a different viewpoint from Todorov who excluded poetry and allegory from the fantastic genre, we consider narrative poems and allegories to be possible forms that represent unknown imagination, given that the poems in question are narrative, not lyric or didactic, and the allegories are a variation of teleological reading of the fantastic. Moreover, some fantastic literature inherits its idiosyncratic narrative art from the mainstream of great epic poetry. Such stories present readers with perfect manifestations of fantastic imagination. Like the verse form of oracles that reserve musical elements of chanting, epic and tragedy originally drew on verse form as mimesis par excellence. According to the historical evolution of fantastic literature, described in the section of periodization, the primitive conception fosters the complex epic style to narrate human nature and fate in relation to gods/God and devils/Satan. Ruling out poetry from the fantastic narrative would appear paradoxical, since fantastic imagination is embodied into synthetic structures germane to musicality. As Goethe illuminated, his epoch was entering into the prosaic age (or the intellectual period in the light of Barfield's evolution of consciousness). Its corollary is the decrease of fantastic epics or poems, which illustrates man's incremental loss of musical and artistic creation of the fantastic. Therefore, the postulate of defining fantastic literature as exclusively narrative prose is too far-fetched. The dream-discourse recovers the pristine "literal" meanings that once split into figurative and abstract meanings and eventually a non-existence of the signified.

The creation of fantastic literature with dream-discourse is in essence teleological. George F. Held expounds the meanings of the *spoude* (earnestness in accomplishment) and the *ethos* in Aristotle's *Poetics* and assimilates the seeds of a teleological ethical perspective in Homer's epics with Plato and Aristotle. This teleological outlook is also exposed in *The Epic of Gilgamesh* [Held, 48]. This teleological interpretation in epic poetry can be extended along the lines of fantastic epics, from Antiquity to the present day. It is coupled with musical imagination to harmonize into the state of *unus mundus*.

In the dream-discourse, human beings dream of being attached to the Archetype or Forms or the Causality of all Becoming. The objects in dreams concern universal unity and semantic unity. Plato tried different figures to explain the arcane third kind (*triton genos*) – chôra. He once described it by the figure of a dreamy state. In this light, the metaphor of dreams as the fantastic rhetoric joins the dreamy space of chôra. In the dream-discourse, all human nature and fate are related to gods/God and their/his relations with other gods or devils/Satan. *The Epic of Gilgamesh* leaves to Gilgamesh's posterity the wisdom related to the interaction between gods/devils and man. The only difference between them is men's mortality. Homer's epics tell us how gods' behaviours and temperaments influence men's actions and fates. Likewise, Virgil's *The Aeneid* narrates the story of the origin of Rome under the interference of gods and the inspiration of the deceased. Ovid's depiction of a similar natural law of metamorphosis in the Universe, gods and men illustrates the teleology of human existence. Dante and Milton wrote from a Christian point of view, from the proposed stage of myth as the fabrication of truth. They presented the correlations between men's world and that of the yonder, the unknown worlds governed by God and Satan. Even the medieval Arthurian legends fit this teleology of human action and destiny in relation to divine power. From the prediction of a true king for Briton to the quest of Holy Grail and the resurrection of the king, the storytelling pivots the principle that human deeds are in interaction with divine power. The epics akin to Germanic or Teutonic myths such as *The Kalevala*, *Elder Edda* and *Beowulf* often inspire readers to dream with the collective unconscious, thus leading to a teleological reading.

Two representative masterpieces that continue this teleological depiction on an epic scale in the Occidental modern times are Goethe's *Faust* and Tolkien's *The Lord of the Rings* with *The Silmarillion*. Different from ordinary Faustian legends, Goethe's creation commences with a discussion, in fact a certain kind of bet, between God and Mephistopheles, whose interlocution sparks the adventurous life of Faust. Not only God and Devil can influence Faust, but also Faust can interact with them. Although he named his work a tragedy, we see it in essence as a fantastic epic because the fourth stage of traditional tragedy as catharsis in *Faust* is euphemized into Tolkienian Consolation. Goethe's epic depiction of the unknown is close to epic poems created from the primitive conception. The other virtuoso, Tolkien, composed a great epic in the 20th century. Different from his predecessors of Christian fantastic literature, Tolkien's writing is an emulation of classical epic permeated with cosmological Christianity within a modern/postmodern frame. His poetics revealing the interior history of reading and imagination is further illustrated in Tolkien's 1953 letter addressed to Robert Murray, a Jesuit priest:

> *The Lord of the Rings* is of course a fundamentally religious and Catholic work; unconsciously so at first, but consciously in the revision. That is why I have not put in, or have cut out practically all references to anything like 'religion', to cults or practices, in the imaginary world. For the religious element is absorbed into the story and the symbolism. [...]
>
> Certainly I have not been nourished by English Literature, in which I do not suppose I am better read than you; for the simple reason that I have never found much there in which to rest my heart (or heart and head together). I was brought up in the Classics, and first discovered the sensation of literary pleasure in Homer. Also being a philologist, getting a large part of any aesthetic pleasure that I am capable of from the *form* of words (and especially from the *fresh* association of word-form with word-sense), I have always best enjoyed things in a foreign language, or one so remote as to feel like it (such as Anglos-Saxon). But that is enough about me. [Tolkien 1995, 142]

Popular readers and movie goers may only regard Tolkien as an excellent fantasy writer and tend to ignore his true poetic value, for example, the embedment of lays, ballads and songs in his prose novels, especially his preference for alliterative metre and the abundant tetrametre that echoes the epic tradition. From the poetic tradition and aesthetic evaluation, Tolkien's creation can be deemed as the first sign of the renaissance of fantastic epic that foresees the coming of the final stage of fantastic literature or poetic language leading to final participation. Just like final participation that is not a simple return to original participation, Tolkien resorted to sub-creation to compose his fantastic epic instead of imitating primitive epics. Epic, history and geography are inseparable in the stage of original participation, whereas in the intellectual and conscious stages, history and geography are abstracted from imagination, as language from concrete figures. The appropriate setting of contemporary fantastic epic is thus a completely imaginary time-space eluding factual, historical and geographical referents.

A similar teleological perspective is also portrayed in Chinese epics *The Investiture of Gods* and *Journey to the West*. In the former novel, gods influence and predetermine men's battles, and the Wise Old Man is authorized to nominate gods; in the latter, the spiritual accomplishment or Jungian individuation of the four nonhuman characters (the monkey king, the pig-spirit, the river-spirit and the dragon-prince or the white steed) and the mission of the monk Xuanzang (to take the Sutras back to the East) are achieved under the predetermination of the Buddha and the Bodhisattva. The focus of this novel is more on man's conflict with himself, which is close to Goethe's *Faust*. Thus, devils play a vital role in the story. This quintessence of synchronicity between gods/devils or Christian

God/Satan and men (in Chinese, often termed as the archetypal fight among ren [men], shen [deities] and muo [devils]) is the spirit of the rhetoric of dream-discourse. The structure of the discourse is decided by the enunciated, viz. the semantic syntax. The staging of fantastic storytelling rendered by the dream-discourse represents a thorough reunification of figurative and literal in language. It further demonstrates the transcendental unity of the spiritual and the material in human life. The last feature of the teleology of dream-discourse resides in the reification of the metaphysical or imaginative "third way." In the fantastic epic, the enunciation that appears more significant in contemporary narration (e.g. the Nouveau Roman) is neutralized by the heterodiegetic narrator. The modernistic and postmodern enunciation cedes to the hypotyposis of the enunciated in the fantasy epic.

We have presented the concept of Jung's collective unconscious and Tolkien's vision of Faerie in our discussion of the imaginary of the fantastic. Following our thesis of fantastic mimesis, the dream-discourse is better understood as a unitary representation of an imagined universe or an imitation of the human collective dream. This collective dream is inspired from the collective unconscious, the imaginary of Faerie or Coleridge's primary imagination. Dream here is germane to mythic imagination but not to the repressed desire (sexual or not), because myth can also be interpreted as the human collective dream. Tolkien's appropriation of myth to theorize his fairy-stories highlights the underlying quality of myth in the creation of stories. This sub-creation represents a second reality of the unknown, like dreams, which signify a second existence or space akin to chôra. According to Jung's analytical psychology, dreams contain both the individual unconscious and the collective unconscious. This vision of multilevel in dreams can also be corroborated by Daoist, Hindu and Buddhist philosophies on dreams. Therefore, dreams possess a universal quality. To elucidate in general terms, the dream in the present rhetorical discourse refers to the deeper level of dream, the layer that is endowed with the key to the communion with chôra, the cradle of primary imagination or the core realm of the unknown. In this light, Tolkien's language related to the figurative Faerie realm is connected with chôra via aesthetic imagination. The dream discourse is to be apprehended *per se* as a figurative structure. This is in contrast to formalistic analysis, characterized by reading figurative expressions literally.

Not all narratives with the dream motif in the story are considered to be with the dream-discourse. A fantastic narrative appropriating dream *as motif* can be a narrative of dream-discourse, of mirror-discourse or a magician's hat-discourse. For example, the surrealistic genre is excluded from the present rhetorical discourse, given that the surrealistic literary form exaggerates strangeness deriving from unreined association or reverie and that it is often a direct copy of dreams. As stated before, Aristotle exposed the danger of this kind of overwhelming strange writing in his *Poetics* while emphasizing the importance of strange or unfamiliar diction, or diction of distance. Goethe was also wary of his reckless beta-thinking (to use Barfield's term) and assumed that the systematic imagination is the true poetics. The same reflection was held by Tolkien, who excluded the dream-like writings of reveries or other similar works of "fancy" (to be understood by Coleridge's definition) from the real creation of fantasy. Consequently, our evaluation of the rhetoric hinges on a synthesis of several theoretical constructs: the structure of the collective unconscious, the structure of Bachelard's material imagination, the synthetic structure of Durand's imaginary systems in relation to the structure of discourse including the enunciated, enunciation and syntax. The dream-discourse cradles the synthetic structure of music and myth. To employ nature's images, the central rhetoric lies in connecting and penetrating the mountains and the seas by the fluidity of a river with the informal or imaginary and mystic logic. The dream-discourse refines language and myth through a comprehensive storytelling that links the two realms, the known and the unknown, as a third way. This process of fantastic mediation, as the countercurrent of the formalizing mediation, can be compared to the alchemy of language that refines imagination and language into the semantic unity and *unus mundus*. The linguistic alchemy, according to the narrative patterns, is further divided into two discourses: external alchemy and internal alchemy.

The Dream-Discourse as External Alchemy

In the dream-discourse, the semantic content integrates naturally into the artistic disposition and narration of the form. The Greek tetralogy of tragedy may be re-interpreted in terms of Tolkien's tetramerous elements of a fairy-story. According to Tolkien, the requisite elements for a successful fairy-story are Fantasy, Recovery, Escape and Consolation. In Greek tetralogy, the first part offers exposition, background and the central theme of the entire work. The second part presents the monstrous actions. The third part develops with a reconciliation of actions. The fourth part refers to the aesthetic reception of the audience who could go home happy [Goethe 1994, 198]. Tolkien's perspective on *fantasy* is different from what readers receive nowadays. He employed the term *Fantasy* to distinguish from *Imagination*, understood as the mental power of image-making. Fantasy is defined as the Art of "the operative link between Imagination and the final result, Sub-creation" [Tolkien 1997, 139]. Tolkien proposed the term Fantasy for the following purpose: "in a sense, that is, which combines with its older and higher use as an equivalent of Imagination the derived notions of 'unreality' (that is, of unlikeness to the Primary World), of freedom from the domination of observed 'fact', in short of the fantastic" [ibid., 139]. And the art of fantasy is "indeed narrative art, story-making in its primary and most potent mode. In human art, Fantasy is a thing best left to words, to true literature" [ibid., 140]. According to Tolkien's theory of fairy-story, the dream-discourse may be taken in the light of holistic *Fantasy*.

On the basis of Bachelard's poetic imaginary, as studied before, the very quality of the dream-discourse is to make readers dream in communion with the collective unconscious. The metamorphic rhetoric lies in the artistic implementation of the converging imaginary schemas, symbols and archetypes. Just as the formation of Durandian clustering symbols that hinges on the dominating reflexes in reaction to time and space, the enunciated setting of fantastic literature appears as the primal constituent of the story background. Fantastic and realistic literature can be distinguished because fantasy with dream-discourse extends from the known world into the unknown. Readers are given an imaginary geography that may link to an unknown time (past, present and future) which converges into a strange but familiar space-time, reminiscent of the unknown. This process is the reverse of the mirror-discourse in which the rhetoric plays on the strange rendering of familiarity, or represents the true meaning of the uncanny. The spatial and temporal construction of dream-discourse appertains to the sphere archetype or Mandala of Jung, material imagination or the denier archetype of Durand. The language thus manifests itself as a reunification of abstract and concrete meanings, a space beyond yet inclusive of antithesis vibrating with the space of chôra. In the dream-discourse, the *mise en scène* of Jung's archetypes is in manner of a whole scale. In a way that reminds us of the metaphor of the sea, this kind of storytelling yields a new reality through complete imitation. The antithesis contrived here is not a counterbalance of polarity like the antithetic rhetoric thriving in the mirror-discourse. Like the *Yi Jing* principle that yin and yang never neatly counterbalance, the antithesis in the dream-discourse is rather a dynamic drive that unfolds the impending plot of the story. The archetypal structure is constructed by hero, shadow, the old man, anima and animus intertwined with the material structure of the five elements (the rudimentary four plus gold). The imaginary images from the diurnal and nocturnal regimes are embodied through the vivid characters, including gods, devils, spirits, and men with decisive weapons and divine instruments. Besides the synchronism and isotopism of the enunciated structure, diachronism is also a decisive factor in fantastic storytelling. Diachronism is concerned with temporality and akin to musicality. The soul that brings storytelling into play is musical imagination of harmonization or musical dialectical harmonization. Musical fluidity appears more important than architectural structure in the art of telling the fantastic. This mystic and musical structure is also characterized in terms of the external alchemy.

To illustrate this mystic and musical structure of the dream-discourse, intertwined with the inner space of the unconscious, we adduce Chinese novels *The Investiture of Gods* and *Journey to the West* as examples of the Eastern rendering of the fantastic epic and Goethe's *Faust* and Tolkien's *The Lord of the*

Rings and *The Silmarillion* as the examples of the Western fantastic epics. The first work represents a Daoist storytelling on an epic scale; the second is an epic grounded in Buddhism and Daoism, related to Indian Buddhism and exerts influence on Japanese culture. Therefore, the novel merits a close examination and analysis. The third one, which Goethe himself characterized as a tragedy, places the emphasis on man interacting with himself under the influence of Devil and God. From this perspective of man's individuation process (man faced with himself), Goethe's epic is quintessentially homogenous to the Chinese *Journey to the West,* which stages a typical process of individuation to reach Nirvana. Finally, Tolkien's work resembles the first Chinese novel in that both touch upon the topic of man interacting with the world, spanning gods, devils, men and animals. The war here is a collective war but not an individual one. These novels inherit the epic tradition couched in human imagination (ever since *The Epic of Gilgamesh*), that gods interact with men and also decide men's fate by means of their free choice and providence.

The Investiture of the Gods and the Symphony of Euphoriant Alchemy

The Investiture of the Gods[58] commences with an archaic poem in metres of seven characters as a summary of Chinese myth from the creation of the Universe to the establishment of the Zhou dynasty. This is the very historical background of the fantastic epic: "Pangu the giant precedes the chaos, *Taiji Liangyi* and *Sixiang* dangle, after Sky of zi and Earth of chou is issued Man of yin [not yin from yin-yang], warding off beasts is the virtue of Youchao sage..." ("混沌 初分盤古先，太極兩儀四象懸．子天丑地人寅出，避除獸患有巢賢...") [3].

---

[58] Here is a synopsis of the story: On the birthday worship of the greatest Chinese goddess Nüwa, the king Zhou (the last king of the Shang dynasty) notices the beauty of the goddess's statue and meditates that he should have such a beauty as his concubine. This lustful desire drives him to compose a sacrilegious poem that he would marry the goddess to serve him in the palace. Irritated by such an insult, Goddess Nüwa decides to punish him as the days of the Shang dynasty are numbered (the king Zhou still has 28 years of life). Thus she sends three female spirits (fox, pheasant and pipa jade) to enchant the king. The king is becoming all the more debauched and cruel under the lure of the fox-spirit. Suggested by the latter, he creates draconian punishments such as *paoluo* [red-hot pillar of brass] and *chaipen* [basin of venomous worms and snakes]. Supported by Arch-Gods Yuanshitianzun and Taishanglaojün [or Lao Zi], Jiang Ziya assists the future king Wu of Zhou to overthrow the tyrant Zhou, who is also assisted by evil men and gods as well as some faithful but ignorant subjects. This evil side is supported by the other Arch-God Tongtianjaozhu. The end of the novel welcomes the victory of the good side and the end of the Shang dynasty. The king of Zhou burns himself in zhaixinglou [star plucking tower]. Jiang Ziya executes and exorcizes the three evil spirits. The novel closes with the investiture of gods by Jiang Ziya to those who die (both good and evil sides) in the battles and the allotment of feuds to the living heroes by King Wu of Zhou.

The novel consists in one hundred chapters (a common number to the zhanghui xiaoshuo ["episodic novel in chapters"]). The first chapter entitled "The king Zhou worships at the temple of Goddess Nüwa" is the trigger to all calamities. The goddess wants to take revenge on king Zhou's sacrilege against her, but finds that he still has 28 years to live. Thus she summons the devils and spirits to his palace and assigns three female spirits to enchant the king. The king's punishment causes the ensuing battles, the establishment of the Zhou dynasty and the future investiture of gods by Jiang Ziya. This investiture was already predestined in heaven. The narrative inception reminds us of the style in Homer's epics. In *The Illad*, Book I entitled "Quarrel, Oath, and Promise" begins with the divine cause of the quarrel between Agamemnon and Prince Achilles: "Among the gods, who brought this quarrel on? The son of Zeus by Leto. Agamemnon angered him, so he made a burning wind of plague rise in the army: rank and file sickened and died for the ill their chief had done in despising a man of prayer" [Homer 1984, 1]. By the same token, gods in *The Odyssey* foresee men's future and frailty, and they use their power to interfere with their actions and decide their fate. Pride seems to be the crucial flaw of men that easily irritates gods. Zeus's discourse on man's refusal of gods' message is a universal truth depicted in epics from both the West and the East:

> 'O the waywardness of these mortals! They accuse the gods, they say that their troubles come from us, and yet by their own presumptuousness they draw down sorrow upon themselves that outruns their allotted portion. [...] Thus Hermes warned him, wishing him well but Aegisthus' heart would not hear reason, and now he has paid all his debts at once.' [Homer 1998, 2]

Like Classical fantastic epics that manifest a complete structure of the collective unconscious with the reverberation of rudimentary elements and with the convergence of symbolic images, *The Investiture of the Gods* is narrated through a semantic structure in harmony with the synthetic structures of mythopoeia.

The trigger of all impending events is considered as the adding of yin yao [the line of yin in the *Yi Jing* trigram] to the original status of all. The following formal metamorphosis of the story and the fate arrangement that takes place in its imaginary setting are associated with the space of the unknown chôra. Since yin of chôra (the initial trigger of all transformation) plays the decisive role in the "becoming," fantastic epics are triggered by the yin symbols such as female goddess, woman, desire and the evil power. Different from the Occidental imaginary of an archetype of the theriomorphic and devouring symbols (e.g. Satan) and from the archetype of the catamorphic symbols (e.g. Hell), the underlying philosophy of *Yi Jing* that glorifies "xuan" (darkness) makes it easier for Chinese people to see light than darkness. This is close to the Durandian nocturnal regime of the imaginary except for the diurnal light being non-antithetic. Therefore, the traditional and genuine Chinese thought does not imagine a hell or purgatory. The conflict between the Jungian Shadow and Light is represented by deteriorated gods and good gods and the men on either side.

From the space of air, heaven, the Arch-Gods Yuanshitianzun and Taishanglaojün (or Lao Zi) take the side Jiang Ziya and the king Wu of Zhou against the other Arch-God Tongtianjaozhu, who allows himself to be misguided by his disciples' calumnies and thus assists the tyrant. Notice that all three Arch-Gods are under the One God Hongjün and the Duo-Gods Fuxi and Nüwa (the insulted goddess in the beginning of the novel). This narrative structure of characterization echoes Lao Zi's *Dao De Jing*: "One [the first change] generates two [the second change], two [the second change] generates three [the third change], and three [the third change] generates all."[59] The three Arch-Gods generate myriads of conflicts and battles on earth. If we consider the figures of gods as Jungian animus, Daoist masters as the disciples of gods can be compared to the archetype of the wise old man, light (Jiang Ziya, like Tolkien's Gandalf) and shadow (Shen Gongbao, Jiang's junior fellow, like Tolkien's Saruman). Parallel to the fight between these two Daoist masters is the antithetic pair of kings: the king Wen and later his son Wu against the king Zhou. Below this structure are gods, immortals, spirits, Daoist masters, alchemists, extraordinary men (*qiren*), officers and soldiers. However, a soul figure of the story is beyond the antithetic dualism that acts as the kinetic power of the plot. This figure is Nuocha, who is reincarnated from the disciple Lingzhuzi (Spiritual Ball) of Taiyi Zhenren (Taiyi immortal) and is born out of a flesh ball from his mother. This sphere image represents the multi-facet of Nuocha: cruel, mischievous, valiant and righteous as man and god.

Characterization by the universal elements (earth, water, fire, air and gold) constructs the structure of material imagination. The figure of fire and air/wind is Nuocha, the third son of Li Jing, who practices Dao with the immortal Du'e of the West Kunlun. The conception of Nuocha in his mother's womb remains for more than three years and he is finally born as a big round flesh ball. The father Li Jing suspects it to be an evil spirit and cuts it with his sword. A child jumps out of the breached ball with a Sky-Earth golden bracelet (the divine qiankun "sky-earth" circle) on his right hand and a Sky Ribbon (red silk ribbon or celestial silk ribbon) around his belly, his eyes blazing with golden light. His master Taiyi grants him two more faqi (divine weapons) – the Fire Spear, the Golden Brick and the Air-Fire Wheel. This fantastic Nuocha later dies for his parents (to

---

[59] Most interpreters, including most Chinese scholars, understand the meanings of "one, two, three" as simple arithmetic numbers. Thanks to the mathematic decoding of *Yi Jing* by Leibniz and the traditional Daoist vision, such as Lao Zi and Lie Zi, we interpret the above numbers as the powers. Therefore, the first change equals the linear power of the number 2 (yang and yin); the second change equals the quadratic power of 2 (yang-yang, yang-yin, yin-yang, yin-yin); the third change equals the cubic power of 2 (the eight basic trigrams of *Yi Jing in toto*).

repent for the catastrophe he caused) and is worshiped as a god by people. In fact, Nuocha kills a son of the dragon king and bullies the king, who in response menaces the life of his parents. Through this episode, Nuocha kills himself to atone for his crime and will be resurrected as Nuocha of Lotus. He is later resurrected by his master from the lotus leaves out of the pond (water) after his furious father breaks Nuocha's golden idol in his temple. This unique character, Nuocha, thus represents the five elements that metamorphose into all. These elements generate and destroy one another. The metamorphosis is not limited to reincarnation. After fulfilling more missions for the future king as a trial of individuation, Nuocha later [Chapter 76] metamorphoses again after eating three fire dates and drinking three cups of wine granted by his master, Taiyi Immortal. He is stunned at the transformation: "He hears the thundering noise from both sides, six hands are sprouting and he has now eight hands in total; three heads are growing out of his neck" [Lu, 770].[60] Not knowing what to do, Nuocha goes to his master and asks how to wield his weapons with these eight hands. His master is quite satisfied and says that "now that you have three heads and six arms (in fact, the Chinese expression of "santou liubei" that describes a man of superhuman power or extremely able and competent), you really deserve to be a disciple of my Golden Light Cave" [ibid., 770]. Now Nuocha holds the Sky-Earth Bracelet in one hand, the celestial Sky Ribbon in another and two fire spears in two hands and still has three bare hands. Then his master complements his gear of divine weapons with the night-dragon divine-fire cover and a pair of Yin-Yang Swords. And Nuocha has evolved into a real "three head six arms." This short episode can further illustrate Barfield's concept of the semantic unity by referring to Chinese language. He assists Jiang Ziya (also Nuocha's master's fellow with a revolutionary mission until the end and accomplishes his Dao trial to reach the status of Nirvana with his mundane body (not through death).[61]

The characters representing the water element are Leizhenzi (Thunder-dragon), Buojian (the soul of Xuanyuan Huangdi's (China's first king and ancestor) general that defeats the monster Ciyou) from the East Sea as a later assistant to the investiture mission, the dragon family of the East Sea and the four saints from Nine Dragon Island of the West Sea. These four saints are able to stride in the waters (shuidun or water-fleeing). The wise old man figure Jiang Ziya is also capable of exercising the skill of striding in the waters. The element earth is represented almost everywhere in the novel, the battlefield of Qishan and the earthly setting. The image of movement is presented by many alchemists with the five-element magic and can swiftly submerge underground (tudun or earth-fleeing), including Jiang Ziya. The symbolic character is the alchemist

---

[60] All the quotations from the novel are my translations from Chinese.

[61] The Daoist conception of immortality is essentially realistic and practical. The practice of alchemy is not for the pursuit of eternal spirit but rather eternal youth and life. Thus it is believed that men can become saints or achieve Dao by keeping the mundane body.

Tuxingsun (Strider of earth) who can "fly" underground many miles overnight and is also a valiant (at first for the bad side) warrior for the future king Wu. The converging images revolving around the four plus one elements bring into action the succeeding episodes of the novel: repetitive recycling and intertwining of fire, air, water and earth. The sequence is not linear but rather cyclical and synthetic. The hypotyposis of unknown phenomena proceeds in harmony with the mutual reinforcement and counteraction among the five elements: gold generates water, water generates wood (air), wood generates fire and fire generates earth. Also, gold counteracts wood, wood counteracts earth, earth counteracts water, water counteracts fire and fire counteracts gold. The Universe is the metamorphosis of the myriad elements of relative values. All these elements can be synthesized into the interaction between yin and yang, which encompasses Durand's imaginary symbols of the diurnal and nocturnal regimes.

Fire remains at the centre of the story as the menacing weapon and image. The king Zhou's fire of sexual desire kindles the Goddess's fire of revenge. The continual lingering of the evil atmosphere as the evil fire accompanied by the three spirits remains as a canopy above the palace. The very chance for the king Zhou to purge his kingdom is the talisman sword given by the alchemist Wunzhongzi (Amidst Cloud) that can exorcize evil spirits. However, the king takes the fox-spirit's (Daji) advice to burn the sword. This fire symbolizes the impossibility of changing the kingdom's doom, which is even aggravated by the later conflagration of the royal temple. The tyrant Zhou creates the cruelest punishment of *paoluo* (red-hot pillar of brass) that will scorch the punished poor. He uses this invention to kill his loyal officers and the virtuous queen. The ensuing battles of the war between the king Wu and the king Zhou continue the fire till the end. As every element is endowed with yin and yang nature, fire also plays the important role of exorcizing evil power. The wise old man Jiang Ziya first demonstrates his supernatural power by burning the pipa-spirit. The group of fox-spirits and other evil spirits invited to join the banquet held by the fox-spirit Daji (now almost the queen) in Chapter 25 are eventually burned and destroyed by the royal general Bigan. The Giant monster Wu Wenhua is ensnared by Jiang Ziya into the mountain and exploded in flame. This is the last inflammation against the evil power before the final doom of the king of Zhou. Fire delivers the final nemesis of the tyrannous king as the denouement where the king Zhou burns himself in his zhaixinglou (Star plucking tower).

Air ignites fire and the plot of the novel is inflamed by the joining of the figures from the unknown realm, heaven and *Xianjing* or Faerie. Gods and xians or immortals are the embodiment of air that decides all. Chapter 15 ascends to the element of air: the council of gods in the Mountain Kunlun (heavenly mountain). The Wise Old Man figure Jiang Ziya, who practices Dao there for forty years (he is now seventy-two), is assigned by his master, the Arch-God Yuanshitianzun, to go back to the earthly world to help the future king of Zhou. With the air from the heavenly mountain, Jiang Ziya encounters the pipa-spirit and burns it to disclose its essence as the jade pipa. However, this air kindles furiously the malicious flame of the fox-spirit. She asks the king to build *chaipen* (the basin of venomous worms and snakes) to punish the incompliant, a concretization of fire, evil, venom and the extreme yin. Failing in advising the king Zhou to redress his tyranny, Jiang Ziya withdraws himself by the River Wei to be a recluse. The element air shifts to the king Wen who accomplishes the book *Zhouyi* (Known as *Yi Jing* today) during his detention by the king Zhou.[62] Though he performs divination by *Yi Jing* oracle to learn that his eldest son was killed and cooked for him to eat to test whether he is an oracle or not, the king Wen eats the meat cake made of his son's flesh for the fate predetermined by Gods. He undergoes a series of fantastic experiences such as spitting three times the meat soup (the meat cake of his son's flesh) from his mouth that transform into three rabbits and jump away (this then corresponds to the saying that the sage does not eat his son) and dreaming of a flying bear that symbolizes his future victory.

The central figure that connects the divine and the mundane in the novel is Jiang Ziya, the archetype of the Wise Old Man that mediates between heaven (as a disciple of an Arch-God and assigned to be in charge of the investiture of the gods) and earth (the advisor to the king of Wen and Wu). The side of good gods often sends a relief force to him, good alchemists come to help him and earthly righteous generals and soldiers converge at his stronghold. He travels by the magic of submerging underground and enters the divine realm. After his first descent to the earthly, he is summoned back to Kunlun Mountain to build the altar for the future investiture [Chapter 37] and goes back to Yuxu Palace (the divine realm of the Arch-God Yuanshitianzun) for counsels [Chapter 38] and gains the Beast Lashing Whip. He can conjure up a blizzard in the middle of July to ward off the attacks from the enemy and utters magic words with his fire umbrella (the true fire of the sun) to melt down the snow into a storm then into an ocean. Defeated by the Ten-immortal Arrays (*zhen*), Jiang Ziya dies with his soul drifting in Kunlun and is later resurrected by god Chijingzi [Chapter 44]. Air also represents qi (breath) that circulates in the body as well as in the Universe. Transitional figures like Jiang often die once and are resurrected to a second life, for example, the aforementioned Nuocha, the metamorphosing Yang Ji, the divine kid Huang Tianhua and his father, the marshal Huang Feihu (Flying Tiger).

The imaginary of the element air makes language a formidable weapon. In Chapter 36, the general Zhang Guifang is a practitioner of black magic. He fights for the tyrant's side. He uses this magic to defeat the marshal Flying Tiger Huang and the general Zhou Ji, who, after hearing the words, "If you, (the name

---

[62] The king Wen is in fact the alleged author of *Zhouyi* [The book of *Yi Jing* from the Zhou dynasty]. He creates the posterior octa-gram of *Yi Jing* (*Hotian Bagua*). Thus the king Wen is considered as an oracle.

of the foe), don't dismount from the horse now, when will be better?" both dismount and fail. The Taiyi Immortal senses this inferior position at Jiang's side and sends his disciple Nuocha to their rescue. He fights against Zhang, who exerts the same spell on him but in vain and is thus badly wounded. Nuocha's immunity from the magic words results from his resurrection out of the lotus. The words are effective on humans who are composed of essence and blood into three hun (logos or animus) and seven puo (anima).[63] If a man hears the magic words, his hun and puo will be strewn everywhere, forcing him to dismount. Nuocha is a metamorphosis of lotus without hun and puo and thus immune to the spells. This episode of language and magic can be considered as a *mise en abyme* of the whole novel's employment of Daoist fulu (symbolic words or incantation). Words are powerful (in Daoist belief) and able to incarnate the abstract sound and writing. This conception is germane to the symbolic meanings in the quasi-mathematic signs of *Yi Jing*. In this light, fantastic storytelling is taken as both literal and figurative. The harmonization of dualism in language, besides the representation of language as real and concrete, is manifest in the communication among gods, alchemists and fantastic men through the use of signified without signifier, the mind's language as telepathy.[64]

However, language can be corrupted for the evil purpose as slander and instigation, like the language appropriated by Melkor (*The Silmarillion*), Sauron (*The Lord of the Rings*) and Mephistopheles (*Faust*) in Occidental fantastic epics. Nevertheless, the idea of the agreement in literal and figurative meanings is retained. In the present circumstance, the magic of words is embodied on the evil side. As stated earlier, all Becoming is triggered by the yin catalysis that connotes the unrighteousness beginning with the king Zhou's lustful desire. From the perspective of narrative discourse, we may crystallize the yin as the interplay of language. All the cruel deeds and crimes of the king Zhou are incited by the language of the fox-spirit Daji, which persists until the doom of the dynasty and the execution of the fox-spirit (who even succeeds in luring the executioner into sparing her life). She fabricates a false reality by evil language that turns the king's head from virtue, and kills most of the honest and loyal subjects. The language of the evil spirit is reinforced by the language of man uttered by a few fawning villains in the palace. On the side of heaven, Dao practitioner Shen Gongbao (Jiang Ziya's fellow), out of fire of jealousy, conspires with the evil side and antagonizes many gods against the good side to help the king Zhou. His evil tongue and hubris make his uttered oath realized: to be plugged at the eye [the crevice of the cliff of the North Sea, the unicorn kilin cliff. The war between

---

[63] In his preface to *Taiyi jinghua zongzhi*, translated as *The Secret of the Golden Flower* by Richard Wilhelm, Jung employs logos to translate "hun," which is translated by wilhelm into animus. Both translate "puo" into anima.

[64] We may refer to Swedenborg's description of the spiritual world where people communicate by the appearance of symbolic images instead of uttering words.

the regiments of Jiang Ziya and the king Zhou is originally at the level of minor gods, immortals, alchemists, spirits and men. However, evil language even permeates the Arch-heaven. The Arch-God Tongtianjiaozhu (of Jiejiao or obstruction branch) is in Chapter 73 misguided by many of his evil disciples with the slander that the disciples of the other two Arch-Gods (of *Daode* or virtue branch and of *Chanjiao* or illumination branch) scorn them as a lower branch and kill their fellows. The God Tongtian thus is enticed to use the most deadly divine array, Zhuxianzhen (god slaughtering array) to take his revenge. In this manner, the evil language unfolds ten chapters of battle among the gods. Even Taishanglaojun (Lao Zi, the Arch-God of virtue) has to join the battle with the other two Gods from the west (Buddha of Jieyin and Zhunti), for they need four gods to fight against the four swords from the dreadful array that slaughter gods (the swords of zhuxian, luxian, xianxian and juexian). Lastly, the Great God or the One Hongjun comes to intercede to stop the formidable array of ten thousand gods. It is evident that the power of language can surpass the wisdom of gods.

The element of water refreshes the smouldering atmosphere caused by the aforementioned evil fire until chapter 10. It is said that the city of Chaoge (capital of the Shang dynasty) had not had rain for half a year. In this chapter, the king Wen chances to encounter a thunder shower while walking in Yanshan. He glimpses a child crying next to a tomb and counts him as a great future general. His companion, alchemist, Amidst Cloud, names the kid Leizhenzi (Thunder-dragon) and will train him to help the king Wen (as Thunder-dragon's foster father) seven years later. Readers will wait until Chapter 21 to see Thunder-dragon come to the rescue of his foster father after the latter escapes from imprisonment by the king of Zhou. Thunder-dragon has metamorphosed into a dragon figure after eating two fairy apricots: "Two wings sprout from his two sides, what is worse, his face changes: the nose raising, face turning blue, hair shifting to red, eyes bulging, teeth protruding his lips like tusks, the body lengthening to two zhang tall (equals 6.6 meters)" [ibid., 210]. His left wing is named wind and right wing thunder. His master Amidst Cloud passes him a golden bar as his divine weapon. Thus Thunder-dragon remains the king's saviour figure. His name is thus charged with the semantic unity of water, wind, rain, thunder, sea, dragon, snake and tiger. He is quite invisible given that he has a face as azure as the sky and body as transparent as water. The element water continues to flow from Chapter 11 to 14 with the episode revolving around the fight between Nuocha and the dragon family of the East Sea as well as between the resurrected Nuocha as god and his father (in his previous reincarnation). Water functions as alleviation of the creeping fire of evil from the palace. Likewise, water also mitigates the ferocity and petulance of Nuocha as he is resurrected through the water lotus. The king Wen of Zhou visits Jiang Ziya by the waters (Weishui) to plead him to be his advisor. In Chapter 44, Jiang uses magic to protect and cover his stronghold Qishan by turning the North Sea upside down, and pouring the waters to ward off the ferocious attacks from the four generals of the Evil Family who manipulate a set of weapons completed in fire, air, earth and water. Later in Chapter 88, white fishes jump into king Wu's dragon boat, which symbolizes the purification and the rebirth of a new dynasty. Like fire, the element water also embraces its yin or negative side. The four saints from Nine Dragon Island of the West Sea are the four divine beasts with the essence of water. They are defeated by the figures and weapons associated with the element earth. The first beast Wangmuo is killed by Jincha, the brother of Nuocha. The others are exterminated by Jiang Ziya's Beast Lashing Whip.

The four primary elements in Daoist imagination condense into various symbols. These can be envisaged from the diurnal and nocturnal regimes proposed by Durand. The Chinese rendering of fantastic imagination into structures is akin to the alchemical structure. Durand places it in the synthetic structure of Messiah. However, Daoist alchemy is more than a simple progressive structure with the myth of Messiah. It is closer to Barfield's concept of semantic unity in language. Daoist alchemy does connect the material and the spiritual, the concrete and the abstract, not through impalpable sublimation but through a real amalgamation of such contraries. Immortality is the goal of Daoist alchemical practice. With a thinking mode underlying an imaginary system based on darkness, the visages of time or death and the symbols against it from the diurnal imaginary are not purely Durandian, not only euphemized but also harmonized by the praise of night. Therefore, the destroying visage of time projected in theriomorphic, catamorphic and nyctomorphic images is harmonized with Nature's law into yin and yang features. For example, gods may assume theriomorphic forms like the numerous disciples and gods or immortals under the Arch-God Tongtian, such as the Goddess Guiling (turtle spirit), Longxuhu (tiger with dragon whisker) and Yuan Hong (ape). The four saints from Nine Dragon Island of the West Sea ride on four divine beasts. Three among the seven great heroes of the novel that attain Nirvana at the end of the novel assume theriomorphic figures: Nuocha (three heads six arms), Thunder-dragon (with a dragon form) and Yang Ji (able to metamorphose into various beasts). If we refer to the final list of the investiture of gods, many are animals or theriomorphic forms. Even the supreme Goddess Nüwa is in fact half-snake half-woman, and Xiwangmu, the Goddess Mother of the West, is also reported as half-leopard half-woman. The imagination of the participation of the animals or vegetation in Daoist alchemy is an extension of the time visage. Animals symbolize movement and time and thus can naturally join in the pursuit of immortality and eternity. The metamorphosis of inanimate objects and the objects' becoming gods bolsters this dream of immortality.

The conception of darkness, death and time towards benevolence in Daoism builds its fantastic storytelling. An alchemist can see in the darkness or discern the identity of evil spirits with his golden eyes. The image of falling or cata-morphism, such as falling into the waters or under the earth, is transformed into magic striding of water and earth (shuidun or water-fleeing) and tudun or wa-ter-fleeing and earth-fleeing). The possible connection between men and gods make heaven accessible and the heroic structure is not a *schizomorphic* one. Accordingly, the diaïretical symbols are concrete gifts from gods after diligent practice of Dao. The alchemical elixir of long life or magical words can resur-rect the dead. Death is not only euphemized into sleep but also reversed into genuine resurrection. Heroes like Jiang Ziya, Nuocha, Flying Tiger Huang and Yang Ji all experience death and live a second life. The nocturnal euphemism of the devouring nyctomorphic images into embedment and container is sublimated by Daoist imagination into alchemical space and power. The caves are tran-scended to dongtian fudi (divine and fairy realm). The metamorphosis into the enemy's belly is a supernatural weapon. The divine palace of Nuocha's master Taiyi Immortal is called Golden Light Cave (Jinguang Dong) and that of Yang Ji's master Yuding Immortal is Golden Glow Cave (Jinxia Dong). The hero Yang Ji lets the sable from the Devil Family devour him as a stratagem to defeat the devils. An inanimate stone can be a goddess, for example, the Shiji Niangniang (the goddess of stone) was originally a stone that was born beyond the cosmos and has become a divine spirit by undergoing earth, water, fire and air. Three isotopisms of images merit a closer investigation: diaïretical divine weapons, the femme fatale against the Grand Mother and metamorphosis as the kinetic gold chain harmonizing all images against death.

The divine weapons and arrays possessed by the characters (divine, human and inhuman) are the myriad incarnations of the five elements, some limited to one element, others embodying several, or even all five. As all yin elements have yang and yang have yin, the extraordinary characters from both good and bad sides can obtain such divine weapons and are able to conjure magic arrays. Most divine weapons are endowed with the material gold, such as Thun-der-dragon's golden bar, Nuocha's golden Sky-Earth Bracelet and Golden Brick and Randeng Immortal's golden Linglong Tower (later passing to his disciple Li Jing). Most of these extraordinary figures possess a pair of golden eyes that can identify the evil spirit. Nuocha's whole gear of divine weapons is the genuine incarnation of fire and air coupled with himself as the incarnation of water and earth. The incarnation of the four elements also features in the Devil Family four generals' weapons [Chapter 40 and 41]: Devil Turquoise with turquoise-cloud sword of the four elements, Devil Red with cosmos pearl umbrella, Devil Sea with earth-water-fire-air pipa and Devil Life with a sable. Their own identities are symbols of the four elements. Their weapons are so ferocious that Jiang Ziya's regiment is temporarily held back until Yang Ji slaughters the evil sable by his magic of metamorphosis and Huang Tianhua uses his firing and golden heart piercing stake to kill the four devils. These four devils have become the four celestial gods of the four elements after the investiture by Jiang at the end of the novel. Jiang Ziya died once in Chapter 44 by the arrays of ten evil gods who side with the king of Zhou and the minister Wen. These lethal arrays manipulate the labyrinthine interactions among the four elements and their philosophy of counteraction. Thus just by making a straw doll with Jiang's name on it can ten evil gods kill the person in reality, given that all things in the Universe are made from the four elements and the concept of *unus mundus* extends to killing through the communion with the four elements, viz. distant murder. In Chapter 76, the Huang brothers (fighting for the evil king Zhou) conjure an array called Ten Thousand Blade Car. The weapon is made of paper with a spinning disk at the centre. Above the car features a four head pennant with words and prints on it, highlighted by the four words: earth, water, fire and air. While they operate the weapon, the climate changes and turns to windy, sinister and foggy, flames suddenly soaring with ten thousands of dashing blades. They prepare three thousand Ten Thousand Blade Cars to attack Jiang Ziya's fortress. It is said that the overwhelming force is competing wind and fire. Just as Jiang and his fellows are besieged by such fierce weapons, the hero Zheng Lun rides on his Golden Eye Beast to pursue the enemy Huang and bumps into them. Zheng penetrates the secret of the magic cars and in the twinkling of an eye, he exercises two rays of white light from his nose and, with a rumbling sound, snorts at the brothers Huang with the white light and defeats them. The brothers fall from their horses and get captured. The aforementioned significant battles in heaven, caused by the ignorance of the Arch-God Tongtian's Gods Slautering Array and Ten Thousand Gods Array, are grounded in the interactions and counteractions of the four elements. Even after Tongtian fails his arrays, he decides to restart and establish earth, water, fire and air to build a new world. This idea is later prohibited by the One God Hongjun. Tongtian finally apologizes for his irrational actions and makes peace with the other gods.

The counteraction of water against fire is manifest in Chapter 64, where fire is neutralized by water. Nuocha has his counterpart in the opposite regiment. The character's name is Luo Xuan, God in Flame from Fire Dragon Island, belonging to the obstruction branch of Arch-God Tongtian. Luo is also enticed by Shengongbao (Jiang Ziya's counterpart) to fight for King Zhou. Different from earth-fleeing (tudun) and water-fleeing (shuidun), Luo Xuan achieves the skill of fire-fleeing (huodun) and tries to burn down Jiang's stronghold area of Xiqi. He can metamorphose into a figure like Nuocha with three heads and six arms, one hand holding a Sky Reflecting Seal, one hand Five Dragon Wheel, one hand Ten Thousand Raven Kettle, one hand Ten Thousand Mile Cloud-Reek Rocket, and the other two hands wielding Flying Reek Sword. Luo Xuan defeats Huang Tianhua's Jade Kilin with his Five Dragon Wheel, but Yang Ji releases his Roaring Sky Dog to harm Luo Xuan, and Jiang Ziya lashes his Beast Lashing Whip that almost forces Luo Xuan to dismount from his Red Reek Steed. Defeated at this first round, Luo Xuan retreats and plots a night raid upon Jiang's stronghold. He uses the fire-fleeing art to ride his Red Reek Steed and launches his Ten Thousand Mile Cloud-Reek Rocket into the city of Xiqi. Just as Jiang is at his wit's end faced with such conflagration, the Dragon Luck Princess (daughter of the Heaven God and the Goddess Mother of the West) from the Sphinx Mountain arrives with her Turquoise Bird. Seeing that the fire is caused by thousands of Flame Ravens, she orders her disciples to spread the Mist-Dew Sky-Earth Net to extinguish the fire. Irritated, Luo Xuan challenges the princess with his Five-Dragon Wheel but hits right into the princess's Four-Sea Phial that ends the weapon of the Fire-Dragon. Then Luo Xuan launches his Ten Thousand Mile Cloud-Reek Rocket, which is captured inside the phial again. Now Luo appears with three heads and six arms to beat the princess with his Sky Reflecting Seal; however, the princess just points at his seal with the Duo Dragon Sword to let fall the seal into the fire. Knowing his disadvantageous situation, Luo escapes with the fire-fleeing. Eventually, Li Jing (Nuocha's father) intercepts Luo Xuan and smashes his brain with his Golden Tower. Fire is eventually quenched by water; the executor of fire or the human incarnation of fire (man equals earth) is quashed by gold.

The last hexagram of *Yi Jing* ends with huoshuiweiji (disharmony of fire and water)[65] to signify that it is not an end but a recommencement. The elements of fire and water thus predominate in the phenomena of counteractions. The novel uses the end of the Shang dynasty as its setting to unfold the changes departing from the unbenefited status of fire against water. Intertwined with the other two elements of air and earth, the catalysis to the whole metamorphoses of the storytelling is embodied in the Goddess Nüwa and the evil fox-spirit Daji. The former is the fire and water with air, the latter the fire and water with earth. Accordingly, the devouring female figure in Durand's diurnal regime of the imaginary is coupled with the figure of the Great or Telluric Mother. Given that the first appearance of yin (or the original status of chôra) launches the universal formation with the interaction and counteractions of the four elements, yin remains the vital factor that ferments the created into eternal metamorphosis. Like the images of fire and water with the dual features of benevolence and malevolence, woman can be the *femme fatale* as well as *femme divine*. The contrast between Nüwa and Daji represents the contrast between god and devil in man.

In the novel, human figures of women are overshadowed by female gods and devils. We learn about the horrible death of the queen Jiang (her two arms are scorched by *paoluo* and one of her eyes is plucked), which is plotted by the

---

[65] Notice that the fire trigram is placed above the water trigram to form the hexagram of fire-water disharmony. On the contrary, if the water trigram goes above the fire trigram, it will be the hexagram of water-fire harmony. The *Yi Jing* philosophy holds that the Universe is always in the process of changing and harmonizing, thus the last hexagram (the 64th) presents the disharmony to predict future harmonies and changes.

cruel Daji. In addition, the latter takes revenge on Flying Tiger Huang (who scratches the face of a fox, in reality Daji) by ensnaring his wife to Star Plucking Tower to let the king Zhou harass her. She jumps out of the tower to defend her virtue. The king's concubine Huang (the sister of Flying Tiger Huang) accuses Daji of murdering Huang's wife and reprimands the king's ignorance and crimes, and then she also jumps out of the tower. Good women are slaughtered indirectly by the fox-spirit. Even the identity of Daji was in fact stolen from an ordinary woman. Daji kills the real woman Daji to appropriate her identity and assume human form. She invents the most notorious punishments for the king Zhou. To avenge her fox friends burned by Bigan, Daji feigns sickness and asks the king to use qichiao linglong heart (delicate seven-aperture heart), to cure her. Only Bigan has such qichiao linglong heart. The king thus orders his minister Bigan to sacrifice for Daji. Her cruel behaviour of killing and devouring (the fox-spirit eats men) is embodied by the two aforementioned penalties: the scorching killing of fire and the devouring killing of water. The vivid depiction of Daji's evil deeds is in fact an animation of the fixed expressions concerning women's potential of being evil. The fixed expressions in Chinese language such as "the most venomous heart is in women" and "women are the water of calamity" are to be taken literally. The fixed expression that "when a country is about to collapse, there must be evil monsters and spirits" is completely staged in the present novel. This fox-spirit Daji combines the three expressions (venomous, water and evil spirit) in one. Her language is also a concretization of the expression "devilish words enchanting the public." Like the powerful magic words used by the gods and alchemists, Daji's language is also overwhelming to the kingdom. She is a parallel figure to Melkor or Sauron who only exerts the power of language to instigate the Maiar, the Elves and Men to misunderstand one another and revolt against the good realm.

The image of the Great Mother reified in the Goddess Nüwa serves as the causality of all Becoming and the termination of the plot. As mentioned earlier, the king Zhou's lustful desire for the Goddess Nüwa is the specific trigger of the collapse of the Shang dynasty. Almighty as she is, she has to obey heaven's number or Providence while taking her revenge. Knowing that the king Zhou still has twenty-eight years to live (this can be consulted from the divine almanac), she thus summons three spirits to enchant him with the proviso of no killing. Therefore, strictly speaking, the evil fox-spirit Daji takes on the mission assigned by the Goddess Nüwa to corrupt the king. However, her wicked nature goes beyond the mission, for she has slaughtered too many people in the most venomous manner. After the first chapter, Daji plays a crucial role along with a regiment of evil gods and spirits to interact and counteract with the power of yang. The devouring images cluster as the decline of the kingdom of Shang culminates. It is not until Chapter 92 that the Goddess Nüwa rejoins the conflict between good and evil. She comes to help Yang Ji to yield the buffalo-spirit Jin

Dasheng and the ape-spirit Yuan Hong of the Plum Mountain (the king of the seven animal spirits). She sends her disciple Turquoise Cloud Child to manipulate the Fuyaosuo (Devil Yielding Rope) and the Yellow Headscarf Hercules to pierce his nose and hammer his back to beat him back into the form of buffalo. Then the Goddess Nüwa grants Yang Ji the divine weapon of Shanhe Sheji Tu (the Country Map) to yield the ape-spirit. He ensnares the ape-spirit into the labyrinth of the map to imprison it and later uses the Devil Yielding Rope to bind it. The Goddess Nüwa appears in time to help conquer the most difficult and fierce evil spirits. Therefore, the tough fox-spirit and her two companions (the pheasant and the jade pipa) who escape the pursuit of Jiang Ziya's heroes will be tamed and yielded by the Goddess Nüwa in Chapter 97. The Goddess uses again the Devil Yielding Rope to bind the three spirits and sends them to Jiang Ziya for the final execution. The three spirits cunningly defend themselves by saying that they just followed the Goddess's order and it is not reasonable for Yang Ji to furiously chase them. The Goddess rebukes them for killing too many innocent and honest people in an abnormally cruel way. They deserve their final penalty according to heaven's law. And thus ends the story of the most wicked and evil female spirits, the cause of all ghastly tragedies. The devouring fatal woman can only be conquered by the Great Mother of cosmos.

Fantastic storytelling featuring strangeness and narration as the central rhetoric of mimesis of the unknown quintessentially resides in metamorphosis as the breath or momentum of the story flows. The inception of Ovid's *Metamorphoses* stages the chaos in the beginning and the ensuing metamorphoses of the extension of the Universe. Likewise, the Chinese fantastic epics, the presently analyzed novel along with *Journey to the West*, commence with poems with a review of the metamorphosis of the Universe from chaos (hundun). Metamorphosis underlies the philosophy of changes in *Yi Jing* and the Daoist secret of alchemy. Therefore, the imagination of metamorphosis euphemizes, harmonizes, transcends and *metamorphoses* the imaginary of time and death. As mentioned earlier, theriomorphic and catamorphic images are transformed into benevolent and divine images by the Daoist *logic*. The only permanence in the Universe is metamorphosis itself and thus death is not death, time is reversible. Metamorphosis as the main syntactical structure of the novel is also represented by characterization, setting and actions. The one hundred chapters of the novel are saturated with all engrossing sundry episodes, chapter after chapter. The space is not confined in three dimensions, it extends to the unknown realm, both ascending and descending space inhabited by different kinds of immortals. Characters undergo their individuation in the process of the battles. The final investiture of gods for the dead men, spirits and gods is a perpetual *mise en abyme* of metamorphosis. Moreover, in the process of the storytelling, the principal characters develop and metamorphose in both material and spiritual ways. For example, Thunder-dragon and Nuocha literally metamorphose into theriomorphic figures;

this is a proof of their achievement. Yang Ji, similar to the monkey king Sun Wukong of *Journey to the West*, can metamorphose into myriads of forms. All these three heroes, along with Li Jing, Jincha, Mucha and Weihu (different from the others that become gods after dying in the battles) metamorphose into gods from their material bodies. As to Jiang Ziya, the vital figure to the establishment of the Zhou dynasty and the executor of the investiture, he has to continue to practice Dao with his earthly identity for some more years. Not only life metamorphoses, history also metamorphoses as the Shang dynasty changes into the Zhou dynasty. In a parallel way, life and death interchange too.

Throughout his life of profound researches of alchemy, Jung eventually turned to *Yi Jing* and Daoism and annotated the Daoist book *The Secret of the Golden Flower* to advance his psychological researches. He sought a connection between matter and spirit from a more "scientific" direction. Therefore, Daoist alchemy provided evidence for his theory of synchronicity. The secret is believed to be the elixir of long life or xiandan (divine pill) and flesh-and-blood immortality. If Durand viewed hypotyposis as the central rhetoric for the synthetic structures that depict vividly beyond temporal confinement, Chinese fantastic literature is the hypotyposis of immortality. The elixir of long life can be a pill, charm, array or magic words. In Chapter 26 and 27, Bigan does not collapse after he digs his heart out for king Zhou to cure the fox-spirit's disease; he can still walk out of the palace because Jiang Ziya predicts that Bigan will encounter such a misfortune and writes him magic words to ward off the danger. The remedy needs to be burned (words written on paper) and mixed with water to drink, under the condition that he can not turn back (interestingly similar to the Western Orpheus's motif). However, no sooner has he turned back out of curiosity to ask, "What if a man without the heart?" as he hears a vegetable peddler shouts that her vegetables are those without hearts, he collapses and dies. The general Huang Flying Tiger also dies once and is resurrected by his son, Huang Tianhua, by filling him with the divine pill and anointing him with the divine ointment on his wounded eyes [Chapter 32]. Nuocha also dies once and is resurrected by his master Taiyi Immortal by reconstructing the stem and leaves of lotus of the pond. Jiang Ziya himself also dies once and is resurrected by Chijingzi (Red Essence) by retrieving his two hun (animus) and six puo (anima) and pouring them back to Jiang's mouth [Chapter 44]. Even the evil spirit jade pipa can come back to life. After being burned down into her original object identity as a jade pipa, the fox-spirit Daji picks up the object and hangs it outdoors. After absorbing the essence of the sun, the spirit is resurrected and continues to harm people.

The above analysis of the novel sheds light on the imaginary and synthetic structure of fantastic narration with the dream-discourse. If we use the Chinese metaphor that the reservoir of the collective unconscious as myth is described as the mountains and the seas (as in the title of the Chinese *Classic of the Mountains and the Seas*), the fluidity and musicality in the temporal storytelling as the rhetoric between the fantastic imagination and the achieved sub-creation can be compared to rivers. The image of rivers represents the temporal linking between the mountains and the seas. Therefore, the dream-discourse is endowed with the attributes of the Durandian musical harmonization, reunification of the contraries, style of history or the progressive structure of Messiah.

Tolkien as a Modern Homer

The incredibly numerous names of gods, immortals, spirits, alchemists and men in *The Investiture of the Gods* reminds us of the myriads of names in Tolkien's *The Silmarillion* and *The Lord of the Rings*. Their writings require an index to check and review all the characters. The Chinese novelist Lu (author of *The Investiture*) and the English novelist Tolkien interestingly demonstrate a universal imagination in creating fantastic epics: the scale of the battles, the universal imaginary structures related to Shadow against Light, the arrangement of the four elements plus the gold element, and the highlight on the diurnal and nocturnal images. The interweaving of shadow and light throughout the narrative movement of *The Lord of the Rings* constructs the underlying semantic structure of the novel. The story begins with the long-expected party of Bilbo's birthday embellished with fireworks and the joy of light. In contrast to the light, the following chapter tells about the shadow of the past, many of the Enemy and the Land of Mordor. The Jungian archetype of shadow is represented as a personified figure before the eyes of the hobbits as well as of readers. Pia Skogemann reckons Tolkien's realm of Faerie to be Jung's collective unconscious and accordingly undertakes a symbolic reading of the trilogy. This development of an allegorical reading of the trilogy by interpreting the four hobbits as representing the four psychological functions is intriguing: thinking (Frodo), intuition (Pippin), sensation (Merry) and feeling (Sam).

Middle-earth is the perilous realm of the collective unconscious. Each of the four hobbits has a numinous experience to begin their processes of individuation. The hobbits, though Halflings, are surrogates of us readers in the real world. With these characters out on their heroic quest in the story, readers will vicariously share their experience as entering the realm of the unconscious to go through a literary individuation. Moreover, the narration on the hobbits confronting the past shadow is a *mise en abyme* of the relationship between the narrated story and readers:

> That name the hobbits only knew in legends of the dark past, like a shadow in the background of their memories; but it was ominous and disquieting. It seemed that the evil power in Mirkwood had been driven out by the White Council only to reappear in greater strength in the old strongholds of Mordor. The Dark Tower had been rebuilt, it was said. From there the power was

spreading far and wide, and away far east and south there were wars and growing fear. Orcs were multiplying again in the mountains. Trolls were abroad, no longer dull-witted, but cunning and armed with dreadful weapons. And there were murmured hints of creatures more terrible than all these, but they had no name. [Tolkien 1999, 57]

Dangers lurk in this passage (reminiscent of Tolkien's Faerie, the *perilous* realm) and the hobbits will launch an adventure that drives them to live the legends. The experience of the hobbits, especially the imaginative Sam, who has long believed in dragons and elves, will enter the marvellous world to witness by himself. We readers, in a parallel manner, will be led through our imagination into the world of legends to undergo Tolkien's tetra-elements (Fantasy, Recovery, Escape and Consolation). The narration starts with the Shire, space of consciousness, through a quest of destroying the one ring into the unconscious, and eventually returns back to consciousness, the scoured Shire. This archetypal structure is evident and complete as an epic model.

With the ensuing plot after the revelation of the shadow of the past, we will learn about the archetypes of anima and animus in their projection onto different characters. Besides the hobbits, Aragorn son of Arathorn goes through his heroic individuation from the identity of the strider to the king of a new era to Middle-earth. Shadow figures such as Gollum, Saruman, Shelob, Balrog and other minions of Sauron concretize the real danger of the collective unconscious, because none of these figures were originally evil. It is sufficient to state that the master of Sauron, Melkor, was at the outset of world creation an Ainur, a Holy One or the offspring of Eru's (the One) thought. In the perilous realm, good forces are benevolent to heroes and help them ward off evil assaults and temptations. This particular conception on good and evil echoes the aforementioned Daoist vision. All evil power derives from good. The archetypes of the Wise Old Man, Anima and Animus are embodied by Gandalf, Galadriel and Elrond. However, this archetypal approach is often reproached for ignoring the literariness of works. Maintaining the values of Jung's theory but being prudent not to fall into the pitfall of undermining the poetics of Tolkien's fantasy art, we will not stop with *archetypocritique* here. The approach we employ in analyzing narrative discourse will emerge gradually from the depth of the sea to the surface. Besides the complete deployment of Jungian archetypes, the dream-discourse pattern is constructed through the Bachelardian imaginary of the four elements and Durandian symbols from both diurnal and nocturnal regimes that form synthetic or dramatic structures. Additionally, the essence of the fantastic rhetoric that refines language to its unity of figures and abstract meanings constructs the central linguistic structure. The alchemy of language serves as the exact eclectic approach, or the third way, to connect Jung's spiritual structure of images.

The core of the *archetypocritical* structure of dream-discourse is the process of individuation. From another angle, the pivot of the structure of material imagination is the interplay of the four elements: air, water, fire and earth. A complete amalgamation of the basic elements in the story will lead to the fifth element. Plato named the fifth element a sphere and Daoism calls it gold or purified element as the secret of the golden flower. Here we would review the concept developed before about myth, chôra and mimesis. Considering Plato's metaphors of the term chôra, we may also interpret the fifth element as the pure and concrete manifestations of chôra itself, the malleable purest material gold. Air connotes language and music, and symbolizes the celestial envoy; it is an element that represents the style of *harmonism*. The story must be fluid with diction in unison with breath, connecting the beginning to the end. In the Silmarillion mythology, air comes first in the creation of the world. In the beginning, Eru, the One, called Illuvatar in Arda, "spoke to them [the Ainur], propounding to them themes of music; and they sang before him, and he was glad" [Tolkien 1999, 3]. Apparently, words and music are prior to the fashioning of the world. Then the subsequent plot of the mythology is structured as the descending of heavier materials. Water and earth will be further separated by Melkor who kindles a great fire. As highlighted earlier, the reading of fantastic literature is like tracing back to the semantic unity of language and myth. Tolkien's trilogy offers a teleological reading of such linguistic alchemy. The trilogy in fact invites a reverse reading. It ends with the return of the king, which means Middle-earth will be henceforth left completely in the hands of men. Tolkien did not tell us the sequel, but we can easily imagine what would follow. He in fact inspired us to conduct a reverse reflection on the story. The ring is the representative material of fire, which is the raiment of Melkor's evil language and fire. Readers have to trace back to the origin of human nature, both good and evil. The narrative closure of the trilogy entails a reference to *The Silmarillion*. Otherwise, the appreciation of the trilogy will fall short of unity. Returning to the shadow and light of the past in Tolkien's mythology is like returning to the origin of human nature. As the four elements are explicitly narrated along the formation of the world in *The Silmarillion*, the elements are incorporated to underlie the imaginary structure of the trilogy.

The incipit of the story is characterized by earth, Middle-earth. The hobbits depart from the Shire and pass hills, mounds, delves, glades, forest and villages. Then they ward off the hunt of Ringwraiths by leaving the land to the waters. With the help of the elves (implication of air), they go through different hardships constructed by the element earth. The element water remains ambiguous in the story. Given that it offers the first mirror to reflect the human image, it gains the attribute of human desire. Thus the mirror (water) of Lothlórien can reveal different levels of the unconscious. The water of the Marshes represents the shadow of death and past. In contrast to these ominous images of water, the deluge caused by Treebeard is an antidote to the evil fire flaring in Isengard. The fire of desire and evil aroused by the ring is the abiding image from material imagination that endures until the denouement of the story, the destruction of the ring with Sméagol the Gollum. The closure of the trilogy offers a double reading. That Sam, Peppin and Merry return to normal peaceful Shire life after the scouring of their hometown signifies a return of the material earth after purification. This makes the structure a complete circle. However, Tolkien implied a return to the lighter material from earth, viz. Frodo's departure with the elves at the Grey Havens. They will return to the realm of air beyond water. This explains why it is necessary to consult *The Silmarillion* to completely understand the mythopoeia of Tolkien. As these characters of Middle-earth return to the blessed land, readers start their quest for exploring the fantastic imagination of Tolkien.

From the abstract structure (Jung's archetypocriticism) to the material imaginary structure, our focus is more on the unconscious level of human imagination. With Bachelard's imaginary system, structures formed with symbolic images will uncover the dream-discourse at the imaginary level of insecurity vis-à-vis the inexorable and ineluctable time. The dream-discourse centres on the art of musicality, which emphasizes musical harmonization and musical dialectic synthesis.

While most modern narrative rhetoric or narratology raves about the narrative art contrived by the complex enunciation and the interplay of speeches, fantasy contents itself with absorbing storytelling related to the unknown realm. However, fantasy works are likely to be criticized as superficial, without psychological depth. For example, Tolkien's fantasy was first criticized by many academic scholars from this perspective. This is indeed another bias generated from the intellectual and conscious stages of human conscious evolution. From the stage of original participation, man perceives an existing unity with Nature. This stage prior to the separation between the percipient and the percept arouses fantastic creation, centring on man embraced by the world and God/gods. A later evolution of consciousness towards science and intellect separates man from Nature, as if he was above it. Psychological literature is an outgrowth of conscious evolution. Likewise, Chinese narrative writings started to delve into the psychology of characters in the 20th century, as China tried to catch up with intellect and science from the West. This also explains why Chinese literature lacks fantasy creation since the last century. Psychologist as he was, Jung showed little interest in psychological literature, but rather turned towards visionary literature, mostly fantasies. By the same token, Durand valued the synthetic structure of myth in his research of the anthropological imaginary. The dream-discourse of the fantastic presents the synthetic structure of the nocturnal imaginary through the rhetoric of hypotyposis, which vividly depicts the unknown of past, future and present.

We have so far analyzed the semantic structure of dream-discourse, viz. the imaginary *dispositio* of fantastic poetics. This analysis will be further enhanced by a formalistic approach of narrative structure and language. Dream-discourse recapitulates poetic elements of epic and saga. The storytelling is authorized by a heterodiegetic narrator with zero focalization, or an omniscient narrator. Since action is the dynamism of the discourse, the employment of overtly narrative monologues or other focalized depiction of characters' thought or psychology will obstruct the fluidity of the story movement. Aristotle's comments on the poet's part in epics may shed light on the dim position of the narrator in the fantastic story of dream-discourse. Aristotle stated:

> Homer deserves praise for many other reasons but particularly because he alone of the poets saw clearly what he was to do. He saw that the poet himself should speak very little, since he is not an imitator if he uses that method. Other poets assume an active role throughout the whole of their poems. [...] But Homer, after a few lines of introduction, immediately brings in a man or woman or some other character – never a characterless person but one with [definite] characteristics. [Aristotle 1970, 52]

The conception of imitation, according to the above quotation, further refers to objectivity. Accordingly, Tolkien's theory of sub-creation may be reckoned to be a response to Aristotle's poetics of mimesis. The fantastic mimesis through the rhetoric of dream-discourse imitates the unknown truth, as Tolkien often termed, the splintered light from God's realm, by an objective and vivid representation. The dream-discourse re-presents the intrusion of the supernatural by the voice of an objective narrator, for the enunciated space here follows Nature's law. This fantastic mimesis is also a *mise en abyme* of readers' reading experience. Because in the sub-creation, characters are similar to us in critical ways, so that we all speculate about the genuineness of myths, legends or fantastic tales.

Note that fantastic literature with dream-discourse represents different layers of human psychology from the unconscious to consciousness. A resort to a realistic narration of the interior thought of the characters will undermine the imaginary structure of the work. It is redundant and tedious to repeat human psyche with ostensive narration of realism. The narrator acts as a minstrel who tells the ongoing plot as chanting. This enhances the rhythm and the musicality of the story flow, the essential element in the temporality of narration. Story signifies past, present and future, a flow of time; music, different from painting, represents the art of time with the beginning, the middle and the end. A painting can be appreciated upside-down or from any spatial angles. In contrast, it is difficult to imagine listening to or playing a piece of music reversely. In compliance with the principle of musical harmonization, the narrator of dream-discourse narrates the time and the space of the story at a vantage point:

The rain, however, did not last long. Slowly the sky above grew lighter, and then suddenly the clouds broke, and their draggled fringes trailed away northward up the River. The fogs and mists were gone. Before the travellers lay a wide ravine, with great rocky sides to which clung, upon shelves and in narrow crevices, a few thrawn trees. The channel grew narrower and the River swifter. Now they were speeding along with little hope of stopping or turning, whatever they might meet ahead. Over them was a lane of pale-blue sky, around them the dark overshadowed River, and before them black, shutting out the sun, the hills of Emyn Muil, in which no opening could be seen. [Tolkien 2001, 515]

The imaginary structure dominated by the antithesis of shadow and light is concretized at the formal level by rich characters and actions. The magnitude of the dream-discourse equals that of epic as Aristotle theorized. He emphasized action when telling a story, linking fact and art, as did Tolkien. The hub of storytelling lies not in the antithesis of good and evil or light and shadow, but rather in the hypotyposis of the interaction of the elements deriving from such universal imagination. The central action of dream-discourse always features a quest, mingled with dangerous trips and wars. In *The Lord of the Rings*, Frodo's quest in company with Sam and the Gollum is parallel to the war waged by good against evil. The essential elements of reversal and recognition proposed by Aristotle concerning the complex tragedy and epic are embodied in Tolkien's fantastic creation. The conflict between Sam and Gollum in relation to Frodo encompasses both features of reversal and recognition. In the same measure, the Strider's life in exile and his later identity as the genuine king Aragorn present the required elements for a complex epic. The spatial magnitude of the work is the imaginary realm Middle-earth. However, confined by the limited scale, Tolkien resorts to embedded stories that bridge the gap of time, mostly via reciting lays, ballads and songs by the voice of the hobbits, Elves, Aragorn and other characters. His obeying the rule of his tetra-elements (Fantasy, Recovery, Escape, and Consolation) makes his creation pertinent to unity.

As Aristotle highlighted the employment of reason in the epic mimesis, Tolkien also insisted that the creation of fairy-stories is a process of reason. Aristotle explained the quality of impossibilities and possibilities: "Poets should choose impossibilities which are probable rather than possibilities which are unconvincing. They should not make their plots from parts which are contrary to reason. The best thing is for a plot to have no part which is at variance with reason" [Aristotle 1970, 53]. Tolkien also stressed the sensible part of telling a fairy-story, especially to distinguish it from the tale that is only a thing imagined in one's sleep. Without reason, Fantasy will perish and become Morbid Delusion: "Fantasy is natural human activity. It certainly does not destroy or even insult Reason; and it does not either blunt the appetite for, nor obscure the perception of, scientific verity" [Tolkien 1997, 144]. In fact, dream-discourse is similar to the composition of music, an art form that is concrete (sensible or audible) and abstract (impalpable), and scrupulous and imaginary at the same time. Durand also views musical imagination of harmonization as the sublime synthetic structure of the imaginary and estimates that myths are closer to such structure. The dream-discourse is created in harmony with musical imagination and reasonable composition.

The uniqueness in dream-discourse is the harmonization of the known and the unknown, the figurative and the literal. The effect of the *mise en abyme* in dream-discourse reflects the audience's frame of mind. Dream-discourse features the characterization of complex art. The hobbits, imaginary beings, are depicted as ordinary people like the reader. It is this imaginary character of hobbits that makes the quest possible. The hobbits embody the third way that enables the completion of a secondary harmony in the storytelling to enter the space beyond and yet inclusive of dualism (chôra). Other characters such as Men, Dwarfs, Elves, the Maiar and the evil creatures converge into a conflux of fantastic symphony.

The folks in Middle-earth undergo a similar stage as readers do in real life. This stage can be compared to the idolatrous stage criticized by Barfield. For most characters in the story, tales are taken as figurative, whereas Sam, literally believes them. Tolkien's sub-creation is a real *mise en abyme* of painting our world, especially in terms of reading fantastic tales. Hobbits, though naïve and simple in comparison with other folks, still somewhat disdain the significance of myth. The argument between Gaffer and Sandyman on the legend of Bilbo's wealth vividly describes this disbelief, while Gaffer stresses the queerness of Bilbo and his influence on Sam who is "crazy about stories of the old days." "Elves and Dragons! I says to him. Cabbages and potatoes are better for me and you. Don't go getting mixed up in the business of your betters, or you'll land in trouble too big for you, I says to him" [Tolkien 1999, 31].

If Frodo represents the sensitivity of a poet predisposed to myth and legend, Sam is the incarnation of the primitive mentality remaining in idolatrous times. Sam delights in taking on the perilous mission overshadowed by the evil power, because he expects to see the Elves and all the other ensuing wonders and dangers. This further harks back to Tolkien's assumption that Faerie is a perilous realm. Though also with a naïve hobbit heart, Frodo appears heavy-laden, for he is intellectually poetic. This explains why Sam is the only character never tempted and twisted to take the ring, except for the oldest being, Tom Bombadil. Hobbits play a transitional role, as a third race, to cross the realm of the collective unconscious. Being depicted as ordinary people compared with the Elves, Hobbits still appear as supernatural or unknown creatures in traditional fairy tales. Moreover, the appearance of hobbits does create wonder for Men, such as Eomer the rider of Rohan and Theoden. Eomer rejects the true existence of "Halflings and considers them to be "only a little people in the old songs and children's tales out of the North," and doubts where they "walk in legends or on the green earth in the daylight?" [Tolkien 2001, 33]. Aragorn's reply in fact reflects Tolkien's vision of myth, legend and truth: "'A man may do both,' said Aragorn. 'For not we but those who come after will make the legends of our time. The green earth, say you? That is a mighty matter of legend, though you tread it under the light of day!" [Ibid., 33]. Theoden calls Merry and Pippin "the folk of legend" and acclaims that "the days are fated to be filled with marvels" on seeing the hobbits.

This marvel aroused by hobbits is enhanced by the scene of Ents. Gandalf's reply to Theoden's inquiry about the origin of Ents offers a lucid explanation about men and the oblivion of myth and tale. This explanation embodies Tolkien's mythical theory developed in "On Fairy-Stories":

> Is it so long since you listened to tales by the fireside? There are children in your land who, out of the twisted threads of story, could pick the answer to your question. You have seen Ents, O King, Ents out of Fangorn Forest, which in your tongue you call the Entwood. Did you think that the name was given in idle fancy? Nay, Theoden, it is otherwise: to them you are but the passing tale; all the years from Eorl the Young to Theoden the Old are little count to them; and all the deeds of your house but a small matter. [Ibid., 185]

Gandalf exposes to the king, and at the same time to readers, the true meaning of myths, legends and tales. His identity of the Maiar is effectively a living testimonial of the truth revealed in songs and ballads about the past ages of *The Silmarillion* mythology. Theoden acknowledges the illumination by the following reflection:

> Long we have tended our beasts and our fields, built our houses, wrought our tools, or ridden away to help in the wars of Minas Tirith. And that we called the life of Men, the way of the world. We care little for what lay behind the borders or our land. Songs we have that tell of these things, but we are forgetting them, teaching them only to children, as a careless custom. And now the songs have come down among us out of strange places, and walk visible under the Sun.' [Ibid., 185]

That truth lies behind the normally ignored myths, legends and fairy tales is the essence of the universal memory. The above quoted passages reveal men's obliviousness to this. Men gradually forget their connection with Nature as human consciousness evolves. Barfield embraced a similar view on man's deviation from Nature, viz. distancing from original participation. This universal memory corresponds to Jung's collective unconscious as well as the concept of universal consciousness. In harmony with the tenet of external alchemy, men achieve success, wisdom, immortality or divinity through gifts from gods/God. We may refer to the above Chinese epic, which is also a paradigm of external alchemy. Similarly, Gandalf raises the issue of human oblivion and points out the very origin of Men. In *The Silmarillion*, Tolkien depicts Man's nature that tends to keep distance from the Valar: "Men have feared the Valar, rather than loved them, and have not understood the purposes of the Powers, being at variance with them, and at strife with the world" [Tolkien 1999, 116]. He also presents the origin of the aforementioned oblivion of Men: "But when he [Felagund or Finrod] questioned him concerning the arising of Men and their journeys, Bëor would say little; and indeed he knew little, for the fathers of his people had told few tales of their past and a silence had fallen upon their memory" [ibid., 164]. As long as we regain our memory in harmony with Nature, including the unknown past, present and future, the external alchemy will be accomplished. This is why we need the fantastic epic with dream-discourse that is able to make us dream and thus remember. Characters in the ring trilogy eventually accomplish their quests and wars, because they are still connected with Nature, for example the hobbits' encounter with Treebeard and Theoden's acceptance of Gandalf's advice. Gandalf the Maiar represents divine power and Nature that makes the external alchemy possible, meanwhile he himself goes through his own internal alchemy. The interactions among the characters of Tolkien's mythology and novels are a typical contemporary *mise en scène* of external alchemy.

An omniscient realist narrator depicts more the minds and emotions of characters and narrates the time and space by obeying the natural law of our known world. It is this emphasis on the human mind that makes man forget. Men's egoism deteriorates their universal memory and accelerates their oblivion. In contrast, an omniscient narrator of fantastic literature with dream-discourse grasps the statures, dispositions and actions of characters of the known and the unknown. The imaginary landscape and time requires a more musical and pictorial language. The dexterousness of the narration lies in beguiling readers to travel smoothly into the perilous land of sub-creation. We may imagine an invisible rhapsodist who embodies the morphology of the enunciated. This is a fluid river with melodious and harmonious curves. The non-action poeticization refines the imaginary essence of language and myth. The dream-discourse as external alchemy captures the imaginary space of chôra or *Liangyi* (the naissance of dualism). The alchemy thus harmonizes antithetic elements to reach a transcendental status of *unus mundus*. The underlying principle of *Yi Jing* or Daoism is in fact dualism, but the wisdom lies in the harmonious momentum out of the antithetic powers. Therefore, in the dream-discourse, the conflict and fight between good and evil is necessary and perpetual.

The Dream-Discourse as Internal Alchemy

Compared with the structure of the external alchemy as a collective accomplishment in the plotting of the fantastic, the dream-discourse as the internal alchemy stresses on the individuation of the hero, whose fate is actually predetermined by God(s) and yet will be accomplished under interaction and counteraction with other gods and devils. In this section, the Chinese epic novel *Journey to the West* by Wu Cheng'en and German epic play *Faust* by Goethe are to be studied to exemplify the structure of the dream-discourse underpinned by internal alchemy. In the discourse of external alchemy, each character, originally integrated as a grain of the Universe, plays his predestinated role to go through his respective individualization. The narrative structure of such an epic story features a sphere of macrocosm serving as an alchemical furnace extending from sky to earth, where characters interact and counteract through continual metamorphosis until the final collective accomplishment. Lu Xixing's *The Investiture of the Gods* and Tolkien's *The Lord of the Rings* manifest this pattern of discourse, which can also be apprehended in the light of Barfield's original participation where the percipient sees himself as one part of the perceived world. The ideal of *unus mundus* in the first type of dream-discourse is accomplished by the collective participation and quest with the help of gods and benevolent spirits. On the other hand, discourse based on internal alchemy features a microcosm where the main character evolves to integrate into the macrocosm. In *Journey to the West*, the striving quest of the monkey Sun Wukong unfolds a linear adventure that eventually returns to the secondary harmony; in similar fashion the linear development of the plot in *Faust* as the life quest of the hero ends with a transcendental return to the Causality.

Journey to the West and Taming the Monkey's Mind

The monkey Sun Wukong is the hero of the novel, albeit the journey refers to the Buddhist monk Xuanzang's pilgrimage to India to obtain religious scriptures (Sutras). More precisely, the novel is a process of internal alchemy of Sun Wukong's taming his "monkey mind" to reach the status of Nirvana. The incipit of the novel resembles that of *Faust* in that neither hero is satisfied with what they presently possess and are thirsty for the ultimate wisdom. The monkey hero, though being the monkey king, laments for his mortality and meditates on the secret of immortality and the ultimate wisdom, whereas Faust, being the most erudite and wisest scholar, deplores the meagerness of human knowledge so as to resort to alchemical means to gain the secret of the Universe.

Like *The Investiture of the Gods*, *Journey to the West* features one hundred chapters, ranging from the birth of the monkey king to his final Nirvana. The narrative discourse is fluid, with the interaction and counteraction of the four elements. The monkey himself is an embodiment of the universal element of earth, for after the poem as a review of the creation myth, the novel begins with narrating a stone monkey born from the crack of a divine rock atop the primitive mountain Huaguo amidst the sea. The monkey is conceived by Nature with the essence of the sun and the moon, the yang and the yin. One day the divine rock bursts open to yield a stone egg like a round ball. The egg is metamorphosed into a stone monkey by the wind. This embodiment of earth (stone) and wind will undergo the tests of fire and water, which will also be incarnated into his fellows of the quest. The monkey has become the king to the herd of monkeys because his might and valour leads him to explore the mysterious cave to find the source of the waterfall. Thus the monkey king discovers a fairyland called Waterfall Cave for the monkey subjects. The monkey king enjoys his subjects' worship and material satisfaction in his kingdom. However, he is disquieted by certain misgivings: Though he is the king of the kings in the kingdom of the monkeys, not controlled by men or other animals, yet he has to submit to the law of Nature, to be governed by the God of Hell after he dies. This desire to surpass Nature's law, death, triggers the successive episodes of the novel spanning from Daoism to Buddhism. An old and wise monkey enlightens the king that only three kinds of men can be immune to reincarnation among the creatures of five worms[66]: Buddha, Immortals and the Divine Saints. Inspired by the ideal of immortality, the monkey king sets off on his quest.

The monkey king becomes a disciple of the Bodhisattva Xu and gains a name from his master. He is henceforth called Sun Wukong (*Wu* means to apprehend; Kong means emptiness), for having a name is significant to the practice of Dao. His innate intelligence makes him the best among his master's disciples and the Bodhisattva endows him with the magic power of seventy-two metamorphoses and a divine instrument – the Somersault Cloud (the magic cloud as transportation that goes one hundred and eight thousand miles per somersault). Never satisfied, Sun Wukong goes to the dragon palace under the sea to extort some weapons from the dragon king of the East Sea. Sun Wukong's overwhelming reputation intimidates the dragon kingdom into offering him whatever he demands since he is not easily satisfied. Sun is eventually satisfied with the divine iron column alleged to be left from the times of the emperor Yu the Great who used it to fathom the river to prevent floods. Curiously, the column, which is 6.6 meters and 8100 kilograms, shrinks into a handy golden staff in the hand of Sun Wukong. Before leaving with the staff, he asks for gear to fit the weapon from the dragon kings of the North, West and South Seas. This monkey of might and main even goes to Hell to delete his name from the book

---

[66] The antique Chinese taxonomy classifies animals into Five Worms: human beings are naked worms, beasts are furry worms, birds are plume worms, fish are scale worms and insects are shell worms.

of life and death to refuse death, and to Heaven to challenge gods and make hay of the celestial space.

He eats divine peaches and many of the elixirs from the palace of the Goddess Mother of the West. None of the heavenly gods is able to tame the monkey until the Bodhisattva Guan Yin who pours her saint water onto Sun's head to stagger and trip him. Nevertheless, the Emperor God's sentence of death for Sun cannot be executed, because Sun has eaten too many elixirs and gains an indestructible "adamant" body. Then Lao Zi proposes to put the monkey into his alchemical furnace to refine the elixirs from his body, which will then be burned to ashes. However, the smart monkey hides himself at the position of xun (wind) (one of the eight basic trigrams of *Yi Jing*) to avoid fire. His body remains intact in the furnace except for his eyes, smoked by the reinforcement of wind and transformed into "fire-gold eyes." Falsely assuming that the monkey has become ashes, Lao Zi opens the furnace and the monkey escapes again. Just as all the gods are at their wit's end, the Gautama Buddha bets with the monkey that if he is able to escape at a somersault of his magic cloud beyond his palm, then he can supersede the palace of Heaven and the Emperor God will move to the West. The almighty Buddha is as boundless as the edge of the Universe and outwits the monkey. The latter is henceforth imprisoned under Five Element Mountain, transformed from Buddha's five fingers metamorphosing into the five elements, gold, wood, water, fire and earth. The naissance, the religious practice and the taming of the monkey ends at the seventh chapter.

From Chapter 8 to Chapter 12, the novel presents the predetermination of the pilgrimage by the Buddha and the Bodhisattvas, the selection of the elite (the imperial monk Xuanzang) and the empire's preparation for his departure. In the meantime, the Bodhisattva Guan Yin has chosen three guardians for the monk Xuanzang in the form of disciples, namely the monkey Sun Wukong, the pig Zhu Bajie or Zhu Wuneng and the Friar Sand or Sha Wujing, together with a white horse transformed from a dragon prince. The emperor Taizong of the Tang dynasty thus grants him the title Tang Sanzang (San means three, Zang means the scripture) for he will obtain the three Buddhist scriptures from India. The chosen guardians are actually divine characters who have erred and been punished by the Emperor God. The Bodhisattva Guan Yin encounters them on her way to the imperial palace and persuades them to take on the mission to protect the monk as atonement for past sins. The sins committed by the monkey out of his mischievousness and pride are illustrated in the beginning chapters. The pig was originally a deity, Tianpeng Marshal from the Milky Way, but was abased into an earthly reincarnation (the reincarnation into the pig form was an accident, for he missed the right spot) because he harassed the goddess of the moon Chang'e. As to the monster Sand, he, originally a deity general from the heavenly palace Lingxiao, was punished and abased by the Emperor God for he inadvertently broke a glass lamp on the occasion of a divine peach party. He turns into a monster in the sand river to suffer from flying blades penetrating his breast every seven days. Out of pain and hunger, he eats one wayfarer every two or three days. The dragon prince, the son of the dragon king of the West Sea, was punished and suspended in the air to be beaten and executed because he burned the bright pearl of the palace. These penitents thus will purge their sins by going through the test of the pilgrimage.

In summary, our postulate of the imaginary structure of the dream-discourse with the array of the four elements that lead back to the pristine status of chôra beyond polar dualism is effectuated in the present novel. The four elements are first embodied in the protectors of the monk Tang Sanzang by the euphemism of the theriomorphic imagination where the devouring animals and monsters are essentially deities and benevolent. The consecutive devouring devils from the caves (they want to eat the flesh of the monk to be immortal) as the *femmes fatales* will be conquered by the protectors and the divine mother figure Bodhisattva Guan Yin. The lurking perils in the darkness represented by the nyctomorphic images are penetrated and illuminated by the fire power of Sun Wukong. The eventual ascension of the fellowship of the pilgrimage is accomplished by the feminine power (the element of water) that harmonizes with the element fire inside Sun. The whole structure of the novel is mirrored in the manifestations of the elements in Sun's divine weapons and instruments as the isotopism of the *diaïretical* symbols which functions as the *mise en abyme* of the plotting grounded in the four elements intertwined with the semantic isotopism from the diurnal and nocturnal regimes.

The divine outfit of Sun Wukong plus himself is the incarnation of the four plus one elements. The first magic his master teaches him is to metamorphose by breathing his hair. This image is related to the element of air that also transforms Sun Wukong into a monkey from the raw stone egg. The element of air, furthermore a symbol of Heaven and ascension, is embodied into his magic cloud of somersault. This divine chariot can transport without any confinement of the three dimensions. His golden staff is flexible, ranging from a miniature needle to a giant column. The malleability of gold evokes the metaphor of the malleable gold employed by Plato to explain the ineffable chôra. The monkey with the substance of earth bears the golden staff, which testifies Daoist philosophy of the five elements, earth generates gold. The golden staff as the treasure of the dragon palace of the East Sea echoes the alchemical law that gold generates water. Besides his golden staff, the monkey later obtains a pair of fire-gold eyes, which identify the devils and will later generate his tears. The element of water is essentially the neutralizing element that will tame Sun Wukong and transcend his fire to a higher status. His fire of petulance and hubris will be mitigated and harmonized by the power of water in the process of his pilgrimage as he encounters the fire of devils. This is why his imprisonment by the Gautama Buddha under the Five Element Mountain does not really tame him and transcend his spirit, since the mountain belongs to earth and earth cannot counteract fire. Therefore, the Buddha asks the Bodhisattva Guan Yin to give the pilgrimage guardian task to Sun Wukong, which unfolds as a whole process of the internal alchemy. Considering the furious temper of the monkey, Guan Yin puts a hoop round his head to help the monk tame the monkey by reciting the hoop spells. This hoop will eventually disappear by itself as Sun Wukong attains the state of water-fire harmonization that transcends to Nirvana. Though Guan Yin employs the hoop to tame Sun, she actually guards the pilgrims in the air, and always arrives in time to help Sun Wukong. She is the incarnation of the element of water, especially the saint water and the figure of divine mother.

The pilgrims undergo eighty-one calamities travelling to India to accomplish the mission of obtaining the Buddhist texts of Sutras. Though the monk Sanzang appears as the main character in the pilgrimage, given that the others are his guardians, Sun Wukong is the actual hero in the book and the eighty one calamities are his own trials. The narrative structure is constructed as a linear development of consecutive episodes with the spatial direction from the east to the west. All the calamities are within the environment of mountains, woods, caves and reclusive villages and houses. The semantic isotopism presents a total image of devouring darkness and night reinforced by the devilish fire of greed and wickedness. The element of earth serves as the substratum of the linear syntax of the journey, which stages the interaction and counteraction among the other three elements. Sun Wukong as the fire incarnation goes through all the tests with the help of air and water to fight against the Shadow of his fire to reach the refinement of the pure gold, the status of Nirvana. The central images of the malicious force are the theriomorphic devils inhabiting the nyctomorphic and catamorphic caves. The pilgrims encounter various spirits and monsters, Sun Wukong being the central figure to fend off attacks from them. Some of them intend to hinder the pilgrimage, whereas others want to eat the flesh of the holy monk to lengthen their life span. The most horrible caves they encounter are those of the spider, buffalo, bull, centipede and the white-bone demon. The most furious mountain is the Flame Mountain. Also, Sun Wukong has to confront his identical double, and the pilgrimage has to face the false double of the holy temple of their destiny.

The demons of spiders, centipedes and the white-bones are the manifestations of the Shadow of water and earth, being the incarnation of the devouring fatal women. On many occasions, Sun Wukong destroys the demons with assistance from other deities. Some of the evil spirits or monsters were not originally wicked; they were the disciples or animals of heavenly Gods and Buddhas or Bodhisattvas. The demons in Chapter 48 and 49 are tough to deal with and just as Sun Wukong is at his wit's end, Guan Yin arrives in time to defeat the unknown demons. Guan Yin explains that these demons were the carps bred in her pond. However, nine years ago they took the advantage of escaping by the tides of a tsunami and occupied the river tended by the white turtle. The monster in the Golden Glisten Cave is even more powerful than the fishes. In Chapter 50, Sun fights against this mighty monster but fails. Many deities such as Nuocha,[67] the thunder gods and the fire virtue god come from Heaven to help him; however, the whole gear of Nuocha's divine weapons and his metamorphosis into three heads and six arms turns out to be impotent. The water attack by the thunder gods and the fire attack by the fire virtue god eventually prove that the demon remains intact. The worst is, this demon even confiscates all the weapons from his enemies, including Sun Wukong's. The latter has no choice but resort to the Gautama Buddha to get orientation. The Buddha refuses to reveal the identity of the demon, out of certain embarrassment, but implies the method to capture it. At last, Sun realizes that the demon is the turquoise buffalo of Lao Zi. Naturally Lao Zi comes to solve the problem and tames his buffalo.

The above examples illustrate that divine animals have the potential to become evil. Also, evil spirits can redress their misdeeds and undertake religious practice, as for example the family of the Bull Demon King and the Iron Fan Princess. We would like to highlight again that the double sides of the four elements are grounded in Daoist yin-yang philosophy from the naissance of yin of chôra. The calamity caused by this family is the climax of the story and the archetype of the fire test throughout the journey. The little Red Kid demon, the son of the bull couple, defeats Sun Wukong with his Samadhi fire or genuine fire. This kind of fire can not be quenched by normal water; therefore, the assistance from the dragon kings of the seas is useless. As usual, Sun has to wait until Guan Yin uses her genuine saint water to quench the genuine fire and tames the kid demon to be her disciple. This fire family is crucial to the pilgrimage, since the pilgrims have to pass Flame Mountain to continue their journey and it is impossible without the help of the plantain-leaf fan of the Iron Fan Princess, which can calm the fire and bring about breeze and rain. Since Sun Wukong fails in borrowing the magic fan (the Princess holds a grudge against him for taking her kid away to Guan Yin), he metamorphoses into a bug to be swallowed by the princess and menaces her by stomping her stomach until she yields the fan. However, she tricks him, giving him a false fan that will actually inflame the fire. Then Sun Wukong fights with the Bull King Demon for the fan again and disguises himself as the Demon to beguile the fan from the princess while the Bull King Demon asks for a truce to join the feast held in the dragon palace of the river. This is a temporary ceasefire by the element water. Then the Bull King Demon in turn tricks Sun Wukong to relinquish the fan by assuming the form of his fellow, the pig Bajie. In order to win the fan, Sun Wukong wages a big war by dragging many deities from heaven to help him. At last, the demon is defeated and Sun obtains the fan and extinguishes the fire to pass the mountain

---

[67] Nuocha is one of the central characters in the aforementioned novel *The Investiture of the Gods*.

path. He even fans the magic fan forty-nine times to quench the fire forever for the people of the region. Wherever there is fire, it is raining heavily; wherever there is no fire, the sun shines. The couplet at the closure of the chapter explicitly expounds the interaction of the elements of fire and water that predominates over the alchemical process of Sun Wukong: "The harmonization of water and fire renders the original amalgamation, the average of fire and water accomplishes the great Dao" (坎離既濟真元合, 水火均分大道成) [Wu, 61].

After the test at Flame Mountain and Thunder Cave (the bull's den), the narrative discourse continues with the linear syntax revolving around mountains, caves, woods, false and haunted temples and houses and the ghost town Fengdu. The above couplet underlying the pivotal imaginary structure continues until the end of the pilgrimage. The theme of double deriving from the polar dualism plays a significant role as a trial of the individualization to dissolve the dualism. The most striving scholar Faust expresses his agony that "Two souls, alas, are dwelling in my breast, / And one is striving to forsake its brother" [ibid., 145]. Likewise, but in a concrete manner, the mighty proud Sun Wukong encounters his double in one of his trials. The double is in fact another type of monkey with six ears to imitate the voice and the physical outlook of the others. The demon makes himself an identical double of Sun that nobody can discern the authentic from the false, including the Emperor God's devil-reflecting mirror, the Bodhisattva Guan Yin, the God of Hell, the monk Sanzang (by means of the loop spells), the Buddha of Hell and his genuine hearing beast (the beast can discern but he fears the revenge of the false Sun Wukong and recommends to see the Gautama Buddha). Eventually only the Buddha is able to openly pick out the false Sun, the six-ear monkey. Apart from the misguiding double image of the hero who practices Dao, the ultimate destination of the pilgrimage can be false. The temple Leiyin of Ling Jiu Mountain (the exact spot where Buddha preached) appears suddenly in the middle of the pilgrimage. The ignorant monk, pig and Friar Sand rejoice over the accomplishment of the pilgrimage, whereas Sun Wukong perceives with his fire-gold eyes the demon who has fabricated the illusion. Despite his insight, he is not able to defeat the demon to make their original forms appear, and thus the monk is not convinced by the demon story of Sun Wukong. Again, the heavenly deities join the battle to help Sun Wukong defeat the demon, but fail. Lastly, they have to go to Mile Buddha to help them because the demon was originally the Buddha's disciple Yellow Brow Kid. Here we encounter another example of the evil figure that was originally divine and good. This is the embodiment of illusion and temptation throughout the alchemical practice. In the process of alchemy, the four elements, not yet coming to the point of complete harmonization, often release their shadow figures, and thus the double of Sun Wukong and the holy temple. The myriad of demons and spirits are in fact the discernible shadow figures of the four elements, especially the element fire.

After the trial of eighty-one calamities, or the test of the old or extreme yang element as fire, the hero Sun Wukong reaches the status of *unus mundus* beyond but from the polar dualism by the neutralization of the genuine water embodied in the image of the Divine Mother Guan Yin. She is tender, patient and benevolent to the petulant monkey fuelled by untamed fire. In fact, the monkey undergoes the transformation gradually, from the inception as a king of hubris despising all, and a monkey with wild mind and hot temper, to a frustrated, helpless and sobbing religious being (e.g. in Chapter 77), until he becomes a wise monkey with the absolute harmonization of water and fire, sainted as the Warrior Buddha. The continual existence and convergence of the juvenile-yang or the element air (the heavenly deities) in the story is combined with the juvenile-yin or the element earth (destructible demons and spirits) to become the supporting elements to the main contrasting elements of fire or the old-yang (the ego and his fire shadow) and water or the old-yin (the Divine Mother Guan Yin). The dream-discourse of the internal alchemy is quintessentially mediated through the rhetoric of hyperbole in the antithetic and heroic structures that are euphemized and surpassed by the power of yin through the rhetoric of hypotyposis of the unknown realm of the incarnation of the four elements. This synthetic structure corresponds to Durand's dialectic synthesis. The hero Sun Wukong returns to the mysterious space of chôra through the interaction and counteraction of the elements that harmonize the polar dualism. The diachronism, synchronism and isotopism of the narrative structures and images converge into the animation and incarnation of the abstract elements. The original harmony without distinction of the abstract and the concrete in language is also restored throughout the hypotyposis of fantastic storytelling. This imaginary structure of the internal alchemy also features in the Occidental fantastic epics. The example par excellence is Goethe's *Faust*, which will be analyzed from the imaginary structure of internal alchemy.

Goethe's *Faust* in Company with Shadow

Goethe's epic play *Faust* transcends the polar dualism in the traditional Faustian legends and literary works. For example, Christopher Marlowe's *Doctor Faustus* tallies with the traditional version of the myth where Faustus allows himself to be guided by Mephistopheles and seals a pact for twenty-four years with his blood. Marlowe ended his play with a horrid death of the hero, uttered by the two scholars: "O, help us heaven, see, here are Faustus' limbs / All torn asunder by the hand of death!" [Marlowe, 82]. This conventional pact-signing process with the devil and the eventually ghastly death does not feature in Goethe's *Faust*. In fact, Goethe's fantastic play goes beyond the conventional Christian perspective to blend with pre-Socratic philosophy and alchemy. Therefore, his

Faust is deemed as a fantastic epic with the narrative rhetoric of dream-discourse, as internal alchemy.

Different from the above analyzed examples of dream-discourse constructed by the external heavenly alchemy, *Faust*, like *Journey to the West*, unfolds the fantastic story by means of internal alchemy. The trigger of the whole story is the epistemological desire for the ultimate unknown truth: Faust craves for knowledge about the workings of the world, "the unknown of the unknown," the limit of the Universe. The monkey from the above Chinese novel is similar to Faust because the monkey Sun challenges the throne of the God Yuhuang (the Emperor God of Daoism) and craves for immortality. According to our definition of the dream-discourse, the triangle of the actions in the fantastic story – God, Devil and Man – underlies the archetype of the imaginary structure. Faust's action is, indeed, in the very beginning, predetermined in heaven that is staged in "Prologue in Heaven." While the three archangels praise the Lord's creation, Mephistopheles scorns it by satirizing that man employs reason "to be more brutish than is any brute" and judging that "men live in dismay." The Lord argues with the devil, but the latter concludes by "No, Lord. I find it still a rather sorry sight. / Man moves me to compassion, so wretched is his plight. / I have no wish to cause him further woe" [Goethe 1990, 87]. Then the Lord bets with Mephistopheles on his peculiarly striving scholar-alchemist Faust: "Tough now he serves me but confusedly, / I shall soon lead him where the vapour clears. / The gardener knows, however small the trees, / That bloom and fruit adorn its later years" [ibid., 87]. From the prologue, the discourse of the Lord clearly shows his confidence in man's salvation and the quest for the ultimate truth. Erring is normal since "Man errs as long as he will strive" and even this is true to the devils as the Lord expresses "I never hated those who were like you [Mephisto]" [ibid., 89]. Different from the above three novels, though homogeneous in the interrelations between god(s), devil(s) and men, *Faust* will unfold as a individuation process or an internal alchemy of the hero along with the guide and misguidance of the incorporation of the Shadow, Mephisto.

Faust's desire for knowledge comes from the quest for the ultimate wisdom or truth deep from his soul. This is different from desiring the power to dominate or to release one's evil side to abuse others, for the Lord regards him as the peculiar one. From this perspective, Faust is indeed part of the elite that strives and errs in the process of his quest for the ultimate truth, just as the quest of the chosen monkey in the Chinese novel. This quest, as mentioned earlier, is an adventure into the collective unconscious of the ego to encounter the furious Shadow to amalgamate the polar dualism and transcend to *unus mundus*. Jung viewed Goethe as a prophet with his wisdom gained from confronting evil: "At last I had found confirmation that there were or had been people who saw evil and its universal power, and – more important – the mysterious role it played in delivering man from darkness and suffering. To that extent Goethe became, in my eyes, a prophet" [Jung 1989, 60]. What makes Goethe's creation of the Faustian legend a distinct and profound work lies in his being a visionary writer, as Jung assessed that Goethe not only drew on the Germanic myth but also his own life to the accomplished creation of *Faust*. The imaginary structure of Goethe's epic can be analyzed as an internal alchemy departing from the triangle relation of God-Devil-Man, through the trial of earth-water-fire-air grounded in the Shadow power, to the accomplishment of individuation or Nirvana. Jung furthermore brings to light the secret of alchemy in *Faust*:

> I regard my work on alchemy as a sign of my inner relationship to Goethe. Goethe's secret was that he was in the grip of that process of archetypal trans-formation which has gone on through the centuries. He regarded his *Faust* as an *opus magnum* or *divinum*. He called it his "main business," and his whole life was enacted within the framework of this drama. Thus, what was alive and active within him was a living substance, a suprapersonal process, the great dream of the *mundus archetypus* (archetypal world). [ibid., 206]

As the universal art and wisdom in *Faust* surpasses the Christian and Germanic boundary and Goethe himself demonstrated rich and universal knowledge of al-chemy, it is more appropriate to interpret the work's quest as a combination of two of the various religious ways in Hindu Yoga. Faust first resorts to Jana Yoga (Nirvana through knowledge pursuit but penetrating the void mirage in knowl-edge) and later shifts to Karma Yoga that orients towards taking action to release man's desires until saturation to penetrate the void in human desires. Thus the story beginning with the light from heaven in the prologue will undergo a whole process in shadow, embodied by Mephisto and Faust's own desires and actions. The trial of the four elements will transcend through the yin element to the space of chôra.

The spatial structure of the play is constructed from heaven to earth through fire as follows: Prologue in Heaven (the Lord and Mephisto's bet, which repre-sents air and fire as true light of the Lord), Night. Faust's Den (Faust's lamenta-tion for the limit of the known knowledge he has so far studied and the first in-vocation of the Earth Spirit. The ignition of Faust's desire fire for knowledge and wisdom that generates Shadow.), Before the City Gate (Faust's continual melancholy and the appearance of Mephisto disguised in a black poodle), Study (I) and (II) (Faust's confrontation with Mephisto and his pact with the devil), Auerbach's Keller (Mephisto's first demonstration of his magic to fool the tav-ern revellers), The Witch's Kitchen (Faust is rejuvenated by the witch's elixir's of youth), Street (Faust's desires find an aim when he sees Margaret or Gretchen. Fire of love kindled is becoming destructive.), Evening (Faust's being lovesick), Promenade (Gretchen's mother hands in the jewellery given by Faust in secret to a priest), The Neighbour's House (Mephisto uses Gretchen's neighbour Martha to approach the girl), Street (Faust plays the role of the witness testifying the death of Martha's husband and thus meets Gretchen at Martha's place), Garden and A Garden Bower (Faust meets Gretchen again and confesses his love to her and kisses her). From the air in Heaven to the secular earth, the element fire blazes with the rustic and naïve damsel.

Wood and Cave (Faust rejoices over his discovery of the secrets of Nature but laments his association with the devil. He tries to repress his desire for Gretchen lest he might hurt her. We are faced here with conflicts among air, earth, fire and water with Shadow), Gretchen's Room (Gretchen's singing a song expressing her love for Faust), Martha's Garden (Gretchen asks Faust about his religious faith but Faust replies with alchemical wit and blinds her with love and gives her a potion to make her mother sleep, which kills her mother.), At the Well (Lieschen talks to Gretchen (already pregnant) about the scandal of Sibyl's being pregnant without marriage, which is a piercing irony), City Wall (Gretchen's prayer to the Mater Dolorosa for help), Night. Street in Front of Gretchen's Door (Gretchen's brother Valentine duels Faust to avenge his sister's virtue and their mother's death but is killed by Mephisto's black magic), Cathedral (Evil Spirit behind Gretchen, seeking for repentance and refuge in the cathedral), Walpurgis Night and Walpurgis Night Dream. Intermezzo (Mephisto takes Faust to the witch's Sabbath of Walpurgis night to distract him from Gretchen's misery. An apparition reminds Faust of Gretchen and Mephisto attempts again to distract Faust by the intermezzo of The Golden Wedding of Oberon and Titania. Faust is completely buried with a total confrontation with Shadow.), Dismal Day and Night. Open Field (Aware of Gretchen's being thrown into the dungeon, Faust rages at Mephisto and forces him to free her), Dungeon (Gretchen, now in a state of insanity, refuses to escape with Faust from the dungeon. The drama ends here with a voice from above that Gretchen "is saved" and her calling "Heinrich! Heinrich!"). Here ends the first part of *Faust*. Eventually, Faust's fire is too strong and burns down the juvenile-yin (the element earth) of Gretchen.

Once triggered in the heavenly space, the story's setting of the first part is grounded in the earthly space intertwined with the shadow figure of Mephisto and the ensuing appearance of witches and other spirits. Different form other Faust figures, Goethe's Faust is a real alchemist who seeks for the ultimate knowledge and truth. He does not sign the contract just for earthly power and wealth but for a real salvation of his soul. Therefore, the content of the contract is different from the previous cases. Instead of a twenty-four year pact, Faust signs with his blood the contract that Mephisto has to wait on and satisfy him until he says, "Abide, you are so fair" (*Verweile doch! Du bist so schön!*) then the devil can take him. Moreover, unlike Marlowe's Faustus who often addresses "sweet or my good or my gentle Mephistophilis," Faust often curses Mephistopheles with "serpent, snake or liar." None of the manifestations of magic arranged by Mephisto satisfy Goethe's Faust until he encounters Gretchen, who arouses his earthly passion. The hero as the Ego undergoing the process of individuation by confronting his shadow, the element of fire embodied by Mephisto (the old-yang of *Yi Jing*), now encounters Gretchen who represents the element of earth or the juvenile-yin (to use the concept of *Yi Jing*). The first part of the drama ends with the tragedy of Gretchen to predict Faust's alchemical trial through the old-yin (water) and juvenile-yang (air) with the basis of fire and earth in the second part of the play.

The predominant element in the first part is earth, whereas the predominating element in the second part of the play shifts to water. The element of air also metamorphoses from dark spirits (such as sorcerers, witches, phantoms and spirits, condemned in the Northern European Protestant dualism) to the spirits and gods of the Greeks who do not have a sense of sin founded upon dualism. Mephisto always blazes as the manifestation of the element air as long as Faust's desire for eternal satisfaction and the ultimate truth glows. Leaving Gretchen and her misery behind at the end of the first part, Faust closes the earthly way for his alchemical accomplishment and turns towards Nature and the unknown past. The fact that the first part of the play is not divided into acts illustrates the antithetic or heroic structure of the diurnal regime mediated through hyperbolic expressions and the various scenes revolving around the element of earth against fire. In contrast, the second part is divided into five acts as Faust brightens his sight and opens a new door to his spiritual and epistemological quest. Readers or audiences are presented with an imaginary natural and remote land, the palace of the emperor and eventually Faust's coastal kingdom Lynceus the Tower Warden, interwoven with the unknown space of the Mothers and the antique past of Greece.

The spatial structure is deployed on the basis of the water-element: In Act I, Charming Landscape – Faust, reclining on a lawn with flowers, weary, restless, seeking twilight sleep. A circle of spirits, moving in the air: charming little figures, (Faust is purged of feelings of guilt and rejoices over the new hope uplifted by the benevolent spirits. This is a transition from the tragedy of Gretchen to Faust's further quest through Nature), The Court of the Emperor, Large Room, Decked out for a Masked Ball and Pleasure Garden (Faust and Mephisto solve the emperor's fiscal problems by proposing paper money. A great carnival celebration is held. Faust and Mephisto perform magic and produce much gold, and the invention of paper money is completed. Gold is a vital image to the process of internal alchemy in the second part of the play.), Gloomy Gallery (The emperor demands to see Helen and Paris. This is beyond Mephisto's scope of business and he gives Faust a key to "the Mothers" to find a tripod to gain the magic to conjure up these past pagans), Brightly Illuminated Halls and Hall of Knights (Faust conjures Helen and Paris up in the name of the Mothers. Out of jealousy, Faust resolves to stop Paris from carrying Helen away by touching him with the key. Following an explosion, Faust loses consciousness).

Act II, High-Vaulted, Narrow Gothic Room, once Faust's Den and Laboratory in the Medieval Style, with Elaborate and Clumsy Machinery for Fantastic Purposes (Mephisto brings the unconscious Faust back to his old study and meets Wagner, who follows Faust's footsteps in the researches of alchemy. He creates a small human figure in the test tube, Homunculus. The artificial man can describe Faust's dream of Leda and mocks Mephisto's scanty vision), Classical Walpurgis Night (like the witch's Sabbath in Part One but with gods, demigods and other figures from ancient mythology instead of Northern European legends. Faust, Mephisto and Homunculus travel to Greek Antiquity. Homunculus seeks to escape the tube and enters a higher state of existence by uniting with the sea, according to the philosophy of Thales and Anaxagoras. The act ends with Homunculus's being shattered on the shell of Galatea.).

Act III, Before the Palace of Menelaus at Sparta and Arcadia (Mephisto in disguise of Phorcyas convinces Helen to seek refuge in the north where Faust awaits her. Faust wins Helen's heart and they have a son named Euphorion, spirit of romantic poetry. He attempts to fly and falls and vanishes. Helen leaves Faust to join him "in the gloomy real").

Act IV, High Mountains, The Foothills and The Rival Emperor's Tent (Faust is impressed by the grandeur of nature. He wants the land from the sea to defy the ocean. Mephisto arranges for him to win the battle for the emperor by magic in exchange for the stretch of coastline).

Act V, Open Country (A wonderer revisits the couple Baucis and Philemon who once gave shelter to him), Palace (Faust, extremely old, sees the couple dwelling on the reclaimed land as an obstacle to his plan. He asks Mephisto and his three assistants to bargain with them and relocate them), Deep Night (Mephisto burns the couple along with the wanderer, which irritates Faust), Midnight (Four gray women, Want, Guilt, Care and Need, enter. Care passes a curse to make Faust blind), Large Outer Court of the Palace and Torches (Faust continues to plan the improvement of the land for his inhabitants. Mephisto makes the blind Faust believe that the workmen are completing his life's work, when they are indeed digging his grave. He anticipates a moment of bliss that he would ask to abide. He voices the sentence in the pact and dies), Entombment (Mephisto, about to take Faust's soul to hell, is distracted by a group of angels rising and bearing off Faust's immortal part), Mountain Gorges. Forest, Rock, and Desert (chorus and chants by the characters from Christian mythology and symbolic figures. Gretchen appears as Una Poenitentium and later One Penitent to praise the soul of Faust and the Divine Mother, Mater Gloriosa says "come, raise yourself to higher spheres!").

Through the experience into natural contact with the four elements or the old-yin and old-yang and the juvenile-yin and juvenile-yang, Faust dissolves the polar dualism and thus returns to the yin part of chôra and back to the state of

Taiji, since the end of the play features the presence of the Divine Mother, Mater Gloriosa, and the spirit of Gretchen leading and praising for Faust:

> UNA POENITENTIUM (formerly called Gretchen. Nestling):
> Incline, incline,
> That art divine,
> Thou that dost shine,
> Thy face in grace to my sweet ecstasy!
> He whom I loved in pain
> Now returns free from stain,
> Comes back to me. [Ibid., 501]

After the Blessed boys approach in circling motion, Gretchen appears again:

> ONE PENITENT (formerly called Gretchen):
> Amid the noble spirits' mirth,
> The newcomer is so engrossed,
> He scarcely knows of his rebirth
> Before he joins the holy host.
> Behold, all earthly ties have peeled,
> The old shroud has dropped off at length,
> While ether's garment has revealed
> The radiance of his youthful strength!
> Grant that I teach him; he appears
> Still blinded by the new day's glare. [ibid., 503]

This is significant in Goethe's creation of Faust's salvation. The inception with the Lord, the very image of the ultimate truth (the primitive yang as *Taiji*) joins the end with the Divine Mother (the very image of the primitive yin of *Liangyi* or chôra). This ideal and mystic space is revealed as the closure of the play:

> CHORUS MYSTICUS:
> What is destructible
> Is but a parable;
> What fails ineluctably,
> The undeclarable,
> Here it was seen,
> Here it was action;
> The Eternal-Feminine
> Lures to perfection. [ibid., 503]

The "Eternal-Feminine" (*Das Ewig-Weibliche*) refers to the yin of chôra as the space of perfection. Mephisto, the Shadow of the old yang or the extreme yang, loses the game because the person he is dealing with is a wise alchemist whose goal is as pure as gold to find the ultimate wisdom but not to fulfil secular desires. Faust, as the ego at the centre of alchemical practice, interacts and counteracts with the four characters as the symbol of the elements: Mephistopheles is the old-yang or fire, Gretchen is the juvenile-yin or earth, Homunculus is the juvenile-yang or air and Helen is the old-yin or water. A persevering creation of the Lord, Faust himself strives for truth until the last second of his life, just like his creator Goethe, who created his *Faust* until the end of his life. He eventually says the words to Mephisto as he envisions a throng "with free men on free ground their freedom share": "Abide, you are so fair! / The traces of my earthly day / No aeons can impair. / As I presage a happiness so high, / I now enjoy the highest moment" [ibid., 469]. His tenacity in seeking truth and fulfilling human will is all the more striking after Care blinds him and the blind Faust replies: "Yet inside me there shines a brilliant light; [...] / Precise design, swift exercise / Will always win the fairest prize; / To make the grandest dream come true, / One mind for thousand hands will do" [ibid., 463]. The pursuit of Goethe's Faust curiously corresponds to Daoist internal alchemy. No original sin exists but God or Dao or Nature's comprehensive love, incarnated by the archetype of yin, the Divine Mother. The purpose of life is not to rebel against God or Nature, but a fulfillment of one's ability gifted by God. The essence is to glorify God by making the most of one's inborn talent. Faust certainly accomplishes it and thus returns to Heaven.

Bachelard associated the element of earth with the hardness of rock and the malleability of clay. Similar to the monkey Sun, born from the hard rock with the toughest will and desire, Faust as an earthly figure embodies the essence of earth in terms of hard will and malleable clay after his combination with Gretchen and Helen. His hardness in will is confirmed as he replies to Care's question "Is Care a force you never faced?" / "Through all the world I only raced: / Whatever I might crave, I laid my hand on, / What would not do, I would abandon, / And what escaped, I would let go. [...] I stormed through life; first powerful and great, / But now with calmer wisdom, and sedate" [ibid., 459]. Here "hand" and "earth" converge as the central images of material imagination that characterize Faust's earthly figure. Joanne Stroud sheds light on Bachelard's imagination of earth in relation to the hand:

> For Bachelard, imagination is the galvanizer of will and supplies the energy to take action: "Where the imagination is concerned, if one is to feel strong one must feel all-powerful. Reveries of will to power are reveries of will to be all-powerful." He illustrates this point by referring to Greek mythology. "To study the labors of Hercules as dynamic reveries, as images of primordial will, serves to cleanse one's core being almost as effectively as if one had been literally cleansed" (*Earth* 26-27). [...] The possibilities of what the hand can accomplish prompt us to engage in activities of the world and to dream that we can conquer whatever is necessary. The capable hand gives us confidence that we can overcome any difficulties.

The hardness of rock in Faust's will is reinforced by Mephisto's fire, but later becomes softened by Gretchen's feminine water permeating in earth to welcome the birth of Homunculus. Faust's eventual amalgamation with the water Helen, only attainable through the key to the Mothers, is further perfected by the implementation of his plan, reclamation of the land from the sea. The quintessence of his success in sublimating the four elements is his glorifying God by making the most of his innate gift that God endows him with. Through his own striving quest, Faust finds the right way without losing his soul. The structure of the two parts of the play is a complete sphere of the *Taiji* archetype. The rhetoric of antithetic hyperbole engrained in rational dualism is euphemized step by step throughout the process of Faust's quest into the shadow and harmonized by the hypotyposis of the imaginary actions and discourse of the devil Mephisto. The semantic isotopism from both diurnal and nocturnal imaginary regimes represents a complete picture of the collective unconscious and the harmonization of *unus mundus*.

Alice Raphael offers her insightful interpretation of Goethe's *Faust II* according to Jung's theories. She points out that Goethe is aware of the power and significance of the unconscious mind by highlighting the mythological and religious images inherent in the human psyche in *Faust II*. She quotes Goethe as proof that the visionary writer is aware of utilizing both the unconscious and consciousness to attain a higher level of being: "Man cannot dwell for long in a conscious state, or in consciousness. He must again take refuge in the unconscious, for that is where his life is rooted" [Raphael, 47]. Following Raphael's insight, we complement her interpretation by the philosophy of Karma Yoga, for the salvation of Faust's soul lies in his accomplishment of Karma Yoga. He enters the darkness of the collective unconscious and faces the evil Shadow of man to attain the golden light. Goethe's poeticization of Faust is indeed a pertinent manifestation of the Daoist *Yi Jing* wisdom and the scripture of *The Secret of the Golden Flower*, the very books, along with *Faust*, that inspired Jung. Jung added a feminine element to the Christian trinity as the key to the arcane alchemy. This feminine element echoes Goethe's "Eternal-Feminine" as the crucial key to Faust's salvation.

The Mirror-Discourse

While the universal dream in the dream-discourse arouses aesthetic imagination, the dream aroused in the mirror-discourse is close to a nightmare. The dream-discourse flows with euphoriant rhythm and musical harmonization, whereas the mirror-discourse reflects and alienates the image with antithetic visualization. Mirror in terms of discourse is taken metaphorically as rendering the real world seemingly unreal by the narration grounded in realism. Instead of using the motif of mirror in the story, the mirror-discourse constructs the fantastic composition as an entire narrative form of ambiguity and duality. Nonetheless, some remarks on the symbols of mirror are requisite to the evaluation of the mirror-discourse. Mirror, according to ancient belief, is magic that reflects, and can hold the soul and the vital force of men. Therefore, the popular customs, even in different cultures, tend to cover mirrors during a funeral, lest the mirror retains the soul and hinders its return to the yonder [Cazenave, 413]. Mirror as retainer of soul or reflection of the true face of man is illustrated in many fantastic tales such as Andersen's "The Snow Queen" and Hoffmann's "A New Year's Eve Adventure." Mirror, with its function to reflect, is the magic teller of truth, for example, the mirror in "Snow-Drop." Devils without a soul, like ghosts and vampires, have no mirror reflection; however, they could opt for entering the mirror and gaze you from the other side so as to absorb your soul, for example the mirror from Maupassant's "Le Horla." As the mirror divulges the devil that lacks a reflection and a soul, it can also reflect the psyche or soul or a second visage of man and thus a second reality.

Fantastic literature with mirror-discourse uncovers the unknown realm by gliding the narration from the known reality to the other side of the mirror. The primitive form of mirror is the surface of water, as one of the four fundamental elements. Water, with the ability of rendering an image, like the attribute of magic in a mirror, signifies divination. Nostradamus, French medieval astrologist and doctor, saw the projection of the future from the surface of water and composed his famous prophetic verses that predict human future until the end of the world. In Tolkien's ring trilogy, the mirror of Galadriel from the well shows the unexpected and makes visible the past, present and future. Mirror's central material image of water redoubles the meanings of mirror with the complex of Narcissus, driven by the schema of falling. The boundary between water, the surface and the world of the percipient is thus blurred. Among the four elements, water is the most complex one. It is a substantial material rich in paradoxical meanings. Bachelard claimed that participation is the essence of water of *hydrant psyche*. Water in the substance connotes a type of intimacy, a type of destiny and a type of rage, which is a material imagination of totality. Water is different from the elements fire and earth; it is indeed the transitory element. This ambiguous feature of water makes it assimilate with the special nature of mirror.

As the mirror-discourse twists the secure and known materials into unknown phenomena, water is

> the essential ontological metamorphosis between fire and earth. The being dedicated to water is a being in vertigo. It dies at each minute, incessantly something of its substance flows out. The daily death is not the exuberant death of fire that pierces the sky with its arrows; the daily death is the death of water. Water flows always, water falls always, it finishes always in its horizontal death.[68] [Bachelard 1942, 13]

With this double nature of transitoriness and transition, water, the hydrant transformation of mirror, is embedded in fantastic literature as the central dialectical spirit of the discourse.

Contrary to the dream-discourse that makes people dream, the mirror-discourse indeed awakens readers from the alleged reality of the known or from the so-called visible world. As D'Annunzio assumes, "The richest events come to us certainly before our soul notices it. And when we begin to open our eyes to the visible, already we have long adhered to the invisible" (*Les événements les plus riches arrivent en nous bien avant que l'âme s'en aperçoive. Et, quand nous commençons à ouvrir les yeux sur le visible, déjà nous étions depuis longtemps adhérents à l'invisible*) [Ibid., 25]. Bachelard interpreted that this adhesion to the invisible grants us "an impression of youth by returning us incessantly the power to fill us with wonder. The true poetry functions to awaken" (*une impression de jeunesse ou de jouvence en nous rendant sans cesse la faculté de émerveiller. La vraie poésie est une fonction d'éveil*) [Ibid., 25]. The rhetoric of mirror revolves around this antithesis of the visible and the invisible, the known and the unknown, and dreaming and awakening. Ambiguity is a function of awakening from the accepted reality to glimpse at another reality from the unknown.

Reading fantastic stories, contrived by the dream-discourse that parallels gazing into the mirror, entices readers to doubt whether the reflected image is authentically the viewer's or the individual's double or his dreadful doppelganger. This unique meaning reflected from mirror is best illustrated by the travelling enthusiast in the postscript of Hoffmann's story "A New Year's Eve Adventure": "What is it that looks out of the mirror there? Is it really I?" This double image is enlarged into literary discourse to represent imitation and thus mimesis. Grounded in the generally accepted conception of mimesis, an imitation of the real world or of what is likely, the mirror-discourse appropriates mimesis

---

[68] *la métamorphose ontologique essentielle entre le feu et la terre. L'être voué à l'eau est un être en vertige. Il meurt à chaque minute, sans cesse quelque chose de sa substance s'écoule. La mort quotidienne n'est pas la mort exubérante du feu qui perce le ciel de ses flèches ; la mort quotidienne est la mort l'eau. L'eau coule toujours, l'eau tombe toujours, elle finit toujours en sa mort horizontale.*

to reverse it to a mimesis of the false reality through the mirror. The semantic syntax of the mirror-discourse centres on the effect of alienating the taken-for-granted reality that slides into the other side of the mirror. The core rhetoric of strangeness thus hinges on the interplay of realistic discourse characterized by ambiguity, including hesitation, absurdity and the Möbius strip – the predominating narrative techniques that just slightly jeopardize rational law. The rhetoric calls forth skepticism about what has been hitherto known to be real and about the illusion of the consciousness.

The mirror-discourse, like the mirror of Galadriel in the ring trilogy, can be regarded as a kind of *mise en abyme* to the dream-discourse. The relativity of mirror-discourse can be further illustrated by Zhuang Zi's tale of "Zhuang Zhou Dreams of a Butterfly," which questions the relative position of the percipient and the percept. As the dreamer of Zhuang Zhou who utters whether it is he who dreams of a butterfly or a butterfly that dreams of him, the mirror-discourse throws in this interplay between the subject and the object to question the reality before the mirror and inside the mirror. Cortázar, as a master of this unique rhetoric, created all his fantastic tales based on this dreamer-butterfly philosophy of Zhuang Zi. His narrative technique is often characterized in Western literature by the occidental term "the Möbius strip." While the dream-discourse abounds in the creative mind in harmony with Nature, thus more in original participation, the mirror-discourse emerges in the age where science and intellect thrive. The former rhetoric emphasizes the *mise en scène* of human collective memory or collective unconscious by sheer hypotyposis of the enunciated elements, whereas the latter rhetoric mirrors the mentality of the intellectual and conscious age of split language and consciousness by the sophistication of narration that stresses on enunciation. The mirror-discourse will be analyzed from three aspects of discourse: the enunciated space-time, from figurative to literal meanings of the enunciated, the significance of enunciation as the formal syntax leading to the content.

Enunciated Space-Time as Interplay of Mimesis and Strangeness

Grounded in the poetics of mimesis in a strict sense and the rhetoric of strangeness, fantastic literature often presents readers with familiar settings and ordinary characters so as to make readers vicariously follow the ensuing plot and sympathize with the main character who will confront the unexpected and inexplicable phenomenon amidst reality. Realism in settings and characters, like the viewer and the setting before the mirror, appears normal at first sight in the reflection. In fantastic tales with the mirror-discourse, the inception with the realistic familiarity of space is a prerequisite for the uncanny or quasi-supernatural to take place. According to Freud, the fantastic originates from disquieting strangeness and familiarity, viz. *Das Umheimliche*. It can occur to characters no matter where and when. Nonetheless, certain spaces are more frequent in the mirror-discourse. The familiar space encompasses geographical space (designated and non-designated), homely space and distant space.

The geographic space refers to the common place that is known geographically by the character as well as the reader. This referential setting highlights the real effect of the story so as to make contrast between the known and the unknown. Nodier announced, "The first essential condition for writing a good fantastic story would be to firmly believe it and nobody believes in what he invents" (*La première condition essentielle pour écrire une bonne histoire fantastique, ce serait d'y croire fermement, et personne ne croit à ce qu'il invente*) [Nodier 1961, 362] in the beginning of his story "Jean-François les Bas-Bleus" (Jean-François the Bluestockings). Therefore, he employed the exact time and place to tell a fantastic tale to make readers believe the story to be a true historical event: "In 1793, there was in Besançon an idiot, a monomaniac, a lunatic" (*En 1793, il y avait à Besançon un idiot, un monomane, un fou*) [Ibid., 364]. In Hoffmann's "A New Year's Eve Adventure," the extradiegetic narrator tells his story in Berlin (in a beer cellar over the Schleusen Bridge, past the Mint) and another story on the intradiegetic level (the manuscript found by the narrator) about how Erasmus Spikher loses his mirror reflection in Italy. Prosper Merimée depicted the story of "The Venus of Ille" as a real event taking place during his historical and archeological investigation: "I was going down the last slope of the Canigou, and, although the sun had already set, I could distinguish on the plain the houses of the little town of Ille, towards which I was making" [Calvino, 263]. The fantastic adventure of the hero in Gautier's "Arria Marcella" takes place in a geographical city of Italy: "A year ago, three young men, three friends who were traveling together in Italy, were visiting the Studii Museum in Naples, where there was an exhibit of various ancient artifacts excavated from the ruins of Pompeii and Herculaneum" [Kessller, 118]. In another story of Gautier, the hero Théodore in "La Cafetière" (The Coffeepot) witnesses the supernatural event in his host's room in Normandy. Nerval's "La Main enchantée" (The Enchanted Hand) travels in Paris across the famous bridge Le Pont Neuf. American writer Washington Irving also settled his tale "The Legend of Sleepy Hollow" in realism: "In the bosom of one of those spacious coves which indent the eastern shore of the Hudson, at that broad expansion of the river denominated by the ancient Dutch navigators the Tappan Zee, [...] there lies a small market town or rural port, which by some is called Greensburgh, but which is more generally and properly known by the name of Tarry Town" [Sandner, 11]. Nathaniel Hawthorne's "Young Goodman Brown" begins with "Young Goodman Brown came forth at sunset into the street at Salem Village" [Calvino, 183].

Like writers of the Romantic period, those of the late 19th and early 20th centuries tended to depart from realistic time-space and shifted into the strange or supernatural realm. In Wilde's *The Picture of Dorian Gray*, the richness of olfaction and later of other sensations serves as an introduction to the ensuing darker and filthier plot surrounding Dorian Gray:

> The studio was filled with the rich odour of roses, and when the light summer wind stirred amidst the trees of the garden, there came through the open door the heavy scent of the lilac, or the more delicate perfume of the pink-flowering thorn. [...] The dim roar of London was like the bourdon note of a distant organ. [Wilde 1994, 7]

The sensational realism is displayed through olfaction, vision, movement and audibility that eventually converge into the geographical designation of space, London. This inception of realism prepares for the gradual transformation of Gray's portrait and the related deterioration of the originally harmonious and natural sensations. As regards London, it seems to be a place of predilection for writers to create uncanny feeling. Stevenson also availed himself of London with its enigmatic streets to weave the mysterious fantastic tale of Dr Jekyll's metamorphosis into Mr Hyde. The labyrinth of doors and windows in gloomy London welcomes strangeness out of familiarity.

London's French counterpart, Paris, is also a common place for French writers to depict strange feelings deriving from realism. Villiers de l'Isle-Adam sets his story of "Véra" in the frame of Paris, Faubourg Saint-Germain. Maupassant's "Night: A Nightmare" takes place in the middle of Paris and the river Seine. Obsessed by the imagery of water, Maupassant depicted many nightmarish experiences around the river Seine. Besides the above tale, the love (eventually fear) of water and the river is ubiquitous in "Le Horla": "I love this house of mine where I grew up. From my windows I can see the Seine flowing alongside my garden, beyond the main road, almost through my house, the great, wide Seine which goes from Rouen to the Le Havre, covered with passing boats" [Maupassant 1998, 313].

Examples of geographical realism can also be found in German literature. For example, Thomas Mann applied the mirror-discourse in his creation of a modern version of the Faustian legend to explore the conventional pact with the devil. The Faust of the twentieth century is a musical genius, Adrian Leverkühn, who confesses to his friend (the narrator) before his death the secret pact he has dealt with the devil. The novel also presents referential time and space: "in Freising on the Isar, on 23 May 1943" [Mann, 5]. In contemporary fantastic literature, Paris is still a favourite place for creating an effect of strangeness, even for non-French writers. Argentine writer Cortázar wrote a weird story in which the character metamorphoses into an axolotl at the Jardin des Plantes in Paris [Cortázar, 3].

If the designated geographical reference of space-time is not employed in the mirror-discourse, the principle of realism in describing the setting always underlies the development of the whole plot, which is oriented into the realm of strangeness and the unknown. Such space is still known to characters and readers in the real world through the description of referential places. In most fantastic stories of mirror-discourse, the strange and seemingly supernatural intrusion happens at the hero's home, especially in his room, the most familiar place to the hero. This uniqueness in the familiarity of space fits the rhetoric of mirror par excellence since the image in the mirror, one's own image, is the most familiar image of the percipient.

The heroine in "Trilby ou le Lutin d'Argail" (Trilby or the Sprite of Argail) of Nodier encounters a Scottish sprite and lets herself be seduced by it in her own house. This seduction while drowsy makes the familiar house unnerving to the heroine. Under the pen of Gautier in "The Beautiful Vampire," Romuald encounters the beautiful vampire Clarimonde around his presbytery and his own room. In "The Sandman," Hoffmann's tragic hero Nathanael suffers from his fear about his father's alchemical master, whom he has imagined to be the dreadful sandman, in his own house and later at the university and his dormitory. Most of Poe's stories are set in the hero's place. For example, in "The Black Cat," the autodiegetic narrator (narrator-hero) tells the horrible events about his cat(s), and murdering his wife that happen in his two houses; the first house was burned down for some mysterious reason. The double in Poe's "William Wilson" follows the autodiegetic narrator from the school room to social places wherever he goes. Russian writer Turgenev's "The Dream" is about the weird dreams of the autodiegetic who sleeps a lot in his room and the strange encounters in the streets around his house. Cortázar's "The Continuity of Parks" presents a story with the rhetoric of Möbius strip par excellence. The incipit of the story is, "He had begun to read the novel a few days before. He had put it down because of some urgent business conferences, opened it again on his way back to the estate by train; [...] he returned to the book in the tranquility of his study which looked out upon the park with its oaks" [Cortázar, 63]. In these examples of home-space, characters often stay tranquilly at home; however, strange phenomena have chosen them and invade their territories. Unexpected and inexplicable incidents are thus triggered in well known and routine settings. With the mirror-discourse, the familiar space belonging to the character ironically becomes strange and unknown. The home-space thus turns into other-space.

In the mirror-discourse, the story may have realistic settings in addition to the home space. In this case, the most common space is the meeting place, such as hotels, bars and the like. Though realistic, these places imply transitoriness that only exists temporarily and thus renders every guest as a passenger. In Petrus Borel's "Gottfried Wolfgang," the extradiegetic narrator finds a manuscript about the dreadful adventure (staying a night with a beheaded female ghost) of a young German in a hotel. In Gautier's "Deux acteurs pour un rôle" (Two Actors for a Role), the devil Mephistopheles meets the hero in a German *gasthof*; later he appears before him in the theatre, another public space. Villiers de l'Isle-Adam also makes use of a public place to create later uncanny feelings. For example, in "Le Convive des dernière fêtes" (The Guest of the Last Parties), the narrator tells about his fearsome experience at the dance hall of the opera. Also, the quasi-supernatural phenomenon in "The Signal-Man" of Charles Dickens takes place on a train. In Well's "The Story of the Inexperienced Ghost," the narrator tells the story told by his late friend, Clayton. His friend met with a poor ghost and learned about the secret passes of ghosts on a Saturday morning at the Mermaid Club. Besides, many of the aforementioned stories with geographical reference are also given a specific place for the strange event to emerge, most of these being hotels and bars. Examples are the hotel in Italy and the beer cellar in Berlin of "A New Year's Eve Adventure" and the hotel in Pompeii of "Arria Marcella."

From the known space of geographical reference and the home-space to meeting place, the realistic effect starts to deviate from the familiarity. The space echoes with the idea of closing and solitude, albeit the public space bears a connotation of lack of privacy. Strangeness is born from this intersection of effervescence and meeting where the presence of other people makes the surroundings all the more unfamiliar for the hero. The weirdest phenomenon is that the hero often enters the zone of the unknown without others' knowledge, though the space is packed with people. The creation of inserting unknown elements into known space will be fermented by the archetypal and symbolic places. The principal archetype among them is water-space, which also connotes the signification of mirror. Archetypes like the forest and mountain are also representative spatial images symbolizing the mythic setting.

Like the taboo in some folk superstitions that warns people not to stare at the mirror at night, the mirror-discourse presents night as a transitional time-space that brews strange elements. Most fantastic tales have seemingly supernatural events happening at night, though the characters are in the centre of realistic space. Night as devouring image of time offers an effective frame of time-space to stage a fantastic plot from realism. According to Durand's imaginary taxonomy, the diurnal symbols tend to converge into heroic or antithetic structures and the nocturnal symbols into mystic or antiphrastic structures. With the nyctomorphic visage of time that devours as theriomorphic symbols, night becomes a central rhetorical element that renders the setting uncanny. The character's vision thus appears strange and unnerving. In the mirror-discourse, night is not euphemized by antiphrasis but instead, is depicted by hyperbolic antithesis. The narration proceeds under the shadow of darkness and mostly reaches a tragic end characterized by the schizomorphic heroic struggle.

In Hoffmann's "The Sandman," Nathanael's feeling of insecurity and fear emerges in his childhood every evening after dinner. This continual image of the sandman as the devouring and dark destructive power also grows up with the hero and haunts him until his tragic end. Gautier's "Arria Marcella" stages the uncanny resurrection of antique Rome when the sky begins to turn obscure. The hero in "The Beautiful Vampire" lives a double life between day and night. He can no longer distinguish his own image from the mirror reflection. Also under the shadow of night, the hero in Hawthorne's "Young Goodman Brown" becomes cynical after his nocturnal journey. Poe's "The Black Cat" makes use of night and the colour black to contrast the profound darkness of human wickedness with ostensive reality and lightness. Under the pen of Mary Shelley, Frankenstein fabricates his monster in the dead of night and hence launches the ensuing miserable incidents. Master of night and water, Maupassant capitalized on nocturnal time and darkness to concoct realistic fantastic tales that waver between the real and the unreal.

Darkness in the rhetoric of mirror-discourse put the first touch of strangeness in the centre of rational realism. The imaginary of the unknown is poeticized by the mirror-discourse through the temporal fermentation of night that further metamorphoses space. Night's very image of darkness is the colour of imagination rooted in the unfathomable unknown. It is like the depth of the looking-glass or the far end of the other side of the water surface. Even if stories do not take place in the middle of the night or after sun sets, the image of darkness still intrudes in the middle of the day, the seed of the uncanny that ignites the fantastic fire. This murky image is the unknown darkness hidden in the mirror and becomes concrete in fantastic tales. The antithesis of day and night or light and dark remains the central rhetoric of the mirror-discourse, which will also orient the enunciated exaggerated expressions, axioms or fixed expressions and modal expressions to create the ambiguous effect of mirror.

Figure and Fantastic Language –
From Figurative to Literal Meanings

From the Todorovian perspective, the ambiguity that results in the hesitation felt by the character and/or the reader derives from the uniqueness of the enunciated figurative expression and the homodiegetic enunciation. The decisive condition for the pure fantastic narration to be possible (according to Todorov's criteria) is to take figurative language *au pied de la lettre* or literally. Figurative language employed in fantastic narratives encompasses exaggeration, fixed expressions and modal expressions or figurative expressions with modal verbs. The unique mirror-discourse with ambiguity, a popular narrative form since the skeptical period of fantastic creation, revolutionizes the tradition of fantastic creation to the extent that certain critics hold this narrative rhetoric as the exclusive condition for fantastic literature. However, the intimate studies of the previous chapters in Part One have expounded the essential meanings and features of fantastic literature. Accordingly, the Todorovian pure fantastic can be deemed as only a special narrative form of the genre. This unique type of discourse indeed represents the imaginary by the implied author and to the implied reader a thinking mode governed by alpha-thinking, which later makes split in beta-thinking. We can interpret the exaggeration in this narrative discourse by Durand's rhetoric of hyperbole that euphemizes the fear deriving from the diurnal imaginary regime. Since the diurnal symbols construct heroic or *schizomorphic* structure, the rhetoric applied to mediate the imaginary and the formalization is pathological [Durand, 485]. As the aforementioned antithesis of darkness and light, the imaginary of devouring theriomorphic darkness or night produces the uncanny and drives the character to utter expressions of exaggeration. This exaggeration weaves by gradation an atmosphere of fear and menace related to the unknown realm. Figurative language starts to take its original forms and meanings from the brink of distancing the habitually perceived known existences. The reversal of taking figurative language literally is in keeping with suspecting the reality of the percipient's own image faced with the mirror reflection.

According to Durand, the rhetoric of hyperbole is the main medium connecting the fantastic imagination from the diurnal regime with the audience by the formalization of meaning. In fantastic writing, like the function of water that conversely awakens, this hyperbole will awaken to its authentic visage of semantism inclusive of concrete and abstract meanings. This exaggeration of sensation is ubiquitous in fantastic tales composed under the mirror-discourse. Through this discourse, the symbolic mirror reflects the tripartite visage of time (theriomorphic, nyctomorphic and catamorphic) and menaces character as the percipient to flee from or fight against it. For certain other characters, the images generated from the nocturnal regime of the imaginary offer a mystic space to embrace them. They perceive the metamorphosis of the diurnal reality as a return to the cradle of maternal night. The story grounded in the nocturnal vision is indeed an incomplete euphemism of mysticism or antiphrasis. This enclosed and individual focalization will confront the surroundings predominated with diurnal symbols and thus entails a rhetoric of mirror hinging on antithesis. The rhetoric of the Möbius strip in most contemporary fantastic stories brings into play the Durandian synthetic structure with the euphemism from the nocturnal imaginary regime to tame the devouring power from the diurnal regime. In this unique plot elaboration, the enunciation plays a vital role in presenting the fantastic story. The enunciated exaggerated expressions are not voiced by the character, but rather by the narrator who implies an impending crystallization of figurative language. Therefore, different types of narration utilize hyperbole to unfold of the plot, ambiguity being the central effect of totality that is focalized by the functioning of visualization.

The Mirror in the Painting – The Rhetoric of *Mise en Abyme*

Like the visual effect created by the painted mirror with the reflected images to the painting, the unique rhetoric of the *mise en abyme* reinforces the visual ambiguity of fantastic narration. Parallel to figurative language that is to be taken literally in the process of plot unfolding, the *mise en abyme* will be taken literally with the denouement of the plot. As the pioneer of fantastic literature with the mirror-discourse (or the generally defined French pure fantastic or low fantasy), Hoffmann masterfully blended German folkloric materials with Romantic poetics and created a unique narrative art of *mise en abyme* in his fantastic storytelling. He thus distinguished himself from his traditional fellow storytellers by the revolutionary narrative techniques characterized by grotesqueness, irony, *mise en abyme* and everyday setting as the narrative frame. Although his "The Sandman" is a landmark of the fantastic genre thanks to the elucidation of Freud's psychoanalytical interpretation, its significance in fantastic poetics is overshadowed by the Freudian psychoanalytical perspective that emphasizes Hoffmann's creative phantasm. Substantially, "The Sandman" is *per se* a *mise en abyme* of the variations of fantastic narration: the rhetoric of epistolary writing, the narrator's meta-narration, the *mise en abyme* that mirrors the whole story, an explicit representation of the rational explication along with the supernatural enigma, the antithesis of metaphor and literal meanings, internal focalization with the hero-victim and a complex enunciation mixed with autodiegetic and heterodiegetic narration. Among others, the *mise en abyme* is an effective and poetic artistry to reinforce and reflect the mirror-discourse.

In the tale, the hero Nathanael, holding a unique opinion on man's creation "directed by some Higher Principle existing without and beyond ourselves" (this statement in fact later can be taken as true), composes a poem which is a perfect *mise en abyme* to the whole story about the unfortunate hero:

> He made himself and Clara, united by true love, the central figures, but represented a black hand a being from time to time thrust into their life, plucking out a joy that had blossomed for them. At length, as they were standing at the altar, the terrible Coppelius appeared and touched Clara's lovely eyes, which leaped into Nathanael's own bosom, burning and hissing like bloody sparks. Then Coppelius laid hold of him, and hurled him into a blazing circle of fire, which spun round with the speed of a whirlwind, and storming and blustering, dashed away with him. [...] But through the midst of the savage fury of the tempest he heard Clara's voice calling, "Can you not see me, dear? Coppelius has deceived you; they were not my eyes which burned so in your bosom; they were fiery drops of your own heart's blood. Look at me, I have got my own eyes still." [...] Nathanael looked into Clara's eyes; but it was death whose gaze rested so kindly upon him. [Calvino, 54]

For Hoffmann, the rhetoric of *mise en abyme* functions as a concentric centre that mirrors the story as a whole. The central spirit lies in Romantic poetics in contradistinction to the prosaic. The quoted poem composed by the hero resonates with his own story created by the author. Eyes, as the core motif throughout the story, are radiated from this created poem to the development of the whole story until the tragic denouement.

Rhetoric of import, the *mise en abyme* contrived by Hoffmann, exerts a great influence on French writers. Mérimée embedded in his "The Venus of Ille" two episodes as the *mise en abyme* to mirror the double interpretation of the story. The hesitation between a natural explication and a supernatural explication characterizes not only the whole story but also the two embedded episodes. In the first episode, two town rowdies, taking the bronze statue of Venus as a wicked object that broke Jean Coll's leg, pass by the statue and talk about taking their revenge to destroy the statue. One of them picks up a stone and the narrator thus describes: "I saw him stretch out his arm and throw something, and immediately after, I heard a loud noise come from the bronze. At the same moment the apprentice raised his hand to his head and cried out in pain. / "She's thrown it back at me! he exclaimed" [Calvino, 271].

The narrator laughs at this superstitious interpretation by explaining that the stone "had obviously rebounded from the metal, and had punished the rascal for the outrage done to the goddess" [ibid., 271]. However, this apparently laughable episode falls into uncertainty when the narrator later chances to closely observe the statue: "He [M. de Peyrehorade] had just noticed a white mark a little above the breast of the Venus. I saw a similar mark on the fingers of the right hand, which I then supposed had been touched by the stone in passing, or else a fragment of it might have been broken off by the shock and hit the hand" [ibid., 277]. The marks on the fingers and above the breast of the Venus open for a double interpretation of the incident, which serves as a perfect *mise en abyme* to the double interpretation of the death of M. Alphonse towards the end of the story.

The other rhetoric of *mise en abyme* is the enigmatic inscription on the pedestal of the statue: CAVE AMANTEM. The decoding of this Latin inscription orients towards two extreme meanings according to the translations of Monsieur de Peyrehorade and the narrator. The former translates as "Beware of him who loves thee; mistrust thy lovers," while the later decodes as "Beware if she loves thee." Since the narrator is a scholar and state inspector from Paris, readers tend to accept his translation instead of the funny translation surmised by the peasant connoisseur or collector of antiques. The inclination for the second translation of the inscription becomes all the more convincing as M. Alphone is seemingly murdered by the Venus statue *who loves him* since he slips his wedding ring on her third finger.

Poe also crafted the technique of the *mise en abyme* to enhance the tension and story plotting of his fantastic tales; "The Fall of the House of Usher" offers an excellent example. The narrator-witness chooses one of Usher's favourite medieval romances to read to him and pass away the terrible night together; ironically this reading of the 'Mad Trist' of Sir Launcelot Canning mirrors the ensuing horrible incident about Madeline of Usher. As the narrator reads about the scene where the hero slays the dragon, the plot of the romance synchronically unfolds the tumults from the vault in Poe's story:

> '[...] And Ethelred uplifted his mace, and struck upon the head of the dragon, which fell before him, and gave up his pesty breath, with a shriek so horrid and harsh, and withal so piercing, that Ethelred had fain to close his ears with his hands against the dreadful noise of it, the like whereof was never before heard.'
>
> Here again I paused abruptly, and now with a feeling of wild amazement – for there could be no doubt whatever that, in this instance, I did actually hear (although from what direction it proceeded I fount it impossible to say) a low and apparently distant, but harsh, protracted, and most unusual screaming or grating sound – the exact counterpart of what my fancy had already conjured up for the dragon's unnatural shriek as described by the romancer. [Poe 1994, 161]

The narrator later resumes his reading of the romance and perceives even more clearly "a distinct, hollow, metallic, and clangorous, yet apparently muffled reverberation" [ibid., 162]. The fantastic incident is later revealed by Usher: "*We have put her living in the tomb*! [...] And now – tonight – Ethelred –ha! Ha! – the breaking of the hermit's door, and the death-cry of the dragon, and the clangour of the shield! say, rather, the rending of her coffin, and the grating of the iron hinges of her prison, and her struggles within the coppered archway of the vault!" [ibid., 162-3]. The gibbering murmur of Usher's words explicitly exposes the synchronicity in the *mise en abyme* of the dragon slaying that mirrors the fantastic resurrection of Lady Madeline.

This narrative technique has become more popular in postmodern writing. Cortázar's "Continuity of Parks" is a live example of presenting the synchronical interplay and the connection between the embedded novel and the novel readers read. The fantastic effect is created through staging the *mise en abyme* as the animation of reading process. The hero of the story is reading a novel which is coincidently (and haplessly) taking place in his real world. Strangeness emerges when the realistic setting of the hero's space turns out to be identical with the setting described in the novel read by the hero. Recognition of the two settings can be certain from the previous gradual vague impression: "At the top, two doors. No one in the first room, no one in the second. The door of the salon, and then, the knife in hand, the light from the great windows, the high back of an armchair covered in green velvet, the head of the man in the chair reading a novel" [Cortázar, 65]. This passage of the setting depiction mirrors the earlier portrayal of the hero's surrounding: "Sprawled in his favorite armchair, its back towards the door – even the possibility of an intrusion would have irritated him, had he thought of it – he let his left hand caress repeatedly the green velvet upholstery and set to reading the final chapters" [ibid., 63-64]. Readers are not given any solution to the end of the story but an open ending with uncertain ambiguity. We readers are not forced into the hesitation for an explication but feel the ambiguity of strangeness like appreciating paintings of the Möbius strip. Such a transgression between the extradiegetic and intradiegetic narrations is further developed by Gérard Genette, who defines the narrative as metaleptic fiction. The present short story of Cortázar is studied to exemplify his theory [Genette 2004, 25-27]. Cortázar brings into play the rhetoric of *mise en abyme* and metalepsis to create a new style of fantastic narration which is in the inception marked by the plurality of "parks" in the title. The *mise en abyme* is a condensed rhetoric of an embedded mirror that enhances the effect of the mirror-discourse. In addition, a more common feature in the mirror-discourse is its reversal from figurative language to its literal meanings, which requires further investigation in the following section.

Expression of Exaggeration or Hyperbole and Repetition

In the literature of realism, metaphor is a main device to vividly depict scenes, actions and characters. In the mirror-discourse of fantastic literature, the rhetoric of exaggeration, personification and other hyperbolic expressions of extreme sensations will lead to the realm of the supernatural. This rhetoric of exaggeration is, as a matter of fact, the corollary of antithesis from the imaginary. In most fantastic works with the mirror-discourse, hyperbole and its procession of pleonasm underscore the poetics of antithesis. Readers are naturally required to exclude a figurative reading of the text.

In the mirror-discourse, hyperbolic expressions often arouse feelings of fear, for example, Nathanael ("The Sandman") uttered that he "was *spellbound* on the spot" [my emphasis, Calvino, 40] when he hides behind the curtain to peep at his father's master or the sandman. As he was haunted by the fear towards the sandman, his melancholic and gloomy expressions about his own life seem to come true later, just as what he once stated: "but to the fact that a *mysterious destiny* has hung *a dark veil of clouds* about my life, which I shall perhaps only break through *when I die*" [my emphasis, ibid., 42]. This dark veil becomes concrete as the mysterious figure of the sandman gradually regains his devilish menace on Nathanael. As related to the ghoulish sandman, eyes are the central motif that connects the webs of story plotting. The hyperbole in the description about eyes is the main expression to be taken literally: "Thousands of eyes were looking and blinking convulsively and staring up at Nathanael; he could not avert his gaze from the table. Coppola went on heaping up his spectacles, while wilder and ever wilder burning flashes crossed through and through each other and darted their blood-red rays into Nathanael's breast" [ibid., 58].

These exaggerated expressions reflect the fear felt by the hero and further echo with the above quoted poem composed by the hero as a *mise en abyme*. The images of "burning flashes," "blood-red rays" and "breast" further drive figurative language to a final literal realization. All these conduct to the later scene of smashing Olimpia (an automaton) into a thousand pieces. The mystery of the sandman's identity is thus demystified by Nathanael's professor:

> " [...] Coppelius – Coppelius – he's stolen my best automaton – at which I've worked for twenty years – my life work – the clockwork – speech – movement – mine – your eyes – stolen your eyes – damn him – curse him – after him – fetch me back Olimpia – there are the eyes." And now Nathanael saw a pair of bloody eyes lying on the floor staring at him; Spalanzani seized them with his uninjured hand and threw them at him, so that they hit his breast. [ibid., 68]

Notice again the images of "bloody eyes" and "breast" and in addition, the riddle-solving identification of Coppola with Coppelius. The hyperbolic depiction of the hero's fear and disquietude is enhanced by the successive style of pleonasm centring on the expressions of eyes.

The exaggerated feeling felt by the hero towards Olimpia is another example of the use of figurative language to be taken literally: "As he touched her cold hand, he felt his heart thrill with awe; the legend of 'The Dead Bride' shot suddenly through his mind. But Olimpia had drawn him closer to her, and the kiss appeared to warm her lips into vitality" [ibid., 63]. The discourse of Nathanael's professor (the owner of the automaton) is also as figurative as literal: "You have had an extraordinarily *animated* conversation with my daughter" [my emphasis, ibid., 63]. In this sentence, "animated" is in fact taken figuratively as well as literally since the automaton seemingly absorbs life from Nathanael little by little from each of his gaze and thus "animates" step by step.

French writer Gautier's romantic fantastic tale of "Arria Marcella" brings into play continual exaggerated expressions to the impending reading of the literal meanings. The picturesque description of the space will be taken literally after the metamorphosis of the village of Pompeii:

> It was one of those halcyon days so common in Naples, when the radiant sunlight and the pellucid air imbue objects with hues that in Northern climes *would appear fantastical*, and which *seem to belong more to the realm of dream than to that of physical reality*. Whoever has just once beheld this golden and azure brilliance will carry it back with him into the mist and fog as an incurable nostalgia.

The resurrected city, having thrown off a corner of its ashy shroud, stood out in all its myriad details in the blinding light of the sun. [my emphasis, Kessler, 120]

The above picturesque and animated figurative language depicting the city proves to be in fact literal language. The city indeed resurrects and stands out in the blinding light of the sun in the middle of the night. This language of exaggeration extends to the details of the city scene. The style of personification in the following passages characterizes the unique language of the mirror-discourse:

He stared at houses whose roofs had fallen in, exposing to a single glance of the eye all their inner mysteries, domestic details passed over by historians, which civilizations carry with them to the grave; at fountains *seemingly* only just run dry; at the Forum, surprised by catastrophe in mid-repair, whose hewn and sculpted columns and entablatures *seem to be* waiting still, in skeletal purity, for some to fit them in proper position; [my emphasis, ibid., 121]
[...] among these sepulchral monuments so richly gilded by the sun, and which, placed as they were right alongside the pathway, *seemed still to be part of life*, inspiring non of that cold repulsion or fantastic terror which is stirred in us by our lugubrious graveyards. [my emphasis, ibid., 123]

The employment of personification and animation to describe the scene is nothing but mediocre; however, in fantastic tales, this very technique often leads to the following supernatural incidents. Gautier utilized figurative language of exaggeration, concerning psychological and physical vision, to stage the fantastic from the diurnal conscious state to the ambiguity of nocturnal state (from the perspective of the hero), to eventually return to the diurnal state where the hero's consciousness is henceforward entrapped by the unknown space and time of oblivion. This illustrates again that the antithetic imaginary, among others diurnal vs. nocturnal, determines the rhetorical style of the mirror-discourse.

Poe, the most important foreign writer that influenced the development of French fantastic literature during the second half of 19th century, expanded the figure of exaggeration to the verge of neurosis. In the narration of the realistic fantastic, the hyperbole is not attributed with clues of reason, like the fear in Nathanael of the sandman is likely related to the obedience and death of his father and the rigid manner of his father's master. In Poe's tales, fear and hatred seem to come out of no sensible reason and thus touches the very deep insecurity of man's imagination. The narrator of "The Tell-Tale Heart" hates and kills the old man just for his vulture eye that causes uncanny feeling; the narrator of "The Black Cat" first cuts one of Pluto's (the black cat) eyes from the socket and then hangs the cat to death. The double in "William Wilson" is absolute abhorrence to the narrator who seems to suffer from claustrophobia and be gnawed by his conscience. Poe employed the rhetoric of hyperbole to extreme in order to

awaken readers from the long accepted secure reality, especially our own identity. Given that "William Wilson" perfectly illustrates the image and meaning of
the mirror-discourse by doppelganger and mirror, its overdose of exaggeration
will be analyzed in detail.

The hyperbolic description of the narrator about the enclosed disquieting
space of his school as a giant image nearly animates the surroundings into a devouring monster. The isotopic images of the Gothic giant related to the dragon
(the Draconian laws of the academy) prepare for the apparition of the narrator's
namesake:

> My earliest recollections of a school-life are connected with a large, ram-
> bling, Elizabethan house, in a misty-looking village of England, where were a
> vast number of gigantic and gnarled trees, and where all the houses were ex-
> cessively ancient. In truth, it was a dream-like and spirit-soothing place, that
> venerable old town. At this moment, in fancy, I feel the refreshing chilliness of
> its deeply-shadowed avenues, inhale the fragrance of its thousand shrubberies,
> and thrill anew with undefinable delight, at the deep hollow note of the
> church-bell, breaking, each hour, with sullen and sudden roar, upon the still-
> ness of the dusky atmosphere in which the fretted Gothic steeple lay imbedded
> and asleep. [Poe 1994 *Selected*, 97]

This is an example of the Durandian diurnal antithetic or schizomorphic structure of mad geometrism. The leading rhetoric is guided by the hyperbolic language confronting spatial insecurity and fear. Throughout the whole story, the
narrator exaggerates the ubiquity of menacing space by hyperbole and pleonasm
of the gigantic image, for example, "From comparatively trivial wickedness I
passed, with the stride of a giant, into more than the enormities of an
Elah-Gabalus" [ibid., 96] and "Oh, gigantic paradox, too utterly monstrous for
solution!" [ibid., 98].

This hyperbolic mad geometrism is intensified as the narrator tells about
peeping at his double. The fantastic emerges as the hyperbolic expressions are
taken literally:

> *My* breast heaved, *my* knees tottered, *my* whole spirit became possessed with
> an objectless yet intolerable horror. Gasping for breath, I lowered the lamp in
> still nearer proximity to the face. Were *these* – *these* the lineament of William
> Wilson? I saw, indeed, that they were his, but I shook as if with a fit of the
> ague in fancying they were not. What *was* there about them to confound me in
> this manner? I gazed; - while my brain reeled with a multitude of incoherent
> thoughts. Not *thus* he appeared – assuredly not *thus* – in the vivacity of his
> waking hours. *The same* name! *the same* contour of person! *The same* day of
> arrival at the academy! And then his dogged and meaningless imitation of *my*
> *gait, my voice, my habits*, and *my manner*! Was it, in truth, within the bounds
> of human possibility, that *what I now saw* was the result, merely, of the habit-
> ual practice of this sarcastic imitation? Awestricken, and with a creeping shud-

der, I extinguished the lamp, passed silently from the chamber, and left at once, the halls of that old academy, never to enter them again. [my emphasis, ibid., 106-107][69]

The figure of repetition thrives in Poe's hyperbolic narration. In the quoted passage, anaphora, as indicated by underscore, enhances the effect of hyperbolic geometrism. The narrator's geometrical madness of the giant shadow blends with fear of his namesake into a vortex of thoughtless folly. This dreadful vortex haunts him till the end of astonishment and horror when he plunges his sword through his namesake's bosom: "But what human language can adequately portray *that* astonishment, *that* horror which possessed me at the spectacle then presented to view?" [ibid., 116] The narrator sees a large mirror stand where none had been perceptible before and sees his own image "but with features all pale and dabbled in blood, advances to meet him with a feeble and tottering gait" [ibid., 116]. He discovers in his antagonist: "[n]ot a thread in all his raiment – not a line in all the marked and singular lineaments of his face which was not, even in the most absolute identity, *mine own!*" [ibid., 117].

The closure with the image of mirror and double, rhetoric of the mirror-discourse par excellence, is perfected by voice. This shift of language style suspends the story in pending ambiguity. If the last speech taken as literally, then the fantastic incident does haunt the narrator as an inescapable giant image:

> It was Wilson; but he spoke no longer in a whisper, and I could have fancied that I myself was speaking while he said:
> *'You have conquered, and I yield. Yet, henceforward art thou also dead – dead to the World, to Heaven, and to hope! In me didst thou exist – and, in my death, see by this image, which is thine own, how utterly thou hast murdered thyself.'* [ibid., 117]

The narration of "William Wilson" impeccably brings into play the diachronic effect of the exaggerated expression of hyperbole and pleonasm.

Similar to Poe's poetics of the fantastic, Maupassant also worked on readers' nerves by an autodiegetic narrator with hyper-sensation. His tales can best express the metaphor of water we use to characterize the mirror-discourse. His representative work of the fantastic, "Le Horla," is a scary story based on the dark imagery of water and mirror that seemingly engenders an ineffable monster or a horrible double. In the beginning of the story, or more precisely, the diaries of the hero, the narrator describes his illness and fear and exaggeratedly describes his waiting for sleep: "Then I go to bed and wait for sleep as if I were waiting for the executioner. I wait for it in terror of its coming, with my heart pounding and my legs trembling" [Maupassant 1998, 316]. This fear is further reflected by the image of water: "when I suddenly fall asleep like a man falling

---

[69] The underlined words in italic were originally emphasized by the author.

into a chasm full of stagnant water to drown" [ibid., 316]. The abstract water image turns out to take shape as the unknown haunting monster possesses the hero: "Someone is in possession of my mind and controlling it!" [ibid., 333] and "He had come back and taken possession of me once more" [ibid., 334]. The hero's hyperbolic expressions concerning water and mirror will be taken literally to touch the ambiguous fantastic spot:

> How frightened I was! Then, all of a sudden, I began to see myself in a mist at the back of the mirror, as if I were looking through a sheet of water; and it seemed to me that this water was slowly gliding from left to right, so that my reflection was becoming clearer every moment. It was like the last stage of an eclipse. What was hiding me did not seem to have clearly defined outlines, but a sort of opaque transparency, growing gradually lighter. [ibid., 341]

Further on, readers almost trust the vision of the narrator since the horror is exaggeratedly expressed in gradation: "I had seen him! The horror of it lingers with me still, making me shudder when I think of it" [ibid., 341]. Just as the narrator says that he is able to see himself completely, readers are surprised by his affirmation of "I had seen him" and this is the first time that the narrator describes the "it" of the Horla as "he."[70] The narrator's attempt to kill "him" only causes another tragedy because he burns his servants alive but only increases his fear to extremity. The end of the story is in fact a perpetual hyperbole of the narrator's fear that lingers in suspension:

> Suppose he was not dead?... Perhaps only time alone has power over that Invisible and Fearful Being. Why should he possess that transparent, unknowable body, that spiritual body, if he too must fear sickness, injury, infirmity, premature destruction?
> Premature destruction? That is the source of all human dread. After man, the Horla. After him who can die any day, any hour, any minute, [...]
> No... no... I know beyond a doubt that he is not dead. ... In that case... in that case... I shall have to kill – myself. [ibid., 343-344]

Given that most of Maupassant's fantastic tales are the embodiment of fear towards darkness and water, the very image of mirror, his other story "Night: A Nightmare" or "La Nuit" merits analysis here. Maupassant's fantastic narration makes much use of hyperbolic expressions reinforced by repetition or pleonasm.

---

[70] This shift from "it" to "him" is the translator's own emphasis. In fact, French language does not make disctinction between the pronouns "it" and "he" or "she." In the French version, the monster is described by "il" (English "it" in masculin) which creates an effect of ambiguity between the object and human. The translator translated with "him" on the scene of the mirror reflection because at this point, the narrator is able to delineate the concrete shape (in reality the monster seems to steal the narrator's own image) of the unknown phenomenon "The Horla."

In this short story, the autodiegetic narrator depicts his nightmarish experience by the river Seine in Paris. The metamorphoses from time to space converge into the eventual effect of the fantastic. The narration begins with a repetition of anaphora "I love" and then the repetition of the preposition "in" to hyperbolize the narrator's extraordinary favourable emotion for night, which ironically turns out to be devouring. If night figures are part of the devouring image of time according to Durand, Maupassant artistically represented the imaginary by his fantastic storytelling of the hero's nocturnal experience. Night, as synecdoche of time, sprawls Paris's space to intrude the whole territory of time. The exaggerated expression about time will be also taken literally to enter the supernatural dimension: "Well, yesterday – was it yesterday? – yes, no doubt, unless it was earlier, a day, a month, a year earlier.... I do not know, but it must have been yesterday, because since then no day has risen, no sun has dawned. But how long has it been night? How long? Who can tell? Who will ever know?" [Calvino, 398]

Maupassant depicts the insecure feeling towards the unknown by a gradual narration with the rhetoric of pleonasm to blur the time at night. The narration later proceeds from the unknown time to the unknown space, leading to the eventual quasi-destruction of the represented character. The successive and repetitive exaggerative expressions of the narrator conduct the story to an open ending of the unknown abyss. The interplay of hyperbole with abundant pleonasm, anaphora, epizeuxis and diacope takes on the vital rhetoric of the story:

> Was the Seine still flowing? I wanted to know, I found the steps and went down. I could not hear the current rushing under the bridge.... A few more steps.... Then sand.... Mud.... then water. I dipped my hand into it. It was flowing... flowing... cold... cold... cold... almost frozen ... almost dried up ... almost dead. [ibid., 402]

The rhetorical employment of hyperbole and pleonasm urges readers to vicariously experience the character's sensation and later to enter into the fantastic dimension of the story. Besides the rhetoric of hyperbole and amplification that construct the mirror-discourse, fixed expressions also create an enigmatic and ambiguous atmosphere in the fantastic narration. These expressions are normally to be taken literally at the denouement of the story.

Set Expressions Apt to be Taken as Literal Meanings

In the mirror-discourse, the figurative language of set expressions and expressions of axioms, proverbs, wish, oath and curse eventually is to be taken literally in a reading involving the passage of time, until the revelation of quasi-supernatural phenomena at the denouement of the story. These expressions can also be regarded as the foreshadowing of impending strange and inexplicable phenomena. For example, in "Arria Marcella," the narrator presents the following conversation to imply the impending metamorphosis of space-time, which will testify to the literal reading of the set expression: "'There is nothing new under the sun,' replied Fabio, 'not even that axiom, since Solomon invented it.' / 'Perhaps there may be something new under the moon,' Octavian added, with a smile of melancholy irony" [Kessller, 122]. The modification of the old axiom by replacing "sun" with "moon" proves to come true later in the story. This axiom and wish was originally planned to be taken literally by the author.

In "The Venus of Ille," the rich intertextual rhetoric of plotting the mysterious story offers the characteristic of reversing the figurative into the literal. The interesting quotations recited by Monsieur de Peyrehorade to show off his pedantry will be later taken literally. In response to the narrator's enquiry about Jean Coll's broken leg, Peyrehorade cites "*Veneris nec praemia nôris*" (quoted from Virgil's *The Aeneid*), which originally meant "And the presence of Venus, you don't known it," to further express "Who hasn't been wounded by Venus in his time?" [Calvino, 269]. The figurative meaning of the expression that refers to love desire will eventually be realized literally when his son is really wounded (and indeed killed) by Venus. In discussing the statue's model with the narrator, Peyrehorade quotes again a sentence from Racine's *Phédre* (Acte I, scène 3), "Venus with all her might has fastened on her prey," [ibid., 273] to follow the comment of the narrator on Venus's ferocious but beautiful expression. Naturally, this figurative rhetoric to perfect the menacing beauty turns out to be fulfilled by the tragedy in which Peyrehorade's own son is the prey fastened upon by the mighty Venus.

Likewise, in keeping with his philosophy of composition, Poe supplemented the rhetoric *mise en abyme* and the hyperbole and pleonasm by the skillful operation of set expression. In the case of the aforementioned "William Wilson," an epigraph is woven into the texture. Poe quoted a passage from William Chamberlayne's *Pharronida* (falsely assumed quotation) as the epigraph of his short story. Moreover, the hero bears the same surname as the quoted poet: "What say of it? what say of CONSCIENCE grim, / That spectre in my path?" [Poe 1994 *Selected*, 96]. The spectre of conscience seems to be implied as the namesake of the hero and gradually takes shape in the story. The following figurative expression uttered by the hero bolsters up this epigraph: "all virtue dropped bodily as a mantle" [ibid. 96]. Poe agilely combined the metaphor of mantle and spectre of conscience and vividly staged it as a spectacle of horror in the story. On the final scene of the story, after the hero plunges his sword through his namesake's bosom, the body of the latter dissipates with nothing left but his mask and cloak (mantle), ringing with the last discourse of conscience.

Villiers de l'Isle-Adam's "Véra" also launches the narration with a proverb "Love is stronger than Death, said Solomon; and it is true that its mysterious power knows no limits" [Kessler, 274]. More often than not, readers take the expression as a metaphor and understand it as the spiritual power stronger than death. However, with the narration focalizing on the vision of the Comte d'Athol, a literal interpretation of the set expression is gradually imposed upon readers until the culmination of the end of the story: "Suddenly, like a reply, a shining object fell with a metallic sound from the marriage bed onto the black fur. A ray of the sinister earthly dawn lit it up…. The lonely man bent down and picked it up; and a sublime smile illumined his face as he recognized this object. It was the key to the tomb" [ibid., 283]

By the same token, the curse cast by the characters in Potocki's *Le Manuscrit trouvé à Saragosse* almost causes a synchronic emergence of the supernatural. Ignorant of the fact that her daughter Blanca was just murdered by the brother of the mother:

> The poor woman was with her daughter and was going to sit down at the table. Seeing her son entering the house, she asked him if Blanca would come for dinner. "Could she come," said Landulphe, "and bring you to hell, with your brother and all your family of the Zampis." The poor mother fell onto her knees and said, "Oh! God! Forgive him for these blasphemies. In this moment, the door opened with a crash, and they saw a haggard ghost enter, torn up with stabs, and yet retaining a horrible resemblance to Blanca.[71] [Potocki, 94]

The above example of a curse reinforces the point that the fantastic realizes the literal meaning of a figurative expression. Although the final rational explanation removes the literary interpretation from the figurative expressions, the embodiment of the quoted passage arouses readers to ponder upon the original figure of language.

Maupassant's saying in "Night: A Nightmare" that "One is finally killed by what one violently loves" seems to be realized towards the end of the story. With the opening of the vivid and jubilant description of the picturesque night, readers are tantalized into the nocturnal promenade with the hero. However, the gradual alienation of time and space makes the enunciation seemingly glide into the other side of the mirror; in this instance, the horrible and stagnant water of the Seine. The ironic figurative expression is eventually made concrete under the ambiguous tone of the hero as victim. This metamorphosis of love and desire into destruction implicitly echoes the pact with the devil. The hero's unusual affection for night is often endowed with dark imagination. This mirrors to some

---

[71] *La pauvre femme était avec sa fille, et allait se mettre à table. Lorsqu'elle vit entrer son fils, elle lui demanda si Blanca viendrait souper. Puisse-t-elle venir, dit Landulphe, et te mener en enfer, avec ton frère et toute ta famille des Zampi ! La pauvre mère tomba à genoux et dit : - Oh ! mon Dieu ! pardonnez-lui ses blasphèmes. Dans ce moment, la porte s'ouvrit avec fracas, et l'on vit entrer un spectre hâve, déchiré de coups de poignards, et conservant néanmoins avec Blanca une affreuse ressemblance.*

extent the unconscious pact with the devilish power. Rejoicing turns into horror. The story seems implicitly to warn readers to be wary of words. Language may not be merely a sign or linguistic expressions. It seems to be able to animate or take shape like magic spells.

This magic power of words is indeed effective and even animates a painting in Wilde's fantastic creation. Deviating from the lively description of the contract deal (Marlowe's representation of a contract formula or Goethe's mutual dialogic consent between Faustus/Faust and Mephistopheles), Wilde averted the blunt depiction of the pact by insinuating the wishful figurative expression. The pact with the devil in *The Picture of Dorian Gray* is implied by a mirror-discourse of the narration. The concrete figure of a devil such as Mephistopheles is absent from the novel. In the mirror-discourse, this devilish pact is enacted in the character's psyche and the devil is in fact a part of the character, like the unconscious shadow. Figurative language thus remains as an important clue to the implied pact. The expression of wish, the unreal conditional expression, will come true and compels readers to receive it literally:

> 'How sad it is!' murmured Dorian Gray, with his eyes still fixed upon his own portrait. 'How sad it is! I shall grow old, and horrible, and dreadful. But this picture will remain always young. It will never be older than this particular day of June... If it were only the other way! If it were I who was to be always young, and the picture that was to grow old! For that – for that – I would give everything! Yes, there is nothing in the whole world I would not give! I would give my soul for that!' [Wilde 1994, 34]

And the fantastic arises when the above wish starts to be realized as Gray encounters the first metamorphosis of his portrait. The complete realization of the wishful expression unfolds the novel to the climactic denouement of the story: "disgusted by the abhorrent picture, Gray seizes the same knife that kills the painter and stabs the picture with it" [ibid., 256]. Ambiguity occurs with the last scene when people find an old man lying dead in Gray's study: "Lying on the floor was a dead man, in evening dress, with a knife in his heart. He was withered, wrinkled, and loathsome of visage. It was not till they had examined the rings that they recognised who it was" [ibid., 256].

The above reading illustrates how set figurative language can function on the enunciated level of discourse to incubate a fantastic tale. Apart from these rhetorical techniques of the interplay between the figurative and the literal, a last skill of the mirror-discourse on the enunciated level merits a close analysis. This is synchronicity of modal expressions.

Synchronicity of Modal Expressions

The synchronic feature of modal expressions is a ubiquitous verbal pattern re-current in the mirror-discourse to create a simultaneous effect of strangeness, disquietude and fear. Almost all fantastic tales with the mirror-discourse use modal words to express an uncertain and unnerving feeling that is synchronic with the unknown intrusion. The most common modal expressions are "as if," "it seems that," "I fancied," "I thought I saw," "I imagined" and so forth. In French literature, here are common conditional figurative expressions: "on eût dit," "on dirait," "ils m'appelleraient," "comme si," etc.

Hoffmann used such expressions to blur the borderline between the known reality and the unknown realm, which further makes reality more fantastic. Such expressions abound in "The Sandman." For example, the hero's feeling or un-certain impression about Olimpia should be taken literally since she is nothing but an automaton. The expressions activate simultaneously with the animation of the automaton's eyes that seem to absorb the hero's eyes or soul: "he *fancied* a light like humid moonbeams came into them. It *seemed as if* their power of vi-sion was now being enkindled; their glances shone with ever-increasing vivac-ity" [my emphasis, Calvino, 59]; "for he *fancied* that she had expressed in re-spect to his works and his poetic genius [...] and even *as if* it was his own heart's voice speaking to him" [ibid., 66]. The gloomy shadow of the sandman or Coppola in fact never dissipates as the hero "*fancied* he detected a gasping sigh *as* of a dying man stealing awfully through the room; his heart stopped beating with fear" [ibid., 59]. From the beginning exaggerated expressions of Nathanael's first confronting Coppelius or the sandman ("I *was spellbound* on the spot") to the end of the story with the modal expression ("Nathanael stopped *as if spellbound*; he bent down over the railing and perceived Coppelius."), readers eventually take the indicative hyperbole of fear "was spellbound" and the modal expression "as if spellbound" literally. They are oriented to accept the haunting existence of Coppelius and his identity as Coppola and the sandman.

Recall the aforementioned story of Gautier, "Arria Marcella." Figurative language is coupled with the literal meanings at a synchronic level as the hero Octavian takes a walk at night while the old city is undergoing its fantastic res-urrection:

> Instinctively and without his being aware of it, *his feet carried him towards the entrance to the dead city.* He pushed aside the wooden bar and stepped in aim-lessly among the ruins. [...] the missing portions [of the broken columns] were filled in by half-tones, and an unexpected beam, *like an evocative touch* in a sketch for a canvas, disclosed an entire ensemble of fallen ruin. *The silent genii of the night seemed to* have restored the fossil city for some fantastical, living reenactment. [...] Occasionally Octavian even *fancied he saw* shadowy human forms moving in the darkness, but they vanished as soon as they reached the

lighted patches. Indistinct sounds, faint muffled whispers, drifted through the
stillness. [my emphasis, Kessler, 129]

From the animation of the expressions of amplification and axiom to the present
synchronicity of modalization, the hero later meets his ideal love and experiences a sensual instance in the fantastic space and time.

In "The Venus of Ille," besides the rhetoric of *mise en abyme* and exaggeration, all the conditional expressions converge to the final supernatural incident
that the statue of Venus animates and murders the bridegroom, who recklessly
leaves his wedding ring on the statue's finger. Being a realistic fantastic writer,
Mérimée made the most of modal expressions to create doubt out of sheer reality.
The story thus deserves a close reading to illustrate the rhetoric in question. The
narrator initially gains the guide's information about the statue, which is described as alive by the guide's figurative language with comparative and modal
expressions: "I tell you it's an idol; you can see from her appearance. She looks
straight at you with her great white eyes.... Anybody'd think she was trying to
stare you out, because you daren't look her in the eyes. [...] She looks wicked...
and she is wicked, too" [Calvino, 265]. If readers stop here, this description with
personification of the inanimate statue appears ordinary, just as the reaction of
the narrator that sees nothing supernatural about the statue. However, this osten-
sibly banal comparison functions as a preparation for the deployment of the final
incident, which orients towards the supernatural.

The victim M. Alphonse's discourse bears tragic irony when he confesses to
the narrator his worry and fear about the statue: "Besides, what would the people
here think of my absent-mindedness? They'd make fun of me and call me the
statue's husband..." [ibid., 283]. This figurative expression proves to be more a
literal expression as M. Alphonse fails to take his ring off the statue's finger and
confesses to the narrator, "'You will laugh at me... but I don't know what is the
matter with me... I am bewitched, dammit! [...] 'No – I – I could not get it off
the finger of that confounded Venus.' / 'Nonsense! You didn't pull hard enough.'
[said the narrator] / 'Yes, I did.... But the Venus... has clenched her finger.'
[ibid., 285]. The fear in Alphonse grows to extremity as he says that the statue is
his wife: "'No, I tell you. The Venus's finger has contracted and bent up; she has
closed her hand, do you hear? ... She's my wife, apparently, because I gave her
my ring.... She won't give it back" [ibid., 286]. The narrator, a rationalist ar-
chaeologist from Paris, always holding a distant and objective perspective towards the statue and its surrounding events, starts to be influenced by the collective fear of the statue: "I shivered suddenly, and for a moment my blood ran cold.
Then a deep sigh he gave sent a breath of wine into my face and all my emotion
disappeared" [ibid., 286]. However, the narrator's natural reasoning of the episode of Alphonse's being bewitched will later collapse in the course of
Alphonse's tragedy.

Towards the end of the story, the modal expressions uttered by the narrator imply a supernatural explanation of the incident of murder: "There was no trace of blood on his clothes. I opened his shirt and found a livid mark on his breast, which extended down his sides and over his back. *It was as if he had been crushed in a band of iron.* My foot stepped on something hard which was lying on the rug; I bent down and saw the diamond ring. [my emphasis, ibid., 288]. The expression "It was as if" (French original version *"On eût dit"*) presents what the supernatural explication suggests as the true causality of the tragedy. As is often the case in fantastic tales with the mirror-discourse, the figurative comparison suggests a supernatural intrusion or explanation to the inexplicable event. The narrator further undertakes a preliminary investigation of the murder and goes round the house to see any suspicious clues. As passing to and fro in front of the statue, he stops to look at it, at this moment, he remains no longer as sober and untouched by the rumours about the statue: "I must admit that *I could not look at its expression of ironical malice without fear,* and my head was so full of the ghastly scenes I had just witnessed that *I felt as I were looking at an infernal divinity* gloating over the misfortune which had befallen the house" [my emphasis, ibid., 289].

The story is all the more driven to a supernatural explanation after the narrator asked the bride about the unfortunate Alphonse. On her nuptial night, she goes to bed before her husband. Then she hears the bedroom door opens and someone come in: "A moment later the bed creaked *as though it were burdened with an enormous weight.* [...] and she felt the touch of something *as cold as ice*" [ibid., 289-90]. The comparative expressions such as "as though" and "as...as" strongly suggest a supernatural murderer. And shortly after this dreadful touch, her husband enters and then "she heard *a stifled cry.* [...] Then she turned her head... and saw, so she says, her husband on his knees by the bed, with his head on a level with the pillow, in the arms of *a sort of greenish giant who was embracing him with all its might*" [ibid., 290]. And Madame Alphonse repeats it over and over to the narrator that she recognizes the murderer as "the bronze Venus, Monsieur de Peyrehorade's statue." It is an option to judge Madame Alphonse as mad in response to the trauma, and deny her testimony as witness. However, readers are rather beguiled into the supernatural interpretation of the mysterious murder. Even the *post scriptum* added to the story suggests the forever infernal power of the statue: *"it would seem that* an evil fate pursues those who possess that piece of bronze [the statue has been melted down by Madame de Peyrehorade]. Since that bell began to ring in Ille, the vines have twice been frost-bitten" [ibid., 292]. It is evident that the application of figurative expressions of condition and comparison functions efficiently in unfolding the mysterious plot by suggesting the supernatural intrusion in the middle of realism.

In similar fashion, the conditional expression is a common rhetoric in Poe's tales that features a homodiegetic narrator as the witness. More often than not, the narrator witnesses the whole process of the hero's horrible and strange experience and focuses his vision on the hero. The common use of conditional "as if" is inclined to be taken literally to make the fantastic possible. The horrible scene towards the end of "The Fall of the House of Usher" is deployed simultaneously with the reading of the unfolding plot of the medieval romance 'Mad Trist' where Ethelred slays the dragon through the continual expressions of modalization:

> "No sooner had these syllables passed my lips, than – *as if* a shield of brass had indeed, at the moment, fallen heavily upon a floor of silver." [...] "I saw that he spoke in a low, hurried, and gibbering murmur, *as if* unconscious of my presence." [...] "*As if* in the superhuman energy of his utterance there had been found the potency of a spell – the huge antique panels to which the speaker pointed threw slowly back, upon the instant, their ponderous and ebony jaws." [my emphasis, Poe 1994, 162-163]

In this manner, Poe dexterously manipulated the figurative expressions, from the aforementioned *mise en abyme*, through hyperbole and culminating with modalization, to make the bleak Gothic house collapse before the eyes of the narrator-witness.

In the situation of a represented narrator who confesses his personal experience, the expressions of modalization appear even stronger in creating consternation, which brews the inescapable supernatural intrusion of the unknown power. Maupassant entrusted his autodiegetic narrator with repetitive speeches of modal expressions in "The Horla." The description of the insecure feeling of being harassed by an unknown being is deployed with numerous modal expressions and comparisons: "I also feel somebody approach me, look at me, touch me, climb on my bed, touch me, kneel on my chest, take my neck between his hands and squeeze... squeeze... with his all his strength, trying to strangle me" [Maupassant 1998, 316]. In the following quotations, the insecure feeling becomes stronger and stronger until the culmination of the nearly delineated visage of the unknown being. "Little by little, however, an inexplicable uneasiness came stealing over me. Some force, it seemed to me, some occult force was slowing me down, stopping me, preventing me from going any farther, calling me back. I felt that distressing impulse to turn back [...]" [ibid., 332]. The rational narrator still doubts whether such hypersensitive perception is a psychological phenomenon: "I feel as if all this had happened to my spiritual being" [ibid., 333] and "Oh, if only I could leave it, if only I could go away, flee and never return! I should be saved, but I can't do it" [ibid., 334]. However, the sensation of this quasi-supernatural intrusion later appears more physical: "I had the impression that a page of the book lying open on my table had turned over by itself. Yet not a breath of air had come in through my window" [ibid., 336]. Eventually, it appears as a perceivable although "invisible" presence, there as a sort of reflection: "as if I were looking through a sheet of water" [ibid., 341]. This dreadful feeling is all the more intense as uncertainty and fear culminate to certainty, which leads to the narrator's resolution to terminate *it.*

Maupassant's "Night: A Nightmare" also applies such expressions to unfold the strange metamorphosis of night into devouring space and time. By the repetition of the ignorance of time, the narrator enunciates the ensuing incident by modal expressions of *feel* and *seem*: "For the first time I felt that something strange was going to happen, something new." "It seemed to be getting cold, that the air was becoming thicker, that night, my beloved night, was weighing heavily upon my heart" [Calvino, 399]. "What could the time be? It seemed to me I had been walking an infinite length of time" [ibid., 401]. The abundant use of comparison with "as" and "like" or simile in portraying the nocturnal scene transforms night into the devouring theriomorphic power. The coloration is vividly brought into play, initially as antiphrasis of the nocturnal imaginary but later returning to devouring diurnal images. The following depiction of the Champs-Elysées impresses readers with effect of animation:

> The chestnut trees, touched with yellow light, look as if they were painted, like phosphorescent trees. The electric bulbs, like pale dazzling moons, like eggs from the moon, fallen from heaven, like monstrous, living pearls, caused the streaks of gaslight, filthy, ugly gaslight and the garlands of colored, lighted glasses to grow pale beneath their pearly, mysterious and regal light. [ibid., 398]

The rhetoric of impressionist depiction of the street scene is ironically imbued with unnerving animated power that emerges synchronically with comparative expressions. This impressionist painting of Paris eventually deforms into muffling darkness, for the narrator's voice finds no echoes: "My voice vanished without an echo, weak, muffled, stifled by the night, the impenetrable night. I yelled: 'Help! Help! Help!' My desperate cry remained unanswered. What time was it? I pulled out my watch, but I had no matches" [ibid., 400]. The menacing night not only mutes the hero but also blinds him: "I resumed my walk like a blind man, feeling my way along the wall with my stick, and every moment I raised my eyes to the heavens, hoping that day would dawn at last. But the sky was dark, all dark, more profoundly dark than the city" [ibid., 401]. The animation of the nocturnal city takes place as the figurative expressions are taken literally.

The conditioning of fantastic emergence by modal expressions creates a synchronic effect of the intrusion of the unlikely and makes the text fantastic. Wilde also made extensive use of such figurative rhetoric to create a *fin-de-siècle* fantastic narration by the uncertain emergence of the first incident of the metamorphosis of Gray's picture, long after the first time he enunciated his wish to exchange his soul to stay forever young and beautiful:

> He started back *as if* in surprise. Then he went on into his own room, looking somewhat puzzled. After he had taken the buttonhole out of his coat, he *seemed to* hesitate. Finally he came back, went over to the picture, and examined it. In the dim arrested light that struggled through the cream-coloured silk blinds, the face *appeared to* him to be a little changed. The expression looked different. *One would have said* that here was a touch of cruelty in the mouth. It was certainly strange. [...] But the strange expression that he had noticed in the face of the portrait *seemed to* linger there, to be more intensified even. [Wilde 1994, 105]

The relation between modal expressions as figurative and the supernatural appearance is functional but not etymological like hyperbolic and set expressions, given that the apparition of fantastic elements is proceeded synchronically by a series of figurative expressions introduced by modalizing formula and comparisons. The reading is thus conditioned by the figurative expressions that precede the event.

The Significance of Enunciation

The above idiosyncrasy of figurative language in the mirror-discourse belongs to the enunciated trait. From the perspective of rhetoric as a whole, the level of enunciation (the instance of narration) that functions between the narrator/implied author and the reader/implied reader plays a crucial role especially in modern/postmodern stories. In realistic fantastic tales, enunciation often decides the reading orientation towards the supernatural or the strange. We will further explore the way enunciation affects the narrative voice and focalization that characterize the mirror-discourse. The importance of enunciation was highlighted by Todorov as he emphasized the uniqueness of first person narration: "In fantastic stories, the narrator usually says "I": this is an empirical fact that we can easily verify" (*Dans les histoires fantastiques, le narrateur dit habituellement "je": c'est un fait empirique que l'on peut vérifier facilement*) [Todorov 1970, 87]. To exemplify his assumption, Todorov adduced fantastic works such as *Le Diable amoureux, Manuscrit trouvé à Saragosse, Aurélia*, the tales of Gautier, the tales of Poe, "La Vénus d'Ille," "Inès de las Sierras," the stories of Maupassant and certain tales of Hoffmann [ibid., 87]. It is evident that, according to the examples quoted by Todorov, most fantastic tales of nineteenth-century Europe manifested a predilection for first person narration. Nonetheless, this selection is by no means exclusive; suffice it to take Gautier's tales and Hoffmann's tales for example. The heterodiegetic narrator (the third person) is also able to render the text ambiguous and make hesitation via mirror-discourse. In fact, the frequently quoted tale, "Véra," by Todorov to manifest the rhetoric of fantastic discourse and the hesitation between an allegorical and a literal reading of the work is narrated by an external narrator. Nevertheless, it is easier for a homodiegetic narrator to make use of the mirror-discourse to arouse doubt in readers, given that a represented character as narrator leaves his discourse open to be judged true or false and thus can create doubt.

Homodiegetic Narrator and the Requirement for a Narrative Pact

The central aesthetics of the mirror-discourse is to place the reader before a dilemma of doubt: believe or not? This skeptical reaction to fantastic narratives mainly derives from a Cartesian worldview. In the fantastic world, the "*Je pense, donc je suis*" (I think; therefore I am) is slightly modified into "*Je pense, donc j'en doute*" (I think; therefore I doubt). The effect of doubt, to doubt reality of the known realm before the mirror, is central to the fantastic tales poeticized by the mirror-discourse. On the other hand, if doubt is ruled out, readers tend to accept for true the unlikely story told by the narrator, for his homodiegesis at the same time suggests credibility. Moreover, the represented character who says "I" makes readers identify with a pronoun "I" that belongs to anyone, any ordinary person. Identifying with the narrator-character is by no means a delimitation of the ambiguous reading of the tale. This identification with the credible narrator will be followed by the stage of authentication, viz. readers still try to find a rational explication with the narrator who experiences the unlikely event. Moreover, this homodiegetic narrator is often an autodiegetic (when the narrator is also the hero) narrator and requires a special connivance between the narrator and the reader or rather implied reader.

The autodiegetic narrator or autodiegetic narrator tells his personal experience by implying elite readers at the start of the tale:

> You ask me, brother, if I have loved; yes. It is a strange and terrible story, and although I am sixty-six years old, I scarcely dare to stir the ashes of that memory. I am reluctant to refuse any request of yours, *but I would not tell such a story to any soul less tempered by experience.*
>
> The events are so strange that I cannot believe that they ever happened to me. For more than three years I was the victim of an extraordinary, diabolical obsession. I, a poor country priest, led every night in a dream (pray God it was a dream!) the life of a lost soul, a voluptuary, a Sardanapalus. [my emphasis, Calvino, 229]

The highlighted clause shows the implication of a narrative pact and also an intention to convince the reader. The social position of the represented narrator as a priest intensifies the credibility of the fantastic tale. This interplay of an autodiegetic narrator opens to doubt. In addition, a credible identity of the speaker leads to the eventual effect of ambiguity and hesitation of the mirror-discourse. The end of the story appears all the more convincing as it is presented as confession from a brother to a catholic seminar: "There, brother, is the story of my youth. Never look on a woman, but go with your eyes fixed on the ground, for chaste and steadfast as you may be, one minute may make you lose Eternity" [ibid., 259].

Among fantastic writers, Poe is a master of manipulating the autodiegetic narrator. This does create realistic fantastic tales with the artistry of sensation. His employment of autodiegetic narration enhances his philosophy of composition to create an effect of totality. Different from the autodiegetic narrator in the romantic fantastic tale that uses abundant modal expressions to unfold the inexplicable incident, Poe's narrator often speaks firmly of what he intends to utter with indicative expressions of exaggeration of his sensations. This affirmative tone of the narrator with hyperbole ironically arouses doubt in readers towards the narrated story. Some examples of his tale's beginnings with the enunciation of the narrator manifest well this unique narrative technique:

> Let me call myself, for the present, William Wilson. The fair page now lying before me need not be sullied with my real appellation. This has been already too much an object for the scorn – for the horror – for the detestation of my race. To the uttermost regions of the globe have not the indignant winds bruited its unparalleled infamy? [...]
>
> I would not, if I could, here or to-day, embody a record of my later years of unspeakable misery, and unpardonable crime. [...] Have I not indeed been living in a dream? And am I not now dying a victim to the horror and the mystery of the wildest of all sublunary visions? [Poe 1994 *Selected*, 96]

The narrator tells his own experience of fighting with his eponymous namesake. The uncertainty about naming in the commencement of the story contrasts the ensuing affirmative tone of the narrator relating each confrontation with his double. Even in the middle of his narration, the narrator elucidates again the naming issue: "In this narrative I have therefore designated myself as William Wilson, – a fictitious title not very dissimilar to the real" [ibid., 101]. Ambiguity lies in the narrator's precarious mental status and the real existence of a mysterious namesake that appears as his conscience.

If the narrator in the above tale appears moderate in relating his horror, the narrators in other tales such as "The Tell-Tale Heart" and "The Black Cat" sound intense and flaming, in a way that drives readers into the realm of darkness, especially the unknown psychological corner. In the beginning of the first tale, the narrator announces with indicative sentences that he is not mad and claims his sanity and acute senses:

> True! – nervous –very, very dreadfully nervous I had been and am; but why will you say that I am mad? The disease had sharpened my senses – not destroyed – not dulled them. Above all was the sense of hearing acute. I heard all things in the heaven and in the earth. I heard many things in hell. How, then, am I mad? Hearken! and observe how healthily – how calmly I can tell you the whole story. [Poe 1994, 221]

The narrator "soberly" describes the detailed process of his murder of the old man and his confession of the crime. He tries to prove to readers the unknown dark power that reigns over him. However, ambiguity in such a genre of narration is even sharper as the narrator firmly addresses his sanity with indicative expressions but is ironically suspected to be mad.

A similar instance happens in "The Black Cat," in which the narrator not only murders his black cat but also his wife for no reason. The story opens with the sober and stable expressions of the narrator:

> For the most wild yet most homely narrative which I am about to pen, I neither expect nor solicit belief. Mad indeed would I be to expect it, in a case where my very senses reject their own evidence. Yet, mad am I not – and very surely do I not dream. But to-morrow I die, and to-day I would unburden my soul. My immediate purpose is to place before the world, plainly, succinctly, and without comment, a series of mere household events. In their consequences, these events have terrified – have tortured – have destroyed me. Yet I will not attempt to expound them. To me, they have presented little but horror – to many they will seem less terrible than *baroques*. [Ibid., 189]

Poe's realistic fantastic narration foresaw the predominating narrative art elaborated by his followers. As mentioned before, the devil will later (towards the end of the nineteenth century) lose its shape to an abstract evil that is a part of mankind. Poe's fantastic tales that depict criminal psychology is revolutionary in fantastic storytelling. The core imaginary of the unknown is grounded in the human nature related to Devil. The doppelganger of "William Wilson" appears as the narrator's conscience when his evil side governs his behaviour. However, in "The Tell-Tale Heart" and "The Black Cat," the double as conscience does not take shape but is incorporated inside the narrator himself as a split personality and is only "visible" by its audible existence. Poe's rhetoric of mirror-discourse makes the mirror image sheer horror uttered through a seemingly paranoiac voice. Readers thus doubt the credibility of the autodiegetic narrator's perception.

Maupassant, who can be regarded as the French counterpart of Poe, staged a represented narrator, either hero or witness, to tell unlikely incidents. Most of his fantastic tales stress the disquieting space-time and material, especially the element water. In the afore-quoted "Night: A Nightmare," the fantastic arises as the

autodiegetic narrator is devoured by the horrible and uncertain power, albeit he
habitually adores night:

> I love night passionately. I love it as one loves one's country or one's mis-
> tress. I love it with all my senses, with my eyes, which see it; with my sense of
> smell, which inhales it; with my ears, which listen to its silence; with my
> whole body, which is caressed by its shadows. [...]
> In the daytime I am tired and bored. The day is brutal and noisy. I rarely get
> up, I dress myself languidly, and I go out regretfully. [...]
> But when the sun goes down a confused joy invades my whole being. I
> awaken and become animated. [Calvino, 397]

The narrator's ostensive euphoria appears unnaturally exaggerated and causes
readers to suspect his credibility as he starts to be uncertain about time, as we
have illustrated before. The impression gained from Maupassant's process of
enunciation assimilates that of Poe's paranoiac genre of narration. Be it the
wicked nature of crime or the devouring unknown being, the realistic fantastic
narration centres on the image of darkness: night and human dark evil.

If Poe's narration is told retrospectively by an autodiegetic narrator, Maupassant's fantastic tale proceeds rather synchronically with the autodiegetic narration, though apparently in an illogical manner. The closure of the above quoted
story exemplifies this illogic: "I fully realized that I should never have the
strength to come up, and that I was going to die there... in my turn, of hunger,
fatigue and cold" [ibid., 405]. This fantastic narration of instant is idiosyncratic
to Maupassant's times that the effect is created by synchronicity. The ambiguity
remains unendingly unresolved since the narrator's stance is open to question.
Possible interpretation will fall between a veritable unknown nocturnal power or
monster that makes time freeze and merely a false vision by a mad speaker. This
is similar to the ambiguity created by Poe's tales.

As stated above, the interplay of doubting the represented narrator and getting convinced by his credible identity also appears with a non-hero homodiegetic narrator, often presented as a witness of the unlikely incident. This kind
of narration serves as a vital technique in many of Mérimée's fantastic tales. The
tale "The Venus of Ille" will be adduced again to illustrate this art of enunciation.
Readers tend to believe all the reports addressed by the narrator as the witness of
the events. The narrator endeavours to find all possible and reasonable explica-
tions for the murder of M. Alphonse and relates the incident in a neutral and rational tone. Precisely because of this, readers are more inclined to accept the supernatural interpretation. Synchronic with the narrator's observation of the
statue, readers also learn numerous indices of the statue's wicked nature and bad
omens. The represented narrator says "I" with his identity as a Parisian scholar
renders the story more convincing and thus attains the effect of doubt, in the
present case, to doubt the untrustworthy reality and rationality.

Science-Fiction writer, Wells also scrupulously employed a unique narrator to tell his fantastic stories to make them credible and doubtful at the same time. Like the stories of *The Time Machine* and *The Island of Dr Moreau* that are told by a narrator-witness, Wells's other fantastic stories are often told by a represented narrator as witness to relate the incidents, through an ambiguous perspective. The uncertain fantastic incidents are indeed invisible to our earthly eyes, according to Nature's law. The invisible phenomena, a ghost and the door to Eden, in "The Story of the Inexperienced Ghost" and "The Door in the Wall," are enunciated by such narrator-witnesses. Telling ghost or supernatural stories through such a voice resembles the feeling returning to listening to tales by the fireside. The stories are told by an average person like us, and yet they are distrustful since we never witness the unlikely, and others may always lie.

Contemporary writer Cortázar used a very new narrative rhetoric to tell a story of perpetual theme, metamorphosis, in "Axolotl." The autodiegetic narrator's enunciation in the inception shocks readers with "Now I am an axolotl":

> There was a time when I thought a great deal about the axolotls. I went to see them in the aquarium at the Jardin des Plantes and stayed for hours watching them, observing their immobility, their faint movements. Now I am an axolotl.
> I got to them by chance one spring morning when Paris was spreading its peacock tail after a wintry Lent. [Cortázar, 3]
> I decided on the aquarium, looked obliquely at banal fish until, unexpectedly, I hit it off with the axolotls. I stayed watching them for an hour and left, unable to think of anything else. [ibid., 3]

Astonished by the indicative statement of "I am an axolotl," readers are forced to grope for the "logic" into the labyrinth woven by the complication of the obscure real and unreal. The narrator's composed tone and unruffled manner, unlike the neurotic predisposition of Poe's and Maupassant's autodiegetic narrators, incites readers to think that maybe the language itself is mad and completely fantastic.

The represented narrator "I" was a common narrative technique employed by many fantastic writers during the nineteenth century. The mainstream literary form of Romantic and Post-Romantic or Symbolist poetry makes the speaker of poetry a first person narrator in fantastic narration. Literary ballads of the period, the speakers of which are naturally homodiegetic, also play an important role in telling fantastic stories in the poetic form. The homodiegetic narration facilitates the identification of the reader with the character, and the authentication together with the character. This interaction often makes the reader hesitate between the supernatural and the natural explanations and thus makes fantastic literature with the mirror-discourse ambiguous, hesitation felt or not.

Heterodiegetic Narrator with Internal Focalization – Following the Hero's Vision

Though ignored by Todorov while treating the enunciation of his theory of fantastic fiction, the heterodiegetic narrator is still important in manipulating the rhetoric of ambiguity and duality in fantastic literature. The interaction of identification between the reader and the represented narrator is not the concern under the present enunciation, yet the urge of authentication in the reader does not dissipate. Malrieu, modifying Todorov's exclusive definition of fantastic literature's homodiegetic narration, claimed that the heterodiegetic narrator in fantastic literature creates an even stronger sense of uncertainty and fear since such a narration denies the voice of the annihilated hero.

> In fantastic literature, the character staged by the third person narration is, literally, the one that can not say "I." The "he" is he who is not able to realize his constituent splitting, who is alienated without knowing it, who is not aware that he is also phenomenon [the supernatural phenomenon]. [...]
> [...] the he is the "no-person," the one that does not enter into the schema of communication, the one with whom, for one reason or other, the communication is cut. Whatever his nature, whatever the reasons for which his actions are told in the third person, it is strange to us, definitively cut from us.[72] [Malrieu, 136]

In the mirror-discourse, a heterodiegetic narrator identifies with the hero's suffering from the inexplicable intrusion of unknown phenomena. The heterodiegetic narration does not follow the narrative code of the conventional third person narration, like in the dream-discourse and the magician's hat-discourse. In the heterodiegetic mirror-discourse, the narrator often identifies with the hero with a specific focalization, usually internal focalization with the hero's vision. This feature is further corroborated by the narrator's abundant use of *free indirect speech*. Therefore, he can voice out for the hero and act as his double. The narrator in Hoffmann's "The Sandman" can perfectly exemplify such kind of non-represented narrator, who yet says "I" as he (the implied author) addresses the implied readers "you":

---

[72] *Dans la littérature fantastique, le personnage mis en scène à la troisième personne est, littéralement, celui qui ne peut pas dire je. Le il est celui qui n'est pas capable de prendre conscience de son dédoublement constitutif, qui est aliéné sans le savoir, qui n'a pas conscience d'être aussi phénomène. [...] / [...] le il, c'est la « non-personne », celui qui n'entre pas dans le schéma de la communication, celui avec qui, pour une raison ou pour une autre, la communication est coupée. Quelle que soit sa nature, quelles que soient les raisons pour lesquelles ses actions sont rapportées à la troisième personne, il est étranger à nous, coupé définitevement de nous.*

> Nothing more strange and extraordinary can be imagined, gracious reader, than what happened to my poor friend, the young student Nathanael, and which I have undertaken to relate to you. Have you ever experienced anything that completely took possession of your heart and mind and thoughts to the utter exclusion of everything else? All was seething and boiling within you; your blood, heated to fever pitch, leaped through your veins and inflamed your cheeks. Your gaze was so peculiar, as if seeking to grasp in empty space forms not seen by any other eye, and all your words ended in sighs betokening some mystery. [Calvino, 48-49]

The narrator in the inception (following the epistolary narration) shows his sympathy for Nathanael and calls for readers' vicarious reading. The identification of the narrator with the hero is reinforced by his use of conditional expression and free indirect speech: "Nathanael felt *as if* a heavy burden that had been weighing him down to the earth was now rolled from off him, *nay, as if* by offering resistance to the dark power which had possessed him, he had rescued his own self from the ruin which had threatened him" [my emphasis, ibid., 56].

Furthermore, the narrator's portrayal of Clara in reality corresponds to Nathanael's own aesthetic viewpoint on her:

> I might now proceed comfortably with my narration, if at this moment Clara's image did not rise up so vividly before my eyes that I cannot turn them away from it, just as I never could when she looked upon me and smiled so sweetly. Nowhere would she have passed for beautiful; that was the unanimous opinion of everyone who professed to have any technical knowledge of beauty. [ibid., 52-53]

It is even difficult to discern the narrator's perspective on artistic creation from Nathanael's own:

> Everything, even his own life, was to him but dreams and presentiments. His constant theme was that every man who delusively imagined himself to be free was merely the plaything of the cruel sport of mysterious powers, and it was vain for man to resist them; [...] the inspiration in which alone any true artistic work [...] was the result of the operation directed inwards of some Higher Principle existing without and beyond ourselves.
>
> This mysterious extravagance was in the highest degree repugnant to Clara's clear intelligent mind, but it seemed vain to enter upon any attempt at refutation. [ibid., 52]

In addition, Nathanael's vision of the sandman or Coppola or Coppelius and his obsession with Olimpia bolstered by the contact of eyes are precisely re-perceived by the narrator through the exuberant diction of figurative expressions like "seem," "as if," and "he fancies." The narrator with this unique status in the story blurs the borderline between the real author, the represented narrator and the other characters. In this manner, readers tend to identify with the unfortunate hero as the narrator does. Even after the hero's death, readers continue to ponder on the horrible and inexplicable story with the narrator on the level of authentication, i.e. trying to find a rational explication to the hero's tragedy. It is clear that the heterodiegetic narrator is by no means a conventional omniscient one. The enunciation of the story is presented with subjectivity which still arouses doubt in the reader.

By the same token, the narrator in "Arria Marcella" obviously shows empathy for Octavian and acts as a spokesperson for him, who is denied speeches. In the circumstance where the narrator enunciates vicariously as the surrogate for the hero, the enunciated often overflows with free indirect speech to further demonstrate the narrator's identification with the hero. Confronting the seemingly metamorphosing space, Octavian's hesitation and doubt is represented by the narrator's discourse in free indirect speech: "Could his friends have had the same idea as he, and were they searching for him among the ruins? These half-glimpsed forms, these faint sounds of footsteps – could it be Max and Fabio chatting as they strolled, and disappearing around a corner?" [Kessler, 129].

The narration's play of mirror that reflects the hero's confusing status serves as the *mise en abyme* of readers' expected reading process of fantastic literature of the mirror-discourse:

> Just a moment before, in the deceiving darkness of night, he had been prey to that unease which plagues even the most intrepid souls *when faced with troubling, fantastic phenomena that reason in powerless to explain.* His vague alarm had turned to profound astonishment; the clarity of his perceptions made it impossible for him to doubt the evidence of his senses, yet what he beheld was *utterly incredible.* – Still unconvinced, he began to make mental note of small details in order to prove to himself that *he had not fallen victim to a hallucination.* – *Surely* these were not phantoms gliding before his eyes, for the brilliant sunlight imbued them with an unmistakable air of reality, and they cast long morning shadows over the sidewalks and the walls. [my emphasis, ibid., 132]

During the hero's visit to the ruin of the Arria family, the vivid depiction of Octavian's feeling seems to be the narrator's own: "Octavian followed behind, *appearing more moved than* his carefree companions by the fate of these mortals dead for two thousand years" [ibid., 123]. The reaction of Octavian after being introduced to the very spot where Arria was found strengthens the ambiguity between the hero's genuine supernatural travel into the past and his own somnambulism. Unable to voice out his keen emotion, Octavian's silence is uttered by the narrator's visualization of such abstract feeling. The narrator's penetration into the hero's mind makes the two merged as one identity. The ambiguous voice enhances the uncertainty of the hero's nocturnal fantastic experience:

> *His chest heaved, his eyes were moist with furtive tears*: this catastrophe, effaced by twenty centuries of oblivion, *moved him as though it were a recent tragedy*. The death of a mistress or a dear friend could not have grieved him more; and while Max and Fabio had their backs turned, *a tear fell*, belated by two thousand years, on the very spot where she *who had awakened in him a retrospective love had perished*, suffocated in the fiery ash of the volcano." [my emphasis, ibid., 125]

From describing the external reactions and traits of Octavian to the clear frame of mind, the narrator continues to speak for the melancholic hero and sees with him. He depicts the thought of the hero that may explain the ensuing incident: "Octavian, sunk in regret at not having been in Pompeii on the day of Vesuvius's eruption, so that he might have rescued the lady with the golden rings and so earned her love, had heard nothing of this gastronomical conversation" [ibid., 125]. The hero's frame of mind is further explored from the perspective of his unique aesthetics for women. Having the narrator associate him with Faust additionally foreshadows the impending metamorphosis of time-space to enable him to see his ideal woman. The narrative tone that describes the hero's comments on women and his fascination with the women in art again blurs the boundary between the narrator and the hero:

> As for Ocrtavian, he readily admitted that reality held no great charm for him. Not that he gave himself up to schoolboy dreams, strewn with lilies and roses like a madrigal by Demoustier, but every beautiful woman was surrounded by too many prosaic and disenchanting accessories [...] Like Faust, he had loved Helen, and his deepest wish was that the undulations of the centuries should bring him one of those sublime incarnations of human dream and desire, whose form, invisible to vulgar eyes, continues to exist in space and time" [ibid., 127-28].

Since the heterodiegetic narrator is profoundly integrated with the hero, readers have reason to distrust the narrator's words. Readers often follow the feelings and thought of the hero to interpret the unexpected intrusion of unknown phenomena. The visibility of the invisible is questioned on both sides of the reader and the hero: "The darkness and solitude was filled with invisible beings that his presence had disturbed, *he had stumbled into the midst of an enigma, a mysterious drama* that *seemed to* await the moment he should leave in order to begin" [my emphasis, ibid., 129]. The narrator's employment of modal expressions to paint the improbable nocturnal encounter with Arria reflects the hero's mind and the reader's doubt: "Exceedingly astonished, Octavian wondered *if he were half asleep*. He asked himself seriously *if* the hallucinations of madness *were not* dancing before his eyes, but was compelled to acknowledge that *he was neither dreaming nor mad*" [my emphasis, ibid., 130].

The tone of the narrator, objective or subjective, often decides the directing discourse of the story. In the mirror-discourse, a heterodiegetic narrator acts as a double of the hero or tells the story with reticence to leave readers doubt and let them search for authentication. This reticence in enunciation is often brought into effect by the play of mirror. The effect of visual confusion further renders the whole narration equivocal. This play of mirror functions in Wilde's *The Picture of Dorian Gray*. Each time Gray stares into his portrait, a variation of mirror image, the narrator's description follows exactly the vision and inner reaction of the hero. Near the end of the story, Gray's contemplation upon the death of Basil is mediated by the narrator's voice to explicitly bring to light the interplay of soul, portrait and mirror. The mirror-discourse is even enhanced by the free indirect speech: "For it was an unjust mirror, this mirror of his soul that he was looking at. Vanity? Curiosity? Hypocrisy? Had there been nothing more in his renunciation than that?" [Wilde 1994, 254]. The frequent use of the free indirect speech, especially while enunciating Gray's viewpoint on art, makes it difficult to distinguish the narrator from Gray:

> Music had stirred him like that. Music had troubled him many times. But music was not articulate. It was not a new world, but rather another chaos, that it created in us. Words! Mere words! How terrible they were! How clear and vivid and cruel! One could not escape from them. And yet what a subtle magic there was in them! [ibid., 26]

This sympathetic narration of the hero's life sustains until the last murder plotted by the hero, to annihilate his own portrait, an ironic mirror-image as foul parody:

> But this murder [of Basil] – was it to do him all his life? Was he always to be burdened by his past? Was he really to confess? Never. There was only one bit of evidence left against him. The picture itself – that was evidence. He would destroy it. Why had he kept it so long? [...] It had brought melancholy across his passions. Its mere memory had marred many moments of joy. It had been like conscience to him. yes, it had been conscience. He would destroy it. [ibid., 255]

However, Wilde's manipulation of heterodiegetic narration is not limited to the ambiguity of the interchangeable identities between the hero and the narrator. At the closure of the story, the narrator completely distances himself from Gray to overlook the final scene of the story. Throughout the repetitive questioning by free indirect speeches, the narrator's conscience seems to be eventually regained after the hero kills his "monstrous soul-life." The narrator thereafter recovers his objective point of view: "Lying on the floor was a dead man, in evening dress, with a knife in his heart. He was withered, wrinkled, and loathsome of visage. It was not till they had examined the rings that they recognised who it was" [ibid., 256]. The narrator's employment of the impersonal pronoun for Gray has completely annihilated the human traits of the hero and has thus extracted from the permeating ambiguity of his identity with the sinful hero.

The Embedded Enunciation

The embedded enunciation in fantastic literature can be regarded as a consequence of meta-enunciation. Influenced by Hoffmann and urged to create a new narrative method to differentiate themselves from the fixed narrative code of fairy tales, Romantic writers of the fantastic intended to revolutionize their narrative skill. The narration is thus represented in the story as a meta-narration. Hoffmann was the first to demonstrate originality in narrative art and was widely copied. The realistic setting in the romantic fantastic is, strictly speaking, not different from fairy tales, for not all of the tales begin with the fixed code of "Once upon a time." Stressing on credibility and authentication of the fantastic story, writers revolutionized the enunciation of the story. They experimented with the homodiegetic, in particular autodiegetic, enunciation, which was thus thriving during the Romantic period. Along with this narrative technique, the embedded enunciation emerged, which is often coupled with a certain kind of meta-enunciation. Hoffmann meditated on an effective way of transmitting the story in the "The Sandman":

> Hence I was most powerfully impelled to narrate to you Nathanael's ominous life. I was completely captivated by the elements of marvel and alienness in his life; but, for this very reason, and because it was necessary in the very beginning to dispose you, indulgent reader, to bear with what is fantastic – and that is not a small matter – I racked my brain to find a way of commencing the story in a significant and original manner, calculated to arrest your attention. To begin with "Once upon a time," the best beginning for a story, seemed to me too tame; with "In the small country town S---- lived," rather better, at any rate allowing plenty of room to work up to the climax; or to plunge at once *in medias res*, "'Go to the devil!' cried the student Nathanael, his eyes blazing wildly with rage and fear, when the weather-glass peddler Giuseppe Coppola" – well, that is what I really had written, when I thought I detected something of the ridiculous in Nathanael's wild glance; and the history is anything but laughable. I could not find any words which seemed fitted to reflect in even the feeblest degree the brightness of the colours of my mental vision. [Calvino, 49-50]

This meditation on fantastic narration by the narrator as the implied author of "The Sandman" interprets the true meaning of the rhetoric of mirror-discourse: "Perhaps, too, you will then believe that nothing is more wonderful, nothing more fantastic than real life, and that all that a writer can do is to present it as 'in a glass, darkly'" [ibid., 50].

The counterpart of Hoffmann in French literature, Nodier, also commented on the fantastic genre and the narrative techniques of telling such stories by the voice of the narrator-author in the tales. In "La Fée aux miettes" (The Fairy of Crumbs), Nodier commented in the section of "To the reader who reads the prefaces" (*Au lecteur qui lit les prefaces*) [Nodier 1961, 167] on the fantastic genre by referring to Homer, Aesop and La Fontaine to demonstrate his faith in literary imagination. He further claimed that "to be interested in the fantastic tale, we have to be made to believe, and an indispensable condition to be made to believe is to believe" (*pour intéresser dans le conte fantastique, il faut d'abord se faire croire, et qu'une condition indispensable pour se faire croire, c'est de croire*) [ibid., 167]. He further illuminated the significant role of a lunatic narrator: "the good and real fantastic story of an epoch without beliefs could only be appropriately placed on the lips of a lunatic" (*la bonne et véritable histoire fantastique d'une époque sans croyances ne pouvait être placée convenablement que dans la bouche d'un fou*) [ibid., 170]. Throughout the author's meta-narration, the selection of Michel from an asylum of Glasgow to tell the story about the crumb fairy implies a scrupulous narrative art for writing a fantastic tale in Nodier's times.

Similar narrative reflections by the narrator-author abound in Nodier tales. In "Jean-François les Bas-Bleus" (Jean-François the Bluestockings), the narrator ponders on the condition for a good fantastic story: "The fantastic is a little out of date, and there is no harm. Imagination abuses too easily the easy resources; and then it does not make the good fantastic that it wants. The first essential condition for writing a good fantastic story would be to firmly believe in it and nobody believes in what he invents" (*Le fantastique est un peu passé de mode, et il n'y a pas de mal. L'imagination abuse trop facilement des ressources faciles ; et puis ne fait pas du bon fantastique qui veut. La première condition essentielle pour écrier une bonne historie fantastique, ce serait d'y croire fermement, et personne ne croit à ce qu'il invente*) [ibid., 362]. Nodier's insight into the fantastic genre and the importance of readers' believing and being made to believe is further developed in "Histoire d'Hélène Gillet" (The Story of Hélène Gillet) by the narrator-author's classifying the fantastic into different categories:

> But if you are curious about fantastic stories, I inform you that this genre demands more good sense and art than we ordinarily imagine; and at first, there are many kinds of fantastic stories.[73] [ibid., 330]
>
> To a true story, the merit of the teller is doubtlessly nothing. If his imagination comes to mix with the story, the embroidery highly risks ruining my canvas.

---

[73] *Mais si vous êtes curieux d'histoires fantastiques, je vous préviens que ce genre exige plus de bon sens et d'art qu'on ne l'imagine ordinairement ; et d'abord, il y a plusieurs espèce d'hisoires fantastiques.*

His principal artifice consists in hiding himself behind his subject.[74] [ibid., 331]

From the above examples of meta-narration in fantastic literature that set forth the technique of embedded narration, numerous fantastic stories that follow take on the artistic multi-level narration. The narrative variations encompass manuscripts or diaries found by a represented character, epistolary narration and the story told to an extradiegetic narrator by another character (intradiegetic narrator).

In the embedded narration of the fantastic, an extradiegetic narrator often finds manuscripts and diaries so as to disclose the unlikely strange story narrated by the intradiegetic narrator in the rediscovered document. Earlier fantastic tales, if not disguised in satire or a fairytale style of narration, often utilized the embedded narration to ward off probable reproach of telling supernatural or irrational stories. Moreover, this kind of narrative technique reinforces the credibility of the story because the first narrator as represented character may lie but the narrator in the concealed and private documents has no reason to lie. Examples of discovered manuscripts appear in the following works: Potocki's *The Manuscrit trouvé à Saragosse*, James's *The Turn of the Screw*, Borel's "Gottfried Wolfgang," etc.

The enunciation performed in "The Turn of the Screw" is even more complicated. At the beginning of the story, a character using first person says, "The story had held us, round the fire, sufficiently breathless, but except the obvious remark that it was gruesome, as, on Christmas eve in a old house, a strange tale should essentially be, [...]" [James, 7]. Then another represented character, Douglas, is asked to tell his friends around the fire a story of "sheer terror." He discloses that the story he is going to share with his friends is written and is laid in a locked drawer. The manuscript is indeed a "woman's. She has been dead these twenty years. She sent [him] the pages in question before she died" [ibid., 8]. The story in question concerns a governess who seems to see a ghost and fights against the forces of evil to protect her pupils. Douglas suggests a psychological interpretation of the perception of the ghost by her repressed passion for her employer, the young and handsome uncle of her pupils. Douglas even comments on the reading of the story in relation to the governess's unrequited love: "The story *won't* tell [who she was in love with], [...] not in any literal, vulgar way" [ibid., 10]. The homodiegetic narrator claims that the present version of the story comes from the manuscript handed by Douglas: "[T]his narrative, from an exact transcript of my own made much later, is what I shall presently give. Poor Douglas, before his death – when it was in sight – committed to

---

[74] *A une histoire vraie, le mérite du conteur est sans doute peu de chose. Si son imagination vient s'en mêler, la broderie risque fort de me gâter le canevas. Son principal artifice consiste à se cacher derrière son sujet.*

me the manuscript [...] he began to read to our hushed little circle on the night of the fourth" [ibid., 11]. Moreover, the title of the story is in fact given by the extra-homodiegetic narrator. Accordingly, the narration of the story possesses three layers of enunciation that imposes the rendering of ambiguity upon readers. The intricate enunciation of the present story is contrived by the writing of the manuscript and a represented character, who narrates to another represented character, who transcribes the situation following the manuscript.

Diaries serve as another efficient way to transmit inexplicable experiences. The diary form is often presented directly without the interference of a character; however, readers may imagine a certain person who finds the diary and discloses it to readers. Maupassant's "Le Horla" is in fact presented in a diary form, written by the hero who suffers from an unknown creature called the Horla. Since the story is presented as a diary, the ambiguity between reading the story as a real event and as the illusion of the mad hero easily emerges. A manuscript or diary kept by an individual may elicit the essential effect of the mirror-discourse, doubt, which is the very effect of the above cited works. However, diaries and letters kept by many writers create a reverse aesthetic effect. This forms a collective witness that turns out to be an objective voice telling the incredible story. Under this circumstance, *Dracula* is taken eventually as a story of a vampire without doubt, albeit doubt permeates the inception of the novel. Therefore, Dracula will be further analyzed in the next section, on the magician's hat-discourse.

Epistolary narration has been popular since the eighteenth century. This unique method served as an appropriate narrative medium for fantastic storytelling during the nineteenth century due to the domination of rationalism that would rebuke fantastic tales for being superstitious or irrational. The decision chosen by the narrator or implied author of "The Sandman" to commence Nathanael's story with letters from many possible sources exemplifies one important feature of telling fantastic tales: credibility. The narrator reasons as below:

> I determend not to begin at all. So I pray you, gracious reader, accept the three letters which my friend Lothair has been so kind as to communicate to me as the outline of the picture, into which I will endeavour to introduce more and more colour as I proceed with my narrative. [...]
> In order to make the beginning more intelligible, it is necessary to add to the letters that, soon after the death of Nathanael's father, Clara and Lothair, the children of a distant relative, who had likewise died, leaving them orphans, were taken by Nathanael's mother into her own house. [Calvino, 50]

With the underlying meta-narration as the theory of telling fantastic tales addressed by the narrator in "The Sandman," Hoffmann used this device in many of his tales.

In "A New Year's Eve Adventure," the story of losing one's mirror reflection is narrated via the manuscript of the character-victim (the little man in brown, Erasmus Spikher) that is received by another character who is shown in the first person. This autodiegetic narrator is also embedded in the journal sent to Hoffmann himself, which is demonstrated in "Foreword by the Editor" and "Postscript by the Traveling Enthusiast." Hoffmann brings into play the *mise en abyme* of reading and telling process both on the enunciating level and in the enunciated content. The narrator seems to be enchanted by and in love with an Italian woman, Julia Giuletta. He comes across a little man in brown and Peter Schlemihl (Chamisso's famous character who loses his shadow under a certain pact with the devil) and meets the little man again in his own room at the hotel. The next morning, the strange man disappears. Just as the narrator reckons the incident to be only "an exceptionally vivid dream," he finds a manuscript: "a fresh manuscript, whose content I am sharing with you, since it is unquestionably the remarkable story of the little man in brown. It is as follows" [Hoffmann 1967, 115]. Then the subtitle of "The Story of the Lost Reflection" is presented. Strictly speaking, the story is narrated on three levels: the editor, the narrator who keeps the journal and the narrator who tells his miserable experience of losing his reflection. Todorov analyzed this tale of Hoffmann as inclining towards allegory in terms of the representation of shadow, reflection and social position. Because Todorov excluded allegory from the fantastic genre, he disqualified this tale from being classified as such. Nevertheless, according to our detailed studies, fantastic literature offers the option of allegorical and literal appreciation, which is also acknowledged by Tolkien. This is indeed a matter of reader-response perspective. The narrative rhetoric of the tale fits well the mirror-discourse and thus creates an effect of ambiguity.

Mary Shelley also employed embedded narration in her Gothic story of *Frankenstein*. Four letters, written by R. Walton to his sister Mrs Saville, head up the core story of Frankenstein. The four letters take on the role of the prologue to the main narrative and help to establish the credibility of the story, since the letters are sent to the captain's sister. Through the letters, the reader may trust the real existence of the scientist Frankenstein, for Walton describes as a matter of fact to his sister his encounter and communication with him. The central enunciation of the story told by Frankenstein to Walton is embedded within the frame of the letter, though readers are presented with the subtitles of fourteen chapters that dilute the impression of reading letters. The enunciation of Frankenstein ends with his resort to Walton to satisfy his vengeance in his death if "the ministers of vengeance should conduct him [the monster] to [Walton]" [Shelley, 595]. Walton continues the narration by four more letters to his sister to tell the sequel to the story of Frankenstein. In the closing letters, Walton encounters the monster created by Frankenstein and reports the monster's annihilating himself to follow his master: "He sprung from the cabin-window, as he said this, upon the ice-raft which lay close to the vessel. He was soon borne away by the waves, and lost in darkness and distance" [ibid., 606]. Just like the end of the monster remains uncertain with the vague billows, the story of Frankenstein wavers in ambiguity to arouse doubt and authentication.

By the same token, Stevenson also resorted to embedded narration to tell his famous uncanny and unlikely fantastic tale of science-fiction. He elaborated his narrative to relate, in a credible manner, the story concerning the tragic event of Dr Jekyll. He endowed the reputed and rational lawyer Mr Utterson with the narrative voice: "a man of a rugged countenance, that was never lighted by a smile; cold, scanty and embarrassed in discourse" [Stevenson, 9]. The credibility of the story is reinforced by the inclusion of a number of documents presented by analeptic narrative. These are Dr Jekyll's will, the closure of the story with Dr Lanyon's Narrative, which in turn contains a letter from Jekyll and Lanyon's response to it, and Jekyll's "Full Statement of the Case." Note that both Lanyon and Jekyll are scientists and are thus credible. The effect created by the above reciprocity of narrative variation, essentially the shift of point of view, creates suspense to intensify the novel's concentration on the double by the gradual uncovering of horror.

Semantic and Formal Syntax – Form Leading to Content

The mirror-discourse contains two elements that eventually converge into syntax of antithesis. These are interpreting figurative language as literal on the enunciated level to bring the supernatural into play, and representing a homodiegetic narrator-character or a heterodiegetic narrator through the vision with the hero This antithesis in reality mirrors Todorov's assumption that the central aesthetics of the fantastic is to demand doubt. The fantastic imposes upon readers the dilemma of "to believe or not to believe" by the antithetic rhetoric of ambiguity. Nevertheless, Todorov interpreted the employment of figurative language in fantastic writings as an illustration of his claim that the fantastic finds its origin in figurative expressions, and that the supernatural is only born from language. Holding a converse perspective from Todorov's interpretation, we conclude that fantastic creation crystallizes the true meanings of figurative language. Reversely, rhetorical language finds its origin in fantastic creation and it is probable that language is born with the supernatural or with the unknown. In like manner, Jung, Bachelard, Durand, Barfield and Tolkien all valued semantic significance of myth as the primeval language, the imagery of which is analogous to that of fantastic imagination.

In light of Jung's imaginary archetypes, the antithetic syntactic structure of the mirror-discourse is grounded in the archetype of shadow against ego. This antithesis generates dynamism of actions in the story. In the mirror-discourse, the protagonist undergoes the experience of opposites in psychological life. This experience reflects the psychological fact that whatever is in the ego complex has its mirror "opposite" in the unconscious. A controlling ego will be matched by disorder in the unconscious. The mirror-discourse in fantastic literature brings into play the looming visualization of the character's monstrous double or the invisible and the unknown realm in/behind the mirror. This visualization as mirage emerges through the unique linguistic employment of figurative language that implies a realization of the meanings. This is also an inversion from modal expressions to certain indicative expressions, i.e. the figurative to the literal. The play of mirror revolves around the ambiguity of "as if the prince was a frog" and "the prince is also a frog" or "the frog seems to contain a potential prince" and "the frog contains a potential prince." This underlying imaginary of the antithetic structure is illustrated by Jung's insight:

> Since conscious thinking strives for clarity and demands unequivocal decisions, it has constantly to free itself from counter-arguments and contrary tendencies, with the result that especially incompatible contents either remain totally unconscious or are habitually and assiduously overlooked. The more this is so, the more the unconscious will build up its counterposition. [Jung 1977, xvii]

More often than not, the rhetoric of mirror-discourse designs a tragic end for the hero. To use Jung's language, this is a representation of the fall of individualization. Different from the accomplishment of individualization represented in the dream-discourse as studied before, the mirror-discourse often reflects the image of destruction and fall.

If material imagination of the four elements constructs a harmonious structure in the dream-discourse, the mirror-discourse accentuates the disorder of the imaginary of water and fire that brings about fall and destruction. The mirror-discourse narratives are deemed as variations of the archetypal complexes of Narcissus and of Prometheus. For example, in "The Sandman," Nathanael's father follows the mysterious and devilish master Coppelius for some unknown experiment and is burned to death. The grown-up Nathanael's lodgement's being burned to ashes forces him to move next door to his professor who also deals with the devilish master named Coppola, who is later disclosed to be Coppelius. The momentum of the plot lies in the focus on vision and eyes, both watery and fiery. The end of the hero is obviously tragic, undergirded by the Narcissus complex that symbolizes a *fall*. Appropriately, Nathanael's death results from *falling* from a tower. The material structure of the mirror-discourse features the disharmony and antithesis of water and fire. The character menaced by the inexplicable intrusion of the unknown power is confused by the reality in/behind the mirror and is often doomed.

In a similar manner, the end of "William Wilson," *The Picture of Dorian Gray*, and *The Strange Case of Dr Jekyll and Mr Hyde* demonstrate the same structure of fall and destruction through elaborate mirror-discourse. The character represented by the mirror-discourse stays before the mirror and may enter it through visualization by language. Vampire figures can also be characterized in terms of mirror-discourse. Vampires do not have mirror reflection, yet still appear, or are still believed to appear, in the realm of our known world. The fantastic story is concerned with the blunt and objective intrusion of creatures like vampires from the unknown realm. The lack of reflection may result from their leaving the mirror to intrude our world.

Durand's theory on the structures of the imaginary explains the way converging images and depictions of uncertainty can be used to present horror and fall. The Durandian syntax of the fantastic story depends on the antithetic structure of the diurnal regime and the interplay between the former structure and the mystic structure of the nocturnal regime. The combination of the above structures saturated by the intrinsic images and expressions of dynamism will resort to the extrinsic dynamism and form a story. This story is far from a harmonious synthetic structure, but is rather a return to antithesis. The rationalism underlying the diurnal imaginary system defies the menace of time and death, thus the images of devouring, falling and ascending emphasize the pathological heroic structure. The central antithetic syntactic structure constructed through the mirror-discourse with equivocacy of transgression is manifest in the following phrasal forms of transgression: the antithesis as fantastic transgression, the ambiguous duality in characters and the inversion as the central rhetoric of transgression.

The first phrasal form of antithesis lies in the juxtaposition of the opposing elements. For example, the story of "The Beautiful Vampire" is presented as entirety of antithesis conjuring ambivalent atmosphere. The French title "La Morte amoureuse" (the English translation of title in fact kills the French rhetoric of oxymoron) begins with a play of oxymoron and the story ensues as the alternation and confusion between the real and the unreal, consciousness and dream, day and night. This antithesis develops further into the contrast between hot and cold, flesh and statue, angel and devil, and eventually, life and death. Similar manipulation of antithesis, especially between the poetic and prosaic, irrational and rational, insanity and sanity, human and nonhuman, constructs the plot of "The Sandman." Hawthorne also employed the antithesis between day and night or consciousness and dream as the central dynamism to function the ambiguity of the mirror-discourse.

The second phrasal structure is the ambiguous duality in characters. Characters themselves function as the plot momentum. Besides the above analysis of the narrator as represented character with ambiguous personality (e.g. Poe's and Maupassant's heroes) on the level of enunciation, the other supporting characters are often endowed with indeterminacy that enhances the narration. Such examples can be drawn from "The Venus of Ille," which features ambiguous characters to converge into two possible explanations for the quasi-supernatural incident. The statue is endowed with a double character, for it is both beautiful and evil. Ambiguity can also be found in the fiancée of M. Alphonse since she is beautiful and somewhat malicious as the statue Venus. The Spanish athlete whose stature and skin tone are assimilated with the statue offers another element for hesitation. This equivocacy across characters suggests a dual reading of the story. Similarly, in other tales Poe used the ambiguity of other supporting characters, including the cat in his "The Black Cat." The obscure identity of the second cat is apt to suggest the return of the ghost of the first cat, hanged by the hero. Likewise, in "Ligeia," duality in the hero's second wife Lady Rowena, who seems to be resurrected from the hero's first wife, suggests the return of his first wife Ligeia. This play of mirror in ambiguity and resurrection of the character was applied even earlier in Wilhelm Jensen's *Gradiva*. The ambivalence of the identity (a simply modern woman or a reincarnation of the model of the statue?) of the heroine, Zoe, evokes the confusion between fantastic appearance and hallucination.

Actions in the stories of the mirror-discourse appear less significant than those represented through the dream-discourse and the magician's hat-discourse. Ambiguity as the principal rhetoric in the mirror-discourse freezes the development of action. Often, description of action is interrupted by speculation, either from the hero or the narrator. The crux is, more often than not, stories along the ambiguous lines linger on the doubt about the antagonist's real existence. Hence, the action hinges on the continual dubious ambiguity until the eventual implausible denouement. Eventually, actions in stories of the mirror-discourse can be interpreted as the solving of an enigma.

Seeing action as enigma solving also explains the fact that detective or mystery stories are derived from fantastic tales with the mirror-discourse. For example, Poe is regarded as the precursor of modern detective stories. Both Robert Louis Stevenson and Sir Arthur Conan Doyle are his admirers. Poe's "The Murders in the Rue Morgue" has been a major influence on Doyle's detective stories of Sherlock Holmes. In *Dr Jekyll and Mr Hyde*, the culminating point of the syntactic structure equals the revelation of Mr Hyde's true identity, which solves the mystery of Dr Jekyll's will drafting, behaviour and gloomy mood. The climax of "The Venus of Ille" arises with the scene of M. Alphonse's murder, which solves the enigmatic duality of Venus's being good or evil, inanimate or animated. Similar to the unfolding of the Jekyll story that closes with the denouement of destruction, Wilde's *The Picture of Dorian Gray* and Poe's "William Wilson," end with the death of the heroes, through their annihilating their doubles and ironically bringing about their own destruction. Unlike the distinct unambiguous solution of the enigma in detective stories, fitting Todorov's criteria for the uncanny or strange story, the ends of the above three stories of double are not veritable enigma solving. A perpetual puzzle of unsolved riddles

continues to impose upon readers or characters who uncover the preliminary solution. The other tales under the same category of the well constructed rhetoric
of mirror produce the same effect of opening to unending ambiguity. For example, the doubt about the grim sandman does not dissipate after the death of Nathanael, and "The Venus of Ille" drives the narrator and readers into a hesitation
for good.

This dubiousness may be apprehended as the ambiguous effect of narrative
in the light of Poe's philosophy of composition. Disdaining the composition under "a species of fine frenzy – an ecstatic intuition," Poe claims a scrupulous
philosophy for composing a good work with artistic totality or unity of effect.
The conscientious composition stressing the *mise en abyme*, the interplay of
figurative and literal expressions and, in particular, the enunciation deliberation
is manifest in the unique effect of the mirror-discourse. The syntactic structure
of the mirror-discourse can eventually be formalized, according to Todorov's
analysis, as one of irreversibility of time with or without gradation. It requires
linear and continual reading and accentuates the time of perception of the work.
It is true that irreversibility is needed at the level of denouement, viz. the destruction of the hero or the unknown phenomenon. However, identification and
authentication couched in the process of reading invite a second reading of the
story, even after the unknotting denouement.

In recapitulation, the mirror-discourse ultimately questions the formalization
of figurative language and arouses readers to return to literal semantism through
the isotopism of modal expressions. The play of visualizing the imaginary invites readers to doubt, and imposes literal crystallization upon modal expressions, from ambiguity of the story to participation of fantastic semantism. The
interplay of figurative expressions through diachronism and synchronism makes
the fantastic story an alchemical furnace that refines language into a semantic
unity of the figurative and the literal. Although underpinned by the imaginary of
the unknown, the syntactic structure of the mirror-discourse hinges on the form,
viz. the elaborate contrivance of the enunciation with the purposely enunciated
expressions of figure. Mirror-discourse represents, through ambiguity, the insecurity and uncertainty of the imaginary that is governed by the subject confronted with time-space, the subject himself, other humans and the nonhuman.
Ambiguity gives rise to doubt and forces us to share fear. Therefore, in the mirror-discourse, it is the form that decides the content. Nonetheless, in harmony
with the teleological creation of fantastic literature studied before, the linguistic
and mathematical form of fantastic tales is the artistic medium for ultimately
revealing spiritual and semantic structures of the universal imaginary of mankind.

The Magician's Hat-Discourse

If the mirror-discourse hinges rather on the form of the tale than its content, the magician's hat-discourse depends on the content to render its unique form. In contrast to the mirror-discourse, the magician's hat explicitly represents fantastic imagery through the rhetoric of hypotyposis, which resembles the hypotyposis in the dream-discourse but varies from it in the way characters, actions and time-space are organized. To use a musical metaphor, the dream-discourse is a symphony, whereas the magician's hat-discourse is a sonata. The former emphasizes the musical harmonization of a holistic narrative unity; the latter rejoices over engrossing storytelling.

As in real life, where the magician's hat is able to make the visible invisible and the invisible visible, the magician's hat-discourse metamorphoses the unknown into the perception of the known by the astuteness of sensational storytelling. This telling about the unknown highlights a certain spot of the collective unconscious. It can be associated with what Aristotle termed as the simple epic or the epic derivative as legend and folktale. Different from the mirror-discourse that uses the modal expression of "as if" to manipulate belief, the discourse of the magician's hat boasts its hypotyposis of the unknown elements to lure its readers into its created ambiance to experience the situation of "what if." As stated before, fantastic works composed with the dream-discourse can be deemed as Aristotelian complex epic, in which the hero achieves individuation. With a slight difference from the dream-discourse, the rhetoric of the magician's hat features a process of partial individuation (in a strict sense, not just mere success in a quest), inasmuch as the representation of the unknown and the characters are on a scale of miniature or microcosm, whereas the dream-discourse constructs poetic macrocosm. In terms of the settings of the fantastic, different from the complete aesthetic secondary time-space of the dream-discourse and from the realistic time-space of the mirror-discourse, the magician's hat-discourse caters to the curious and magic taste of readers. It craftily metamorphoses realistic settings into the unknown realm or brings imaginary creatures into our realistic settings.

The main distinctive features that discriminate the present discourse from the first two types are the close focus on the particular and the absence of ambiguity in representing unknown elements. In accordance with the aforementioned metaphor of the immense sea vis-à-vis the spindrifts, the magician's hat-discourse can be seen as the perfect *mise en abyme* to the dream-discourse. *La fantastique* is mediated by the rhetoric of the magician's hat and incarnated into legends, fairy tales, folklores, ballads, most Chinese *zhiguai* or *shenguai*, Arabian tales and fables. The magician's hat dexterously transforms all elements mainly through hypotyposis, interplaying either with antithesis or antiphrasis, before the eyes of a variety of audiences, who may be superstitious, unsuperstitious or skeptical. Many critics of fantastic literature embrace a strict and limited perspective and are inclined to exclude the fantastic works narrated through the rhetoric of the magician's hat, viz. under the rhetoric of hypotyposis to transmit the imaginary. They often prefer the narratives of mirror-discourse that fabricates uncertainty and ambiguity as the essence of fantastic narration.

This bias can be emphasized again in the light of Durand's theories of the imaginary and Barfield's conscious evolution. The rationalistic spirit engrained in alpha-thinking corresponds to the attachment of the isotopism of images that cluster into the schizomorphic structures of the diurnal regime. Accordingly, most critics agree on the tragic end as a common closure for fantastic narratives; on the contrary, narratives with happy endings are often dismissed from the corpus for fantastic theorization. Critics with such a vision try to group them under the category of fairy or supernatural tales or the marvellous (*"le merveilleux"* proposed by French critics). However, the category of the fantastic discourse akin to the fairy tale is not as simple as critics have stated. Variations exist among the realistic fantastic, the Kafkaesque fantastic, fairy tales, Tolkienian fairy-stories, oriental supernatural stories, and fables. These various forms and contents of the fantastic also feature common elements raised in strictly defined fantastic fiction, such as themes of double and monstrosity. Since the human imagination is dominated by confrontation with time and death, the representation of fantastic imagination will naturally depend on the diurnal and nocturnal orientation of the anthropological imaginary. For example, a vampire story can be narrated by means of mirror-discourse centring on hesitation and ambiguity (e.g. Gautier's "The Beautiful Vampire"); it can also be narrated by means of the magician's hat-discourse (e.g. most modern vampire stories like the classic *Dracula* and contemporary famous vampire chronicles created by Anne Rice). Therefore, an exclusive definition of the fantastic genre that merely stresses the uniqueness of narrative enunciation would contradict the universal imagination of men and thus probably lead the studies of fantastic literature into an impasse.

Many authors like the mirror-discourse because their imagery focuses on the aesthetics of death within the diurnal regime. This is under the influence of their cultural background. The notion of the aesthetics of death is well expounded in Michel Guiomar's theory. He distinguishes the fantastic from the marvellous by the tendency of imagination faced with death. He claims that the fantastic is dramatic and tragic and always finishes badly; in contrast, the marvellous is happy and beneficial. While the fantastic uncovers the extremity of human condition, the problem of which is death, the marvellous disregards or gets out of braving the problem. Consequently, "the marvellous is a lie of man to himself, the fantastic is a lie of the Universe to man" [Guiomar, 259]. By the same token, Guiomar distinguishes these two genres by the reader's situation: a solitary and isolated state for the reader of the fantastic, a collective and shared experience for the reader of the marvellous. The situation of readers of the fantastic reminds us of the Romantic themes. This individual state of the hero and the reader in the fantastic coincides with the individualistic and confidential tendency of Romanticism. It is true that the aesthetics of death plays a vital role in the rendering of tragic or comic end of fantastic imagination; however, fantastic or marvellous creation is more than a linguistic lie with an antithetic ending. Our earlier investigation of the imaginary underlying the poeticization of fantastic creation reveals that the essence of the genre resides in the unknown, not simply related to death. Therefore, the magician's hat-discourse, a distinctive technique of storytelling that generally corresponds to French marvellous narration, will be raised as a significant rhetoric that differentiates from the mirror-discourse.

Most French critics interpret the marvellous as one identical form, for example, "Once upon a time" is often referred to as a fixed incipit and the happy ending is considered as invariable. Different from this conventional viewpoint, Todorov discerned the variations of the marvellous genre. He defined the pure marvellous as a genre without limitation. In the case of the marvellous, supernatural elements provoke no particular reaction in either the character or in the reader [Todorov 1970, 59]. The fairy tale is only one of the varieties of the marvellous. He further distinguished the pure marvellous from other neighbouring marvellous kinds listed as follows: (1) the hyperbolic marvellous (e.g. *The Arabian Nights*), (2) the exotic marvellous (with depiction of unknown creatures), (3) the instrumental marvellous (staging elements like the magic carpet or the healing apple), and (4) the scientific marvellous (featuring supernatural powers such as magnetism) [ibid., 60-62]. This enumeration of various marvellous narratives, with the substratum of the supernatural, calls for further research of the narrative art that forms the marvellous. It is evident that Todorov had not considered fantasy (the most popular genre in our times along the lines of the fantastic) in his classification of the marvellous. According to the historical and realistic manifestation of the fantastic/marvellous genre, Todorov's well-defined fantastic literature proves to cover a minor form in comparison with the major form of the fairy-story, fantasy and even science-fiction. In this light, for the comprehensiveness of the studies of the fantastic genre, we propose a third rhetoric, the magician's hat-discourse, to encompass the different forms underpinned by the imagination of the unknown.

With emphasis on images deriving from the Jungian shadow archetype, the central dynamism of the story resides in the conflict of thesis and antithesis. The shadow figure can intrude into the setting recognized by the reader to challenge the protagonist and thus launching the ensuing adventure or strife. It is possible that the protagonist enters the unknown realm to encounter his/her shadow figure and thus unfolds the impending experience of strangeness. The other kernel archetypes as animas or animus, the wise old man and the Self are alternative to the rhetoric. For example, the frog holds potential for metamorphosing into a prince and vice versa. The above contrast launches the storytelling by drawing images from the unknown realm. In a parallel manner, as the mirror-discourse is characterized by metamorphosing respectively from the elements of water and fire, the magician's hat-discourse mainly revolves around any of the Bachelardian elements, a hypotyposis with the quality of air, earth, fire and water, which is connected to the diurnal or nocturnal imaginary regime. Metamorphosis in this third rhetoric includes all variations of material imagination to animate *la fantastique*. The magician's hat-discourse places more stress on the pleasure of mimesis that results in bewitching storytelling. Despite the examples with a tragic ending (based on the antithetic structure of the diurnal regime encountering the nocturnal), it often corresponds to the last of Tolkien's claimed elements for fairy-stories: consolation or Euchatastrophy. Different from the mirror-discourse whose content is rather defined by the form, the form of the explicit and vivid storytelling of the magician's hat-discourse mainly depends on the semantic elements or the content. The manipulation of the enunciation will cede to the significant levels of the enunciated and the syntax.

In the enunciation of the magician's hat-discourse, like in the dream-discourse, the narrator is mainly neutral and objective. The play of mirror is not considered essential to create doubt. On the other hand, the narrator (often the implied author) tells the stories to make believe (or without believing it, a paradoxical thesis proposed by Todorov) or to make the reader aware of the unknown realm. With the central rhetoric of hypotyposis incorporated into the mystic structure of nocturnal imagery, as opposed to the uncovering of uncertainty in diurnal schizomorphic structures, the magician's hat-discourse accentuates the representation of the story instead of paying attention to the narrator. This mode of enunciation is akin to that in the dream-discourse. Therefore, the enunciated takes on the decisive form of the fantastic. Spatial imagination will pilot our analysis of the rhetoric in question. It is divided into three aspects: (1) time-space grounded in the realism of man's law, (2) fables of the nonhuman and the discourse from theriomorphic space, and (3) language in harmony with Nature's law as spatial particles of chôra.

Time-Space Grounded in the Realism of Man's Law

This spatial selection of fantastic tales under the third rhetoric category is a frequent source of disagreement among theorists of the fantastic genre. Though often disregarded by French scholars, since the creation under such narrative technique is scanty in France, supernatural tales with a realistic setting are numerous in other cultures: the Arabian *Thousand and One Nights*, the majority of Chinese fantastic tales, English fantasy and ghost or vampire stories and Latin American fantastic tales of magical realism. Compared with the setting represented in the tale of the mirror-discourse, where the realistic traits prepare for the intrusion of implausible strangeness to intrigue readers to doubt, the realistic setting in the magician's hat-discourse serves as a striking contrast to the explicit depiction of the unlikely intrusion. It arouses readers' primitive imagination to believe, in reality, to vibrate with the very semantism of human imagination. The effect of strangeness, implausibility and absurdity is all the more intense in the fantastic stories narrated through the magician's hat-discourse, for example, Kafka's *Metamorphosis* and Gogol's "The Nose." It is also questionable to limit the definition of fantastic literature to realistic setting with ordinary characters when considering fairy tales. In addition, it is incorrect to consider fairy tales to commence with a fixed narrative code and thus delineating the genre simply by an identical start: "Once upon a time" or "There was once."[75] However, most tales start similarly to realistic fiction, and unfold a more surprising and strange plot by the rhetoric of hypotyposis on the unknown dimension. The beginning of Andersen's "The Little Mermaid" offers no sign of any supernatural intrusion: "Far out to sea the water is as blue as the petals on the loveliest cornflower and as clear as the purest glass. But it is very deep, deeper than any anchor rope can reach" [Andersen, 39]. The choice of water-space may be analogous to the mirror-discourse that prepares for the impending insecurity. Another tale of Andersen's can also exemplify this realistic feature, "The Shadow": "In the hot countries the sun can burn properly. People become as brown as mahogany all over; in the very hottest countries they are even burnt into negroes – but it was only to the hot countries that a learned man from the cold one had come" [Calvino, 317]. The inception of the tale, albeit realistic and sunny, conceals an impending horror under the sun – the betrayal of the hero's own shadow.

The difference between the tales under the mirror-discourse and the magician's hat-discourse with an analogous inception then is due to the different treatment of actions and characters. If some of Andersen's tales are still set in the narrative incipit with "There was once," despite the above examples, tales of Brothers Grimm and of Oscar Wilde are more enframed under realism. The Grimms' "Hansel and Grettel" starts narration in this manner: "Hansel one day took his sister Grettel by the hand, and said, 'Since our poor mother died we have had no happy days; for our new mother beats us all day long, and when we go near her, she pushes us away'" [Grimm, 126-127]. Likewise, the Grimms begin "The Nose" with a realistic question: "Did you ever hear the story of the three poor soldiers, who, after having fought hard in the wars, set out on their road home, begging their way as they went?" [ibid., 238]. This kind of interro-

---

[75] The Chinese version of "Once upon a time" or "很久很久以前 henjiu henjiu yiqian" is in fact translated from Western tales. The Chinese *zhiguai* or fantastic tales are not characterized by such a phrase; however, the narration of the supernatural phenomena is direct and certain. The alienation of time-space is not necessary for depicting the allegedly unreal events.

gation by the narrator is also employed in the mirror-discourse, for example, in Nodier's "Trilby ou le lutin d'Argail" (Trilby or the Sprite of Argail). A similar technique of storytelling is utilized by Wilde, who opens "The Nightingale and the Rose" *in medias res* with the student's lamentation: "'She said that she would dance with me if I brought her red roses,' cried the young Student; 'but in all my garden there is no red rose'" [Wilde 1994 *Happy*, 23]. The introduction of "The Happy Prince" is not different from any other realistic fantastic tales: "High above the city, on a tall column, stood the statue of the Happy Prince. He was gilded all over with thin leaves of fine gold, for eyes he had two bright sapphires, and a large red ruby glowed on his sword-hilt" [ibid., 9]. Readers have thus far no indication of the future animation of the statue.

In Chinese literature, the setting, whether in realistic or fantastic stories, is grounded in realism or with a realistic spatial beginning. This often causes polemic, among French critics, on whether Chinese *zhiguai* stories are fantastic or not, given that the narrative rhetoric accentuates the hypotyposis of the unknown realm rather than lingering on the ambiguous doubt about unknown existence. The Chinese rhetoric of telling ghost stories is similar to English narrative rhetoric, which centres on the weaving of horror instead of the speculative thinking on the existence of ghosts. The circumstances of such Gothic horrors will further spotlight on the space of an isolated or haunted house or place and the nocturnal time. Bram Stoker thus presented the place of the story in "The Judge's House": "When at the end of three hour's journey he [the hero Malcolm Malcolmson] alighted at Benchurch, [... which] was a market town" [Stoker 2003]. The hero, with a predilection for quietness to prepare for his examination, stumbles across a haunted Gothic house: "It was an old, rambling, heavy-built house of the Jacobean style, with heavy gables and windows, unusually small, and set higher than was customary in such houses, and was surrounded with a high brick wall massively built" [ibid.]. Curiously, numerous Chinese ghost stories present a student/literatus on his way to the capital for the official examination. The encounter with ghosts, devils or other spirits takes places at haunted places like hotels, old houses, temples or luxurious houses metamorphosed from tombs. However, the narrative style of Chinese ghost stories is rather plain and simple compared with the vivid depiction of emotions and creepy scenes in Western works. The focus of Chinese fantastic tales is akin to that of Western fairy tales: depiction of the communication and interaction among humans and imaginary phenomena. In this manner, myriads of fantastic tales, set in realistic setting, actually differ in unfolding the plots.

The first narrative mode to be analyzed here is characterized by its reciprocity with the mirror-discourse, a modern rhetoric deriving from romantic fantastic fiction. However, the proliferation of fantastic tales with the mirror-discourse has gradually saturated the genre, and readers may be satiated by the thriving narrations of ambiguity and hesitation. Therefore, a return to fairy storytelling or ghost stories, viz. a straightforward narration of the supernatural or the implausible unknown phenomenon, later breakthroughs the pending doubt of the ambiguous open ending. Writers are no longer satisfied with an instant of glimpse of the dissimulation of the mirror image; they explore the other side of the mirror, just like Alice entering the looking-glass. In the magician's hat-discourse, the apparent initial doubts provoked from modal expressions are simply a narrative tactic to conduct to the ensuing testimony of other witnesses, which will dissipate doubts. Stoker, the Gothic virtuoso, offered us examples drawing on such a narrative technique par excellence: *Dracula* and "The Judge's House."

From Modal to Indicative Expressions as from the Known to the Unknown Realm

Modal expressions first render ambiguous the strange intrusion amidst reality, thus creating doubt between a supernatural and natural reception. The realm of the unknown is imposed upon readers through linguistic play from the figurative "as if it were" to the dissipation into the indicative "it is." Using Durand's language, the thriving diurnal images constructing heroic or schizomorphic structures, mediated through the hyperbolic antithetic rhetoric, will undergo a process of linguistic purification to return to the pristine semantic unity of literature and myth. The metamorphosis of rhetoric proceeds from hyperbole to antiphrasis and eventually to the synthetic structure as hypotyposis. *Dracula* of Stoker is a typical fantastic story that combines both the narrative art of ambiguity and of lucidity. Different from Gautier's above quoted story, "The Beautiful Vampire," which weaves the plot under the obscurity of the blurring of day and night or consciousness and dreams, *Dracula* presents a blunt and direct depiction of the image of the Un-Dead. The idiosyncratic narration through collective journals, diaries and letters as witness surrounding the intrusion of the vampire(s) makes the novel a classic vampire story. The narrative artisty resides in the hypotyposis of all unlikely events. Oscar Wilde even acclaimed the novel as "the most beautiful novel of the century" (*le plus beau roman du siècle*) [Sadoul, 8].

The novel couples mirror-discourse with the magician's-hat discourse through using the techniques of embedded narration, and initial expressions of modalization, to transform along the narrative process into the dissipation of ambiguity. The story commences with Jonathan Harker's journal under the shadow of the mirror-discourse with abundant modal expressions. For example, "the wolves began to howl *as though* the moonlight had had some peculiar effect on them" [my emphasis, Stoker 1994, 23], "His [the driver] hand actually *seemed like* a steel vice" [ibid., 24], "his hand [Dracula] grasped mine with a strength which made me wince, an effect which was not lessened by the fact that it *seemed* as cold as ice" [ibid., 26], "I doubted if it were not the same person [as

the driver] to whom I was speaking" [ibid., 26], "There *seemed* a strange stillness over everything; but as I listened I heard, *as if* from down below in the valley, the howling of many wolves" [ibid., 29], and "I am all in a sea of wonders. I
doubt; I fear; I think strange things which I dare not confess to my own soul"
[ibid., 29]. The hesitation felt by Harker towards the mysterious existence of the
Count, human or monster, eventually dissipates as the latter explicitly menaces
him, controls his sending letters and imprisons him in his castle, which is affirmed by the end of Harker's journal that indicates his ending his life: "At least
God's mercy is better than that of these monsters, and the precipice is steep and
high. At its foot man may sleep – as a man. Good-bye, all! Mina!" [ibid., 69].

The doubt created throughout Harker's journals is intensified by the introduction of a bloodthirsty lunatic patient Renfield, narrated in the diary of Dr
Seward. The latter diagnoses the patient as a certain undeveloped homicidal ma-
niac. The enigma surrounding Renfield will be dissolved as the doubt about
Lucy's becoming a vampire dissipates and as the horrible nature of the Count is
uncovered by Professor Van Helsing. Stoker's selection of Dr Seward to lead the
principal narration of the story is by no means fortuitous. If the inception of
Harker's journals is more doubt-provoking (since he travels to an exotic and insecure country and the fear may be caused psychologically), the narration of Dr
Seward is in contrast credible since readers may notice his being scientific and
rational in the course of all incidents.

The most excellent part of *Dracula*'s narration lies in Professor Van
Helsing's being voiceless. His faith in the real existence of the supernatural
Un-Dead may be considered as a prejudice from his obsessive researches about
vampires. This fact would jeopardize the storytelling of the vampire into incredible, despite his status of being a professor. Accordingly, telling the vampire
story through the voice of Dr Seward, a credible and rational skeptic of supernatural beings, will further authenticate the story. Furthermore, Mina, the secondary recorder of the development of the vampire hunting and hunted, is represented as a trustworthy storyteller since her profession of assistant school mistress implies rationalism and honesty. The narrations of Jonathan, Mina and Dr
Seward, initially separately presented, later converge together to clearly delineate the portrait of the Un-Dead or *nosferatu* (as they call it in Eastern Europe).
This polyphonic narration is essentially pivoted by Dr Seward's account. In fact,
the doctor initially distrusts Van Helsing's assumption that the deceased Lucy
would feed on her prey. He even suspects that Van Helsing hides the corpse of
Lucy to show them the empty coffin. Their later discovery of a stray child in the
clump of trees whose throat is without a scratch or scar of any kind makes the
doctor say triumphantly to Van Helsing that Lucy is dead for good without becoming what the professor terms as Un-Dead. However, this instant victory of
rationalism and skepticism proves to further authenticate the existence of Lucy
as Un-Dead in Chapter XVI:

> When Lucy – I [Dr Seward] call the thing that was before us Lucy because it
> bore her shape – saw us she drew back with an angry snarl, such as a cat gives
> when taken unawares; then her eyes ranged over us. Lucy's eyes in form and
> colour; but Lucy's eyes unclean and full of hell-fire, instead of the pure, gentle
> orbs we knew. [ibid., 253]

After seeing Lucy walking as Un-Dead out of her tomb with their own eyes,
Seward, Arthur and Quincey, who love Lucy, take on the tough job with Van
Helsing to annihilate the "demon in Lucy's shape." Arthur, Lucy's fiancé, is
consented to be the blessed hand to set Lucy's soul free. The narration presents a
detailed and explicit history and nature of the Un-Dead [ibid., 257] followed by
the vivid description of Lucy Un-Dead's annihilation:

> Arthur placed the point over the heart, and as I looked I could see its dint
> in the white flesh. Then he struck with all his might.
> The Thing in the coffin writhed; and a hideous, blood-curdling screech
> came from the opened red lips. The body shook and quivered and twisted in
> wild contortions; the sharp white teeth champed together till the lips were cut
> and the mouth was smeared with a crimson foam. [ibid., 258-9]

Though the existence of Lucy-vampire is witnessed by the four men and the existence of other vampires is perceived by Jonathan, the fact is, no proof can be
offered but witness record. This is the realm of the unknown, for science yet is
not able to prove the phenomenon.

Anyway, the novel is inclined to make us believe in vampires (as is the intention in the marvellous writing) through the voice of the assistant school mistress Mina: "There are such beings as vampires; some of us have evidence that
they exist. Even had we not the proof of our own unhappy experience, the
teachings and the records of the past give proof enough for sane people. I admit
that at the first I was sceptic" [ibid., 283]. The denouement of the novel fits to
what Tolkien proclaims as necessary, Euchatastrophy. In the vampire story, this
Euchatastrophy will be the destruction of the monster Un-Dead:

> But, in the instant, came the sweep and flash of Jonathan's great knife. I
> shrieked as I saw it shear through the throat; whilst at the same moment Mr
> Morris' bowie knife plunged in the heart. It was like a miracle; but before our
> very eyes, and almost in the drawling of a breath, the whole body crumbled
> into dust and passed from our sight. [ibid., 448]

The postscript enhances the whole narrative artisty of the unknown monster
vampire, by the further affirmation of the lawyer Jonathan Harker seven years
after the narrated incident:

It was almost impossible to believe that the things which we had seen with our
own eyes and heard with our own ears were living truths. Every trace of all
that had been was blotted out.
[...]
We were struck with the fact that, in all the mass of material of which the record is composed, there is hardly one authentic document! nothing but a mass
of type-writing, except the later note-books of Mina and Seward and myself,
and Van Helsing's memorandum. We could hardly ask anyone, even did we
wish to, to accept these as proofs of so wild a story. Van Helsing summed it all
up as he said, [...]
'We want no proofs; we ask none to believe us! [ibid., 449]

Jonathan's statement in the note indeed shows the narrative technique of a vampire story. This narrative reflection also echoes the underlying attitude of the
magician's hat-discourse. Stoker excelled in telling horror stories in an objective
and neutral way, either by epistolary or omniscient narration, to weave the plot
from doubt and uncertainty to the affirmed intrusion of the unknown phenomenon. Horror is thus confirmed. In the case of *Dracula*, the narration transforms
from skepticism about madness or illusion to the concrete figure of the
Un-Dead.

By the same token, in Stoker's "The Judge's House," the confirmation of
horror glides from skepticism and doubt to the hero's death caused by the ghost
of the Judge. The narration goes through local superstition, Malcolmson's start,
the odd thrilling sensation through the hero, to the final hunting by the ghost of
the Judge. Like Stoker, English writers tend to employ similar rhetoric process
of telling horror or ghost stories. For example, A. N. L. Munby's "The Stranger
in the Mist" tells a fantastic story of a kind ghost that helps the hero Giles, who
is caught in the mountains. The omniscient narrator and the out-of-date map as
"the object of proof" make the story a genuine ghost story. Appearing more authentic than the previous story, E. F. Benson's "The Confession of Charles
Linkworth" offers collective witness of a ghost (who was a criminal and executed) by the prison officer Draycott, the doctor and the chaplain. The ghost
telephones and asks for confession from the chaplain to repent for his crime.
According to our researches of ghost stories, besides the Asian styles of telling
horrible or sentimental ghost stories, for example, the charming female ghosts in
Chinese tales (e.g. "Xiao Qian") or the spine-chilling Japanese Samara series
(*The Ring* in English adaption), English writers are one of the rare Europeans
who explicitly narrate ghosts and their interactions with men without resorting
to the mirror-discourse to create doubt.

Hyperbolic Language Brings the Figures into Action

With the magician's hat discourse, the voice is mostly that of the omniscient narrator, in fact, the implied author. The narrator will tell the fantastic story in a way that completely controls the juggling of the magician's hat. This is, in addition, as we noted before, a positive quality evaluated by Aristotle, who valued the non-interference of the poet, i.e. the narrator in the storytelling. The narrative discourse is a smooth line of hypotyposis, whether it leads to a tragic or happy ending. This hypotyposis of the unknown is based on the rhetoric of hyperbole that reversely retrieves the body of the implicit metaphors, such as metonymy and synecdoche. The narrative space and time still reside in realism, but strangeness is exaggerated to the extent of absurdity. This type of modern storytelling of the fantastic exists only in the intellectual and conscious ages. The outer world and the others, including the family, are as abstract as language itself. The substance of our known world completely metamorphoses into an unknown situation. Besides the traditional magical causality of unlikely phenomena, absurdity often plays the role of causality in modern tales. Gogol's fantastic tales represent the first reflection of such strangeness and absurdity in the 19th century, whereas Kafka's tales represent the strangeness or alienation of the 20th century.

Gogol's narrative art of the fantastic manifests itself as avant-garde in his own times, the heyday of Romanticism. His fantastic tales show few characteristics of the Romantic temperament. For example, "The Nose" offers a good example of the magician's hat-discourse juggling with absurdity as modern (or even postmodern) magic. In the story, the "nose" that symbolizes the social position and represents the body as a synecdoche (initially taken as *figurative* language) appears as a genuine living *figure*. Different from conventional fantastic works such as the romantic fantastic or the fairy tale that possesses an internal logic throughout the narration, Gogol mocked all possibilities of logic and created his revolutionary tales of the fantastic. Under his narrative art, the perceivable phenomenon or our known world is *per se* strange and weird through the abstraction and formalization of society. Man himself is no more important than one's social title, just as language has become idolatrous. Gogol employed the magician's hat-discourse to satirize his Russian society as well as to purify language. His hyperbolic rhetoric abolishes the distinction and inverts the relationship between tenor and vehicle. The figures of synecdoche and hyperbole are metamorphosed into their literal meanings. Readers are presented a Nose-figure that menaces his master's (the hero) social position and identity. The narration of the rhetorical figure recovers its body and challenges the sign of the ego. The metaphor and metamorphosis are put into play to banalize the improbable or inconceivable.

Each chapter of the story offers an independent improbable incident. The first incident begins with the incredible event that the barber Ivan Yakovlevich finds a nose in his breakfast hot roll. Then the same morning, Collegiate Assessor Kovalev (the hero) is bewildered to find that there is nothing but a bare smooth surface instead of his nose. In Chapter 3, thirteen days later, the hero wakes up to find his nose back in the right place. The narrator of the story completely controls the plotting of the story by explicitly voicing out the absurd and the unknown towards the end the first chapter: "Ivan Yakovlevich turned ashen…. But here the incident becomes befogged and it is completely unknown what happened after this point" [Calvino, 202]. Chapter 2 deploys another fantastic event concerning the meeting between the hero and his lost nose. Readers are told that an "incredible sequence of events unrolled before his eyes" and the hero is even more astonished:

> A combination of horror and amazement swept over Kovalev when he recognized the stranger as his own nose. At this eerie sight, everything swayed before his eyes. But although he could hardly stand on his feet, he felt compelled to wait until the nose returned to the carriage. He waited, shaking as though he had malaria. [ibid., 205]

The nose-figure can even enter the cathedral and pray. The hero himself has to scrape up all his courage to address his nose. The metamorphosis of the figure here arrives at its culminating point where the transformation of the synecdoche regains its flesh and blood by a final identification of language. After the hero tries to explain his situation of losing his nose, the nose-figure replies:

> "I don't see anything," the nose said. "Kindly come to the point."
> "Sir," Kovalev said with dignity, "I don't know how to interpret your words. The matter is quite clear, I believe. Unless you are trying … Don't you realize that you are my nose?"
> The nose looked at the major and frowned slightly.
> "You're mistaken, sir. I'm all on my own. Moreover, there couldn't possibly have been close relations between us. Judging by your dress, you must be employed by the Senate, or possibly but the Ministry of Justice, whereas my field is science."
> And having said this, the nose turned away and resumed his prayers. [ibid., 206]

We readers, as well as Kovalev, are completely at a loss. The hyperbolic expressions continue to contrive the all the more absurd and fantastic story as the hero resorts to press, doctor and police to solve the problem of his lost nose. Eventually in Chapter 2, the police return his lost nose. Nevertheless, the hero fails in putting the nose back. He even incredibly suspects that Mrs. Podtochina (who wants to marry her daughter to the hero) has exerted witchcraft on his nose. This nonsense creates a supernatural sensation in the public. The second chapter thus ends with the narrator's comment: "Following these events ... but here again, things become beclouded and what followed these events has remained completely unknown" [ibid., 222]. The nonsense continues until the last chapter where the hero has his nose back, "as though nothing had happened." The story closes with a meta-narration on the genre of the absurd fantastic:

> Now, that I [narrator] cannot understand. It's absolutely beyond me. But strangest of all, the most incomprehensible thing, is that there are authors who can choose such subjects to write about. This, I confess, is completely inexplicable, it's like... no, no, I can't understand it at all. [...]
> However, when all is said and done, and although, of course, we conceive the possibility, one and the other, and maybe even... Well, but then what exists without inconsistencies? And still, if you give it a thought, there is something to it. Whatever you may say, such things do happen – seldom, but they do. [ibid., 226]

Logic is defied as the central structure of the story. Gogol's art of telling absurd *unknown* phenomena is characterized by hyperbolic and humorous expressions. The fantastic adventure of the hero and his nose's recuperating its *figure* proposes a new perspective on the true meaning of symbols (the nose as a symbol of sex and social rank) and metaphors (the animation of the synecdoche of nose). Gogol's deconstruction of logic in his story arouses a converse process of the formalization of *la fantastique*. He de-formalized the abstract and arranged the meeting between the concrete and the abstract.

Likewise, this rhetoric of hypotyposis on the unknown by hyperbolic expressions is employed in Nerval's *La Main enchantée* (The Enchanted Hand). Readers are agape at the walking hand, departing from its executed master, by the bridge Pont Neuf of Paris. The black magic in the story makes a radical shift of the language; we thus enter the concrete from the abstract meaning of the hand as only a part of the body. The synecdoche regains its flesh and blood, like the nose in Gogol's story. The figure of fragmentation returns to a concrete existence by hyperbolic expressions and absorbing storytelling. Nerval's miserable story reminds us of the pathos-arousing metamorphosis that befalls Gregor Samsa, penned by Kafka.

The inception of the story dissolves any possibility of Todorovian hesitation about the unlikely incident: "As Gregor Samsa awoke one morning from uneasy dreams, he found himself transformed in his bed into a gigantic insect" [Kafka, 89]. The omniscient narrator tells this strange story at a vantage point and penetrates even this insect's thought: "What has happened to me? he thought. It was no dream. His room, a regular human bedroom, only rather too small, lay quiet between the four familiar walls" [ibid., 89]. The narrative discourse centres on the hypotyposis of the unknown situation: "What if one really transforms into a nasty insect." The narration is initiated with the figurative language of "uneasy dream" and the hyperbole of metamorphosing into an insect, which gradually takes on the rhetoric of euphemism of miniaturization. The figurative expression of describing someone as an insect has become concrete here and traced back to the unknown nature of human relations and existence. The abstract thought throughout the story (the repetition of "he thought") proves to be insignificant. Gregor's difficulty in movement and the eventual denial of language raise the solemn issue of the sign and the meaning. This metamorphosis manifests as a de-formalization back to figure as literal. The process inspires readers to consider how signs decide meanings, as the insect annihilates the existence of Gregor. In contrast, the identity of the insect shows that abstract logic still requires concrete appearances. In Kafka's story, logic is again defied, as in Gogol's story. Absurdity appears as a modern magic. If Gogol's Kovalev loses only his nose, Gregor loses his entire body and transmutes into an unknown identity. Allegorical reading may interpret the insect as a figure referring to the hero's nasty position in society. Even so, the present discourse explores the unknown situation through fantastic storytelling. The nightmare (at first as an uneasy dream) of the poor hero turns out to be reality, an unknown and impalpable realm in the middle of realism. The hero does enter into the other side of the mirror (not merely a visual obsession) and is not able to come out of it. The absence of hesitation and ambiguity (the hero doubts in the beginning, but the narrator immediately tells what happens exactly) puts this story into the category of the magician's hat-discourse.

In the discourse of mirror, the unbearable and unknown incident often disappears as the hero wakes from his dream or nightmare. In the present discourse, it is impossible to return to take everything as figurative: "What about sleeping a little longer and forgetting all this nonsense, he thought, but it could not be done, for he was accustomed to sleep on his right side and in his present condition he could not turn himself over" [ibid., 89]. Gregor tries to comfort himself that the unlikely change is the morning's delusions and will gradually fall away. And the change in his voice is a precursor of a severe chill. The reaction of the hero's family indicates that the sign is more significant than the love between the family members. Gregor's endeavour to retrieve the proof of his real being and position in his family eventually fails, since idolatry decides man's perception and conception, even his family later take the insect as insect. Kafka's storytelling often arouses further meditation on the relationship between signs and meanings. He also revolutionized the traditional narration of bestiary by his imaginary relativity. In this Kafkaesque fable of the fantastic, the hypotyposis does not focus on the anthropomorphosis of the unknown animals but rather on theriomorphic imagination of the unknown men.

The state of *unus mundus* in language (the abstract in the concrete) remains for a longer period of time in Chinese culture, since the stage of original partici-

pation lasted until the beginning of the 20th century. Moreover, Barfield, on
many occasions, illustrated the eclectic conception of language by adducing
Chinese language. Under such a thinking mode, Chinese fantastic tales with the
motif of metamorphosis, without any magic causality like the case in Gogol or
Kafka's stories, highlight the mysterious and unknown power in Nature as harmony but not the absurdity or pathos of human existence. In Li Fuyan's "Zhang
Feng," the eponymous hero metamorphoses into a tiger while travelling in the
forest. He takes it naturally and adopts the nature of a tiger to eat men, though he
recognizes that the victims are from his village. The story is permeated with
Daoist vision of man's existence in relation to Nature. The consciousness remains in original participation where man is a part of Nature and the aggran-
disement of human individualism is absent. The affirmative mode of depicting
the story emphasizes the art of telling the impending unknown plot of the
metamorphosis and the circumstance of *what if* a man changed into an animal.
Without any magic indication or obsession with the figure of tigers, the hero
"found himself changed into a tiger with brindles of bright colours" after rolling
on the lovely and cozy meadow by a tree. Without meditating on the strange and
inexplicable transformation, "he looks at his sharp claws and teeth, tries his
strength and finds that he is unparalleled in the world." He eats the officer Zheng
from Fuzhou. After relishing his meal, the tiger Zhang Feng thinks that he
should go back to the very spot where he first changed into a tiger to resume his
human form (it is narrated that he had a dreamy consciousness of his human
identity). The story even closes with the hero's exile into the west for the son of
his victim learns about the truth of his father's death and tries to take his revenge.
The officer judges that the killing is not deliberate since Zhang was a tiger and
suggests the exile of the hero.

The tradition of Chinese fantastic fiction accentuates storytelling rather than
dialectic speculation. Writers are not bothered by the causality of the metamorphosis but craft the ensuing actions. This extroverted orientation of poeticizing
the imagination of the unknown dilutes the inclination of the introverted abstraction of human behaviour and language. Language can be as imaginary as *la fantastique*. According to a Chinese metaphor, a man compared to a tiger may
eventually become a tiger. The logic of language retains the pre-logic or informal logic. This vision of semantic unity in language and worldview originates
with Daoism, especially Zhuang Zi's philosophy on metamorphosis and the human form. He claimed that he was not afraid of transforming into a rat or an insect because all beings belong to and are integrated into the Universe as a whole,
which can also be understood as the Jungian *unus mundus*. Zhuang Zi combined
the fantastic or the strange with the inter-transformation (not exclusively reincarnation) of all beings in the Universe. Chinese hyperbolic language in the magician's hat-discourse is mitigated into a natural language by the rhetoric of

euphemism derived from the nocturnal imaginary regime that man is a grain in great Nature.

Fables of the Nonhuman and the Imagined Discourse from Theriomorphic Space

Our inclusion of this narrative form in fantastic literature appears more questionable in comparison with other neighbouring sub-genres of fantastic literature. Todorov, in his theory of fantastic fiction, excluded any possible allegorical reading of the fantastic from his scope of the genre. He was ready to rule out tales with allegorical implications, such as "William Wilson" and "A New Year's Eve Adventure," not to mention the luculent allegories of beast tales. According to our exploration of fantasy, beast fables are represented under the *inventio* of a harmonious integration of the diurnal theriomorphic imagination into the nocturnal mystic or antiphrastic structures. The animal images are associated with the imaginary of time, and thus music and language. Music is an artistic representation of temporality and movement, which is related to animation. Language is also endowed with the quality of music (the sound) and temporality (time and linear expression). The premise that language originates with myth and metaphor also entails a surmise that the origin of the figure of anthropomorphosis and personification is to be found among animals.

Based on our thematic studies of the fantastic, the narrative form of bestiary illustrates the image of the subject vis-à-vis movement, particularly animals and their language. This may derive from the motif in many folktales, in which a man chances to understand conversation among the animals, and laughs at them. In many of these stories, the man's wife forces him to reveal the reason for his laughter, and once the reason is uncovered, the man dies. This reveals an ongoing curiosity and imagination of mankind to crack the code of animals' language, or more exactly, human language. It is sensible to suppose that the imagination of telling beast tales is couched in the imagination of and desire for a universal language. The behaviour and mentality of animals feature an important part in conceptualizing the unknown. Some writers content themselves with hypotyposis of the animal world for delightful imitation; certain others view the unknown realm of the animals as an identical reflection of the human world; while still others use the unknown realm of animals to satirize our known world. Though writers' attitudes are at variance, a common characteristic of allegory is attributed to the tales. By the same token, the imagery of the animated finds its counterpart in the imagery of the inanimate. The construction of this type of tales manifests itself as a narration of imitation of the human world through decoding nonhuman into human language.

In fantastic tales, the world of animals or objects resembles ours. For example, the French *Fables* of La Fontaine and *Le Roman de Renart* (The Romance of the Fox) represent the animals' world as ours. The former work offers a moral to conclude each tale in verse; the latter satirizes the cunning character, the fox, with political discourse. "The Bremen Town Musicians" from the Grimms' tales tells about how deserted animals encourage each other and become musicians. Andersen staged a teapot's monologue in "The Teapot." For a multi-faceted author like Wilde, his fantastic creation is realized into different forms of the mirror-discourse (*The Picture of Dorian Gray*) and the magician's hat-discourse, e.g. "The Canterville Ghost" and "The Nightingale and The Rose," and now a fable of objects and animals, "The Remarkable Rocket." Wilde wisely combined the objects and animals together to enable their communication. As the title indicated, the hero is in fact a Rocket, who discourses like a philosopher, or rather a politician, with other kinds of fireworks – Roman Candle, Catherine Wheel, Rocket, Cracker, Bengal Light and Fire-balloon. After all his companions have triumphantly gone into the sky, the ignored rocket remains and continues to discourse with the animals, the Frog, the Dragon-fly, the Duck and the Goose. This is piercing satire on philosophers and politicians who discourse incessantly (we may refer to the irony in "The Nightingale and the Rose"). The end of the story makes the Rocket a veritable mockery: 'I knew I should create a great sensation,' gasped the Rocket, and he went out" [Wilde 1994 *Happy*, 73].

It is important to note that the narration of beast and object fables often excludes communication between men and animals or objects. This is a unique imitative creation of the Universe of nonhuman beings. Once the speech granted to animals or objects, the interlocution among them and humans is impossible, though human characters and discourses are still represented in the tales. The rule of the storytelling resides in the alternative of human and nonhuman discourses. However, it is this very reason that, in the absence of satire, Tolkien rules out bestiary from his compass of fairy-story:

> The magical understanding by men of the proper languages of birds and beasts and trees, that is much nearer to the true purposes of Faërie. But in stories in which no human being is concerned; or in which the animals are the heroes and heroines, and men and women, if they appear, are mere adjunct; and above all those in which the animal form is only a mask upon human face, a device of the satirist or the preacher, in these we have beast-fable and not fairy-story. [Tolkien 1997, 117]

Since Tolkien's theory emphasizes the storytelling of Faerie (more on the imaginary space) related to man, the reflection of human behaviour and language into animals and objects appears much of homo sapiens. However, in the process of telling stories of the nonhuman, writers effectively instill the imagination of the unknown into the animals. Here the archaic memory of theriomorphism is brought into play. The fantastic diction launches the imagination that inspires readers to step back to the unity of man and other beings. Though rich in satire and allegory, fables offer a third way into the status of the linguistic *unus mundus* beyond the dualistic view of man vs. the nonhuman. Barfield regarded allegory as "a natural development from myth rather than its enemy" [Barfield 1988, 86]. He also hypothesized that we might well experience a "rediscovery of allegory" [ibid.] with the coming of final participation and the advent of a new and less literal conception of language.

The imaginary revolving around time and the production of theriomorphic symbols are all the more conspicuous in Chinese fables about the astrological animals. The twelve animals participate in the race held by the Daoist Emperor God, Yuhuang Dadi. The imaginary space of animals is connected with the divine space and the communication is not barricaded. This is a story of the competition among animals and their relationship with gods. The combination of animals with the semantism of time (movement and animation) and the combination of the race with acceleration and speed echo the convergence of the animation and the symbolic number twelve. The Chinese measurement of time is antique, twelve "hours" (*shichen*) a day and a cycle of twelve terrestrial years (*dizhi*) of the twelve animals that won the race. This beast fable manifests the origin of the unitary meanings in language related to animals and time.

The fables of the present day incorporate science, economics and politics to penetrate into the unknown realm of animals and the unknown extent of human nature. George Orwell's *Animal Farm* brings to light the imaginary language and thinking of pigs in relation to men. Aside from the satire on communism and church, the interaction among the various animals brings us back to the original status of figurative language concerning animals. The pigs' discourse is tightly related to politicians, who represent theriomorphic imagination and the devouring time. For example, the regulation for the mob: "The seven commandments" are summarized into "Four legs good, two legs bad." The way the pigs manipulate polarity by language leaves a clue of linguistic severance. It seems that politicians are as eternal as time in human history, both in the East and the West. If politicians avail themselves of the language of sophistry as rhetoric to discourse, many bestiaries purify language and urge a rediscovery of the allegoric language. The discourse of animals is also appropriated in science-fiction. Mikhail Bulgakov's *The Heart of a Dog* explores the speech and thinking of a dog and eventually of a half-beast-half-man. This is a 20th century Frankenstein experiment that shifts from life creation with fragments of corpse to a live animal (a bedraggled street dog). Similarly, Herbert Adam's books such as *Watership Down* are also wonderful examples of animals reflecting human foibles. The universal theriomorphic imagination remains in our scientific age, which arouses our archaic memory of theriomorphism. Animals' and objects' language is *per se* a representation of semantic unity that keeps on requiring rediscovery.

From the realm of man's law in the previous section to animal's law, hyperbolic language regains the flesh and blood of figures through the rhetoric of euphemism from the nocturnal imaginary. The language voiced by animals arouses human imagination to re-participate with Nature. According to recent scientific studies, one critical difference between man and ape is the use of language for the purpose of peace, thus a unification of the disparate. However, contemporary idolatry of language keeps severing the semantic unity. We may conclude this section by Coetzee's heroine's (*Elizabeth Costello*) comment on language and realism. She refers to Kafka's fable "A Report to an Academy" to illustrate the ambiguity between man and ape in identifying the narrator:

> The word-mirror is broken, [...] The words on the page will no longer stand up and be counted, each proclaiming "I mean what I mean!" The dictionary that used to stand beside the Bible and the works of Shakespeare above the fireplace, where in pious Roman homes the household gods were kept, has become just one code book among many. [Coetzee]

Language in Harmony with Nature's Law: Spatial Particles of Chôra

While the first narrative mode of the magician's hat-discourse is grounded in the realistic space governed by man's law and the second in the space appertaining to the imaginary law of the nonhuman, the present pattern of the discourse is ruled under Nature's law. The images converge into this specific discourse by the extrinsic momentum of musical harmony. In compliance with our interpretation of chôra as a space of harmonious oxymoron, the idea of spatial particles of chôra refers to the imaginary spaces that transcend the antithetic dualism. They are in connection with the material imagination of the four elements. Unknown creatures or phenomena appear natural to characters from the known realm, where a room for the unknown is always spared, viz. open to the reception of contradictions. This appears as an inversion of the rhetoric of litotes: "the unknown or the unreal is not impossible." Thus, gods or ghosts can not be proved nonexistent. Faced with the immense power of Nature, especially the overwhelming features of time and death, man submits to the unknown power by the rhetoric of euphemism or the *mise en miniature* (rendering in miniature). Besides the imaginary of subject-object interrelations, the hypotyposis of the unknown time and space juggles a variation of metamorphoses. The storytelling travels into the unknown past and future; it also enters into the unknown realm of the present in resonance with water, air, earth and fire. The forbidden realm of Faerie or Chinese *Fudi Dongtian* (both exist in the West and East) co-exists with man's realm. The make-believe of this sublime and transcendental space can be associated with the fifth element, which Plato views as a sphere and Chinese Daoism names gold, obtained by the sublimation of alchemy.

The spatial characteristic of the discourse governed by Nature's law is represented as a microcosm of the dream-discourse that represents a macrocosm by the style of fantastic epic. The story is represented as sub-creation, a second imaginary world with characters from the unknown realm. The narration, like the complex dream-discourse, hinges on the underlying interplay between gods, angels, spirits, devils and men. Realistic settings are integrated with the realm of the unknown. The representation of a harmonious cosmos as ultra-space under Nature's law corresponds to Shelley's perception of poetic diction: "in the footsteps of nature." Tolkien employs the image of splintered light with refraction of God's light to shed light on mythopoeia. The discourse in question reflects the splintered particles departing from chôra. This unknown but transcendental space beyond yet inclusive of dualism with perpetual metamorphosis is only accessible through aesthetic imagination rooted in primary imagination.

Barfield saw a possible medium to enter final participation, i.e. poetic diction. The core spirit of the diction lies in the magic power of figurative language with real figure that purifies and recovers the true visage of metaphor, through metamorphosis, and reaches metaphysics. The magician's hat-discourse here features a vivid imitation of the mysterious unknown:

> *Figure and figurative* [...] may justly be applied, owing to the perceptual or aesthetic, the pictorial, form in which these unitary meanings first manifest in consciousness. Not an empty 'root meaning to shine', but the same definite spiritual reality which was beheld on the one hand; and on the other hand, in what has since become physical light; not an abstract conception, but the echoing footsteps of the goddess Natura – not a metaphor but a living Figure. [Barfield 1973, 88-89]

Realism Replete with Wonders

Similar to the motif in Gogol's "Nose" where the part of the body outwits the master, Andersen's "The Shadow" is told by means of a slight spatial difference in narrative discourse from the tales rooted in realistic space. In the realm of the story, the shadow that assumes a personal identity is regarded as a natural phenomenon. For example, the Shadow (the hero's shadow that assumes human form) states to the princess that the scholar is his shadow and she actually talks to the Scholar-shadow. Under Nature's law, personification or anthropomorphosis is concretized by the vivid depiction of the narration. Different from the absurd and happy ending of "The Nose," the hero-scholar ends up with the execution plotted by his own shadow. The Shadow in the story is no longer a symbol of human evil nature and the phantasm of desire; it takes on a figure as a new born man. Many years after the Shadow left the scholar (the shadow was sent by the scholar to peep at the maiden in the house opposite), it returns to visit the scholar as a well-dressed man: "I've become so much of a body that I've actually got flesh and clothes; you never expected to see me in such fine condition. Don't you recognize your old shadow?" [Calvino, 320]. The maiden opposite is in fact Poetry and the shadow stays there for three weeks to absorb everything that has been sung and written as if staying for three thousand years. The description of the Shadow's birth as a man after the baptism of poetry is an allusion to the scene in Eden after Adam and Eve eat the fruit of knowledge: "I became a man. When I came out I was matured, but you were no longer in the hot countries. I was ashamed, as a man, to go about as I was. I needed boots and clothes and all the human paraphernalia that make a man recognizable" [ibid., 323]. The Shadow has become realistic and materialistic, whereas its master remains faithful to "the true and the beautiful and the good [that] most people appreciated it as a cow does roses" [ibid., 324].

The exchange of identities between the scholar and the Shadow starts with the exchange of addressing expressions. The scholar addresses his shadow from "thou" to "you" but the Shadow addresses his master from "you" to "thou." Eventually everybody takes the scholar as "the shadow" of the Shadow. This is an illustration of the manipulation of language and the right of discourse. The end of the story is tragic, for the scholar refuses the offer of the Shadow (a hundred thousand rix-dollars a year) to be his shadow and insists on revealing the truth to the princess. However, the scholar is finally executed as a mercy killing for he is considered mad. The Shadow gradually takes his figure and language and eventually denies his master's identity and voice. This animation of the fragmentary part of the body helps "clean the window" of our vision on synecdoche and metonymy in figurative language by the inverse rhetoric process of euphemism faced with the imaginary of time, the dark power of shadow.

Tolkien accepted the use of satire in telling fairy-stories with the exception of satirizing the magic itself. It is undeniable that irony and satire are frequently revealed between the lines of the fantastic, according to all the works so far analyzed and mentioned from the discourses of dream, mirror and the magician's hat. Many writers demonstrate their artistry of irony in fantastic writings. Wilde is particularly a master of irony and satire in telling stories, via narration (fiction) or showing (play). The irony and satire in the afore-studied novel of *The Picture of Dorian Gray* is based on the central magic object, the portrait of the hero, taken as a "foul parody." Wilde's art of narrative discourse of the magician's-hat is consummate. His storytelling technique of the Gothic ghost story "The Canterville Ghost" is a vivid resurrection of the conventional romance and fairy tale. The narrative space in the story features a belief in ghosts among the people: "When Mr Hiram B. Otis, the American Minister, bought Canterville Chase, every one told him he was doing a very foolish thing, as there was no doubt at all that the place was haunted" [Wilde 1994 *Lord*, 45]. This reception of the haunted house is the very feature in English fantastic writing that differs from French writing, as Jacque Finné highlights in his research of theories of the fantastic. Wilde's parody resides in the imitation of the Gothic setting and the "spooky" appearance of the ghost against the materialistic spirit of the Americans that show no sign of fear, and reversely frighten, hoax and menace the ghost. The hub of the fantastic is not in the meditation or hesitation on the authentication of the ghost, but rather in the interaction between the modern and capitalist men, and the antique and classic ghost.

The ghost stories we have so far studied centre on the deployment of haunting power and the depiction of menace and fear without communication between human and the nonhuman. The expectation of horizon lies in authenticating the existence of the ghost and the pathetic fate of the ghost's victim. The present story of Wilde deals with the horizon where men and ghosts co-exist. The focus is placed on all possible interactions that could take place between men and ghosts, "what if" ghosts, or other alleged supernatural beings existed. This story can be termed as a melodious and euphoriant parody of the Gothic ghost story by drawing on the narrative art of the fairy tale.

Wilde initially reminded readers by the subtitle "Hylo-idealistic romance" that the ghost story in question combines the materialistic and the idealistic in the romance style. Under such a premise, the author elaborated the rhetoric of hypotyposis in telling the unknown phenomenon: the materialistic humiliation of the ghost (prosaic style) and the sympathy and love for the poor ghost (romantic style). The word "ghost" in the fantastic represents the existence of the concrete meaning. The *hylo*-existence of the Canterville ghost is completely ignored and abstracted by the *hylo*-characters, the Otis family apart from Virginia. The conventional description of the Gothic climate of the story becomes a sharp contrast to the reaction of the Americans: "As they entered the avenue of Canterville Chase, however, the sky became suddenly overcast with clouds, a curious stillness seemed to hold the atmosphere, a great flight of rooks passed silently over their heads, and, before they reached the house, some big drops of rain had fallen" [ibid., 47].

The blood stain on the floor is nothing but a red stain in the eyes of modern Americans:

> Mrs Otis caught sight of a dull red stain on the floor just by the fireplace and, quite unconscious of what it really signified, said to Mrs Umney, 'I am afraid something has been spilt there.'" The latter replies that blood has been spilt on that spot. Mrs Otis's reaction is unexpected to readers: "'How horrid,' cried Mrs Otis; 'I don't at all care for blood-stains in a sitting-room. It must be removed at once.' [ibid., 47]

This incident of "the blood-stain" is followed by more sensational appearances of the ghost with different creepy properties. However, though accepting the fact that a ghost does exist, the Otis family just regard it as a commercial opportunity (they think of exhibiting the ghost in USA) and impose human rules on the ghost. The latter is even humiliated many times by the family, especially the naughty twins, to the point that he laments his miserable existence.

Compared with the Shadow in the previously discussed story that embodies human evil and desire, the miserable Canterville ghost embodies death and the abstract past that is being debased into a phantom-wise sign. The depiction of the ghost's physical and horrid traits (a conventional figure as literal) is starkly contrasted to the insulting reaction of the modern Americans. The hypotyposis of Wilde's language on the picturesque portrayal of the ghost echoes with musical rhythm and rhymes that make the story a return to the fount of language, metaphor and myth: "His eyes were as red as burning coals; long grey hair fell over his shoulders in matted coils; his garments, which were of antique cut, were soiled and ragged, and from his wrists and ankles hung heavy manacles and rusty gyves. [...] he fled down the corridor, uttering hollow groans, and emitting a ghastly green light" [ibid., 50]. Following the blood-stain and this gruesome appearance, the existence of the ghost will be incrementally humiliated by the family and be impelled to his space of impasse:

> Just, however, as he reached the top of the great oak staircase, a door was flung open, two little white-robed figures [the twins] appeared, and a large pillow whizzed past his head! There was evidently no time to be lost, so, hastily adopting the Fourth Dimension of Space as a means of escape, he vanished through the wainscoting, and the house became quite quiet. [...]
> Never, in a brilliant and uninterrupted career of three hundred years, had he been so grossly insulted. [ibid., 50]

The most striking irony is manifest in the encounter of the authentic ghost and the fake one: "Right in front of him was standing a horrible spectre, motionless as a carven image, and monstrous as a madman's dream!" [ibid., 55]. Under the narrative virtuosity of Wilde, the ghost's nightmare is in fact the materialistic numbness and superficialness of man. This "naïve" ghost is effectively hoaxed by the American twins. Throughout the narration, readers are impressed by the poetic style of the ghost in contradistinction to the prosaic style of the Americans. The ghost's representation of archaic, graceful and pedantic language is even conspicuous in his vow of revenge for this disgracing prank. He utters his oath like a knight but chance plays a joke on him aright:

> he ground his toothless gums together; and, raising his withered hands high above his head, swore, according to the picturesque phraseology of the antique school, that when Chanticleer had sounded twice his merry horn, deeds of blood would be wrought, and Murder walk abroad with silent feet.
> Hardly had he finished this awful oath when, from the red-tiled roof of a distant homestead, a cock crew. He laughed a long, low, bitter laugh, and

waited. Hour after hour he waited, but the cock, for some strange reason, did
not crow again. [ibid., 57]

Though he finds his vigil in vain, his erudite spirit makes him consult several
books of ancient chivalry, "of which he was exceedingly fond, and found that,
on every occasion on which his oath had been used, Chanticleer had always
crowed a second time" [ibid., 57]. The vivid description of the failure and frustration of the ghost against the victory and shallowness of the American family
leads readers back to a reflection of the meanings of language and its figures, as
the narrator comments: "[The Americans] were evidently people on a low, material plane of existence, and quite incapable of appreciating the symbolic value of
sensuous phenomena" [ibid., 57].

The narrator's addressing himself "I" illustrates his position as the im-
plied-author who shows sympathy for the ghost. The narrator "I" is in reality
heterodiegetic. He does not question the existence of the supernatural phenomenon; instead, he utilizes hypotyposis of the imaginary interaction between
man and ghost by bringing into play the euphemism on the ghost and hyperbole
on the man. The impending incidents of the ghost as a victim of *a ghost story*
culminate at the final blow "on the 19th September" preceded by his being tri-
pled by strings and butter-slide and his catching cold because of a heavy jar of
water falling right down on him, though he did make concessions. Eventually
the ghost renounces his nocturnal expedition but he still lives in the house, albeit
the Otises consider that the phenomenon has disappeared. The abstraction of the
figure of language undergoes a parallel waning process of the figure of the ghost.
However, the purification of language will be effectuated by pure imagination.
Out of the materialistic family there is an angel figure with an innocent heart,
Virginia. She feels sorry for the ghost and decides to mourn for the ghost. From
chapter five to the end of the story, the narrative style shifts to romantic fairy
tale, like the poetic part of Wilde's "The Nightingale and the Rose" in contradistinction to the prosaic narration on the interaction between the student and the
girl. The ghost reveals the secret of making a ghost sleep and the Garden of
Death in a poetic language:

> 'Far away beyond the pine-woods,' he answered, in a low dreamy voice, 'there
> is a little garden. There the grass grows long and deep, there are the great white
> stars of the hemlock flower, there the nightingale sings all night long. All night
> long he sings, and the cold, crystal moon looks down, and the yew-tree spreads
> out its giant arms over the sleepers.' [ibid., 64]

The brave Virginia accepts the voyage into darkness to mourn for the ghost and
helps him regain peace. From man's vision, Virginia has disappeared for the
whole day since her entering the unknown realm beyond three-dimensional
space. She reappears at midnight without revealing to anyone the secret between

her and the ghost. The end is happy, because the sweet Virginia has become the heir of the treasure of the Canterville and gets married with her cavalier Duke of Cheshire.

If we compare the present story with Wilde's *The Picture of Dorian Gray*, the differences between the mirror-discourse and the magician's hat-discourse are evident. Mirror-discourse creates ambiguous disquietude and doubt in the existence of the unknown metamorphosis of the portrait, whereas the magician's hat stages the objective witness of the ghost by the unfriendly and friendly interaction between the ghost from the unknown realm and men from the known realm. The spatial logic of the present story complies with Nature's law; viz. the appearance of the ghost is accepted as natural. However, the realm of the unknown related to Love and Death is only visible to those who keep a simple heart. The enunciated literal language is here another illustration of a return to the figurative origin: animation of hyperbole and euphemism are metamorphosed by hypotyposis.

Wilde's poor ghost tricked by men is reminiscent of other such stories where the supposed furious and horrid imaginary creatures are depicted as victims. In Chinese fantastic tales, ghosts are also vulnerable to the hoax of man. Cao Pi's (187-226) "Zong Dingbo Catches a Ghost" tells a story about such a naïve ghost and a cunning man. The doubt and desire to authenticate the existence of the ghost in the mirror-discourse cedes to the hypotyposis of the ensuing unknown actions after the hero's encounter with the unknown phenomenon. In Chinese language, it is often termed as fantastic out of the fantastic (qi zhong qi). The start of the story is an explicit recognition of the ghost's existence: "When he was young, Zong Dingbo met a ghost one night. He asked, "Who are you?" The ghost answered, "I'm ghost" and asked in return. Dingbo lied to it, "I'm ghost, too" [Cao]. The Cartesian style of scandalous feelings towards this supernatural intrusion is absent in most of Chinese fantastic fiction, and this is also true in traditional Japanese fantastic tales. Through a series of lies, the hero gets the Achilles' heel of ghosts: "fear being spat on by man." Then towards the end of their journey approaching the town Wanshi, the hero catches the ghost and carries it on his head. Arriving in the town, the ghost has metamorphosed into a goat and the hero spits on it lest it changes again. He sells the ghost/goat for fifteen hundred coins. The hero never fears the ghost or doubts about its authenticity. The author's main concern is to tell an extraordinary story, as fantastic as possible.

In the discourse of the magician's hat, a ghost is as concrete as a goat. The hyperbolic and repetitive expressions of doubt and ambiguity in the mirror-discourse (the pathological expressions) where the existence of ghosts is revealed through the enunciation process, are absent here. The magician's hat-discourse brings into play the vivid rhetoric underpinned by the *mise en minature* or euphemism of the imaginary process. The pathological structures are often transformed into mystic and euphemistic structures through the magician's hat-discourse; it often has a happy ending, poetics based on euphoria.

Figures as *Figures*

Under this category, fantastic storytelling extends to a thorough crystallization of symbols and metaphors. The discourse centres on the returning of figures to real *figures* through animated narration. The sublimation of the ghost into peaceful sleep in "The Canterville Ghost" represents the alchemy of language through imagination and love. The image of the nightingale in the ghost's discourse about the Garden of Death employed as a metaphor by the ghost is animated and granted the speech as a real figure in another tale of Wilde's, "The Nightingale and the Rose." This combination of concrete and abstract meanings in fantastic storytelling is parallel to the process of Eucharist of language: to refine language and recover the gold of figures in metaphor and myth. This kind of narrative art tells stories that enunciate Symbols in fantastic literature and also undergoes such a semantic purification.

In Wilde's "The Nightingale and the Rose," we enter into the unknown realm of the nightingale's and other plants' and animals' world. We learn from the discourses of the bird the semantic unity of love, nightingale and rose:

> "Here at last is a true lover," said the Nightingale. "Night after night have I sung of him, though I knew him not: night after night have I told his story to the stars, and now I see him. His hair is dark as the hyacinth-blossom, and his lips are red as the rose of his desire; but passion has made his face like pale ivory, and sorrow has set her seal upon his brow." [Wilde 1994 *Happy*, 24]

The Nightingale as an animal character in the fantastic story also uses figurative language, which renders the whole narrative discourse a thorough hypotyposis of the unknown Nature, e.g. the dialogues among the animals and plants. The idealistic and romantic Nightingale decides to sacrifice her life for the student (for she thought that this is a true lover). The vivid and musical birth of the rose is depicted with figurative and animated language, enhanced by the figure and speech of the Rose-tree:

> And when the Moon shone in the heavens the Nightingale flew to the Rose-tree, and set her breast against the thorn. [...] All night long she sang, and the thorn went deeper and deeper into her breast, and her life-blood ebbed away from her.
> She sang first of the birth of love in the heart of a boy and a girl. [...] [ibid., 28]

The personification of the rose's blossoming process against the sacrifice of the Nightingale is further developed into two more steps, coupled with the song of love at different levels:

> But the Tree cried to the Nightingale to press closer against the thorn. [...]
> So the Nightingale pressed closer against the thorn, and louder and louder grew her song, for she sang of the birth of passion in the soul of a man and a maid. [...]
> So the Nightingale pressed closer against the thorn, and the thorn touched her heart, and a fierce pang of pain shot through her. Bitter, bitter was the pain, and wilder and wilder grew her song, for she sang of the Love that is perfected by Death, of the Love that dies not in the tomb. [ibid., 29]

The pale Nightingale's death is in sharp contrast with the naissance of the crimson rose, "Crimson was the girdle of petals, and crimson as a ruby was the heart" [ibid., 29]. The end of the story shockingly unveils the Professor's daughter's being material and the student's ruthlessly throwing the rose into the gutter, gone over by a cart-wheel. The poetic language is eventually murdered by the prosaic language. Wilde's fantastic discourse of the magician's hat evokes the semantic unity of music, concrete and abstract meanings.

Nature's law makes all phenomena possible through the magician's hat-discourse. Man may interact with the nonhuman without language. On the other hand, man is endowed with the secret of language to communicate with the nonhuman. This style of storytelling takes readers back even farther to the original participation with semantic unity, which includes the understanding of Nature's language. Chinese fantastic tales offer a great variety of communication and interaction between man and the nonhuman. Nevertheless, the Chinese imagination has developed a system compliant to Nature's law, but is grounded in the human Dao. Accordingly, the nonhuman characters often take on human form to get into contact with man, including sexual intercourse. The Daoist thinking mode even inspires writers to depict the marriage between man and the nonhuman, as well as their offspring.

Pu Songling is one of the great Chinese masters of the fantastic. His vivid description of the relations between the hero and the nonhuman woman is unsurpassed. Under his consummate narrative art, all the eponymous flowers as heroines. The purple peony bloom (in the tale "Gejin"), the white peony bloom ("Xiangyu"), the chrysanthemum ("Huangying") and the lotus ("Hehua sanniangzi") become wives to the heroes. In the first story, the hero Chang Dayong is fascinated by peony blooms and composes poems for the flowers. In order to let his planted peony blossom, he has run out of money. Such affection moves the purple peony bloom so much that she metamorphoses into an exquisite damsel with unparalleled beauty (宫妆艳绝) to meet the hero. Because of his love for the flower, the hero almost withers to death. The peony-woman Gejin uplifts him with cold and fragrant drink with medicine smell (藥氣香冷), in reality, essence of peony bloom. Afterward, the hero regains his energy and strength, and relishes a sexual relation with Gejin. The description is as sensual as erotic: "her jade-wise skin starts to expose, warm fragrance flows, between the nesting and touching, feeling the breath and sweat transpiring with scent, no smell is not perfume" (玉肌乍露, 熱香四流, 偎抱之間, 覺鼻息汗熏, 無氣不馥) [Pu]. Gejin even gives the hero money to go home and introduces her sister to his brother. Each flower-woman gives birth to a child to their husband. However, as often is the case in the Chinese fantastic narration grounded in Confucianism (the Confucians believe that nonhuman spirits are abnormal and evil), the hero doubts the abnormal identity of his wife and tries to get the truth from her. The story ends with the parting of both flower-women by the rebuke: "Three years ago, moved by your passion, I dedicated my body and life to you; now that you suspect me, how can we continue our relation?" (三年前感君見思, 遂呈身相報; 今見猜疑, 何可復聚!) [ibid.] Both throw their children outside and disappear. The very places where the children fall grow two peonies that blossom the same year, one purple, one white.

The Confucian ethics and Daoist imagination inspire Chinese fantastic writers to focus on vividly depicting possible plot development after the encounter between the hero and the nonhuman. This perpetual conception of Nature and the central spirit of Daoist aesthetics, stressing animation, defer the abstraction of Chinese language. Similar to the story of the peony-woman Gejin, the other stories with flower-women all spend a sensual life or moment with the heroes. The story of "Xiangyu" even portrays spiritual and faithful love between the flower and the hero. They undergo life and death together. The beauty of the peony-woman also possesses different visages: flower, nymph, flower-soul and flower-beauty.

This narrative hypotyposis of the actions between man and the nonhuman in Chinese fantastic literature continued for many centuries until the beginning of the 20th century. The nonhuman refers to gods, ghosts, flower-spirits, fox-spirits and myriads of others. The fox-spirit is quite idiosyncratic in Chinese literature and also Japanese literature under the influence of the former. Different from Western fables concerning foxes, e.g. the French *Le Roman de Renart*, the Chinese fantastic foxes are as sophisticated and versatile as the semantic meanings of the word fox.[76] In contemporary Chinese language, the term "狐狸精" (fox-spirit) has reduced and abstracted into a pejorative sense of "waitress," like the debasement of the word "rose" in English. However, in fantastic storytelling, foxes are depicted with iridescent colours, especially by Pu. Foxes bear a double semantic unity, both positive and negative. They can be evil and harmful as well as good and benevolent. Pu Songling often depicted the female fox-spirits as

---

[76] The fox-spirit Daji in the aforementioned *The Investiture of the Gods* from the dream-discourse embodies one of the meanings revolving around the word fox.

wise, cute and faithful women. They are aesthete, especially appreciating the literary art of those heroes who fail the national examination (like Pu himself). As regards male fox-spirits, they are endowed with three different characters: cunning, erudition and humour. Unfortunately, the contemporary meaning for "老狐狸" (old fox) has reduced into "a cunning person, or being cunning". It is evident that fantastic tales offer the forgotten semantic unity in language. The accelerating changes in Chinese language splitting the concrete and the abstract meanings are becoming obvious in our times. This can be elucidated in the light of Barfield's theory of human evolution of consciousness. Chinese people experienced their intellectual and rational stage in the 20th century shortly after an abrupt irruption with original participation. Overnight they forsook their traditional philosophy, archaic or classic language, wisdom and their so-called superstitions to embrace Western culture, among others, science, rational thinking and self-consciousness. The radical movement of modern Chinese (bai hua wen or modern prosaic Chinese) has launched a century's interruption of fantastic creation along the lines of conventional *zhiguai* stories. Interestingly, in contrast, many Western writers, such as Borges, Cortázar and Ursula Le Guin, created their unique style of fantastic tales under the influence of Daoism or Chinese *zhiguai*, whereas contemporary Chinese writers seek their Muses in Western culture and literature.

Lacking the imagination based on reincarnation featuring in Chinese literature, Western fairy tales bring into play the communication and interaction between men and the nonhuman by a direct description with the magical metamorphosis of animals and objects into human forms. For example, in one of the Brothers Grimm stories, "The fisherman and his wife," the world is larger than our perceived realm and it is in harmony with Nature's law. The fish speaks to the fisherman and reveals his identity as an enchanted prince to plead with the man to release him. The fish-prince communicates with the fisherman seven times without transforming into human form and grants him many boons (in fact demanded by the fisherman's greedy wife). The musician in "The Wonderful Musician" speaks and tricks the animals (a wolf, a fox and a hare) while fiddling around, looking for some company. In Andersen's tales, the nonhuman are able to discourse without assuming human form, for example, in "The Nightingale," the Chinese emperor communicates with the authentic nightingale that is truly faithful to the king and comes back to sing for him while the king is seriously ill. The storks in "The Marsh King's Daughter" play the role of narrator to tell the story and the truth concerning the misfortune (betrayed by her two sisters) of the heroine. Their narrative discourse plays a double role by using animals' language to stage the figurative language as literal. With the magic time and space, the storks themselves metamorphose and the heroine glides into an unknown realm of the future time-space on the night of her wedding. However, the right of speech is sometimes considered a taboo for nonhuman beings; for example, the heroine in "The Little Mermaid." In order to adopt human form to meet her charming prince, the mermaid cedes her sweet voice to the sorceress. This dilemma between choosing the human form and the voice or speech is rare in Eastern culture. The significance of language as a unity of body and form or of concrete and abstract is highlighted as the mermaid vaporizes into the air. This Western style of the magician's hat-discourse is more compliant to Nature's law than Chinese tales, since the latter still centralize on man's Dao to certain extent.

The Sheer *Mise en Abyme* of Chôra – The Unknown Space-Time and Faerie

The rhetoric mediating between the fantastic imagination and the formalization of logic can be sublimated into the *literal figure* from the perspective of time and space. Durand's theory of the imaginary develops from the isotopism of images appertaining to time and space. Bachelard's material imagination spans the known and the unknown realm. Jung's third way of synthesizing the two antithetic realms is creative imagination, which is indeed the synchronicity of various spaces. Barfield valued the aesthetic imagination that connects the archaic past and the imaginary future. His historical surmise that verbal inflections exist without a root echoes the synchronism of a semantic unity. Tolkien's proposal of sub-creation in the fairy-story extends to the unknown space (Faerie) and time (the unknown space renders time flexible and synchronic). With the present discourse of the magician's hat, the momentum that activates the plotting of the story lies in creating a Euclidean space through temporal imagination.

This kind of space can be one saturated by magical logic. Therefore, time can be frozen and stopped by sleep as in "Rose-Bud" to escape death. The magic of one of the fairies alleviates the curse of the uninvited revengeful fairy on the princess. The rhetoric of euphemism to escape death from the nocturnal imaginary of Durand is vividly depicted by the fantastic embodiment. The sleep and awakening after one hundred years echoes with the imaginary of death and resurrection. This interplay of figurative and literal recovers the true visage of language, for example, the semantic unity of the word "sleep." The poetic diction of simile that death is often compared to sleep may be in reality the literal meaning of the word in its semantic unity. This rhetoric of euphemism dominated by the pre-logic of fantastic imagination is often concretized in the fantastic tales with the motif of the *mise en miniature*. The stories such as the Grimms' "Tom Thumb," Hoffmann's "The Nutcracker" and Nodier's "La Fée aux miettes" (The Fairy of Crumbs) are the concrete representation of such rhetoric that mediates human fantastic imagination into formalized logic. The rhetoric of euphemism that moderate death via sleep and of miniaturization as antiphrasis will metamorphose into the synthetic structure, based on the hypotyposis of the unknown future and past as well as the invisible space.

Based on the theory of the imaginary, time plays a crucial role in conjuring up the myriads of fantastic images. Temporality makes the unknown space of chôra arcane and ineffable. However, time also offers the traces (like the traces left by the manifestations of the four elements departing from chôra) that man can track archetypes of the unknown realm where the antitheses co-exist in harmony. With the development of quantum physics and relativity, this temporal-spatial imagination continues, and plays an essential role in fantastic creation in modern times. The rhetoric of hypotyposis employed to mediate fantastic imagination into the formalization of what is conceivable ranges from musical imagination to the structure of Messiah. Like the invisible space calculated in algebra, fantastic literature imagines the unknown space through a vivid rhetoric of storytelling based on its informal logic. In literary tradition, the imagination of Arcadia has existed ever since the beginning of humanity. This imaginary space appears both in Chinese and Western literature. The Chinese equivalent to this Greek term is "Daohua yuan," which means the garden of peach blossoms. The quintessential idea of such a spatial imagination resides in the desire for a peaceful land without violence. This echoes with one of the possible origins of the naissance of language, to retain peace against violence. However, the initial dream for such a utopian space often turns out to be dystopia. The numerous works based on dystopia make such writings a sub-genre of imaginary literature. Since the gist of the present work is rhetoric of the fantastic discourse rendered by imagination, the focus will fall on imagining the unknown, invisible time and space, rather than on social criticism. The present investigation will go through the imagination of the unknown or invisible space, from conceptions of future and past to the imagery of a forbidden land, Faerie.

Though most critics of fantastic literature view science-fiction as a unique narrative genre distinctive from the fantastic or fantasy, we count it as a variation of fantastic storytelling uniquely popular in the times of technology, according to the perspective of the evolution of consciousness. Our technological epoch is the later period of the intellectual and conscious age where science and technology decide our lifestyle and thinking mode. The narrative style drawing on the rhetoric of the naïve representation of imaginary creatures like Homer's epics or *Beowulf* or the solemn religious work like *The Divine Comedy*, or Chinese *Journey to the West* does not allure the reader as much as science-fiction or contemporary fantasy. As the earlier science-fiction *Frankenstein* focuses on death and life creation, science-fiction towards the end of the 19th century shifted to the imagination of time and space beyond death and enhanced the narrative art with updated scientific knowledge. Considered as the father of modern science-fiction (or rather science-fantasy) writing, Jules Verne's fascination with the unknown space, the outer-space and the mysterious past hidden in certain space is rendered into absorbing stories.

Verne's novel *Twenty Thousand Leagues under the Sea* freely depicts the imaginary undersea world, fantastic but based on geographical realism. The whole novel is driven by vivid description, giving momentum to images related to the archaic records of mountains and seas. The inception of the novel explicitly announces the coming of the fantastic adventure on the sea:

> The year 1866 was marked by a strange occurrence, an unexplained and inexplicable phenomenon that surely no one has forgotten. [...]
> The fact was that for some time a number of ships had been encountering, on the high seas, 'an enormous thing,' described as a long, spindle-shaped object that was sometimes phosphorescent, and infinitely larger and faster than a whale. [Verne, 13]

Readers' horizon of expectation surrounds a certain undersea monster as the narrator continues to tell in Chapter III that he "had had no more thought of chasing the sea unicorn than of finding the Northwest Passage." The narrator's vocation is to "pursue this annoying monster [killer narwhal] and rid the world of it" [ibid., 25]. The title of Chapter VII, "An Unknown Species of Whale" harks back to our choice of the decisive term *unknown* that defines fantastic literature in this book. The narrator discreetly uses the term "unknown" to refer to the monster instead of "supernatural," though he keeps on designating it as "the monster."

As readers are still entrapped in the horror of the monster ("I thought of the monster! ... But where had that voice come from? ... The times are long past since Jonah's taken refuge in the bellies of whales!" [ibid., 53]) With the Biblical allusion, the enunciated "this monster is made of steel" starts to hint that the unknown monster is proved to be nothing but the submarine *Nautilus* directed by Captain Nemo. And obviously, the narrator (Professor Aronnax) and his colleagues of the *Abraham Lincoln* are abducted by their original prey (their mission is to hunt the unknown ship). The focus of the novel in fact shifts to the imaginary voyages narrated by the abducted professor under the sea. The professor views the fantastic phenomena throughout his voyage as "natural" phenomena "unknown" to the scientists on earth. In this manner, the setting of the novel agrees with Nature's law, the "supernatural" parts remain as the "unknown" realm awaiting scientific discovery. He himself also emphasizes: "I am a writer whose business it is to record thing that appear impossible, yet are incontestably real. This was not a dream. I saw and felt what I am describing!" [ibid., 263]. In less than ten months, the narrator covers twenty thousand leagues to witness wonders in the Pacific and Indian Oceans, the Red Sea, the Mediterranean, the Atlantic, and the North and the South Polar Seas. Through his adventure under the sea with Captain Nemo, Aronnax reconsiders the credibility of human knowledge and the approximation of the antique people's conception and perception.

The novel refers to Plato's Atlantes and leads us to the extraordinary and imaginary trip to this lost world. Plato's dialogue between Timaeus and Critias was inspired by Solon who mentioned that the first Athenian city – Saïs – had been invaded and partly destroyed by the Atlantes. Atlantis is often taken as a metaphor since the lost continent has never been rediscovered. Jules Verne resurrects the life of language by bringing the professor to travel throughout various historical wonders of Nature. The narrator does see and touch the lost continent.Atlantis with Nemo. It is reported as "extending from the twelfth degree of latitude to the fortieth degree north" [ibid., 266].

Likewise, the conversation between Nemo and the narrator on the name of the Red Sea is also a reflection on language. The captain answers Aronnax's question on the origin of the name by adducing a chronicler of the fourteenth century:

> This imaginative person claims that its name was given to the Red Sea after the passage of the Israelites, when Paraoh perished in the waters that closed about him at Moses' command:
>> *En signe de cette merveille,*
>> *Devint la mer rouge et vermeille.*
>> *Non puis ne surent la nommer*
>> *Autrement que la rouge mer.*
>> "To commemorate that marvel,
>> The sea turned red and vermilion;
>> What else could one call it then,
>> Except the Red Sea!" [ibid., 219]

Finding the poet's explanation satisfactory, Aronnax insists on the captain's personal opinion. The captain's opinion is quite simple: "'Red Sea' is a translation of the Hebrew word 'Edom' and, if the ancients gave it this name, it was because of the special colour of these waters. "[...] I remember having seen the Bay of Tor completely red, like a lake of blood"" [ibid., 219]. The fact and the name converge as the red colour is explained by the microscopic algae, *trichodesmia*. And the very spot where Moses crossed with his people is proved by the captain to be sand-bound. Other fantastic locales, including giant sea monsters such as their genuine fighting against an enormous squid-like monster, described by the narrator, are by the same token a trace back to the semantic unity of language as myth, metaphor and truth, the idea embraced by Barfield, Tolkien and other theorists of the imaginary.

The tales and records in Chinese *Shanhai Jing* (*The Classic of Mountains and Seas*) describe sundry unknown creatures and locales. Scholars often consider the content of the book nothing but the outgrowth of fantastic imagination. However, more archeological explorations discover more and more evidences of the factuality of these mythic and fantastic records. The imaginary creature of dragon exists in the language of ancient people of both Chinese and European culture. Recently, archeological discoveries have gradually revealed the myste-rious visage of the dragon, the alleged imaginary monster in many European ep-ics and divine creature in Chinese fantastic literature. The return of language's semantic unity is not only taking place in the vivid depiction of the imaginary space but also in the storytelling of time as extra-space.

Verne's English counterpart, H. G. Wells, dedicated a rich imaginary treas-ure based on his scientific knowledge. His "The New Accelerator" explains the existence of an invisible extra-space formed under ultra-light speed. Based on the imaginary of time and space and the intellectual background of quantum physics, Wells created his relativity in fantastic storytelling. In the story, the hero and his friend take the accelerator drug and move with the speed of light. Speeding this condition, other objects and people appear to them to move at a snail's pace, almost motionless. In fact, according to Todorov, this kind of tale is termed as the instrumental marvellous, the story of what could be possible in the future. The imaginary of temporality against space is not modern in fantastic writing. In many tales concerning the imaginary realm of Faerie or Chinese *Xianjing* or *Fudi Dongtian*, men experience a radical lapse of time as they leave from the unknown realm for their own world. Daoist records already explain that one day in fairyland equals one generation (normally one hundred years) in the secular world. It seems that one day, such temporal and spatial imagination (time is calculated "differently" in the fantastic realm) could meet in science.

The magician's hat-discourse sometimes manifests as an entire *mise en abyme* to the dream-discourse. The imagination of the unknown past is depicted through dreamy images as a sub-creation on the level of microcosm. Irish writer Lord Dunsany excelled at such a discourse in narrating the poetic tale "The Sword of Welleran." Similar to the style in the fantastic in the dream-discourse, the language is that of a grand style with many archaic words. The toponyms and patronymics in the story are imbued with an unknown and remote atmos-phere. Though the narrator says "I," the narrator is more an implied author who tells the story from an objective point of view. The initial description of the set-ting is followed by the heterodiegetic narrator:

> Where the great plain of Tarphet runs up, as the sea in estuaries, among the Cyresian mountains, there stood long since the city of Merimna well-nigh among the shadow of the crags. I have never seen a city in the world so beau-tiful as Merimna seemed to me when I first dreamed of it. It was a marvel of spires and figures of bronze, and marble fountains, and trophies of fabulous wars, and broad streets given over wholly to the Beautiful. [Silverberg, 26]

The dream mentioned in the story echoes the rhetoric of the *mise en abyme* of the dream-discourse. The story bears both metaphorical and literal meanings. The narrator's dream is the key to the imaginary of the unknown, which also re-fers to the realm of Jungian collective unconscious. The narrator names himself a dreamer and addresses "you" to the implied reader. The story time is 100 years back from the present time of enunciation. The war in the dream and the fortress city in the past in the dream of the narrator is like many concentric circles. The collective unconscious is represented by the rhetoric of condensed storytelling that connects the inhabitants with deceased heroes and guarding deities. This imagination of microcosm is enhanced by the archetypal images of sea, mountains and woods, which give a sense of history in space and time. The narrative is rhythmic like the rhythm in dream or the rhythm from the remote and arcane chôra.

The inhabitants of the city Merimna get connected with their deceased heroes and enter the battlefield to defend their beautiful city in dreams. Simultaneously, readers' aesthetic imagination is aroused to get in contact with the human collective unconscious. The narration of the story is unique in its concentric dreams. The action of war takes place in the dreams of the inhabitants, who are dreamed by the narrator who inspires us readers to dream. After Merimna's people awake from their dream of the bloody battle, they also awake from their eternal dream that the six heroes of Merimna are alive protecting the city:

> Thus wept the people of Merimna in the hour of their great victory, for men have strange moods, while beside them their old inviolate city slumbered safe. But back from the ramparts and beyond the mountains and over the lands that they had conquered of old, beyond the world and back again to Paradise, went the souls of Welleran, Soorenard, Mommolek, Rollory, Akanax, and young Iraine. [ibid., 41]

The heroes' names as language and their statues as symbols to the inhabitants eventually lead to a concrete existence and an abstract spiritual emblem as well. The only connection between the abstract and the concrete is dreams, in reality fantastic storytelling. Tolkien's interesting story of "The Farmer Giles of Ham" also tells a story from the imaginary unknown past that seemingly reveals the truth in semantic unity of language and myth. The dragon Chrysophylax, the stupid giant (the one that "had started all the trouble one summer's night long before") and the loony but lucky farmer Giles live the history of Ham and tell the story of the name "the Lord of Ham" and "the Lord of Tame," which later derives into Thame. Myth, truth and history are converged by the imaginary images into the hypotyposis of the unknown past.

By the same token, fantastic storytelling extends to the imagination of time in the future. This is a popular topic in contemporary fantastic creation, especially in science-fiction. The story can be a travel into the past and the future by an imaginary invention, for example, Wells's *The Time Machine*, which demonstrates the eternal truth of human nature through time. In the year 802,701 AD, violence seems outwits everything and language also splits into fragile peace (spoken by the Eloi) and strong violence (uttered by the Morlock). The issue of men's wicked nature is commonly raised in science-fiction that depicts the un-known future. Arthur C. Clarke envisioned in 1968 the future world by telling a story of voyage into the outer space in *2001: A Space Odyssey*. Although this future has now become our past, the combination of temporal and spatial imagi-nation with human evolution from apes and the imagery of the universal light or "God" is a 20th-century idiosyncrasy. With the magician's hat-discourse, authors are free to juggle all kinds of scenes through hypotyposis of the unknown future. This imagination of the unknown future attracts more contemporary writers. For example, Isaac Asimov's Foundation series vividly depicts an unimaginable fu-ture that even integrates religion with science and psychology.

The last category of the magician's hat-discourse compliant to Nature's law is governed by the imaginary of time transcending to the forbidden realm or the imaginary setting of sub-creation. Authors represent the collective unconscious by painting and chanting the unknown realm. Such an imaginary unknown realm is in fact perilous (as Tolkien characterized it) and forbidden to the ordinary and mediocre, i.e., only the elites can enter the forbidden space. In Chinese fantastic tales, the *Xianjing* or *Fudi Dongtian* is only reserved for those who have *xiangu* (fairy bones) or have the potential to succeed in the practice of Dao, which is germane to true or primary imagination. This is very close to the state of return-ing to original participation, a harmonization of antithetic dualism. The follow-ing is a synthetic definition of Daoist *Xiangjing* or Faerie:

> In order to become *xian* (divine and immortal), Daoism constructs a space in-habited by deities, named *Xianjing*. This is the embodiment of the Daoist creed. These divine places spanning (1) heaven, such as *sanqingjing* (Realm of three main gods), (2) the sea, such as the ten continents and three islands, (3) moun-tains and caves, such as the ten major *dongtian*, thirty-six minor *dongtian* and seventy-two *fudi*. The word *dong* means its quasi-homophone *tong*, which sig-nifies "connect or communicate." Therefore, the spatial term *dongtian* also re-fers to "communicate or connect with heaven." In order to accomplish Daoist practice, the earthly deities and fairies live in *Dongtian Fudi* to get connected with the celestial deities and thus get access to heaven. The word *fu* means "bliss" and *di* means "earth." Those who live in *fudi* can live for several gen-erations. Daoist practice normally refers to alchemy, consisting of external al-chemy (*waidan*) and internal alchemy (*neidan*).[77]

The motif of heroes who tumble into the fairy realm abounds Chinese fantastic literature. This can be a short visit, a sensual experience, a marriage between the fairy and the human, and a spiritual enlightenment. In the fairy realm, nonhuman creatures are also endowed with certain divine colours and with language and

---

[77] This explanation is combined from Ren Jiyu's *Zongjiao Cidian* (Dictionary of Religion), Ching Xitai's *Zhongguo Daojiao* (Chinese Daoism) and Hu Fushen's *Zhonghua Daojiao Dacidian* (Chinese Daoist Dictionary).

special ability. If the chosen one who has entered the realm and later reveals the locale to the ordinary people, the gate of the realm will be forever shut from him. In the realm of fairy, we may encounter evil creatures, termed as *jing* or spirits. They also possess supernatural magic power from their practice of Dao but they are still practicing Dao. This traditional Chinese vision sees no hell, i.e., evil spirits also live in the unknown realm, which is similar to the peril in Faerie. Tolkien's definition of Faerie with its restriction and peril is very close to this Daoist taboo:

> The realm of fairy-story is wide and deep and high and filled with many things: all manner of beasts and birds are found there; shoreless seas and stars uncounted; beauty that is an enchantment, and an ever-present peril: both joy and sorrow as sharp as swords. In that realm a man may, perhaps, count himself fortunate to have wandered, but its very richness and strangeness tie the tongue of a traveler who would report them. And while he is there it is dangerous for him to ask too many questions, lest the gates should be shut and the keys be lost. [Tolkien 1997, 109]

Faerie or *Xianjing* represented in the story with the magician's hat-discourse is a glimpse of the collective unconscious. The fascination of Chinese people with immortality, especially among emperors and scholars, makes the stories of *Xianjing* idiosyncratic to Chinese fantastic storytelling. The tale from the collection of *Hou Soushen ji* (*Post* In Search of Gods and Spirits), "Liu Chen and Ran Zhao," is the paradigm of the *Xianjing* narrative pattern which is re-created by various arts of embellishment.

In this story, the two heroes go to Tiantai Mountain to search for herbs, but get lost. They chance to intrude on the realm of shenxian (deities) and encounter two extraordinarily beautiful damsels. The lucky heroes thus spend a wonderful time with the fairies (without knowing the fairies' real identity) and have stayed for half a year. Although the two damsels ask them to stay by implying that they come here because of their spiritual fortune or karma and should enjoy such happiness, both heroes, still attached to secular family, insist on going home. They return home only to see their offspring of seven generations after them. This is an archetypal narration of the lapse between the divine time and the secular time. In this story, six months seemingly equal seven hundred earthly years. The story ends with the quest for Dao. Both heroes try to track back to the fairyland but in vain. In the end, they decide to forsake the secular life and practice Dao in the mountains.

A variation developed from this archetypal story of "encountering fairy or gods in Faerie" is created by Pu Songling. He excelled his narrative art by modifying the story into "Pianpian" in which the two damsels from the above tale are changed into a nymph of the banana tree, named Pianpian, and the heroes are modified into a hero named Luo Zifu. In this late version, the hero is invited by the heroine to stay at her place overnight. Then the couple get married and have a child. After the child grows up, the hero always shows his secular attachment. The heroine thus cut paper into three donkeys to ride them home. Later, the hero misses his wife and goes back with his son to the cave; however, they can see nothing but yellow leaves. The forbidden realm of the divine beings can only be reached by chance and luck but never be found with human vision.[78] This concept of passivity concerning encountering the divine harks back to Marion's assumption of passivity in "vision" the icone. The idea of passivity and the forbidden fairy realm can be exemplified in many fantastic tales, both in the East and the West.

The fantastic imagination of the unknown fairy realm also informs Western literature. As in the aforementioned definition of Tolkien, Faerie is also endowed with secret as a forbidden realm. Like the alchemical imagination, the substance of gold being the sublimating key to the absolute realm (we may refer to the book *Taiyi jinghua zongzhi*, translated as *The Secret of the Golden Flower* by Richard Wilhelm and annotated by Jung), gold is also the magic key in Western stories. For example, in Hoffmann's "The Golden Pot," the golden pot spans the earthly and the fairy realms. In MacDonald's "The Golden Key," the golden key allows the boy (named Mossy) to get access to the realm of rainbow whence the shadows fell. Tolkien's "Smith of Wootton Major" features a tinsel star (wrapping a small silver star) and serves as the key to get connected with Faerie.

The magician's hat-discourse in *Twenty Thousand Leagues under the Sea* utilizes hypotyposis of the imaginary Atlantis from a geographical and archeological perspective, whereas in "The Golden Pot," Atlantis is described as a golden fairyland of the salamander family. This fairy realm is only accessible through certain magic power. The story is deployed through the conflict between the good and evil magic (the fight between the Salamander Lindhorst and the old witch Liese) and between the poetic and the prosaic (the conflict between the hero Anselmus and the bourgeois Conrector family; also the contrast between Serpentina and Veronica). The magic golden pot is in fact the dowry of Serpentina who is deeply in love with the hero and vice versa. Towards the end of the story, this imaginary realm is also shown through the narrator's personal visit. The transitional space is the azure chamber (the exact place where the hero undergoes a season of instruction) of Lindhorst Archivarius. The latter mounts into the golden goblet (filled with liquor) held in the narrator's hand and vanishes in the blaze. Even the heterodiegetic narrator partakes of the precious drink and glides into the fairyland of Atlantis.

---

[78] The Confucian writers are inclined to write about the motif of the supernatural women giving birth to children, especially a boy. Given that having a son to continue the family blood complies with the "family Dao," supernatural women, such as fox-spirits or ghosts, will be accepted by the parents of the hero or the society after they give birth to a child.

The golden (flower) pot, possessed by the snake spirit Serpentina, is coupled with the fire lily and the power of transition between two realms. The bad witch (who recovers the quill of the black Dragon) desires the golden pot to perfect her power. Hoffmann vividly tells interactions among the witch, the mediocre people, the poetic hero and the divine beings from Atlantis. The painting of the golden garden of Atlantis resembles that of a Daoist or Buddhist heaven. Above all, the aesthetic imagination with poetic language is at the centre of the storytelling. For example, the elite with a particular taste beyond the secular standard can have the hand of Serpentina, the owner of the golden pot. The hero's original writings are criticized and corrected by the Salamander who instructs him for a season to catch the sublime status of poetic language. Even the closure of the story explicitly reveals to readers the secret of Atlantis:

> Were you not even now in Atlantis; and have you not at least a pretty little copyhold farm there, as the poetical possession of your inward sense? And is the blessedness of Anselmus anything else but a living in poesy? Can anything else but poesy reveal itself as the sacred harmony of all beings, as the deepest secret of nature? [Hoffmann 1993, 70]

It is obvious that this fairyland is forbidden to those who lack poesy.

The dominating material in Hoffmann's story is the element fire (the salamander) with golden images. Likewise, MacDonald's "The Golden Key" also places fire as a central motif that leads to the imaginary realm of rainbow, related to light. Rainbow can be regarded as a universal archetype that links the earthly and the heavenly. In Chinese myth, the greatest goddess Nüwa refines the penta-colour (or rainbow) stone to make up the hole in the sky. In the Biblical myth, God appears as rainbow in promise to Noah and his offspring. In Greek myth, Iris (rainbow) is a messenger between heaven and earth. In Irish myth, leprechauns bury treasure at the end of rainbow. In "The Golden Key," the rainbow refines figurative meanings as its literal meanings and recovers its semantic unity. Other elements signified by language also regain their pristine meanings. The storytelling is more a mystic teaching (as Tolkien criticized in his "On Fairy-Stories") than a description of the unknown.

The beginning accords with the convention of fairy tale: "There was a boy who used to sit in the twilight and listen to his great-aunt's stories" [Anderson, 22]. The heterodigetic narrator explicitly states the differences between the real world and Fairyland: "things that look real in this country look very thin indeed in Fairyland, while some of the things that here cannot stand still for a moment, will not move there" [ibid., 23]. The boy learns from his aunt about the golden key (he can find it if he reaches the place where the end of the rainbow stands) and takes it seriously. Living near the border between Fairyland and man's realm, he finds the golden key upon a bed of moss and is thus called Mossy. A parallel episode is taking place with a girl, Tangle (the name is taken from her being untidy). Guided by the fairy fish, she meets the fairy Grandmother and is educated to keep clean. The two children reunite and are sent out from the fairy's house for their quest, to find the hole to the golden key. They encounter people of shadows and want to find the country from which the shadows come. The imagination of time lapse takes place in this story, as the two children settle for the quest in the valley (the sea of shadows), "Mossy's hair was streaked with gray, and Tangle had got wrinkles on her forehead" [ibid., 35]. From this valley of shadows, they lose each other and undertake their individual adventure. Guided by the fish, now an aëranth, Tangle encounters the Old Man of the Sea, the Old Man of the Earth and the Old Man of the Fire. The structure is a conspicuous rendering of the rudimentary elements of man's imagination. On the other hand, Mossy encounters directly the Old Man of the Sea and is guided by the flying fish to the end of the rainbow. There he finds the hole of sapphire to his golden key and enters the rainbow (representing the element of air), where he reunites with Tangle (guided there by a serpent).

The end of the story is enhanced by the sounds of Aeolian music and their continual going up to the country whence the shadows fell. The universal images of caves related to divine power as in Daoist *Xianjing* or Faerie are found in this story. Moreover, the imagination of time lapse is represented here: "For seven years [...] seemed to her like seven hours" [ibid., 41]. The magician's hat-discourse under this category is a sheer *mise en abyme* of the dream-discourse since it touches upon universal elements underlying our imagination (water, earth, fire and air). The storytelling is a recovery of the multi-meanings in language where concrete and abstract is a unity of *unus mundus* as Tangle observes: "For she knew there must be an infinite meaning in the change and sequence and individual forms of the figures into which the child [the Old Man of the Fire] arranged the balls, as well as in the varied harmonies of their colours, but what it all meant she could not tell" [ibid., 40].

The narrative structure that MacDonald utilized to depict Fairyland and the interaction between the divine and secular men is quite similar to Chinese narration, both highlighting more a symbolic depiction of wisdom. However, Tolkien is not satisfied with this kind of storytelling and finds the story "ill-written, incoherent, and bad, in spite of a few memorable passages" [Anderson, 21]. Inspired by this "ill-written" tale, Tolkien himself created a fairy-story, "Smith of Wootton Major," to demonstrate his ideal and consummate art of a true storytelling of fantasy.

The beginning of Tolkien's story is already distinct from the stereotyped one of "The Golden Key": "There was a village once, not very long ago for those with long memories, not very far away for those with long legs. Wootton Major it was called because it was larger than Wootton Minor, ..." [Tolkien 1998, 147]. The golden pot and the golden key are now metamorphosed, under the art of Tolkien, into a tinsel star, which wraps a silver star from Faery. Tolkien availed himself of telling the passing of the talisman by the Twenty-four Feast. The King of Faery (Alf) is disguised as a cook called Prentice. The kid who has the piece of cake with the star inside inadvertently swallows it. The description of the discovery of the magic star and the possession of the artistic power (e.g. craftsmanship) illustrates Tolkien's definition of Fantasy. The boy hears the dawn-song of the birds, passing on like a wave of music into the West:

> 'It reminds me of Faery,' he heard himself say; 'but in Faery the people sing too.' Then he began to sing, high and clear, in strange words that he seemed to known by heart; and in that moment the star fell out of his mouth and he caught it on his open hand. [...] there the star stayed in the middle of his forehead, and he wore it for many years. [ibid., 155]

The boy grows up and obtains the name of Starbrow. He is privileged to enter the realm of Faery, though plenty of evils, "he was as safe as a mortal can be in that perilous country. The Lesser Evils avoided the star, and from the Greater Evils he was guarded" [Ibid., 157]. Thus the hero travels for years between his home and Faery. He meets and converses with the Faery Queen and King "as a learner and explorer, not a warrior." Eventually, the Twenty-four Feast has come again and the Master Cook (now Prentice, later disclosed to be King of Faery) asks Starbrow to pass the fay-star to next elite child. They both choose Tim, the little great grand-son of the old Nokes.

The closure of the story is a funny one that leaves readers to linger with the music of Faery and the ludicrous figure of Nokes (who was indeed once frightened by the Faery King's appearance after he mocked Faery): "But old Nokes thumped his stick on the floor and said roundly: 'He's [Prentice] gone at last! And I'm glad for one. I never liked him. He was artful. Too nimble, you might say'" [Ibid., 178]. This jocose end harks back to the humorous tone that ends the story "Farmer Giles of Ham":

> But at last, waking suddenly, he [the dragon Chrysophylax] set off in search of that tallest and stupidest of the giants, who had started all the trouble one summer's night long before. He gave him a piece of his mind, and the poor fellow was very much crushed.
>
> 'A blunderbuss, was it?' said he, scratching his head. 'I thought it was horseflies!' [Ibid., 57]

The Semantic as Formal Syntax Based on Hypotyposis

The vivid storytelling of the known as semantic existence is the essential art of the magician's hat-discourse. The imaginary substratum resides in Durand's nocturnal regime with isotopic symbols that construct the mystic structures of the imaginary, based on the basic rhetoric of antiphrasis or euphemism that extends to hypotyposis. This third pattern of discourse forces readers from the outset into a frame of realism concerning the representation of the unknown, whether the setting is as realistic, or completely unheard-of to readers. The reigning rhetoric is grounded in antiphrasis and antithesis and their mutual interplay. Such imaginary structures decide the ending, tragic or happy, of the stories. Most storytelling predominated by images from the diurnal regime orients to a tragic ending, for example, "The Judge's House." Fantastic images from the nocturnal regime converge into antiphrasis and further extend to synthetic structures. They orient towards a happy ending. For example, most of the tales with space-time under Nature's law have a happy ending, albeit after surmounting dangers or catastrophe.

In the mirror-discourse, the rhetoric lies in causing doubt and authentication and the reading of the stories is often considered irreversible (not exclusively since the fantastic diction plays an important role to arouse aesthetic imagination). In contrast, the magician's hat-discourse invites repetitive reading or recitation, like the musical repetition in the art of fantastic diction. For example, "The Canterville Ghost" with its multi-climaxes of the "spooky" appearances and the continual interaction and conversation between the ghost and Virginia, transcends the linear reading of the dialectics of the menace and the exorcism of the ghost to a third possible harmony. The reading process metamorphoses into the alchemy of language when the figurative and the literal converge and reunite again. To employ a Chinese epithet of describing the hypotyposis of narrative art, the magician's hat-discourse starts with telling the unreal as real and ascends to the state of telling the secondary "real" as the extra-unreal out of the unreal. The imaginary route to the unknown and arcane chôra is in fact not far. Metaphysics is closer to our perception as the metamorphosis of language comes nearer to metaphor and thus retrieves its figures.

Conclusion

The rhetoric of fantastic literature aims at offering a universal narrative scheme for stories grounded in the universal roots of imagination. We reconsider the essential meanings of rhetoric along the lines of Aristotle to develop our analysis of fantastic rhetoric. Therefore, both writers' and readers' *Weltanschauungen* are vital to the appreciation and reception of fantastic works, especially when it comes to world literature. In compliance with intimate studies of theories and critiques from different linguistic cultures and of the imaginary of fantastic literature, the rhetoric of the fantastic takes on the function of storytelling striding across both fact and imagination, as highlighted by Aristotle, in the poetics of mimesis. In the arguments of our theory in the section of the representation of *Yi Jing* and chôra, metamorphosis features as the essence of the narrative momentum that develops into myriads of forms. The importance of strangeness in the art of *lexis* or diction first manifests itself in the narrative discourses of fantastic literature, apart from strangeness on the lexical level. Fantastic literature is quintessentially poeticized through the storytelling of strangeness. Though pertinent to the principle of strangeness, fantastic literature appears as a sensible art, given that the contrivance of storytelling requires Reason. The similarity between fantastic storytelling and musical composition links to the origin of man's mythopoeia in verse chanting and music.

Accordingly, all the three patterns of fantastic rhetoric, the dream-discourse, the mirror-discourse and the magician's hat-discourse, tell stories, whether complex or simple. In the first narrative pattern, we are presented with fantastic epics created from the collective memory of the unknown past. Whether the structure is external alchemy or internal alchemy, the dream-discourse represents the human collective dream in communion with chôra. It is a complete symphony of musical harmonization of storytelling through hypotyposis, taken literally. The mirror-discourse is the outgrowth of our intellectual and conscious ages. Readers are presented with unending doubts concerning unknown phenomena. The central aesthetics of ambiguity with hyperbolic expressions arouses readers' imagination to awaken from the languish reality that has long been appropriated. Symbolic images hinging on the diurnal regime dominate the present discourse, thus engendering the antithetical and schizomorphic structures. The last, but no the least, the magician's hat-discourse is indeed the recovery of the lost epics and myths. This narrative pattern regains its popularity in the present day. Not many writers are competent in creating a comprehensively and scrupulously structured fantastic epic like Tolkien in our times, for we are in an age of splintered consciousness and language. However, the magician's hat-discourse still functions to arouse our aesthetic imagination to trace back to the original harmony. This harmony can be found in arcane space long dreamed by everyone – chôra or *Liangyi* or *De*. This is the space of oxymoron that welcomes the polar antithesis but amalgamates it into the harmony of *unus mundus*. In a word, fantastic literature activates our imagination that continues the fire of metamorphosis. Through seizing the figures of metaphors by the rhetorical storytelling of the fantastic, this metamorphosis sublimates into the realm of unknown metaphysics.

Bibliography

Theories and Critiques: Books, Journals and Encyclopedia

Anglard, Véronique. 1997. *Humain et inhumain*. Paris: Editions Nathan.
Apter, T. E. 1982. *Fantasy Literature: An Approach to Reality*. Bloomington: Indiana UP.
Aristotle. 1970. *The Poetics of Aristotle*. Trans. Preston H. Epps. Chapel Hill: The U of North Carolina P.
Aristotle. 1980. *Poétique*. Trans. Roselyne Dupont-Roc and Jean Lallot. Paris: Éditions du Seuil.
Aristotle. 1991. *Rhétorique*. Trans. Charles-Emile Ruelle. Paris: Le Livre de Poche.
Attery, Brian. 1980. *The Fantastic Tradition in America: From Irving to Le Guin*. Bloomington: Indiana UP.
Bachelard, Gaston. 1942. *L'Eau et les Rêves*. Paris: José Corti.
Bachelard, Gaston. 1943. *L'Air et les songes. Essai sur l'imagination du mouvement*. Paris: José Corti.
Bachelard, Gaston. 1984. *La Poétique de la rêverie*. Paris: PUF.
Bachelard, Gaston. 1985. *La Psychanalyse du feu*. Paris: Gallimard.
Bachelard, Gaston. 1993. *La Formation de l'esprit scientifique. Contribution à une psychanalyse de la connaissance*. Paris: Vrin.
Baldick, Chris. 1987. *In Frankenstein's Shadow: Myth, Monstrosity and Nineteenth-Century Writing*. Oxford: Clarendon Press.
Barfield, Owen. 1967. *History in English Words*. London: Lindisfarne Books.
Barfield, Owen. 1967. *Romanticism Comes of Age*. Middletown: Wesleyan UP.
Barfield, Owen. 1973. *Poetic Diction: A Study in Meaning*. Middletown: Wesleyan UP.
Barfield, Owen. 1988. *Saving the Appearances: A Study in Idolatry*. Middletown: Wesleyan UP.
Baronian, J.-B. 1977. *Un nouveau fantastique*. Lausanne: Editions l'âge d'Homme.
Baronian, J.-B. 1978. *Panorama de la littérature fantastique de la langue française*. Paris: Stock.
Barron, Neil (ed.). 1990. *Fantasy Literature: A Reader's Guide*. New York /London: Garland.
Barthes, Roland. 1970. *Mythologie*. Paris: Éditions du Seuil.
Belevan, Harry. 1980. *Théorie du fantastique*. Centre international de documentation sur la littérature de l'étrange, no. 27. Bruxelles: Editions Recto-verso, "Ides et Autres."
Belzane, Guy. 1990. *La Métamorphose*. Paris: Editions Quintette.
Bergez, Daniel. 1996. *L'Explication de texte litteraire*. Paris: Dunod.

Bernard, Jean-Louis. 1971. *Dictionnaire de l'insolite et du fantastique*. Paris: Editions du Dauphin.

Berthelot, Anne. 1996. *Arthur et la Table Ronde*. Paris: Découvertes Gallimard.

Berthelot, Francis. 1993. *La Métamorphose généralisée : du poème mythologique à la science-fiction*. Paris: Nathan.

Bertin, Johanna. 2004. *Strange Events and More: Canadian Giants, Witches, Wizards, and Other Tales*. Alberta: Altitude publishing Canada Ltd.

Bessière, Irène. 1974. *Le Récit fantastique: la poétique de l'incertain*. Paris: Larousse.

Birzer, Bradley J. 2002. *J. R. R. Tokien's Sanctifying Myth: Understanding Middle-earth*. Wilmington: ISI Books.

Bleiler, Everett Franklin. 1985. *Supernatural Fiction Writers: Fantasy and Horror*. New York: Scribner.

Bloom, Harold (ed.). 1995. *Modern Fantasy Writers*. New York and Philadelphia: Chelsea House Publishers.

Bloom, Harold. 1982. *Agon: Towards a Theory of Revisionism*. New York and Oxford: Oxford UP.

Boothe, Wayne C. 1983. *The Rhetoric of Fiction*. London: Penguin Books.

Borges, J. P. 1980. *Manuel de zoologie fantastique*. Paris: C. Bourgeois.

Boulos Hage, Renée. 1993. *La quête de l'androgyne dans le récit fantastique français du XIX siècle*. Paris: La pensée universelle.

Boyer, Robert H./Kenneth J. Zahorski (eds.). 1984. *Fantasists on Fantasy: A Collection of Critical Reflections*. New York: Avon Books.

Bozzetto, Roger. "William Morris: naissance de l'heroic-fantasy." October 2002. <http://www.noosfere.com>.

Bozzetto, Roger. 1992. *L'Obscur objet d'un savoir : fantastique et science-fiction*. Aix-en-Provence: Publications de l'Université de Provence.

Bozzetto, Roger and Arnaud Huftier. 2004. *Les Frontières du fantastique: Approches de l'impensable en littérature*. Valenciennes: Presses universitaires de Valenciennes.

Bridge, Kathryn. 2004. *Extraordinary Accounts of Native Life on the West Coast*. Alberta: Altitude publishing Canada Ltd.

Brisson, Luc. 1998. *Plato: The Myth Maker*. Trans. Gerard Naddaf. Chicago: The U of Chicago P.

Brooke-Rose, Christine. 1981. *A Rhetoric of the Unreal: Studies in Narrative and Structure, Especially of the Fantastic*. Cambridge: Cambridge UP.

Brooks, Terry et al. 1998. *The Writer's Complete Fantasy Reference*. Cincinnati: Writer's Digest Books.

Brunel, Pierre. 1992. *Mythocritique: Théorie et parcours*. Paris : PUF.

Bulver, Kathryn M. 1995. *La Femme-démon: figurations de la femme dans la littérature fantastique*. New York/Paris: Peter Lang.

Burgin, Victor et al. 1986. *Formation of Fantasy*. London/New York: Methuen.

Caillois, Roger. 1966. "Préface – De la féerique à la science-fiction." *Anthologie de la littérature fantastique*. Paris: Gallimard.

Caillois, Roger. 1979. *Approches de l'imaginaire*. Paris: Gallimard.

Campany, Robert Ford. 1996. *Strange Writing: Anomaly Accounts in Early Medieval China*. Albany: State U of New York P.

Card, Orson Scott. 1990. *How to Write Science Fiction and Fantasy*. Cincinnati: Writer's Digest.

Carroll, Noel. 1990. *The Philosophy of Horror*. New York: Routledge.

Cassirer, Ernst. 1946. *Language and Myth*. Trans. Suzanne K. Langer. New York/London : Harper & Bros.

Cassirer, Ernst. 1955. *The Philosophy of Symbolic Form*. New Haven/London: Yale UP.

Castex, Pierre-Georges. *Le conte fantastique en France: de Nodier à Maupassant*. Paris: José Corti, 1987.

Cazenave, Michel (ed.). 1996. *Encyclopédie des symbols*. Trans. from *Knaurs Lexikon der Symbole*. Paris: Le Livre de Poche/La Pochothèque.

Chanady, Amaryll Beatrice. 1985. *Magical Realism and the Fantastic: Resolved versus unresolved antinomy*. New York/London: Gerland.

Chelebourg, Christian. 2000. *L'Imaginaire littéraire: Des Archétypes à la poétique du sujet*. Paris: Editions Nathan/HER.

Chen, Wenxin. 1995. *Zhongguo chuanqixiaoshuo shihua* (*History of Chinese chuanqi fiction*). Taipei: Zhengzhong Bookstore.

Cheng, Yizhong. 1990. *Tangdai xiaoshuo shihua* (*History of Tang fiction*). Beijing: Wenhuayishu.

Chesterton, Gilbert Keith. 1955. *The Everlasting Man*. New York: Doubleday Image Books.

Chevrel, Yves/Camille Dumoulié. 2000. *Le Mythe en littérature: Essais offerts à Pierre Brunel à l'occasion de son soixantième anniversaire*. Paris: PUF.

Cornwell, Neil. 1990. *The Literary Fantastic from Gothic to Postmodernism*. New York: Harvester Wheatsheaf.

Cortàzar, Julio. 1986. *Entretiens avec Omar Prego*. Paris: Gallimard.

Couty, Daniel. 1989. *Le Fantastique*. Paris: Bordas.

Cumings, E. K. 1934. *The Literary Development of the Romantic Fairy Tale in France*. Bryn Mawr: Pennsylvania.

Dars, Jaques. 1965. *Quelques aspects du fantastique dans la littérature chinoise des Tang et des Song: les histoires de démons et de fantômes du Tai-ping Guang-ji*. Thèse de doctorat. Université de Paris.

Day, William Patrick. 1985. *In the Circles of Fear and Desire: A Study of Gothic Fantasy*. Chicago: U of Chicago P.

Dessons, Gérard. 1995. *Introduction à la Poétique: Approche des Théories de la Littérature*. Paris : DUNOD.

Diables et demons d'Eurasie. 2003. *Revue IRIS,* 25. Grenoble: Université Stendhal.

Dictionnaire Hachette Multimédia Encyclopédique. 1998. CD-ROM. Paris: Hachette Livre.

Dong, Wanhua. 1976. *Cong Liaozhai zhiyi de renwu kan Qingdai de kejuzhidu han songyuzhidu (The System of Mandarinal Examinations and of judiciary of the Qing Dynasty Through the Characters in* Liaozhai zhiyi. Taipei: Association of Taixinshuini.

Du Bellay, Joachim. 1967. *Défense et illustration de la langue française. Les Regrets, Les Antiquités de Rome.* Paris: Gallimard.

Dubost, Francis. 1991. *Aspects fantastiques de la littérature narrative médiévale (XIIème-XIIIème siècles).* Paris: Librairie Honoré Champion.

Dumoulié, Camille. 1995. *Cet obscur objet du désir : essai sur les amours fantastique.* Paris: Ed. l'Harmattan.

Duperray, Max (ed.). 1990. *Du fantastique en littérature : Figures et figurations.* Aix Marseille: Publications de l'Université de Provence.

Durand, Gilbert. 1992. *Les Structures Anthropologiques de l'Imaginaire.* Paris: DUNOD.

Durand, Gilbert. 1996. *Introduction à la mythodologie: mythes et sociétés.* Paris: Editions Albin Michel, S.A..

Durand, Gilbert. 1998. *L'imaginaire symbolique.* Paris: Quadridge/PUF.

Ehrsam, Jean. 1985. *La littérature fantastique en France.* Paris: Hatier.

Eliade, Mircea. 1988. *Aspects du mythe.* Paris: Gallimard.

Eliade, Mircea. 1995. *Méphistophélès et l'androgyne.* Paris: Gallimard.

Fabre, Jean. 1992. *Le Miroir de sorcière: Essai sur la littérature fantastique.* Paris: J. Corti.

Fang, Zhengyao. 1990. *Zhongguo xiaoshuo piping shilue (History of Criticism on Chinese Fiction).* Beijing: Shehuei kexue.

Fernandez, Irène. 2002. *Et si on parlait... du* Seigneur des Anneaux. Paris: Presses de la Renaissance.

Finné, Jacques. 1980. *La literature fantastique: Essai sur l'organisation surnaturelle.* Bruxelles: Editions de l'université de Bruxelles.

Fontanier, Pierre. 1968. *Les Figures du discours.* Paris: Flammarion.

France, Peter. 2001. "Folklore and Literature: The Editor as Author." *NewComparison: For Peter France Writing and Rewriting Folklore, Fairytale and Literature* 31. Lancaster: Uniprint.

Furst, Lilian R. 1969. "Romanticism in Historical Perspective." *Comparative Literature, Matter and Method.* Ed. A. Owen Aldridge. Urbana: U of Illinois P, 61-89.

Gaudin, Colette (ed. & trans.). 2005. *On Poetic Imagination and Reverie: Gaston Bachelard.* Putnam: Spring Publications.

Genette, Gérard. 1972. *Figures III.* Paris: Éditions du Seuil.

Genette, Gérard. 1976. *Figures*. Paris: Éditions du Seuil.
Genette, Gérard. 1979. *Figures II*. Paris: Éditions du Seuil.
Genette, Gérard. 2004. *Métalepse: De la figure à la fiction*. Paris: Éditions du Seuil.
Geoffroy-Menoux, Sophie. 2000. *Introduction à l'études des texts fantastiques dans la littérature anglo-américaine*. Paris: Editions du Temps.
Goens, Jean. 1993. *Loups-garous, vampires et autres monstres*. Paris: CNS Editions.
Goethe, Johann Wolfgan von. 1994. *Essays on Art and Literature*. Princeton: Princeton UP.
Gordon, Rae Beth. 1992. *Ornament, Fantasy and Desire in Nineteenth-Century French Literature*. Princeton: Princeton UP.
Grant, Patrick. "Tolkien: Archetype and Word." *Crosscurrents*. 29 Sept. 2004. <http://www.crosscurrents.org/tolkien.htm>
Griswold, Charles. "Rhetoric and Poetry." *Standford Encyclopedia of Philosophy*. 5 Oct.2005 <http://plato.stanford.edu/contents.htm>.
Grivel, Charles. 1992. *Fantastique – Fiction*. Paris: PUF.
Guiomar, Michel. 1993. *Principes d'une esthétique de la mort : les modes de présences, les présences immédiates, le seuil de l'Au-delà*. Paris: Librairie générale française.
Guo, Pu (ed.) 2002. *Shanhai Jing (The Classic of Mountains and Seas)*. Taipei: Taiwan Guji.
Guo, Yuwen. 1985. Liaozhai zhiyi *de menghuan shijie (The Dreamy Universe in Liaozhai zhiyi)*. Taipei: Taiwan xuesheng.
Harper, Douglas (ed.). 2001. *Online Etymology Dictionary*. <http://www.etymonline.com>.
Hart, L. David. 1999. "The Classical Jungian School." *The Cambridge Companion to Jung*. Cambridge: Cambridge UP, 89-100.
He, Xianming. 1993. *Zhongguoren de siwangxintai (The Chinese Mentality faced with Death)*. Shanghai: Shanghai wenhua.
Hegel, Georg Wilhelm Friedrich. 1963. *Leçon sur la philosophie de l'histoire*. Paris: Librairie Philosophique J. VRIN.
Held, George F. 1995. *Aristotle's Teleological Theory of Tragedy and Epic*. Heidelberg: Universitätsverlag C. Winter.
Hellens, Franz. 1991. *Le Fantastique réel*. Bruxelles: Editions Labor.
Heller, Terry. 1987. *The Delights of Terror: An Aesthetics of the Tale of Terror*. Urbana: U of Illinois P.
Herder, Johann Gottfried Von. 1968. *Reflections on the Philosophy of the History of Mankind*. Chicago: U of Chicago P.
Hoad, T. F. (ed.). 2003. *The Concise Oxford Dictionary of English Etymology*. Oxford: Oxford UP.

Hocke, Gustav René/Cornélius Heim et al. 1977. *Labyrinthe de l'art fantastique, le maniérisme dans l'art européen.* Paris: Denoël Gonthier.

Holy Bible: King James Version Classic Companion. 2003. Thomas Nelson Inc.

Hou, Zhong Yi (ed.). 1986. *Zhongguo lidai xiaoshuo cidian (Dictionnary of Chinese Fiction).* Kunming: Yunnan Renmin Press.

Huang, Muochou. 1985. *Cong* Liaozhai zhiyi *tandao Pu Songling de sixiang-shiye (Exploration of the world of Pu Songling's thought through Liaozhai zhiyi).* Taipei: Tianshan.

Huang, Zexin. 1993. *Zhongguo de gui (Chinese Ghosts).* Beijing: Guojiwenhua.

Hume, Kathryn. 1985. *Fantasy and Mimesis: Responses to Reality in Western Literature.* London/New York: Methuen.

Hunter, Lynette. 1989. *Modern Allegory and Fantasy: Rhetorical Stances of Contemporary Writing.* Basingstoke: Macmillan Press.

Irwin, W. R. 1976. *The Game of the Impossible: The Rhetoric of Fantasy.* Urbana: U of Illinois P.

Iser, Wolfgang. 1993. *The Fictive and the Imaginary: Charting Literary Anthropology.* Baltimore/London: The Johns Hopkins UP.

Jackson, Rosemary. 1991. *Fantasy: The Literature of Subversion.* London/New York: Routledge.

Jaffé, Aniela. 1982. *Apparitions, fantômes, rêves et mythes.* Paris: Mercure de France.

Jauss, Hans Robert. 1978. *Pour une esthétique de la reception.* Trans. C. Maillard. Paris: Gallimard.

Jimenez, Marc. 1997. *Qu'est-ce que l'esthétique?* Paris: Gallimard.

Jin, Ronghua. 1984. *Liuchao zhiguai xiaoshuo qingjiedanyuan fenleisuoyin (Classified Index of the plots of zhiguai from the Six Dynasty).* Taipei: UP of Wenhua.

Jung, C. G. 1968. *The Archetype and the Collective Unconscious.* London: Routledge.

Jung, C. G. 1971. *Les Racines de la conscience: Etudes sur l'archétype.* Paris: Buchet/Chastel.

Jung, C. G. 1971. *Psychological Types. Collected Works 6.* Princeton: Princeton UP.

Jung, C. G. 1977. *Mysterium Coniunctionis. Collected Works 14.* Princeton: Princeton UP.

Jung, C. G. 1978. *Psychological Reflections.* Princeton: Princeton UP.

Jung, C. G. 1989. *Memories, Dreams, Reflections.* London: Vintage.

Jung, C. G. 1993. *Psychologie de l'inconscient.* Paris: Le Livre de Poche.

Jung, C. G. 1995. *L'Ame et la vie.* Paris: Buchet/Chastel.

Kearney, Richard. 2002. *On Stories.* London: Routledge.

Kennard, Jean E. 1975. *Number and Nightmare: Forms of Fantasy in Contemporary Fiction.* Hamden: Archon Books.

Kingsley, Peter. 2003. *Reality*. Inverness: The Golden Sufi Center.

Kroeber, Karl. 1988. *Romantic Fantasy and Science Fiction*. New Haven/London: Yale UP.

Kugler, Paul. 1997. "Psychic Imaging: A Bridge between Subject and Object." *The Cambridge Companion to Jung*. Cambridge UP, 71-85.

Lacassin, Francis. 1991. *Mythologie du fantastique : les rivages de la nuit*. Monaco/Paris: Editions du Rocher.

Langer, Susanne K. 1979. *Philosophy in a New Key: A Study in the Symbolism of Reason, Rite, and Art*. Cambridge/London: Harvard UP.

Le Fantastique contemporain. 2002/2003. *Revue IRIS / Les Cahiers du Gerf*, 24. Grenoble: Université Stendhal.

Le Guin, Ursula K. 1989. *The Language of the Night: Essays on fantasy and science fiction*. New York: Putnam's.

Le Mythe en littérature: Essais en hommage à Pierre Brunel. 2000. Paris: PUF.

Le Robert – Dictionnaire Historique de la langue française. 1992. Paris: Dictionnaire Le Robert.

Lei, Quming. 1990. *Liaozhai yishu tonglun* (*The Art of* Liaozhaizhiyi). Shanghai: Sanlian Bookstore.

Leibniz Gottfried Wilhelm, Freiherr von. 1994. *Writings on China*. Trans. Daniel J. Cook/Henry Rosemont. Chicago: Open Court.

Lem, Stanislaw. 1985. *Microworlds: Writings on science fiction and fantasy*. London: Secker & Warburg.

Levy-Bruhl, L. 1992. *Surnaturel-nature mentalité primitive*. Paris: PUF.

Li, Fengmao. 1986. *Liuchao sui tang xiandaolei xiaoshuo yanjiu* (*Studies of alchemical tales from the Six, Sui and Tang Dynasties*). Taipei: Taiwan xuesheng.

Li, Jie. 2005. "Shilun zhongguo gudai siyanshi de chansheng (*Attempt to Comment on the Naissance of Chinese Antique Poems of Tetra-character*)." *Sibei dire minzuxueyuan xuebao* (*Journal of the Second Northwest university for nationalities*) 2. <http://www.wanfangdata.com.cn/qikan/ periodical.Articles/xbdemzxyxb-zxshkxb/xbde2005/0502/050223.htm>

LI, Kunhai. 1980. *Tangdai chuanqi ji liaozhai* (*The chuanqi of Tang Dynasty and Liaozhai*). Taipei: Sanbuo.

Li, Shoujü. 1995. *Huxian xinyang yu hulijing gushi* (*Belief in Fox-Gods and the Stories of Fox-Spirits*). Taipei: Taiwan xuesheng.

Lie, Zi (A New Translation of *Lie Zi*). 1991. Trans. Wangshou Zhuang. Taipei: Sanmin Bookstore.

Lin, Zaiyong. 1991. *Guaiyi: Shenhuqishen de zhihui* (*The Strange et Superextraordinary: The Fantastic Wisdom*). Hangzhou: Zhejiang renmin.

Little, T. E. 1984. *The Fantasts*. Amersham: Avebury.

Long, Charles H. "Mythology." *The Encyclopedia Americanan* 19: 699-706. Danbury: Grolier, 1998.

Lovecraft, H. P. 1973. *Supernatural Horror in Literature*. New York: Dover Publications.

Lu, Runxiang. 1991. *Tanhu shuogui lu* (*Discourse on Foxes and Ghosts*). Taipei: Yuanliu.

Lu, Xun. 1992. *Zhongguo xiaoshuo shilue* (*History of Chinese Fiction*). Taipei: Fengyun shidai.

Luo, Jingzhi. 1986. *Pu Songling jiqi Liaozhai zhiyi* (*Pu Songling and his Liaozhai zhiyi*). Taipei: Guoli Bianyiguan.

Ma, Xiaohong. 1988. *Tian, Shen, Ren - Zhongguo chuantong de zaoshen yundong* (*Sky, Gods, Men – The Activity of Gods' Creation in the Traditional Chinese Culture*). Beijing: Guoji wenhua.

Mabille, Pierre. 1977. *Le miroir du merveilleux*. Paris: Editions de Minuit.

Mac Killen, Anne. 1920. *Le roman terrifiant ou roman noir*. Paris: Champion.

Main, Roderick. (ed.). 1998. *Jung on Synchronicity and the Paranormal*. Princeton: Princeton UP.

Maingueneau, Dominique. 1993. *Éléments de linguistique pour le texte littérature*. Paris: DUNOD.

Malrieu, Joël. 1992. *Le Fantastique*. Paris: Hachette.

Manlove, Colin. 1975. *Modern Fantasy: Five Studies*. New York/London: Cambridge UP.

Manlove, Colin. 1983. *The Impulse of Fantasy Literature*. London: MacMillan Press.

Manlove, Colin. 1990. "The Elusiveness of Fantasy." *The Shape of the Fantastic: Selected Essays from the 7th ICFA*. New York: Greenwood Press, 53-4.

Manlove, Colin. 1999. *The Fantasy Literature of England*. London: MacMillan Press.

Mao, Feng. 1998. *Shenmi zhuyi shixue* (*Poetics of Mysticism*). Beijing: Shenghuo dushu xinzhi sanlian Bookstore.

Marion, Jean-Luc. 2001. *De Surcroît*. Paris: PUF.

Mathews, Richard. 2002. *Fantasy: The Liberation of Imagination*. New York /London: Routledge.

Matthey, Hubert. 1915. *Essai sur le merveilleux dans la littérature française depuis 1800*. Lausanne: Payot.

Mellier, Denis. 1999. *L'Écriture de l'excès: Fiction fantastique et poétique de la terreur*. Paris: Honoré Champion.

Mellier, Denis. 2000. *La littérature fantastique*. Paris: Éditions du Seuil.

Meng, Shaorong/Zhang Xingqiang. 1995. *Lishishangde liandanshu* (*The History of Alchemy*). Shanghai: Shanghai keji jaoyu Press.

Milner, Max. 1960. *Le diable dans la littérature française de Cazotte à Baudelaire*. 2 Vols. Paris: José Corti.

Milner, Max. 1982. *La fantasmagorie: Essai sur l'optique fantastique*. Paris: PUF.

Mode, Heinz. 1977. *Démons et animaux fantastiques*. Paris: Kogan.

Monard J./M. Rech. 1974. *Le merveilleux et le fantastique*. Paris: Delagrave.

Muchembled, Robert. 2000. *Une histoire du diable: XIIe-XXe siècle*. Paris: Éditions du Seuil.

Naddaf, Gerard. 1998. "Translator's Introduction." *Plato: The Myth Maker*. Chicago: The U of Chicago P.

Nandris, Grigore. 1969. "The Historical Dracula: The Theme of his Legend in the Western and in the Eastern Literatures of Europe." *Comparative Literature: Matter and Method*. Urbana: U of Illinois P, 109-143.

Nicholas, Jolley (ed.). *The Cambridge Companion to Leibniz*. Cambridge: Cambridge UP.

Nodier, Charles. 1989. *Du Fantastique en Littérature*. Paris: Barbe Bleue.

Onions, C. T. (ed.). 1996. *The Oxford Dictionary of English Etymology*. Oxford: Oxford UP.

Ouyan, Jian. 1997. *Zhongguo shenguai xiaoshuo tongshi* (*A General History of Chinese Fantastic Fiction*). Nanjing: Jiangsu Education Press.

Penzoldt, P. 1952. *The Supernatural in Fiction*. London: Nevill.

Perelman, Chaïm. 1989. *Rhétoriques*. Bruxelles: Université de Bruxelles.

Peters, F. E. 1967. *Greek Philosophical Terms: A Historical Lexicon*. New York: New York UP.

Piégay-Gros, Nathalie. 1996. *Introduction à l'intertextualité*. Paris: DUNOD.

Plato. *Ion*. 1998. 15 July 2005 <http://www.gutenberg.org/author/plato>.

Plato. *Timaeus*. 1998. 15 July 2005 <http://www.gutenberg.org/author/plato>.

Poe, Edgar Allan. *Philosophy of Composition*. 3 Feb. 2006 <http://xroads.virginia.edu/~HYPER/poe/composition/html>.

Ponnau, Gewenhaël. 1987. *La folie dans la littérature fantastique*. Paris: Editions CNRS.

Pozzuoli, Alain/Jean-Pierre Krémer. 1992. *Dictionnaire du fantastique*. Paris: J. Grancher.

Praz, Mario. 1977. *La chair, la mort et le diable dans la littérature du 19ème siècle : le romantisme noir*. Paris: Editions Denoël.

Price, Charles P. 2003. "Eucharist." *Encarta Encyclopedia Deluxe*. CD-ROM. Redmond: Microsoft Corporation.

Punter, David. 1980. *The Literature of Terror: A History of Gothic Fictions from 1765 to the Present Day*. London/New York: Longman.

Puzin, Claude. 1984. *Le fantastique*. Paris: Editions Fernand Nathan.

Qian, Dongfu. 1982. *Tang Song guwen yundong* (The Movement of the classic *"guwen"* in Tang and Song Dynasties). Shanghai: Shanghai guji.

Rabkin, Eric S. 1976. *The Fantastic in Literature*. Princeton: Princeton UP.

Raphael, Alice. 1965. *Goethe and the Philosopher's Stone*. London: Routledge and Kegan Paul.

Raymond, François (ed.). *Emergence du fantastique*. Paris: Lettres modernes.

Raymond, François. *Les Maîtres du fantastique en literature*. Paris: Bordas, 1994.

Retinger, J. H. 1908. *Le conte fantastique dans le romantisme français*. Paris: Grasset.

Richter, Anne. 1984. *Le fantastique féminin : un art sauvage*. Bruxelles: Editions Jacques Antoine.

Riffaterre, Michael. 1971. *Essai de stylistique structurale*. Paris: Flammarion.

Riffaterre, Michael. 1979. *La Production du texte*. Paris: Éditions du Seuil.

Rimmon-Kenan, Shlomith. 1983. *Narrative Fiction: Contemporary Poetics*. London/New York: Routledge.

Rochefort-Guillouet, Sophie. 1998. *La Littérature fantastique en 50 ouvrages*. Paris: Ellipses.

Rozas, Ricardo Romera Rozas. 1995. *Introduction à la littérature fantastique hispano-américaine*. Paris: Editions Nathan.

Salman, Sherry. 1997. "The Creative Psyche: Jung's Major Contributions." *The Cambridge Companion to Jung*. Cambridge UP, 52-70.

Sandoz, Claude. *Cours "Tradition classique"* 20 May 2004. <http://www.unine.ch/antic/latinenseignement.html>.

Sartre, J. P. 1981. "Aminadab ou le fantastique considéré comme un langage." *Critiques littéraires (Situations I)*. Paris: Librairies des Champs-Elysées.

Schlobin, Roger C. (ed.). 1982. *The Aesthetics of Fantasy Literature and Art*. Notre Dame: U of Notre Dame P.

Schneider, Marcel. 1985. *Histoire de la littérature fantastique en France*. Paris: Librairie Arthème Fayard.

Schuhl, Pierre Maxime. 1969. *L'Imagination et le merveilleux, la pensée et l'action*. Paris: Flammarion.

Segal, Robert A. (ed.) 1998. *Encountering Jung on Mythology*. Princeton UP.

Shi, Yuliang. 1996. *Guaiyi shijie de jiangou (The Construction of the Fantastic Universe)*. Taipei: Wenjin Press.

Shippey, T. A. 2000. *J. R. R. Tolkien: Author of the Century*. London: Harper-CollinsPublishers.

Siebers, Tobin. 1984. *The Romantic Fantastic*. Ithaca/London: Cornell UP.

Siganos, André. 1993. *Le Minotaure et son mythe*. Paris: PUF.

Siganos, André. 1999. *Mythe et écriture: la nostagie de l'archaïque*. Paris: PUF.

Skogemann, Pia. 2004. "Introduction to *A Jungian Interpretation of Tolkien's The Lord of the Rings*." 27, June 2005. <http://www.cgjungpage.org/ index.php?option=com_content&task=view&id=541&Itemid=40>.

Smitherman, Daniel J. 2001. *Philosophy and the Evolution of Consciousness: Owen Barfield's* Saving the Appearances. San Jose/New York: iUniversity Press.

Steinmetz, Jean-Luc. 1990. *La Littérature fantastique*. Paris: PUF.

Stokes, John. 1992. *Fin de siècle, fin du globe: Fears and Fantasies of the Late Nineteens*. Basingstoke/Hampshire: Macmillan.

Stroud, Joanne. "Gaston Bachelard: The Hand of Work and Play." Fall 1998. <http://www.dallasinstitute.org/Programs/Previous/FALL98/talktext/joan neb.htm>.

Swinfen, Ann. 1984. *In Defense of Fantasy: A Study of the Genre in English and American Literature since 1945*. London: Routledge & Kegan Paul.

Tadie, Jean-Yves. 1987. *La Critique littéraire au XXe siècle*. Paris: Pierre Belfond.

Teichmann, Elisabeth. 1961. *La Fortune d'Hoffmann en France*. Genève: Droz.

Tennyson, G. B. (ed.). 1999. *A Barfield Reader: Selections from the Writings of Owen Barfield*. Hanover/London: Wesleyan UP.

Todorov, Tzvetan. 1970. *Introduction à la littérature fantastique*. Paris: Éditions du Seuil.

Todorov, Tzvetan. 1992. *Introduction to Poetics*. Tran. Brooks Peter. Minneapolis: U of Minnesota P.

Tolkien, J. R. R. 1995. *The Letters of J. R. R. Tolkien*. Ed. Humphrey Carpenter. London: HarperCollinsPublishers.

Tolkien, J. R. R. 1997. *The Monsters and the Critics and Other Essays*. London: HarperCollinsPublishers.

Toursel, Nadine/Jacques Vassevière (ed.). 2001. *Littérature: textes théoriques et critiques*. Paris: Éditions Nathan/HER.

Trail, Nancy H. "Fictional Worlds of the *Fantastic*." *Academic Search Elite* Summer91, Vol.25, Issue 2.

Vax, Louis. 1974. *L'art et la littérature fantastique*. Paris: PUF.

Vax, Louis. 1979. *Les chefs-d'oeuvre de la littérature fantastique*. Paris: PUF.

Vax, Louis. 1987. *La Séduction de l'étrange*. Paris: Quadrige/PUF.

Villani, Arnaud. "Entre mythos et logos: les deux puits de la vérité." *Questions philosophiques*. 2, Aug. 2005 <http://philosophie.scola.ac-paris.fr/questionsphilosophiques.htm>.

Wang, Guoliang. 1994. *Weijin nanbeichao zhiguai xiaoshuo yanjiu* (*Study of zhiguai in the Six Dynasties*). Taipei: Wenshizhe.

Wang, Jinglin. 1992. *Gui shen de moli – Han minzu de guishen xinyang* (*The Charm of Ghosts and Gods – Chinese Poeple's Belief in Ghosts and Gods*). Beijing: Sanlian Press.

Watson, Greer. 2000. "Assumptions of Reality: Low Fantasy, Magical Realism, and the Fantastic." *Journal of the Fantastic in the Arts* 11.2,164-172.

Weisstein, Ulrich. 1988. *Comparative Literature and Literary Theory*. Taipei: Bookman Books, Ltd.

Wellek, René/Austin Warren. 1949. *Theory of Literature*. New York: Harcourt Brace.

Wilpert, Gero von. 1979. *Sachwörterbuch der Literatur*. Berlin: Alfred Kröner Verlag Stuttgart.

Wu, Yifang/Wu Xieyao. 1999. *Yi Jing baishitong (Handbook of Yi Jing)*. Chengdu: Sichuan renming chubanshe.

Xiao, Dengfu. 1989. *Hanweiliouchao fodao liangjiao zhi tiantang diyu shuo (The Conception of Heaven and Hell in the Religions of Buddhism and Daoism from the Six Dynasties)*. Taipei: Taiwan xuesheng Bookstore.

Xu, Hualong (ed.). 1994. *Zhongguo gui wenhua dacidian (Dictionary of Chinese Culture of Ghosts)*. Guangxi minzu Press.

Yang, Winston L. Y./Peter Li/Nathan K. Mao. 1978. *Classical Chinese Fiction: A Guide to its Study and Appreciation*. London: George Prior Publishers.

Ye, Qingbing. 1976. *Tan xiaoshuo gui (Discourse on the Ghosts in the Fiction)*. Taipei: Huangguan.

Ye, Qingbing. 1986. *Tan xiaoshuo yao (Discourse on the Spirits and Devils in the Fiction)*. Taipei: Huangguan.

Yin, Dengguo. 1988. *Zhongguo shen de gushi (Tales of Chinese Gods)*. Taipei: Shijie wenwu.

Young-Eisendrath, Polly/Terence Dawson (ed.). 1999. *The Cambridge Companion to Jung*. Cambridge: Cambridge UP.

Yu, Rujie. 1992. *Xian, gui, yao, ren – Zhiguai chuanqi xinlun (A New Critique of Chinese Fantastic Tales)*. Beijing: Zhongguo gongren Press.

Zeyl, Donald. "Timaeus." *Standford Encyclopedia of Philosophy*. 5 Oct. 2005 <http://plato.stanford.edu/contents.htm>.

Zhang, Changgong. 1951. *Tang Song chuanqi zuozhe jiqi shidai (The Novelists Chuanqi of Tang and Song Dynasties and their Epoch)*. Beijing: Shangwu Press.

Zhang, Jueren. 1985. *Zhongguo gudai liandanshu: Zhongyi danyao yanjiou (Chinese Ancient Alchemy: Studies of Chinese Alchemical Medicines)*. Taipei: Mingwen Bookstore.

Zhang, Qicheng. 1999. *Yidao: Zhonghua wenhua zhugan. (The Dao of Yi: The Essence of Chinese Culture)*. Beijing: Zhongguo Bookstore.

Zhang, Qin. 1999. *Daojiao lianyang xinlixue yinlun (Introduction to the Psychology of Daoist Alchemy)*. Chengdu: Bashu Bookstore & Press.

Zhu, Shaohua. 1993. *Shanggu shenhai xilie xiaoshuo (Fiction of Antique Myth)*. Shenyang: Liaoning Education Press.

Zondergeld, Rein A./Holger E. Wiedenstried. 1998. *Lexikon der Phantastischen Literatur*. Stuttgart: Weitbrecht.

Literary Works of the Fantastic

Adams, Richard. 2001. *Watership Down*. New York: Perennial Classics.

Aesop. 1991. *Aesop's Fables*. Trans. George Fyler Townsend. <http://www.gutenberg.org/etext/21>.

Andersen, Hans Christian. 1994. *Fairy Tales*. London: Penguin Books.

Anderson, Douglas A. (ed.). 2003. *Tales Before Tolkien: The Roots of Modern Fantasy*. New York: Ballantine Books.

Apuleius. 1999. *Apuleius: The Golden Ass*. Trans. P. G. Walsh. Oxford: Oxford UP.

Asimov, Isaac. 1992. *Foundation Trilogy*. New York: Bantam Books.

Asimov, Isaac. 1995. *Gold: The Final Science Fiction Collection*. New York: HarperPrism.

Balzac, Honoré de. 1997. *Melmoth réconcilié suivi de Jésus-Christ en Flandre*. Paris: Flammarion Librio.

Balzac, Honoré. 1972. *La Peau de chagrin*. Paris: Le Livre de Poche.

Balzac, Honoré. 2003. *L'Elixir de longue vie, suivi de "El Verdugo."* Paris: Le Livre de Poche.

Barbey d'Aurevilly. 1993. *Les Diaboliques*. Paris: Pocket.

Baum, L. Frank. 1995. *The Wonderful Wizard of Oz*. London: Penguin Books.

Beuwulf. 1999. Trans. Burton Raffel. New York: Penguin Signet Classic.

Borel, Pétrus. 1985. *Champavert : contes immoraux*. Paris: Le chemin vert.

Borges, Jorge Luis. 1964. *Labyrinths: Selected Stories & Other Writings*. New York: A New Directions Book.

Bradbury, Ray. 1991. *The Martian chronicles*. Paris: Livre de Poche.

Bradbury, Ray. 1995. *Fahrenheit 451*. New York: Ballantine Books.

Brown, Dan. 2000. *Angels and Devils*. New York: Pocket Books.

Brown, Dan. 2006. *The Da Vinci Code*. New York: Anchor Books.

Bulgakov, Mikhail. 1999. *The Heart of a Dog*. Trans. Michael Glenny. London: Harvill Press.

Calvino, Italo. 1998. *Fantastic Tales: Visionary and Everyday*. New York: Vintage International.

Carroll, Lewis. 1994. *Alice's Adventure in Wonderland*. London: Penguin Books.

Carroll, Lewis. 1994. *Through the Looking Glass*. London: Penguin Books.

Cazotte, Jacques. 1997. *Le Diable amoureux*. Paris: Flammarion Librio.

Cervantes Saavedra, Miguel de. 2003. *Don Quixote*. Trans. Walter Starkie. New York: Penguin Signet Classic.

Chamisso, Adelbert von. 2004. *Peter Schlemihl, The Shadowless Man*. <http://www.gutenberg.org/etext/5339>.

Chesterton, G. K. 1994. *Father Brown Stories*. London: Penguin Books.

Clarke, Arthur C. 2000. *2001: A Space Odyssey*. New York: New American Library.

Coelho, Paulo. 2002 *Devil and Miss Prym*. New York: HarperCollins*Publishers*.

Coelho, Paulo. 2002 *The Alchemist*. New York: HarperTorch.

Coelho, Paulo. 2006 *Pilgrimage*. New York: New York: Harpertorch.

Coetzee, J. M. 2003. *Elizabeth Costello*. London: Penguin Books.

Cortázar, Julio. 1967. *Blow-Up and Other Stories*. New York: Pantheon Books.

Dante, Alighieri. 1998. *The Divine Comedy*. Trans. C. H. Sisson. Oxford: Oxford UP.

Dao, Qian. 1985. *Soushenhouji (Sequel to In Search of Gods and Spirits)*. Taipei: Editions Muduo.

Darrieussecq, Marie. 1998. *Truismes*. Paris: Gallimard.

Datlow, Ellen/Terri Windling (ed.). 1999. *The Year's Best Fantasy and Horror: Twelfth Annual Collection*. New York: St. Martin's Griffin.

De Lorris, Guillaume. *Le Roman de Rose*. Paris: Livre de Poche.

Dickens, Charles. 1990. "The Signal-Man." *Stories of Mystery: Nouvelles fantastiques*. Paris: Le Livre de Poche.

Dickens, Charles. 1991. *A Christmas Carol*. New York: Dover Publications.

Ding, Wangdao. 1991. *Zhongguo shenhua ji zhiguai xiaoshuo yibaipian (One Hundred Stories from Chinese Myths and Fantastic Tales)*. Taipei: Taiwan Commercial.

Doyle, Arthur Conan. 2000. *Extraordinary Tales: Histoires extraordinaires*. Paris: Pocket.

Dumas, Alexandre. 1980. *Histoire d'un mort racontée par lui-même*. Paris: Union générale d'édition.

Dumas, Alexandre. 1980. *Les mille et un fantômes*. Paris: Genève Ressources.

Dunsany, Lord. 2004. *The Sword of Welleran and Other Tales*.
   <http://www.gutenberg.org/etext/10806>.

Dunsany, Lord. 2005. *The Book of Wonder*.
   <http://www.gutenberg.org/etext/7477>.

Eco, Umberto. 1990. *Foucault's pendulum*. Trans. William Weaver. New York: ballantine Books.

Ende, Michael. 1985. *Momo*. New York: Puffin Books.

Erckmann-Chatrian. 1987. *Contes fantastiques*. Paris: NéOSocoInvest.

Funke, Cornelia. 2005. *Inkheart*. New York: Scholastic Inc.

Gaiman, Neil. 1998. *Neverwhere*. New York: Avon Books.

Gaiman, Neil. 2000. *Stardust*. New York: Avon Books, INC.

Gan, Bao. 1982. *Soushen ji (In Search of Gods and Spirits)*. Taipei: Liren Bookstore.

Gautier, Théophile. 1993. *Récits fantastiques*. Paris: Bookking International.

Goethe, Johann Wolfgan von.1990. *Goethe's Faust*. Trans. Walter Kaufmann. New York: Anchor Books.

Gogol, Nicolas. 1998. *Nouvelles de Petersbourg*. Paris: Gallimard.

Grass, Gunter. 1993. *The Tin Drum*. Trans. Ralph Manheim New York: Knopt.

Green, Roger Lancelyn. 1975. *Myths of the Norsemen*. Middlesex: Puffin Books.

Grimm, Jacob and Wilhelm. 1996. *Grimms' Fairy Tales*. New York: Penguin Books.

Guiomar, Michel. 1993. *Principes d'une esthétique de la mort*. Paris: Librairie générale française.

Haggard, H. Rider. 2000. *King Solomon's Mines*. <http://www.gutenberg.org/etext/2166>.

Haggard, H. Rider. 2006. *She*. < http://www.gutenberg.org/etext/3155>.

Hartwell, David G. (ed.) 1994. *Shadows of Fear*. New York: A Tor Book.

Hawthorne, Nathaniel. 1996. *Mosses From An Old Manse*. <http://www.gutenberg.org/dirs/etext96/manse10.txt>.

Hesse, Herman. *The Fairytales of Hermann Hesse*. Trans. Jack David Zipes. New York: Bantam Books.

Hesse, Hermann. 1996. *Siddhartha*. Trans. Hilda Rosner. Taipei: Bookman Books Ltd..

Hoffmann, E. T. A. 1967. *The Best Tales of Hoffmann*. New York: Dover Publications.

Hoffmann, E. T. A. 1977. *Selected Letters by E. T. A. Hoffmann*. Ed. Johanna S. Sahlin. Chicago: U of Chicago P.

Hoffmann, E. T. A. 1993. *The Nutcracker and the Golden Pot*. New York: Dover Publications.

Hoffmann, E. T. A. 2003. "Beethoven's Instrumental Music." *Hoffmann's Writing on Music*. Cambridge: Cambridge UP, 96-102.

Homer. 1984. *The Iliad*. Trans. Robert Fitzgerald. Oxford: Oxford UP.

Homer. 1998. *The Odyssey*. Trans. Walter Shewring. Oxford: Oxford UP.

Hong, Mai. 1982. *Yijianzhi (Weird Tales)*. Taipei: Mingwen Bookstore.

Irving, Washington. 1994. *Rip Van Winkle and other stories*. New York: Puffin Books.

James, Henry. 1994. *The Turn of the Screw*. London: Penguin Books.

James, M. R. 1995. *Collected Ghost Stories*. Hertfordshire: Wordsworth Editions Limited.

Janin, Jules. 1979. *Contes fantastiques et contes littéraires*. Paris-Genève: Ressources.

Jarvie, Gordon (ed.). 1992. *Scottish Folk and Fairy Tales*. London: Penguin Books.

Kafka, Franz. 1971. *The Complete Stories*. Ed. Nahum N. Glatzer. New York: Schocken Books.

Kessler, Joan C. (ed.). 1995. *Demons of the Night: Tales of the Fantastic, Madness, and the Supernatural from Nineteenth-Century France*. Chicago: U of Chicago P.

360 *Bibliography*

La Fontaine, Jean de. 2006. *Fables de La Fontaine.* <http://www.gutenberg.org/etext/17941>.

La Vénus d'Ille : une œuvre / Prosper Mérimée. L'objet magique : un thème / Balzac, Maupassant, Wilde, Poe. 1990. Paris: Hatier.

Lang, Andrew. 1996. *The Red Fairy Book.* <http://www.gutenberg.org/etext/540>.

Lang, Andrew. 2005. *The Blue Fairy Book.* <http://www.gutenberg.org/etext/503>.

Lao Zi. 1981. *Lao Zi (Lao Zi: A New Translation).* Ed. Peilin Yu. Taipei: Sanmin Bookstore.

Le Fanu, Joseph Sheridan. *Camilla.* <http://www.gutenberg.org/etext/10007>.

Le Guin, Ursula K. 1975. *A Wizard of Earthsea.* New York: Bantam Books.

Le Guin, Ursula K. 1991. The Left Hand of Darkness. New York: Berkley Publication.

Le Roman de Renart. 2000. Paris: Gallimard.

Lie Zi. 1991. *Lie Zi (Lie Zi: A New Translation).* Ed. Wanshou Zhuang. Taipei: Sanmin Bookstore.

Lewis, C. S. 1994. *The Lion, the Witch and the Wardrobe.* New York: HarperCollins*Publishers.*

Li Fuyan/Sengru Niu. 1989. *Xuanguailu, Xuxuanguailu : Zhongguo lidai biji xiaoshuo xuanyi (Selected Fantastic Tales of Niu Sengru and Li Fuyan).* Hangzhou: Zhejiangguji.

Li, Fang et al. (eds.). 1981. *Taipingguangji (The Great Collection from the Epoch of Peace).* Taipei: Wenshizhe.

Li, Fengmao (ed.). 1994. *Shanhai Jing: Shenhua de guxiang (The Classic of Mountains and Seas: The Native Land of Myth).* Taipei: Shibao Wenhua.

Lin, Yisheng. 1978. *Zhongguo guiguai gushi (Chinese Fantastic Tales).* Taipei: Zhuangyan.

Liu, An. 1994. *Huainan Zi.* Taipei: Shibao Wenhua.

Liu, Yonglian (trad./ed.). 1990. *Zhongguo zhiguai xiaoshuo xuanyi (Chinese Fantastic Tales with Modern Chinese Translations).* Beijing: Baowentang.

Lonnrot, Elias. 1999. *The Kalevala: An Epic Poem after Oral Tradition.* Trans. Keith Bosley. Oxford: Oxford UP.

Lorrain, Jean. 1987. *Histoires de masques.* Saint-Cyr-sur-Loire: Christian Pirot.

Lovecraft, H. P. 1999. *The Call of Cthulhu and Other Weird Stories.* New York: Penguin Books.

Lu, Xixing. 1991. *Fengshen Yanyi (The Investiture of the Gods).* Taipei: Sanmin Bookstore.

MacDonald, George. 1999. *The Complete Fairy Tales.* London: Penguin Classics.

MacDonald, George. 2006. *The Light Princess and other Fairy Stories.* <http://www.gutenberg.org/etext/18811>.

Malory, Sir Thomas. 2001. *Le Morte d'Arthur.* New York: Penguin Signet Classic.

Mann, Thomas. 1999. *Doctor Faustus.* New York: Vintage Books.

Marlowe, Christopher. 2001. *Doctor Faustus.* New York: Penguin Signet Classic.

Marquez, Gabriel Garcia. 1970. *One Hundred Years of Solitude.* Trans. Gregory Rabassa. New York: Harper & Row.

Matheson, Richard. 2001. *I am Legend.* London: Gollancz.

Maupassant, Guy de. 1991. *Contes fantastiques Complets.* Ed. Richter Anne. Paris: Marabout.

Maupassant, Guy de. 1998. *A Day in the Country and Other Stories.* Trans. David Coward. Oxford: Oxford UP.

Mérimée, Prosper. 1995. *Colomba et autres nouvelles.* Paris: Bookking International.

Meyrink, Gustav. 1991. *The Angle of the West Window.* Trans. Mike Mitchell. Cambridge: Dedalus.

Meyrink, Gustav. 1994. *The Opal and Other Stories.* Trans. Maurice Raraty. Cambridge: Dedalus.

Meyrink, Gustav. 1995. *The Golem.* Trans. Mike Mitchell. Cambridge: Dedalus.

Milton, John. 2004. *Paradise Lost.* Oxford: Oxford UP.

Morris, William. 1994. *The Well at the World's End: A Tale.* <http://www.gutenberg.org/etext/169>.

Morris, William. 1995. *A Dream of John Ball: A King's Lesson.* <http://www.gutenberg.org/etext/357>.

Morris, William. 2006. *The Story of Sigurd the Volsung and the Fall of the Niblungs.* <http://www.gutenberg.org/etext/18328>.

Munby, A. N. L. 1949. *The Alabaster Hand and Other Ghost Stories.* London: D. Dobson.

Naugrette, Jean-Pierre (ed. & trans.). 1998. *Stories of Mystery: Nouvelles fantastiques.* Paris: Le Livre de Poche.

Needler, George Henry (Trans.). 2005. *The Nibelungenlied.* <http://www.gutenberg.org/etext/7321>.

Nerval, Gérard de. 1972. *Aurélia – Les Chimères – La Pandora.* Paris: Le livre de poche.

Nerval, Gérard de. 1995. *La Main enchantée.* Paris: Le Livre de Poche.

Niou, Sengru/Fuyan Li. 1989. *Xuanguailu, Xuxuanguailu : Zhongguo lidai biji xiaoshuo xuanyi (Selected Fantastic Tales of Niou Sengru and Li Fuyan).* Hangzhou: Zhejiangguji.

Nodier, Charles. 1961. *Contes.* Ed. P. G. Castex. Paris: Editions Garnier.

Nodier-Balzac-Gautier-Mérimée: Récits fantastiques. 1998. Paris: Pocket.

●

Orwell, George. 1950. *1984*. New York: Penguin Signet Classic.
Orwell, George. 1996. *Animal Farm*. New York: Penguin Signet Classic.
Ovid. 1998. *Ovid: Metamorphoses*. Trans. A. D. Melville. Oxford: Oxford UP.
Palumbo, Donald (ed.). 1986. *Erotic Universe: Sexuality and Fantastic Literature*. New York: Greenwood.
Paz, Octavio. 1999. "The Blue Bouquet." *Short Shorts: An Anthology of the Shortest Stories*. New York: Bantam Books.
Perrault, Charles. 1999. *Contes*.<http://gallica.bnf.fr/ark:/12148/bpt6k101479h>.
Poe, Edgar Allan. 1994. *Selected Tales*. London: Penguin Books.
Poe, Edgar Allan. 1994. *Tales of Mystery and Imagination*. Denmark: Wordsworth Editions Ltd.
Potocki, Jean. 1958. *Manuscrit trouvé à Saragosse*. Paris: Gallimard.
Pratchett, Terry. 2000. *The Color of Magic*. London: HarperTorch.
Pratchett, Terry. 2001. *The Light Fantastic*. London: HarperTorch.
Pu, Songling. 1996. *Liaozhai zhiyi*. Taipei: Dazhongguo Bookstore.
Pu, Yinghua (ed.). 1996. *Tang Song chuanqi* (Chuanqi of Tang and Song Dynasties, Translated into Modern Chinese). Taipei: Taiyang.
Pyle, Howard. 1986. *The Story of King Arthur and his Knights*. New York: Penguin Signet Classic.
Qu, Yiu, et al. 1974. *Jiandengxinhua*. Taipei: Shijie Bookstore.
Rabelais, François. 1999. *Pantagruel*. Paris: Pocket.
Rabelais, François. 2004. *Gargantua*. Paris: Gallimard.
Rice, Anne. 1997. *Interview with the Vampire*. New York: Ballantine Books.
Rowling, J. K. 1999. *Harry Potter and the Sorcerer's Stone*. New York: Scholastic.
Sadoul, Barbara (ed.). 1996. *La Dimension fantastique: 13 nouvelles d'Hoffmann à Claude Seignolle*. Paris: Flammarion Librio.
Sadoul, Barbara (ed.). 1997. *Les Cent ans de Dracula: Huit nouvelles de Goethe à Lovecraft*. Paris: Flammarion Librio.
Sadoul, Barbara (ed.). 1998. *La Dimension fantastique: 6 nouvelles d'Honoré de Balzac à Theodore Sturgeon*. Paris: Flammarion Librio.
Sadoul, Barbara (ed.). 1999. *La Dimension fantastique: 10 nouvelles de Flaubert à Jodorowsky*. Paris: Flammarion Librio.
Sand, George. 1977. *Contes d'une grand'mère*. Paris: Editions d'aujoud'hui.
Sandner, David and Jacob Weisman. (ed.). 2001. *The Treasury of the Fantastic: Romanticism to Early Twentieth Century Literature*. Berkeley: Frog, Ltd.
Schwob, Marcel. 1993. *Vies imaginaires*. Toulouse: Éditions Ombres.
Schwob, Marcel. 1996. *Coeur double*. Toulouse: Éditions Ombres.
Schwob, Marcel. 1999. *Le Roi au masque d'or*. Paris: Le Livre de Poche.
Seignolle, Claude. 1994. *Contes fantastique de Bretagne*. Paris: Terre de Brume.
Shelley, Mary. 1994. "Frankenstein." *Four* Gothic *Novels*. Oxford: Oxford UP.

Sigfusson, Saemund and Snorre Sturleson. 2005. *The Elder Eddas of Saemund Sigfusson; and the Younger Eddas of Snorre Sturleson.* <http://www.gutenberg.org/files/14726/14726.txt>.

Silho, Léa. 2004. *La Tisseuse: contes de fées, contes de failles.* Paris: Oxymore.

Silverberg, Robert (ed.). 1999. *Legends: Short Novels by the Masters of Modern Fantasy.* New York: A Tor Book.

Silverberg, Robert and Martin H. Greenberg (ed.).1990. *The Mammoth Book of Fantasy All-Time Greats.* London: Robinson Publishing.

Sir Gawain and the Green Knight. 2001. Trans. Burton Raffel. New York: Penguin Signet Classic.

Songren zhiguai xiaoshuo: Tales of Chinese Monsters in A. D. 960-1200. 1988. Taipei: Dongfangwenhua.

Spenser, Edmund. 1980. *The Faerie Queene.* London: Longman.

Stevenson, Robert Louis. 1994. *Dr Jekyll and Mr Hyde.* London: Penguin Books.

Stoker, Bram. 1994. *Dracula.* London: Penguin Books.

Stoker, Bram. 2003. *Dracula's Guest.* < http://www.gutenberg.org/etext/10150>.

Suzuki, Koji. 2002. *Guishui guaitan (Stories of ghost water).* Taipei: Taiwan jiaochuan shudian.

Suzuki, Koji. 2004. *Qiye guaitan (Weird Tales of Seven Nights* or *Ring series).* 4 vols. Taipei: Shangzhou Press.

Tangdai chuanqi xuanyi (Selected Tales of Chuanqi from Tang, Translated into Modern Chinese). 1989. Shanghai: Shanghaiguji.

Tennyson, Alfred Lord. 2003. *Idylls of the King and a New Selection of Poems.* New York: Penguin Signet Classic.

The Epic of Gilgamesh. 1972. Trans. N. K. Sandars. London: Penguin Books.

Tolkien, J. R. R. 1995. *The Hobbit or There and Back again.* London: HarperCollins*Publishers.*

Tolkien, J. R. R. 1998. *Tales from Perilous Realm.* London: HarperCollins*Publishers.*

Tolkien, J. R. R. 1999. *The Fellowship of the Ring.* London: HarperCollins*Publishers.*

Tolkien, J. R. R. 1999. *The Silmarillion.* London: HarperCollins*Publishers.*

Tolkien, J. R. R. 2001. *The Two towers.* London: HarperCollins*Publishers.*

Tolkien, J. R. R. 2003. *The Return of the King.* London: HarperCollins *Publishers.*

Tournier, Michel. 1972. *Vendredi ou les limbes du Pacifique.* Paris: Gallimard.

Troyes, Chrétien de. 1991. *Arthurian Romances.* Trans. William W. Kibler. London: Penguin Classics.

Troyes, Chrétien de. 2002. *Roman de la Table ronde.* Paris: Livre de Poche.

Twain, Mark. 1983. *A Connecticut Yankee in King Arthur's Court.* New York: Bantam Books.

Verne, Jules. 1994. *Twenty Thousand Leagues Under the Sea*. London: Penguin Books.

Verne, Jules. 2003. *Autour de la Lune*. <http://www.gutenberg.org/etext/4717>.

Verne, Jules. 2003. *Voyage au centre de la terre*. <http://www.gutenberg.org/etext/4791>.

Verne, Jules. 2004. *20000 lieues sous les mers*. <http://www.gutenberg.org/etext/5097>.

Verne, Jules. 2004. *Les Indes-Noires : suivi de un hivernage dans les glaces*. <http://www.gutenberg.org/etext/5081>.

Villiers de l'Isle-Adam, Auguste de. 1993. *L'Eve future*. Paris: Gallimard.

Villiers de l'Isle-Adam, Auguste de. 1995. *Contes Cruels*. Paris: Gallimard.

Virgil. 1981. *The Aeneid of Virgil: A Verse Translation*. Trans. Allen Mandelbaum. Toronto: Bantam Books.

Vyasa. 2005. *Mahabharata* vol. 1-6. Trans. Huang Baosheng et al. Beijing: China Social Science Press.

Walpole, Horace et al. 1994. *Four* Gothic *Novels: The Castle of Otranto, Vathek, The Monk, Frankenstein*. Oxford/New York: Oxford UP.

Wang, Meng'ou. 1971/73/74. *Tangren xiaoshuo yanjiu* (*Annotated Anthology of the Fiction from Tang Dynasty*), 3 vols. Taipei: Yiwen.

Wang, Pijiang (ed.). 1988. *Tangren xiaoshuo* (*Fiction of Tang People*). Shanghai: Shanghaiguji.

Wang, Shizhen. 1994. Shenxian zhuan (*Legends of Immortals*).Taipei: Shibao Wenhua.

Weis, Margaret (ed.). 1998. *A Magic Lover's Treasury of the Fantastic*. New York: A Time Warner Company.

Well, "The Story of the Inexperienced Ghost,"

Wells, H. G. 1984. *The Time Machine*. New York: Penguin Signet Classic.

Wells, H. G. 2002. *The Invisible Man*. New York: Penguin Signet Classic.

Wells, H. G. 2004. *Selected Stories of H. G. Wells*. New York: Modern Library Edition, 2004.

White, T. H. 1987. *Once and Future King*. New York: Berkley Publication.

White, T. H. 1987. *The Book of Merlyn*. New York: Berkley Publication.

White, T. H. 1988. *Sword in the Stone*. New York: Random House.

Wilde, Oscar. 1994. *Lord Arthur Savile's Crime and Other Stories*. London: Penguin Books.

Wilde, Oscar. 1994. *The Happy Prince and Other Stories*. London: Penguin Books.

Wilde, Oscar. 1994. *The Picture of Dorian Gray*. London: Penguin Books.

Wolfram, von Eschenback. 1980. *Perzival*. London: Penguin Books.

Wu, Cheng'en. 1994. *Xi You Ji* (Journey to the West). Taipei: Guiguan.

Xiao, Haibo/Shaoqing Luo (trad./ed.). 1992. *Liuchao zhiguaixiaoshuo* (*Zhiguai from the Six Dynasties*). Taipei: Jinxio.

Xu, Zihong. 1994. *Zhou Yi* (*Yi Jing*). Taipei: Diqiou Press.

Yourcenar, Marguerite. 1976. *L'Oeuvre au noir*. Paris: Gallimard.

Yuan, Ke. 1993. *Huafeng xianying: shenyi pian* (*Chinese Culture Series: Myths and Legends*). Taipei: Shuquan Press.

Zelazny, Roger. 2002. *The Last Defender of Camelot*. New York: iBooks.

Zhang, Yiuhe (ed.). 1984. *Tang Song chuanqi xuan* (*Selected Tales from Tang and Song Dynasties*). Taipei: Mingwen Bookstore.

Zhou, Nengqie. (trad./ed.). 1985. *Chatuben Tangdai chuanqi cuanyi* (Selected *chuanqi* Tales from Tang Dynasty with Illustrations and Translations into Modern Chinese). Xuchang: Zhongzhouguji.

Zhuang Zi. 2005. *Zhuang Zi* (*Zhuang Zi: A New Translation*). Ed. Songhui Zhang. Taipei: Sanmin Bookstore.

Zipes, Jack (ed.). 1997. *Arabian Nights: A Selection*. Trans. Sir Richard F. Burton. London: Penguin Books.

Author / Title Index

Subject Index

Arbeiten zur Literarischen Phantastik
Eine Schriftenreihe der Universität Leipzig

Herausgegeben von Elmar Schenkel and Alexandra Lembert

Band   1   Fanfan Chen: Fantasticism. Poetics of Fantastic Literature. The Imaginary and Rhetoric.
2007.

www.peterlang.de